ESSENTIAL READINGS IN SOCIAL PROBLEMS

ESSENTIAL READINGS IN SOCIAL PROBLEMS

FIRST EDITION

Edited By Yawo Bessa

University of North Carolina – Pembroke

cognella®

SAN DIEGO

Bassim Hamadeh, CEO and Publisher
Peaches diPierro, Associate Acquisitions Editor
Alisa Munoz, Senior Project Editor
Susana Christie, Senior Developmental Editor
Abbey Hastings, Production Editor
Asfa Arshi, Graphic Design Assistant
Greg Isales, Licensing Coordinator
Natalie Piccotti, Director of Marketing
Kassie Graves, Vice President of Editorial
Jamie Giganti, Director of Academic Publishing

Copyright © 2022 by Cognella, Inc. All rights reserved. No part of this publication may be reprinted, reproduced, transmitted, or utilized in any form or by any electronic, mechanical, or other means, now known or hereafter invented, including photocopying, microfilming, and recording, or in any information retrieval system without the written permission of Cognella, Inc. For inquiries regarding permissions, translations, foreign rights, audio rights, and any other forms of reproduction, please contact the Cognella Licensing Department at rights@cognella.com.

Trademark Notice: Product or corporate names may be trademarks or registered trademarks and are used only for identification and explanation without intent to infringe.

Cover image: Copyright © 2019 iStockphoto LP/Halfpoint.

Printed in the United States of America.

CONTENTS

INTRODUCTION

As an instructor of social problems, I have always wanted to assign additional readings to help my students deepen their understanding of topics covered in the textbook. Sometimes, I just wanted them to read about different topics covered in the lecture from a source other than their textbook. In each case, I used to spend a tremendous amount of time searching for the perfect articles for my students. Perfect articles, from my perspective, are articles that nicely relate to the chapters we are covering in the class and are easy to understand for most beginner college students. It is within this general context that I had the idea of designing this current reader. That is, this reader is a fruit of years of time-consuming search for suitable articles for my students. As such, the reader will be an excellent supplemental material for other instructors teaching social problems.

Instructors teaching social problems will find this reader very helpful for three main reasons. First, colleagues teaching social problems will love the simplicity of the design of this reader. Second, they will love the clarity of the sentences within this reader. Third, they will be appreciative of the fact that it covers all the major topics contained in most textbooks for social problems. Not only instructors but also students taking social problems will appreciate the content of this reader, as the articles were selected with students in mind. For students, this reader will provide a better understanding of various topics discussed in the class from materials other than their regular textbook.

The text contains a total of six units: (1) The Sociological Perspective and Social Problems; (2) Structural Inequality and Implications; (3) Deviance, Sexuality, and Crime; (4) Race, Ethnicity, and Social Problems; (5) Environmental Problems; and (6) Approach of Solutions to Social Problems. These six units represent the major topics of this reader and are subdivided into chapters, which in turn contain one or several readings. It is worthwhile noting that each reading is preceded by a succinct overview describing the main idea, the rationale for its inclusion in the reader, and a brief takeaway.

At the beginning of each section is an introduction, followed by a selection of relevant and current articles about the topic. At the end of each section is a list of engaging and thought-provoking post-reading questions. These post-reading questions will help instructors in assessing their students' understanding of the selected articles. For students, these questions will give the opportunity to think critically about the material they read.

UNIT 1

THE SOCIOLOGICAL APPROACH AND SOCIAL PROBLEMS

Introduction

Social problems belong to a sub-field that uses conceptualization, methodology, and theories of sociology applied to phenomena defined as problematic by a segment of the population in society. An investigation into social problems starts with critical curiosity, concern, skepticism, and passion. That is, curiosity, concern, skepticism, and passion are important starting points for a study of social problems. Even more important than these starting points is the concept of "sociological imagination." Coined by C. Wright Mills, this concept refers to the mental ability that allows us to make connections between social structure and individual conditions. This concept allows us to make a link between public issues and personal troubles as well as between curiosity, concern, skepticism, and passion in a way that makes sense. In other words, sociological imagination enables us to systematically link these four central concepts to formulate social theories. In turn, social theories will be helpful in analyzing social problems for a deeper understanding of their origins and their impact as well as the determination of appropriate solutions.

Fulfilling the Promise: Infusing Curiosity, Concern, and Passion with Sociological Imagination

Devereaux Kennedy

Devereaux Kennedy, "Fulfilling the Promise: Infusing Curiosity, Concern, and Passion with Sociological Imagination," *Exploring the Roots of Social Theory and Inquiry: Making Sense of Social Life*, pp. 1-8, 181-187. Copyright © 2018 by Cognella, Inc. Reprinted with permission.

It is not theoretical questions that first interest people in social study. It is curiosity about social life and how it works; concern for social problems and how to solve them; passion against social injustices and a desire to right them. If social study dampens this curiosity, concern, and passion, it betrays you. If social study shows you how to harness and employ that curiosity, concern, and passion, it does you a service.

Curiosity

When you study social life in a systematic and disciplined manner, it's important to periodically remind yourself why you do so. How did your journey start, and why do you continue it? Such journeys usually begin with curiosity. Why are things the way they are? Have they always been that way? Are they this way everywhere? How might they be different? Peter Berger (1963, 19), in his classic *Invitation to Sociology*, points to "the curiosity that grips any sociologist in front of a closed door behind which there are human voices. If he [or she] is a good sociologist, [she or] he will want to open that door, to understand these voices. Behind each closed door he [or she] will anticipate some new facet of human life not yet perceived and understood."

The limits of all of our experiences are such that the recognition of changes in our life and that of those around us don't necessarily tell us about what's happening to people outside our immediate vicinity. Are the changes happening to us peculiar to our neighborhood, region, class, ethnic or racial grouping, nation, or area of the world? When did these changes begin? How long have they been going on? Where will they lead? This is the curiosity out of which an interest in social study begins.

Margaret Kovach's interest in social life began with curiosity about her own origins. Her education was a portal to self-discovery. Her birth parents were Plains Cree and Salteaux. Her adopted parents were Eastern European. "I was a native kid who grew up round and about a small rural Saskatchewan town. I was loved but conflicted, questioning where I belonged, trying to stay at distances yet needing connection" (2009, 5).

Alison Wolf's upbringing was very different from that of Margaret Kovach, but of course for her, as for all of us, it was "normal." She "grew up in prosperous, peaceful southern England … where it was simply taken for granted that we would all go on to college … because it was normal for my school and for my friends, only years later did I realize how few women, even in our baby-boomer generations, did academic, let alone post-graduate degrees or how few had done so previously" (2013, xi). It was only later that she realized that hers was a "hinge generation." "My generation didn't see this coming. But then, as students or young professionals, we didn't or couldn't survey what society as a whole was doing. What was normal was what we, as privileged sub-group, did" (xii). It is only now that she is able to put what was happening to her and women like her into a global social context. It is only now that she realizes that hers was a hinge generation (xv).

The curiosity that initiates our interest in social life is usually mixed with an "unhealthy" dose of skepticism. Again, Peter Berger: "The first wisdom of sociology is this—things are not what they seem" (1963, 23). I say "unhealthy" because such curiosity and skepticism isn't always helpful in everyday situations. Much of our everyday interactions with others is based on routine. We do the same things in the same way, every day. We rarely think about what is involved in taking the bus, buying groceries, riding the elevator, or hanging out with our friends. We don't have to think about how these things happen or what it takes to make them happen. We just do them.

Indeed, for everyday encounters with others to come off successfully, it is important not to think too carefully or deeply about what is really going on. We accept that the people we interact with are who they appear to be. They, in turn, accept the self we present to them as the real us. Irving Goffman (1967) tells us that this kind of mutual acceptance seems to be a basic structural feature of interaction, especially the interaction of face-to-face talk. Think too carefully about our routines as we perform them, question them too deeply, and they will be hard to do.

What might be unhealthy and destructive in everyday life can be important for the student of social life. The surface of social life is rarely, if ever, all there is. Beneath that surface are layers and layers of social meaning. Our everyday routines are rarely as simple as they appear. They are often not as secure as they seem. The tacit knowledge, practical consciousness, and unreflective negotiation that goes into riding the bus, having a meal in a restaurant, riding the elevator, buying groceries, or hanging out with our friends is the object of study of a whole branch of sociology known as **ethnomethodology**.

ETHNOMETHODOLOGY

Study of how everyday life interactions happen. Ethnomethodologists view everyday life interactions like going to the grocery store, eating at a restaurant, taking a bus ride as artful accomplishments involving shared background knowledge, tacit understandings and negotiation between the participants in such interactions.

Often our curiosity is piqued by something that seems out of the ordinary in our routine. As a civil rights attorney, Michelle Alexander saw her job as resisting attacks on affirmative action. One day she was rushing to catch a bus when she "noticed a sign stapled to a telephone pole that screamed in large bold print: 'The Drug War is the New Jim Crow'" (2012, 3). Her first reaction was that the comparison was absurd. Yet it made her curious.

Concern

Oh—something ain't right
Oh—something ain't right

—"Something Ain't Right," David Byrnes

Sometimes the desire to systematically study social life begins with the feeling or conviction that "something ain't right." The charge for riding the bus doubles and the service is reduced. The price of groceries rises dramatically. Our eyes fix on the people busing tables and washing dishes at the restaurant where we are having a meal. Thinking about their lives spoils the meal. Rowdy kids cut in front of an elderly woman in line for the elevator. When she complains, they push her down and laugh. Everyone else in line pretends not to notice. Our routines are interrupted. Things don't seem to be working the way we think they should or the way they used to. We wonder what has gone wrong, why things cost so much, why some people make so little, and why other people behave so badly.

Charles Murray (2012, 288) remembers that when he was growing up in the 1940s and 1950s there was a code governing the behavior of "gentlemen":

> I understood the code for males to go something like this: To be a man means that you are brave, loyal and true. When you are in the wrong you own up and take your punishment. You don't take advantage of women. As a husband, you support and protect your wife and children. You are gracious in victory and a good sport in defeat. Your word is your bond. It's not whether you win or lose but how you play the game. When the ship goes down, you put the women and children in the lifeboats and wave good-bye with a smile.

Murray admits that the above is crammed with clichés. But, he argues, "they were clichés precisely because boys understood that this was the way they were supposed to behave.... The code of the American gentleman has collapsed, just as the parallel code of the American lady has collapsed" (2012, 288–89). He thinks the collapse of this code is a bad thing. He's concerned about why it has collapsed and what the consequences of its collapse will be.

Passion

Something about the way things are doesn't seem just or fair. Parents sometimes rhetorically ask their kids, "Who said that life was fair?" They add, "When you get older you'll understand." For some of us, our parents' words aren't enough. Just because things aren't fair doesn't mean that we have to accept that unfairness. When we get older we still don't understand why social injustice has to exist. We want to know how social injustices can be addressed. Just because life isn't fair doesn't mean it can't be made fairer and more just.

In the Prologue of *Indigenous Methodologies*, Margaret Kovach says, "I get angry about the racism that Indigenous people experience. I am writing this here because it drives my work.... The writing comes from the heart, it comes from who I am and all that I am.... It comes from my own need and longing to engage with my Nehiyaw and Salteaux ancestry, and to say to my academic world that my culture counts" (2009, 5–8).

In the Preface to *The New Jim Crow*, Michelle Alexander (2012) identifies the readers for whom she has written her book:

> People who care deeply about racial justice but who, for any number of reasons, do not yet appreciate the magnitude of the crisis faced by communities of color as a result of mass incarceration. In other words, I am writing this book for people like me—the person I was ten years ago. I am also writing it for another audience—those who have been struggling to persuade their friends, neighbors, relatives, teachers, coworkers, or political representatives that something is eerily familiar about the way our criminal justice system operates, something that looks and feels a lot like an era that we supposedly left behind, but who have lacked the facts and data to back up their claims. It is my hope and prayer that this book empowers you and allows you to speak with greater conviction, credibility and courage.

Charles Murray directs his book *Coming Apart* at a very different audience, and has very different things to say than does Michelle Alexander. But he too is passionate about what he perceives as prevailing social wrongs, including the dysfunctionality and irresponsibility of the new American upper class:

> Personally and as families its members are successful. But they have abrogated their responsibility to set and promulgate standards. The most powerful and successful members of their class increasingly trade on the perks of their privileged positions without regard to the seemliness of that behavior. The members of the new upper class are active politically, but when it comes to using their positions to help sustain the republic in day-to-day life, they are AWOL. (2012, 294)

Using Your Sociological Imagination to Make Connections

If interest in the systematic study of social life begins with curiosity, skepticism, concern, and passion, it doesn't end there. Curiosity needs to be sated; skepticism and suspicion justified or allayed; social wrongs righted. This requires the acquisition of particular kinds of knowledge and the use of a particular form of imagination—what C. Wright Mills (1959) called the **sociological imagination**.

By the sociological imagination, Mills meant that quality of mind which enables people who possess it to make connections between personal troubles and social issues. Troubles occur within or between individuals sharing the same immediate social environment. Losing a job; doing badly at school; failing at marriage or a relationship; even committing a crime, getting arrested, and being put in prison can certainly be understood in very immediate and personal terms. People lose jobs all the time because they screw up at work or can't get along with their bosses and coworkers. We sometimes do badly at school because we are too lazy to study or would rather party. People sometimes treat their partners with a lack of respect and fail to put the time and attention into a relationship necessary to make it work. Sometimes it really is our fault.

Often, however, it isn't—or isn't completely. When businesses close or stop hiring, when millions of people get laid off and you lose your job, that isn't your fault. When the dropout rates in urban public schools rise and the academic performance of the students who remain drops precipitately, something more is at work than student laziness. When the divorce rate rises dramatically, clearly more is at work than couples failing to make the compromises necessary for a successful marriage. When people decide to drive while drunk or stoned, they place themselves and others at risk. Surely, they should be held accountable for their actions. Yet the need for accountability doesn't explain why some people are held more accountable than others. While people of all races appear to use and sell illegal drugs at about the same rate, black men are imprisoned for drug offenses at rates twenty to fifty times greater than those of white men (Alexander 2012, 7). Sometimes personal problems are connected to public issues.

"An issue is a public matter: some value cherished by publics is felt to be threatened. Often there is a debate about what that value really is and about what it is that really threatens it" (Mills 1959, 8). Murray thinks that the core values, the "founding virtues" that made America great, indeed exceptional—industriousness, honesty, marriage, and religiosity—are being threatened (2012,130). Alexander thinks that the incarceration of poor African American males for drug offenses is not about an increase in crime or drug abuse. It is rather the result of "a stunningly comprehensive and well-disguised system of racialized social control that functions in a manner strikingly similar to Jim Crow" (2012, 4).

Certainly, making connections between personal troubles and social issues requires gathering the relevant facts, and exercising our reasoning capacity to make sense of those facts. But making sense of the social world requires more than facts and reasoning. It requires a quality of mind that will help us "to use information and develop reason in order to achieve lucid summations of what is going on in the world and of what is happening in [ourselves]" (Mills 1959, 5). When we do this, we use our sociological imagination to theorize.

Theory and Theorizing: A Different Way of Looking at Social Theory

Too often, in my view, social theories and the work of social theorists are separated from both what the theories are about, and how social theorists employ those theories to make sense of the social world. In an important sense, all thoughtful students of social life are theorists. They create and present theoretical constructions, pictures of social reality, as explanations for social problems. These problems, they argue, exist because the social world looks and works like this. To solve these problems, they argue, the social world needs to look different and to work differently.

Examples of Theorizing

Here I have selected four works as examples of theorizing. I don't assume that the readers of this book will have read the studies analyzed in it, only that they could read and understand them, and works like them. The studies analyzed here focus on key contemporary social phenomena—history, race, culture, class, gender, and indigenous peoples. They do so, however, from widely different perspectives. Charles Murray is an unabashed man of the right and his book has been influential in conservative circles. Michelle Alexander is a proud woman of the left and her book is very influential in the liberal-left community. Alison Wolf is an accomplished British economist, educator, and journalist. Her book does one of the things important books on social life should do—examines the unexpected and potentially negative consequences of positive social developments.

The subtitle of her well-reviewed book is "How the Rise of Working Women Has Created a Far Less Equal World." Margaret Kovach is a member of the Plains Cree and Salteaux peoples of the Great Plains in southern Saskatchewan. Hers is the only book of the four which could be considered a work of theory, but the indigenous theories and methods she discusses are not ones ordinarily covered in books or courses on theory. [...]

Suggested Further Readings

Berger, Peter. 1963. *Invitation to Sociology*, 164–177 (Sociology as a Humanistic Discipline). Garden City, New York: Doubleday Anchor Books.
Mills, C. Wright. 1959. *The Sociological Imagination*, 3–25 (The Promise). New York: Oxford University Press.

Bibliography

Alexander, Michelle. 2012. *The New Jim Crow: Mass Incarceration in the Age of Colorblindness*, rev. ed. New York: The New Press.
Berger, Peter L. 1963. *An Invitation to Sociology*. Garden City, NY: Doubleday Anchor Books.
Goffman, Irving. 1959. *The Presentation of Self in Everyday Life*. New York: Anchor Books.
Kovach, Margaret. 2009. *Indigenous Methodologies: Characteristics, Conversations, and Contexts*. Toronto: University of Toronto Press.
Mills, C. Wright. 1959. *The Sociological Imagination*. New York: Oxford University Press.
Murray, Charles. 2012. *Coming Apart: The State of White America, 1960–2010*. New York: Crown Publishing.
Wolf, Alison. 2013. *The XX Factor: How the Rise of Working Women Has Created a Far Less Equal World*. New York: Crown Publishers.

Discussion Topics

1. What does C. Wright Mills mean by "sociological imagination"? How does this concept relate to social problems?
2. What is a social theory? In addition, what are some roles social theories play in the analysis of social problems?
3. According to the author, what are the steps involved in the process of theorizing?
4. Select a social theory with which you are familiar, and apply it to a specific problem in the United States.

CONCLUSION

This article explains the important role that sociology plays in the investigation of social problems. The contribution of sociology to social problems is unique through its perspective, which is sociological imagination. Coined by C. Wright Mills, the concept of sociological imagination refers to the ability to establish a link between "biography" and "history." That is, sociological imagination enables us to understand that our personal troubles are connected to public issues. In a sense, this unique perspective of sociology allows uncovering or discovering the influential effects of social structure on social problems, which leads to theory formulation: theorizing. A social theory can be defined as a systematic, disciplined, and logical explanation of social phenomena, such as social problems. The process of theorizing occurs in three major steps: (1) Identify a problem ("the something ain't right"); (2) Describe the nature of the problem, its manifestation, and implications; and (3) Provide a description of how the problem can be solved and the impact of the solution on society.

UNIT 2

STRUCTURAL INEQUALITY AND IMPLICATIONS

Introduction

Defined as patterned by social interaction or social arrangement, social structure reflects the inequality between social classes. Conflict theorists postulate the existence of inequality between the bourgeoisie and the proletariat. The bourgeoisie is the class we commonly refer to as "haves" and the proletariat "have nots." Other terms used to illustrate this dichotomy in the US society are the "1 percent" and the "99 percent." The difference between the 1 percent and the 99 percent resides in the unequal possession of resources. The 1 percent is characterized by access to an extremely large amount of resources, while the 99 percent is characterized by the lack of them. This explains the inequality in society and the accompanying gap between the "1 percent" and the "99 percent."

The implications of inequality are far reaching in society. For Chuck Collins, in his article titled "How Inequality Wrecks Everything We Care About," inequality is at the source of the constant conflict between the "1 percent" and the "99 percent." Given the pervasiveness of inequality, only the "1 percent" is benefiting from the economic system that has been purposefully designed for them. Armed with the economic resources, the "1 percent" can afford to exert heavy weight on the political system. In fact, the "1 percent" has undeniable impacts on the democratic system of the United States; consequently, the political system is also biased in its favor, which undermines the votes at the ballot box. Having the control of the political and economic systems, the "1 percent" can effectively skew all the other sectors of the society and the social structure to its advantage. Since the social structure is designed to the detriment of the "99 percent," the poor are more likely to be sick, less likely to have access to healthcare, more likely to live in inner cities vs. suburbs, less likely to enjoy equal opportunity and justice, and more likely to be dependent on social welfare programs. In one short word, inequality is the source of several social problems, including poverty, which is the main topic of investigation by John Iceland.

In "Causes of Poverty," John Iceland is interested in understanding the factors associated with poverty. To reach this goal, he uses three different theories: culture of poverty, neoclassical economics, and social stratification. For the proponents of the culture of poverty theory, poor individuals suffer from poverty because of their culture, characterized by laziness, instant gratification, and lower moral values. Iceland finds this explanation unsatisfactory because poor Americans are part of American society, and therefore share the main culture in the United States. Compared to culture of poverty, neoclassical economics theory is based on the assumption that poverty can be traced to the individual's family background and educational level. That is, the economic well-being can be linked to an individual's traits. Thus, neoclassical economics is criticized for its individual-level orientation and failure to take into consideration the potential impacts of other social factors, such as the political, social, and economic systems. While neoclassical economics is exclusive, social stratification is more inclusive for postulating that social structure and its biases constitute the major cause of poverty. Using a general sociological stratification theory, Iceland established that inequality in social structure leads to racial, ethnic, and gender inequalities, which are the three major correlates of poverty.

While Iceland discusses in some depth racial, ethnic, and gender inequalities, Cohen dedicated a whole article to the topic. In his article titled "Gender Inequality," Philip Cohen discusses gender inequality in terms of economic inequality with its impacts on women's employment, income, and wealth. For him, the gender pay gap can be explained through differential employment levels between men and women, their work experience, occupation, level of education, and employer discrimination. The pay gap women experience sheds light on the differential incomes and wealth between them and their male counterparts. Even though women are more economically well-off in the United States than most women in other societies, gender inequality is still prevalent in this country. Gender inequality is not specific to the US society; it is a global or international problem that also exists in other countries.

Global inequality is the focus of Oded Galor's article titled "The Long Shadow of History: The Biogeography Origins of Comparative Economic Development." This article explains the factors that contributed to the progression from stagnation to economic growth, from less developed to developed economies using a unified growth theory. This theory also discusses how historical, prehistorical conditions, and regional and genetic diversities affect the interaction between human capital and economic development across countries. Ultimately, this theory explains the stratification on a global level along with its ensuing global inequality.

How Inequality Wrecks Everything We Care About

Chuck Collins

Chuck Collins, "How Inequality Wrecks Everything We Care About," *99 to 1: How Wealth Inequality Is Wrecking the World and What We Can Do about It*, pp. 59-67, 132-134. Copyright © 2012 by Berrett-Koehler Publishers. Reprinted with permission.

Editor's Introduction

In this article titled "How Inequality Wrecks Everything We Care About", the author Chuck Collins explores the topics of inequality and its implications on health, economy, and the democracy in the United States. This article was chosen to be included in this text because it deals with one of the major causes of social problems, which is inequality. After reading this article, you will have a better understanding of the conflicting relationship between the 1 percent and the 99 percent, and why these two classes are living in a parallel world.

The reality is that U.S. society is polarizing and its social arteries are hardening. The sumptuousness and bleakness of the respective lifestyles of rich and poor represents a scale of difference in opportunity and wealth that is almost medieval—and a standing offense to the American expectation that everyone has the opportunity for life, liberty and happiness.

—Will Hutton (b. 1951)

Inequality is wrecking the world. Not just poverty, which is destroying the lives of billions of people around the planet, but also inequality—the accelerating gap between the 99 percent and the 1 percent.

The Inequality Death Spiral

According to research in dozens of disciplines, the extreme disparities of wealth and power corrode our democratic system and public trust. They lead to a breakdown in civic cohesion and social solidarity, which in turn leads to worsened health outcomes.

Inequality undercuts social mobility and has disastrous effects on economic stability and growth. The notion of a "death spiral" may sound dramatic, but it captures the dynamic and reinforcing aspects of inequality. And these inequalities were a major contributing factor to the 1929 and 2008 economic downturns. What follows is the case against inequality.

Inequality Wrecks Our Democracy and Civic Life

Inequality is disenfranchising us, diminishing our vote at the ballot box and our voice in the public square. As dollars of the 1 percent displace the votes of the 99 percent as the currency of politics, the 1 percent wins. Not every time, but enough so that the tilt continues toward the agenda of the 1 percent.

The money of the 1 percent dominates our campaign finance system, even after efforts at reform. To run for U.S. Senate—or to win additional terms in the Senate after being elected—politicians must raise an estimated $15,000 a day in campaign contributions. To do this efficiently, politicians have to spend a lot of time courting people in the 1 percent, attending $1,000-a-plate fund-raising dinners and listening to their concerns and agenda. This means less time shaking hands in front of the Costco or Cracker Barrel. We all respond to the people we are surrounded by, and politicians are no different.

Elections do matter. Politicians care about votes on Election Day, and they campaign for those votes and work to get supporters to the polls. But candidates for the U.S. Congress know that every other day of the year they have to think about money.

The corporate 1 percent dominates the lobbying space around federal and state policies. In the last thirty years, the ranks of official lobbyists have exploded. In 1970, there were five registered lobbyists for every one of the 535 members of Congress. Today there are twenty-two lobbyists for every member.[1]

Who lobbies for the 99 percent? There are impressive organizations out there, such as Public Citizen and the Children's Defense Fund, that stand up, wave their arms, and say, "Hey, what about the 99 percent?" But they are severely underresourced, outgunned, and outmaneuvered by the organized 1 percent.

Inequality Makes Us Sick

The medical researchers have said it. And now a growing body of public health research is arriving at the same conclusion: inequality is making us sick.

The more inequality grows between the 1 percent and the 99 percent, the less healthy we are. Unequal communities have greater rates of heart disease, asthma, mental illness, cancer, and other morbid illnesses.

---

1. According to the Center for Responsive Politics, there were 12,220 registered lobbyists in 2011. This is 22.84 lobbyists for every one of the 535 members of Congress. Center for Responsive Politics, "Lobbying Database," www.opensecrets.org/lobby/index.php?ql3 (accessed January 3, 2012).

Of course, poverty contributes to all kinds of bad health outcomes. But research shows that you are better off in a low-income community with greater equality than you are in a community with a higher income but more extreme inequalities.

Counties and countries with lower incomes but less inequality have better health outcomes. They have lower infant mortality rates, longer life expectancy, and lower incidences of all kinds of diseases. Counties with higher average incomes but greater disparities between rich and poor have the opposite indicators. They are less healthy places to live.[2]

Why is this so? According to British health researcher Richard Wilkinson, communities with less inequality have stronger "social cohesion," more cultural limits on unrestrained individualism, and more effective networks of mutual aid and caring. "The individualism and values of the market are restrained by a social morality," Wilkinson writes. The existence of more social capital "lubricates the workings of the whole society and economy. There are fewer signs of antisocial aggressiveness, and society appears more caring."[3]

Inequality Tears Our Communities Apart

Extreme inequalities of wealth rip our communities apart with social divisions and distrust, leading to an erosion of social cohesion and solidarity. The 1 percent and the 99 percent today don't just live on opposite sides of the tracks—they occupy parallel universes.

New research shows that we're becoming more polarized by class and race in terms of where we live. A 2011 report based on U.S. Census data notes, "As overall income inequality grew in the last four decades, high- and low-income families have become increasingly less likely to live near one another. Mixed income neighborhoods have grown rarer, while affluent and poor neighborhoods have grown much more common."[4] As this distance widens, it is harder for people to feel like they are in the same boat.

High levels of inequality lead to the construction of physical walls. In many parts of the world, the members of the 1 percent reside in gated communities, surrounded by security systems and bodyguards. More than 9 million households in the United States live behind walls in gated communities, similar to the statistics in polarized societies such as Mexico and Brazil. Over a third of new housing starts in the southern United States are in gated communities.[5]

2. For a good overview of health and inequality issues, see Sam Pizzigati, *Greed and Good: Understanding and Overcoming the Inequality That Limits Our Lives* (New York: Apex Press, 2004), 311–30. Also see Dr. Stephen Bezruchka's website, Population Health Forum (http://depts.washington.edu/eqhlth), for information on global and U.S. health and inequality information. Also see Stephen Bezruchka and M. A. Mercer, "The Lethal Divide: How Economic Inequality Affects Health," in M. Fort, M. A. Mercer, and O. Gish, eds., *Sickness and Wealth: The Corporate Assault on Global Health* (Boston: South End Press, 2004), 11–18.

3. See Richard Wilkinson, *Unhealthy Societies: The Afflictions of Inequality* (London: Routledge, 1996).

4. Sean F. Reardon and Kendra Bischoff, "Growth in the Residential Segregation of Families by Income, 1970–2009," Stanford University, US 2010 Project, Russell Sage Foundation, and American Communities Project at Brown University, November 2011, www.s4.brown.edu/us2010/Data/Report/report111111.pdf (accessed January 3, 2012).

5. Edward J. Blakely and Mary Gail Snyder, *Fortress America: Gated Communities in the United States* (Washington, DC: Brookings Institution Press, 1997); and Justice Policy Institute study, as reported in Jesse Katy, "A Nation of Too Many Prisoners?" *Los Angeles Times*, February 15, 2000.

The relationship between the 1 percent and the 99 percent is characterized by fear, distance, misunderstanding, distrust, and class and racial antagonisms. As a result, there is less caring and a greater amount of individualistic behavior. Part of how people express care is support for public investments in health infrastructure and prevention that benefit everyone. As societies grow unequal, support for such investments declines.

Solidarity is characterized by people taking responsibility for one another and caring for neighbors. But for solidarity to happen, people must know one another and have institutions that transcend differences in class, culture, and race. In communities with great inequality, these institutions don't exist and solidarity is weakened.

Inequality Erodes Social Mobility and Equal Opportunity

Inequality undermines the cherished value of equality of opportunity and social mobility. Intergenerational mobility is the possibility of shifting up or down the income ladder relative to your parents' status. In a mobile society, your economic circumstances are not defined or limited by the economic origins of your family.

For many decades, economists argued that inequality in the United States was the price we paid for a dynamic economy with social mobility.[6] We didn't want to be like Canada or those northern European economies, economists would argue, with their rigid class systems and lack of mobility.

But here's the bad news: Canada and those European nations—with their social safety nets and progressive tax policies—are now more mobile than U.S. society. Research across the industrialized OECD countries has found that Canada, Australia, and the Nordic countries (Denmark, Norway, Sweden, and Finland) are among the most mobile. There is a strong correlation between social mobility and policies that redistribute income and wealth through taxation. The United States is now among the *least* mobile of industrialized countries in terms of earnings.[7]

Inequality Erodes Public Services

The 99 percent depends on the existence of a robust commonwealth of public and community institutions. As Bill Gates Sr., the father of the founder of Microsoft, wrote,

> The ladder of opportunity for America's middle class depends on strong and accessible public educational institutions, libraries, state parks and municipal pools. And for America's

6. Wojciech Kopczuk, Emmanuel Saez, and Jae Song, "Earnings Inequality and Mobility in the United States: Evidence from Social Security Data Since 1937," *Quarterly Journal of Economics* 125, 1 (February 2010): 91–128, http://ideas.repec.org/a/tpr/qjecon/v125y2010i1p91-128.html (accessed January 3, 2012).

7. OECD, "A Family Affair: Intergenerational Social Mobility Across OECD Countries," *Economic Policy Reforms: Going for Growth*, www.oecd.org/dataoecd/2/7/45002641.pdf (accessed January 3, 2012). Also see the Pew Charitable Trust's Economic Mobility Project (www.economicmobility.org) and their study "Chasing the Same Dream, Climbing Different Ladders: Economic Mobility in the United States and Canada," January 2010, www.economicmobility.org/reports_and_research/other/other?id=0012 (accessed January 3, 2012).

poor, the ladder of opportunity also includes access to affordable health care, quality public transportation, and childcare assistance.[8]

Historically, during times of great inequality, there is a disinvestment in the commonwealth.[9] There is less support provided for education, affordable housing, public health care, and other pillars of a level playing field. By contrast, in 1964, a time of relative equality, there was greater concern about poverty; in fact, we launched the War on Poverty to further reduce disadvantage.

Today, as the 1 percent delinks from our communities, it privatizes the services it needs. This leads to two bad outcomes. First, because the 1 percent does not depend on commonwealth services, it would rather not pay for them. They often prefer tax cuts and limited government, which leave them more of their money to spend on privatized services.

Second, the quality of life for the 99 percent suffers when the wealthy don't have a personal stake in maintaining quality public services. As we've seen, the 1 percent has tremendous clout. Its members have the ear of elected officials, command over charitable dollars, dominance of media ownership, and networking connections that are sometimes called "social capital." In a democratic society, good government and strong public institutions require civic engagement by everyone. But when those with the biggest amount of political power, largest number of connections, and greatest capacity don't have a stake, a cycle of disinvestment occurs.

The cycle of disinvestment begins when public services start to deteriorate after the withdrawal of tax dollars and the participation of the powerful. For example, if someone doesn't use the neighborhood public swimming pool because he or she belongs to a private club or spends summers at a private beach house, that person doesn't have a stake in ensuring that the public swimming pool is open all summer, clean and well maintained, and staffed with qualified lifeguards. When services deteriorate and the powerful no longer participate, it leads to a decline in political support and resources, which in turn leads to a cycle of further disinvestment.

This lack of stake is even more visible in terms of public education, where the withdrawal of the 1 percent and even the top 30 percent of families has contributed to severe disinvestment in some school districts. This triggers a vicious circle of budget cuts, stakeholders pulling out, and declining public support for education.

The cycle of disinvestment accelerates when it becomes rational to abandon public and community services if one can afford to do so. Those who can get out do so, in a rush-to-the-exits moment. Families in the 99 percent work extra hard to privatize the services they need until there is a wholesale withdrawal from the public sphere.

If you can't depend on the bus to get to work, you buy a car. If you can't rely on the local public schools to educate your child, then you stretch to pay for private schools. If you can't depend on the lifeguards to show up at the public pool, then you join the private pool. If you can't depend on the police to protect your neighborhood, you hire a private security service or move to a gated community. The cycle of disinvestment continues and the costs of privatized services rise, trapping the remaining families in poor schools and neighborhoods lacking services.

8. Bill Gates Sr. and Chuck Collins, *Wealth and Our Commonwealth: Why American Should Tax Accumulated Fortunes* (Boston: Beacon Press, 2003).
9. Ibid., 19–22.

Inequality Undermines Economic Growth

Remember the last time in history that the 1 percent had such a large share of the wealth pie? It was 1929, the eve of the Great Depression. Economic historians argue that this was not a coincidence. Too much inequality contributes to economic instability.

The corollary is that periods of shared prosperity have greater economic growth and stability. The period after World War II, 1947 to 1977, is often cited as a case study of a high-growth and high-equality period.

Making such comparisons is fraught with danger—we're not just comparing apples and oranges, we're comparing bicycles and dump trucks. The period after World War II was unprecedented in terms of the dominant and unrivaled role the United States played in the global economy. But international comparative data that look at inequality and economic performance reinforce this story. More-equal societies do better on most indicators.

The conventional wisdom, espoused in the 1960s by economists such as Arthur Okun of the Brookings Institution, was that there was a trade-off between growth and equity: policies that increased equality would slow economic growth, and aggressive pro-growth policies would worsen inequality. But this thinking is now being turned on its head.

Research by the International Monetary Fund (IMF) and the National Bureau of Economic Research point to the fact that more-equal societies have stronger rates of growth, experience longer economic expansions, and are quicker to recover from economic downturns. According to Jonathan Ostry, an economist at the IMF, trends toward unequal income in the United States mean that future economic expansions will be just one-third as long as they were in the 1960s, prior to the widening of the income divide. Less-equal societies are more vulnerable to both financial crises and political instability.[10]

In volatile markets, investors become gun-shy, even those in the 1 percent. When they perceive that financial markets are rigged in favor of insiders and the politically connected, they take their money somewhere else. "You're going to lose a generation of investors," observed Barry Ritholtz, an investor researcher with Fusion IQ. "And that's how you end up with a 25-year bear market. That's the risk if people start to think there is no economic justice."[11]

Many economists have drawn parallels between 1929 on the eve of the Great Depression and the 2008 economic meltdown. Raghuram Rajan, a former chief economist for the IMF, argues that both depressions were preceded by periods of extreme inequality. In his book *Fault Lines: How Hidden Fractures Still Threaten the World Economy*, Rajan observes that during the decade prior to both economic downturns, the 1 percent captured a gigantic percentage of income gains and wages were stagnant for the majority of Americans. Meanwhile, government policies and private corporate practices encouraged easy access to credit and borrowing among the poor and middle classes. Household debt nearly doubled during both periods.[12]

Did inequality play a role in the 2008 economic meltdown? [...]

10. David Lynch, "How Inequality Hurts the Economy," *Business Week Insider*, November 16, 2011, www.businessweek.com/magazine/how-inequality-hurts-the-economy-11162011.html?campaign_id=rss_topStories (accessed January 3, 2012).

11. Ibid.

12. Raghuram G. Rajan, *Fault Lines: How Hidden Fractures Still Threaten the World Economy* (Princeton, NJ: Prince ton University Press, 2010).

Discussion Topics

1. What is meant by "… the extreme disparities of wealth and power corrode our democratic system"?
2. Discuss the link between inequality and health problems in the United States.
3. This article argues that "… the 1 percent and the 99 percent … occupy parallel universes." What does this statement mean? How can we bridge the gap between the two?
4. Discuss how inequality can negatively affect economic growth in the United States.

The Long Shadow of History: The Biogeographical Origins of Comparative Economic Development

Oded Galor

Oded Galor, "The Long Shadow of History: The Biogeographical Origins of Comparative Economic Development," *Demographic Change and Long-Run Development*, ed. Matteo Cervellati and Uwe Sunde, pp. 29-41. Copyright © 2017 by MIT Press. Reprinted with permission.

Editor's Introduction

This article on "The Long Shadow of the History: The Biogeographical Origins of the Comparative Economic" by Oded Galor discusses the different stages of the economic progress at the global level. This article was included in this text because it explains international economic inequality using the theoretical perspective of unified growth theory. After reading this article, you will have a better understanding of the impacts of the biographical factors on economic inequality at the global level and the relationship between the level of diversity and economic development.

Introduction

The transition from an epoch of stagnation to an era of sustained economic growth has marked the onset of one of the most remarkable transformations in the course of human history. While living standards in the world economy stagnated during the millennia preceding the Industrial Revolution, income per capita has undergone an unprecedented twelve-fold increase over the past two centuries, altering the distribution of education, health, and wealth across the globe.

The improvement in standards of living has not been universally shared among individuals and societies. Variation in the timing of the take-off from stagnation to growth has led to a vast, worldwide divergence in income per capita. Inequality, which had been modest until the nineteenth century, has widened considerably, and the ratio of income per capita between the richest and the poorest regions of the world has been magnified from a moderate 3:1 ratio in 1820 to a staggering 15:1 ratio in 2010.

Throughout most of human existence, the process of development was marked by Malthusian stagnation—resources generated by technological progress and land expansion were channeled primarily toward an increase in population, providing only a minimal contribution to the level of income per capita in the long run. While cross-country variations in technology and land productivity were reflected in differing population densities, their effect on variation in living standards was merely transitory (Ashraf and Galor 2011).

In contrast, during the past two centuries, various regions of the world have departed from the Malthusian trap and witnessed considerable growth in income per capita. The slow-down in population growth during the demographic transition has freed productivity gains from the counterbalancing effect of population growth and enabled technological progress and human capital formation to pave the way for an era of sustained economic growth.

Growth and Comparative Development

The transition from an epoch of Malthusian stagnation to an era of sustained economic growth and the corresponding divergence in income per capita across the globe have been the center of intensive research during the past two decades. The inconsistency of the predominant theories of economic growth regarding some of the most fundamental characteristics of the growth process and their limited ability to shed light on the origins of the vast global disparity in living standards have led to the development of a unified theory of economic growth that captures the growth process in its entirety.

The advancement of unified growth theory has been fueled by the conviction that the understanding of global variation in economic development would be fragile and incomplete unless the prevailing theory of economic growth reflected the principal driving forces behind the entire process of development and captured the central role that historical factors have played in producing the current disparities in living standards.[1] Moreover, the theory has been fostered by the realization that the hurdles faced by less-developed economies would remain obscure unless the factors that facilitated the transition of the currently developed economies from stagnation to growth were identified and modified to account for the differences in the growth structure of less-developed economies in an interdependent world.

Unified Growth Theory

Unified growth theory provides a fundamental framework of analysis for the evolution of individuals, societies, and economies during the *entire* course of human history (Galor 2011, 2005; Galor and Weil 2000; Galor

---

1. Clearly, the understanding of the contemporary world would be limited and incomplete in the absence of a historical perspective. However, the intensity of recent explorations into the interaction between economic development and economic history could be attributed to increasing frustration with the failure of the ahistorical branch of growth theory to capture some of the most fundamental aspects of the growth process.

and Moav 2002; Galor and Mountford 2008).[2] In a *single* analytical framework, the theory captures the main characteristics of the process of development: (*i*) the epoch of Malthusian stagnation that characterized most of human history, (*ii*) the escape from the Malthusian trap and its associated spike in the growth rates of income per capita and population, (*iii*) the emergence of human capital formation in the process of development, (*iv*) the trigger for the onset of the demographic transition, (*v*) the emergence of the contemporary era of sustained economic growth, and (*vi*) the divergence in income per capita across countries.

Unified growth theory explores the fundamental factors that have contributed to the remarkable transition from stagnation to growth and examines their significance to the understanding of the contemporary growth process of developed and less-developed economies. First, it unveils the factors that have generated the Malthusian trap. What accounts for the epoch of stagnation that has characterized most of human history? Why did episodes of technological progress in the preindustrial era fail to generate sustained economic growth? Why has population growth counterbalanced the expansion of resources per capita that could have been generated by technological progress?

Moreover, the theory uncovers the forces that triggered the take-off from stagnation to growth. What is the origin of the sudden spurt in income per capita and population growth rates during the course of industrialization? What was the source of the striking reversal in the positive relationship between income per capita and population growth that existed throughout most of human history? Would the transition to the modern state of sustained economic growth have been feasible without the decline in population growth? What are the hurdles faced by less-developed economies in their attempts to transition to a sustained-growth regime?

Unified growth theory suggests that the transition from stagnation to growth has been an inevitable by-product of the process of development. It argues that the inherent Malthusian interaction between the rate of technological progress and the size and composition of the population accelerated the pace of technological progress and ultimately raised the importance of education in coping with the rapidly changing technological environment. The rise in industrial demand for education significantly reduced fertility rates. It enabled economies to divert a larger share of the fruits of factor accumulation and technological progress to the enhancement of human capital formation and income per capita, paving the way for sustained economic growth.

The theory further explores the dynamic interaction between human evolution and the process of economic development and advances the hypothesis that the forces of natural selection played a significant role in the evolution of the world economy from stagnation to growth (Galor and Moav 2002; Galor and Michalopoulos 2012). The Malthusian pressures have acted as the key determinant of population size and conceivably, via natural selection, have shaped the composition of the population. Lineages of individuals whose traits were complementary to the economic environment generated higher levels of income and thus a larger number of surviving offspring, and the gradual increase in the representation of their traits in the population contributed to the process of development and the take-off from stagnation to growth.

2. See also Hansen and Prescott 2002; Cervellati and Sunde 2005; Lagerlöf 2006.

Origins of the Global Disparity in Living Standards

Unified growth theory sheds new light on the origins of the perplexing divergence in income per capita across developed and less-developed regions during the past two centuries. What accounts for the sudden take-off from stagnation to growth among some countries in the world and the persistent stagnation in others? Why has the positive link between income per capita and population growth reversed its course in some economies but not in others? Has the transition to a state of sustained economic growth in advanced economies adversely affected the process of development in poorer ones? Have variations in prehistorical biogeographical factors had a persistent effect on the composition of human capital and economic development across the world?

The theory unveils the principal economic forces that have generated the remarkable transition from stagnation to growth and underlines their significance to understanding the contemporary growth process of both developed and less-developed economies. Moreover, it sheds light on the role of historical and prehistorical characteristics in the divergence of income per capita across regions of the world during the past two centuries.

The theory advances the understanding of three fundamental aspects of comparative economic development. First, it identifies the factors that have governed the transition from stagnation to growth and have thus contributed to the observed worldwide differences in economic development. Second, it highlights the persistent effects that variations in historical and prehistorical conditions have had on the composition of human capital and economic development across countries. Finally, it uncovers the forces that have sparked the emergence of convergence clubs and explores the characteristics that have determined the association of different economies with each club.

The first layer of unified growth theory explores the underlying forces that have determined the timing and pace of the transition from an epoch of Malthusian stagnation to an era of sustained economic growth and have thus contributed to the disparity in economic development across countries. Country-specific characteristics that have affected the intensity of the pivotal interaction between the rate of technological progress and the size and composition of the population have generated variations in the transition from stagnation to growth and contributed to the gap in income per capita across countries.

Variation in rates of technological progress has reinforced the differential pace of the emergence of demand for human capital, the onset of the demographic transition, and the shift from stagnation to growth and has thus contributed to the divergence in income per capita during the past two centuries. In particular, worldwide variation in the pace of technological progress has been triggered by cross-country differences in: (*a*) the stock of knowledge and its rate of creation and diffusion among members of society; (*b*) the level of protection of intellectual property rights, its positive effect on the incentive to innovate, and its adverse effect on the proliferation of existing knowledge; (*c*) financial constraints and the level of competitiveness of the innovation sector; (*d*) the composition of cultural and religious attributes and their effect on knowledge creation and diffusion; (*e*) the composition of interest groups in society and their incentives to block or promote technological innovations; (*f*) the level of human diversity and the degree to which it complements the implementation and advancement of new technological paradigms; (*g*) the propensity to trade and its effect on technological diffusion; and (*h*) the abundance of natural resources essential for an imminent technological paradigm.

Once the technologically driven demand for human capital emerged during the second phase of industrialization, the prevalence of characteristics conducive to human capital formation has determined the swiftness of its accumulation, the timing of the demographic transition, the pace of the transition from stagnation to growth, and the observed distribution of income in the world economy. Thus, variations in country-specific characteristics that have contributed to human capital formation have differentially affected the timing and pace of the transition from agriculture to industry and comparative economic development as a whole.

In particular, global variation in human capital formation has been influenced by cross-country differences in: (*a*) the prevalence of human capital–promoting institutions and policies (e.g., the availability, accessibility, and quality of public education); (*b*) the ability of individuals to finance the cost of education as well as the foregone earnings associated with schooling; (*c*) the impact of inequality levels and of the degree of credit market imperfections on the extent of underinvestment in education; (*d*) the stock of knowledge in society and its effect on the productivity of investment of human capital; (*e*) the composition of cultural and religious groups in a society and their effects on the incentives of individuals to invest in human capital; (*f*) the impact of geographical attributes on health and thus human capital formation; (*g*) the propensity to trade and the patterns of comparative advantage regarding the production of skill-intensive goods; and (*h*) preferences for educated offspring that may reflect cultural attributes, the composition of religious groups, and social status associated with education.

In its second layer, unified growth theory highlights the direct, persistent effect that deep-rooted factors, determined as early as tens of thousands years ago, have had on the course of comparative economic development from the dawn of human civilization to the modern era. In particular, the theory captures the thesis that some differences in the process of development across the globe can be traced to biogeographical factors that led to regional variation in the timing of the Neolithic Revolution (Diamond 1997). Moreover, the theory is consistent with the thesis that the exodus of modern humans from Africa, fifty to seventy thousand years ago, appears central to understanding comparative economic development across the globe (Ashraf and Galor 2013a).

In its third layer, unified growth theory advances the understanding of the existence of multiple growth regimes and the emergence of convergence clubs (i.e., groups of countries among which the disparity in income per capita tends to narrow over time). The theory attributes these phenomena to variation in the position of economies across the distinct phases of development. It suggests that the differential timing of take-offs from stagnation to growth has segmented economies into three fundamental growth regimes: (*i*) slowly growing economies in the vicinity of a Malthusian steady state, (*ii*) fast-growing countries in a sustained-growth regime, and (*iii*) economies in transition from the first regime to the second. Moreover, it suggests that the presence of multiple convergence clubs may reflect a temporary state as endogenous forces may ultimately permit members of the Malthusian club to shift their positions and join the members of the sustained-growth club.

Persistence of Prehistorical Biogeographical Conditions

Theories of comparative development highlight a variety of proximate and ultimate factors underlying some of the vast inequities in living standards across the globe. The importance of geographical, cultural, and institutional factors, human capital formation, ethnic, linguistic, and religious fractionalization, colonialism, and globalization has been at the center of a debate regarding the origins of the differential timing of transitions from stagnation to growth and the remarkable transformation of the world income distribution during the last two centuries. While theoretical and empirical research have typically focused on the effects of such factors in increasing and sustaining the divergence in income per capita in the postindustrial era, attention has recently been drawn toward some deep-rooted factors that have been argued to affect the course of comparative economic development. This research argues that deep-rooted factors, determined thousands of years ago, have had a significant effect on the course of economic development from the dawn of human civilization to the contemporary era.

Regional Variations in the Onset of the Neolithic Revolution

Variation in productivity and standards of living across the globe during the course of development can be traced to the biogeographical factors that led to regional variation in the timing of the Neolithic Revolution (Diamond 1997). Accordingly, the emergence and subsequent diffusion of agricultural practices were primarily driven by geographic conditions such as climate, continental size and orientation, as well as the availability of wild plant and animal species amenable to domestication. In particular, favorable biogeographical endowments that were associated with a larger variety of domesticable species of plants and animals as well as the diffusion of agricultural practices contributed to the emergence of agriculture, giving some societies the early advantage of operating with superior production technology and generating resource surpluses. They permitted the establishment of a non food-producing class, whose members were crucial for the development of written language and science and for the formation of cities, technology-based military powers, and nation-states. The early dominance of these societies persisted throughout most of history, being further sustained by geopolitical and historical processes, such as colonization.

As depicted in figure 3.1, the timing of agricultural transitions is indeed instrumental to the understanding of precolonial economic development, as captured by population density in the year 1500 CE (Ashraf and Galor 2011). However, evidence suggests that over the past five hundred years, the initial dominance produced by an earlier transition to agriculture has dissipated, and the timing of agricultural transitions has no significant effect on the contemporary level of income per capita (Ashraf and Galor 2013a).[3]

3. The finding of persistent effect on contemporary income (e. g., Olsson and Hibbs 2005; Putterman 2008) does not hold once unobserved heterogeneity that is captured by continental or regional fixed effects is accounted for.

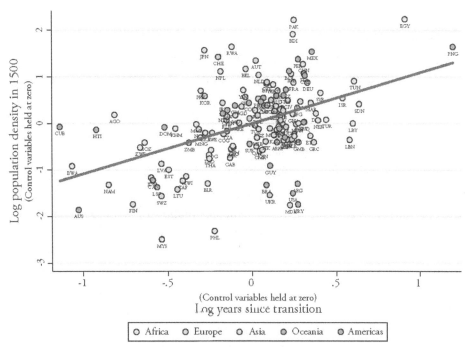

FIGURE 3.1   Years elapsed since the Neolithic Transition and productivity in the year 1500 CE. Conditional on land productivity, geographical factors, and continental fixed effects.

Ashraf and Galor 2011.

Regional Variations in Genetic Diversity

Variation in productivity and standards of living across the globe during the course of development can be traced to the effect of the migratory distance from the cradle of the anatomically modern human in east Africa to the degree of genetic diversity among indigenous populations across the globe (Ashraf and Galor 2013a). In particular, in the course of the exodus of *Homo sapiens* out of Africa, variation in migratory distance from the cradle of humankind in East Africa to various settlements across the globe affected genetic diversity and has had a long-lasting, hump-shaped effect on the pattern of comparative economic development that is not captured by geographical, institutional, and cultural factors.

Ashraf and Galor (2013a, 2013b) establish that the level of genetic diversity within a society has a hump-shaped effect on developmental outcomes in the precolonial and modern eras, reflecting the trade-off between the beneficial and the detrimental effects of diversity on productivity. While the intermediate level of genetic diversity prevalent among the Asian and European populations has been conducive for development, the high degree of diversity among African populations and the low degree of diversity among Native American populations have been a detrimental force in the development of those regions.

The hypothesis rests upon two fundamental building blocks. First, the migratory distance from the cradle of humankind in East Africa had an adverse effect on the degree of genetic diversity within ancient indigenous settlements across the globe. Following the prevailing hypothesis, commonly called the serial founder effect, it is postulated that, in the course of human expansion over Earth, as subgroups of the populations of parental colonies left to establish new settlements further away, they carried with them only a subset of the overall genetic diversity of their parental colonies.

Second, there exists an optimal level of diversity for economic development, reflecting the interplay between the conflicting effects of diversity on the developmental process. The adverse effect pertains to the detrimental impact of diversity on the efficiency of the aggregate production process of an economy. Heterogeneity increases the likelihood of miscoordination and distrust, reducing cooperation and disrupting the socioeconomic order. Greater population diversity is therefore associated with lower total-factor productivity, which inhibits the ability of a society to operate efficiently with respect to its production possibility frontier. The beneficial effect of diversity, conversely, concerns the positive role of diversity in the expansion of a society's production possibility frontier. A wider spectrum of traits is more likely to be complementary to the development and successful implementation of advanced technological paradigms. Greater heterogeneity therefore fosters the ability of a society to incorporate more sophisticated and efficient modes of production, expanding the economy's production possibility frontier and conferring the benefits of increased total-factor productivity.

Higher diversity in a society's population can therefore have conflicting effects on the level of its total-factor productivity. Aggregate productivity is enhanced in one respect by an increased capacity for technological advancement while diminished in another by reduced cooperation and efficiency. However, if the beneficial effects of population diversity dominate at lower levels of diversity and the detrimental effects dominate at higher levels (i.e., if there are diminishing marginal returns to both diversity and homogeneity), the theory would predict an inverted-U relationship between genetic diversity and developmental outcomes throughout the developmental process.

The historical analysis suggests that, controlling for the influence of land productivity, the timing of the Neolithic Revolution, and continent fixed effects, a 1% increase in diversity for the most homogenous society in the sample would raise its population density in 1500 CE by 36%, whereas a 1% decrease in diversity for the most diverse society would raise its population density by 29%. Further, a 1% change in diversity in either direction at the predicted optimum of 0.683 would lower population density by 1.5%.

The contemporary analysis indicates that the genetic diversity of contemporary national populations has an economically and statistically significant hump-shaped effect on income per capita (figure 3.2). This hump-shaped impact is robust to control for continent fixed effects, ethnic fractionalization, various measures of institutional quality (i.e., social infrastructure, an index gauging the extent of democracy, and constraints on the power of chief executives), legal origins, major religion shares, the share of the population of European descent, years of schooling, disease environments, and other geographical factors that have received attention in the empirical literature on cross-country comparative development.

The direct effect of genetic diversity on contemporary income per capita, once institutional, cultural, and geographical factors are accounted for, indicates that: (*i*) increasing the diversity of the most homogenous country in the sample (Bolivia) by 1% would raise its income per capita in the year 2000 CE by 41%; (*ii*) decreasing the diversity of the most diverse country in the sample (Ethiopia) by 1% would raise its income per capita by 21% (*iii*) increasing Bolivia's diversity to the optimum level prevalent in the United States would increase Bolivia's per capita income by a factor of 5.4, and (*iv*) decreasing Ethiopia's diversity to the optimum level of the United States would increase Ethiopia's per capita income by a factor of 1.7. Moreover, the partial $R2$ associated with diversity suggests that residual genetic diversity explains about 16% of the cross-country variation in residual log income per capita in 2000 CE, conditional on the institutional, cultural, and geographical covariates in the baseline regression model.

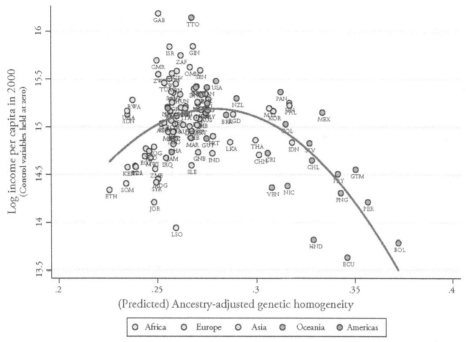

FIGURE 3.2   Genetic diversity and income per capita in the year 2000 CE. Conditional on geographical, cultural, and institutional factors and continental fixed effects.

Ashraf and Galor 2013a.

Looming Challenges

Unified growth theory has planted the seeds for a renaissance in the fields of economic growth and economic history. It has generated novel testable predictions that enabled researchers to revisit their interpretations of existing evidence while guiding them in their important mission of data collection. Recent research on the validity of the Malthusian hypothesis, the sources of the demographic transition, and the role of human capital in the advancement of industrialization is an early indication of the potential impact of unified growth theory.

Further, the theory suggests that exploring the role of cultural, institutional, and geographical factors in the differential pace of the transition from stagnation to growth and the emergence of a great disparity in economic development across the globe could generate significant insights about the growth process and comparative economic development. In particular, the hypothesis that the pace of the transition from stagnation to growth has been influenced by cultural and institutional factors, which may have evolved in response to the economic incentives that the process of development has generated, could benefit from further exploration. Have the institutional and cultural factors that have been associated empirically with the disparity in economic development been the oil that lubricated the wheels of development once economies emerged from the Malthusian trap, or were they the initial trigger that set those wheels in motion?

Finally, the most promising and challenging research in the field of economic growth in the next decades will be: (*i*) the examination of the role of historical and prehistorical factors in the prevailing disparity across the globe and (*ii*) the analysis of the interaction between human evolution and the process of economic development. The exploration of these vast and largely uncharted territories may revolutionize the understanding of the process of economic development and the persistent effect that deep-rooted factors have had on the composition of human capital and economic outcomes across the globe, fostering the design of policies that could promote economic growth and poverty alleviation.

References

Ashraf, Q., and O. Galor (2011): "Dynamics and Stagnation in the Malthusian Epoch", *American Economic Review*, 101, 2003–2041.

———(2013a): "The 'Out of Africa' Hypothesis, Human Genetic Diversity, and Comparative Economic Development", *American Economic Review*, 103, 1–46.

———(2013b): "Genetic Diversity and the Origins of Cultural Fragmentation", *American Economic Review*, 103, 528–533.

Cervellati, M., and U. Sunde (2005): "Human Capital Formation, Life Expectancy, and the Process of Development", *American Economic Review*, 95, 1653–1672.

Diamond, J. M. (1997): *Guns, Germs and Steel: The Fates of Human Societies*, New York W. W. Norton & Co.

Galor, O. (2005): *Handbook of Economic Growth, volume 1*, From Stagnation to Growth: Unified Growth Theory, Elsevier, 171–293.

———(2011): *Unified Growth Theory*, Princeton, NJ: Princeton University Press.

Galor, O., and S. Michalopoulos (2012): "Evolution and the Growth Process: Natural Selection of Entrepreneurial Traits", *Journal of Economic Theory*, 147, 759–780.

Galor, O., and O. Moav (2002): "Natural Selection and the Origin of Economic Growth", *Quarterly Journal of Economics*, 117, 1133–1191.

Galor, O., and A. Mountford (2008): "Trading Population for Productivity: Theory and Evidence", *Review of Economic Studies*, 75, 1143–1179.

Galor, O., and D. N. Weil (2000): "Population, Technology, and Growth: From Malthusian Stagnation to the Demographic Transition and Beyond", *American Economic Review*, 90, 806–828.

Hansen, G. D., and E. C. Prescott (2002): "Malthus to Solow", *American Economic Review*, 92, 1205–1217.

Lagerlöf, N.-P. (2006): "The Galor-Weil Model Revisited: A Quantitative Exercise", *Review of Economic Dynamics*, 9, 116–142.

Olsson, O., and D. A. Hibbs, JR. (2005): "Biogeography and Long-Run Economic Development", *European Economic Review*, 49, 909–938.

Putterman, L. (2008): "Agriculture, Diffusion, and Development: Ripple Effects of the Neolithic Revolution", *Economica*, 75, 729–748.

Discussion Topics

1. How does the unified growth theory explain economic inequality on the global level (between countries)?
2. Identify and explain how biogeographical factors contribute to economic inequality internationally.
3. Explain the relationship between the level of diversity and economic development.
4. What are the weaknesses or the limitations of the unified growth theory?

Causes of Poverty

John Iceland

John Iceland, "Causes of Poverty," *Poverty in America: A Handbook*, pp. 70-97, 165-173, 181-199. Copyright © 2012 by University of California Press. Reprinted with permission.

Editor's Introduction

This article titled "Causes of Poverty" by John Iceland deals with poverty, its causes, and its impacts on society. This article was selected to be included in this text because it explains why poverty is prevalent in some groups than others using general sociological theories of stratification, and it discusses the pattern of stratification across gender, race, and ethnicity. After reading this article, you will understand that poor are poor not because they are not doing enough, but because of the existence of inequality in the social structure.

I t is commonly believed that individual failings or wayward values propel people into poverty. In the 1960s, anthropologist Oscar Lewis wrote:

> By the time slum children are age six or seven they have usually absorbed the basic values and attitudes of their subculture and are not psychologically geared to take full advantage of changing conditions or increased opportunities which may occur in their lifetime.[1]

A 2001 poll in the United States asked: "In your opinion, which is the bigger cause of poverty

---

1. Oscar Lewis, *La Vida* (New York: Random House, 1966), quoted in Schiller, *Economics of Poverty and Discrimination*, p. 127.

today—that people are not doing enough to help themselves out of poverty, or that circumstances beyond their control cause them to be poor?" Responses were nearly evenly split between "people not doing enough" (48 percent) and "circumstances" (45 percent). More affluent people were more likely to believe that poor people themselves were not doing enough, while the poor were more likely to point to circumstances rather than themselves. The same poll also showed that about two-thirds of Americans believe that the poor have the same values as other Americans, and about a fifth thought they had lower moral values.[2]

In the social sciences, neoclassical economic theory also emphasizes the role of individual-level traits, such as family background and educational level, in affecting people's economic well-being. For example, many studies have shown that people who invest in their education or skills can expect higher incomes. This view dominates economic research on poverty in the social sciences. Alice O'Connor has argued that "the ubiquity of the neoclassical model as a way of explaining the causes and consequence of poverty—alternately labeled human capital, social capital, or cultural capital—indicates the extent to which that central theoretical framework still prevails. So, too, does the overwhelming emphasis on individual-level attributes as the 'causes' of poverty, an emphasis that avoids recognition of politics, institutions, or structural inequality."[3]

While neoclassical economic studies are informative, as both human capital traits and individual actions do affect outcomes, researchers who conduct these types of inquiries today often overlook, as O'Connor noted, the enormous impact of social, economic, and political systems on poverty. In this chapter I discuss the underlying structural cause of poverty, including why poverty is more prevalent among some groups than others. I begin with a brief discussion of general sociological theories of social stratification. I then examine the role of the economy and low-wage work in explaining patterns of poverty, analyze changing patterns of racial and ethnic stratification, and finally, discuss gender norms, family structure, and culture and their impact on poverty.

Social Stratification

The term social stratification here refers to a set of social and economic institutions that generate inequality and poverty. Inequalities have played themselves out in various ways in different social systems, past and present. David Grusky posits that modern industrial societies have egalitarian ideologies that run contrary to extreme forms of stratification found in caste, feudal, and slave systems. Nevertheless, inequality continues to be a prominent feature in advanced economies.[4]

Many of the concepts used to understand stratification today come from sociological theorists of the nineteenth and early twentieth centuries. Karl Marx focused on the role of economic systems in producing inequality. Briefly, he argued that stratification in industrial societies is generated by conflict between two opposing classes: the bourgeoisie and proletariat. The former are the owners of the means of production—the

2. Lichter and Crowley, "Poverty in America: Beyond Welfare Reform," p. 19.

3. O'Connor, *Poverty Knowledge*, p. 143.

4. David B. Grusky, "The Contours of Social Stratification," in *Social Stratification in Sociological Perspective*, ed. David B. Grusky (Boulder, CO: West-view Press, 1994), p. 11.

capitalists—and the latter are the workers.[5] The bourgeoisie exploit the proletariat by keeping the surplus value—profit—generated by the work.[6]

Max Weber, whose main body of work dates to the early twentieth century, held that the concept of class alone was not enough to understand stratification. He proposed a triumvirate of concepts: class, status groups, and parties. He defined status groups as communities, often distinguished by a specific lifestyle and value system. If the line between groups is rigid, a status group is a closed "caste." Status groups gain power through the monopolization of goods or control of social institutions. The third concept, parties, refers to political power. Weber makes the distinction between the three concepts in the following way: "Whereas the genuine place of 'classes' is within the economic order, the place of 'status groups' is within the social order ... 'parties' live in a house of 'power.'"[7]

The concepts of class, status, and party continue to have resonance in discussions of the causes of poverty today. Below I discuss the role of the market system (factors relating to "class") in generating both prosperity and poverty, as well as the social forces ("status") that produce unequal outcomes for different groups. Chapter 7 discusses the effect of policy ("party") on poverty.

The Effect of Economic Processes on Poverty

Economic processes affect trends in poverty in two ways. First, economic growth determines absolute increases and declines in average standards of living. Second, economic inequality affects the distribution of income. A common analogy is that economic growth determines the size of the pie, while inequality affects the size of each slice. I now discuss the impact of each of these on poverty.

Economic growth here refers to increases in overall levels of national income. Economic growth is a function of changes in the size of labor supply, human and capital investment, and technological improvements. The U.S. economy experienced all three of these over the last two centuries. The country's population grew from a mere 3.9 million in 1790, to 76.2 million in 1900, to 281.4 million in 2000.[8] Likewise, whereas only 25 percent of people twenty-five years and older had four years of high school in 1940 (the first year in which the Census Bureau collected these figures), 83 percent had achieved this level by 1999.[9] Technological shifts, in the form of the industrial revolution and, more recently, the Information Age, propelled by computer technology, have also contributed to advances in productivity and growth.[10]

Figure 4.1 shows the trend in both poverty rates, using an absolute poverty standard, and the gross domestic product (GDP)—the output of goods and services produced by labor and property located in the

5. Karl Marx, "Classes in Capitalism and Pre-capitalism," reprinted in *Social Stratification in Sociological Perspective*, pp. 69–78.

6. Karl Marx, "Value and Surplus Value," reprinted in *Social Stratification in Sociological Perspective*, pp. 80–82.

7. Max Weber, "Class, Status, Party," reprinted in *Social Stratification in Sociological Perspective*, p. 121.

8. U.S. Census Bureau, "Population and Housing Counts: 1790–1990," Selected Historical Census Data, Population and Housing Counts Internet report, CPH-2-1, table 16 (www.census.gov/population/www/censusdata/pophc.html), 1993; U.S. Census Bureau, "DP-1. Profile of General Demographic Characteristics: 2000," Census 2000 summary file 1 (SF 1), 100-Percent Data Quick Table, American FactFinder tabulation (factfinder.census.gov), 2000.

9. U.S. Census Bureau, "Percent of People 25 Years Old and Over Who Have Completed High School or College, by Race, Hispanic Origin and Sex: Selected Years 1940 to 1999," Educational Attainment Historical Tables, table A-2, Internet release data (www.census.gov/population/socdemo/education/tableA-2.txt), 15 September 2000.

10. See Bluestone and Harrison, *Growing Prosperity*.

United States—over the 1947–2000 period.[11] As expected, the figure shows a negative correlation between GDP growth and poverty, particularly in the 1947–1973 period. In 1947, by one estimate, the poverty rate was well over 30 percent. By 1973 it had declined to 11.1 percent. Over that period, the GDP rose from 1.5 trillion to 4.1 trillion, in constant 1996 dollars. Note that, when we observe slight dips in the GDP, as during the recessions of 1973–1974, 1981–1982, and 1991–1992, we see corresponding spikes in the poverty rate. Evidence from developing countries around the world also indicates that there is a very strong relationship between economic growth and absolute poverty rates.[12]

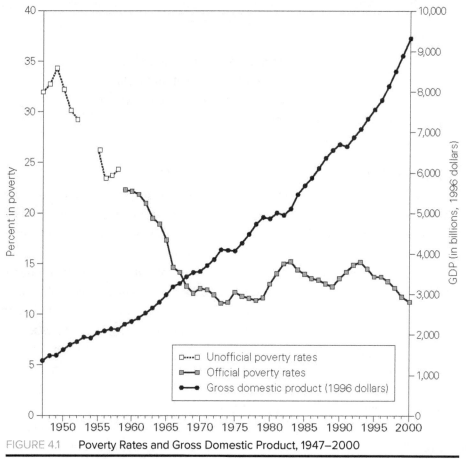

FIGURE 4.1   Poverty Rates and Gross Domestic Product, 1947–2000

GDP data from Bureau of Economic Analysis, "Gross Domestic Product, in Current Dollars and in Chained (1996) Dollars," Times Series Estimates of Gross Domestic Product

The figure also suggests that the relationship between income growth and poverty slowed beginning in the 1970s. This weakening relationship has been noted by a number of studies. Some believe that growing inequality may have also played a role in persisting high rates of poverty after 1970.[13]

11. While the official time series of poverty statistics begins in 1959, researchers have extended the time series backward, using the constant official threshold (adjusted only for inflation), as defined by Mollie Orshansky in the mid-1960s.
12. World Bank, *World Development Report 2000/2001.*
13. See, for example, Robert Haveman and Jonathan Schwabish, "Economic Growth and Poverty: A Return to Normalcy?" *Focus*

Moreover, the rate of GDP growth slowed after 1973. While the economy grew at an average annual clip of 3.9 percent in the 1950s and 4.4 percent in the 1960s, it grew at only 3.2, 2.7, and 2.5 percent rates in the 1970s, 1980s, and 1990s (through 1998), respectively.[14] It has been estimated that a 1 percentage point fall in unemployment reduces the poverty rate by 0.4 points, and a 1 percent change in median earnings reduces absolute poverty by 0.16 percentage points.[15] Hence, the slowing of economic growth had negative consequences for further poverty reduction.[16]

But [...] one caveat to these findings is that the relationship between economic growth and poverty, using a relative or subjective poverty standard, is less straightforward than when we use the absolute poverty standard discussed here. When using relative poverty measures, we find that, as general living standards rise, so do the poverty thresholds, resulting in a much weaker association between income growth and poverty. Inequality therefore tends to have a larger association with trends in relative poverty rates.

Income inequality results from economic systems that foster the accumulation of money and assets in one segment of society, often at the expense of another, or from broad-based economic shifts that produce instability and disruption in the labor market. Inequality is built into today's market system, as its foundation rests on people's ability to accumulate capital. To paraphrase Marx, business owners favor having inexpensive labor to maximize their profits (to reap surplus value).

However, it should be noted that the market is not necessarily a zero-sum game—economic growth potentially benefits large segments of society. Average standards of living rose in the United States dramatically over the twentieth century (as measured by per-capita income), as have life expectancies. Still, stratification and inequality generated by the market are phenomena that continue to cause concern among many observers in the United States and abroad. In my view, an economic system—any system—needs to be able to moderate inequality to retain its popular support and legitimacy.

Aside from the issue of how capital is distributed, economic disruptions, which are common in the market system, can also help produce economic instability and inequality. For example, in the nineteenth century, the United States was largely rural, and a majority of people were engaged in farm-related activities. Industrialization, accompanied by urbanization, changed this; many workers in the countryside and in small towns, such as farmers, unskilled laborers, and skilled craftsmen, were displaced by the mechanization of agriculture and the mass production of other goods. These workers, left with few relevant skills, became a mobile surplus of labor. One consequence was widespread poverty in many American cities and towns.[17]

At the turn of the twentieth century, economic instability in the United States continued. This was the era of the consolidation of large corporations. While these corporations provided stability for many workers in core industries, such as the automobile industry, workers involved in more marginal industries were particularly susceptible to low wages, unemployment, and poverty.[18] The conflict between capital and labor reached a

20, 2 (1999): 1–7; Rebecca Blank, "Why Has Economic Growth Been Such an Ineffective Tool against Poverty in Recent Years?" in *Poverty and Inequality: The Political Economy of Redistribution*, ed. Jon Neil (Kalamazoo, MI: W. E. Upjohn Institute for Employment Research, 1997); Blank, *It Takes a Nation*.

14. Bluestone and Harrison, *Growing Prosperity*, pp. 28–30.

15. Richard Freeman, "The Rising Tide Lifts …" *Focus* 21, 2 (2000): 27–31.

16. Danziger and Gottschalk, *America Unequal*.

17. Sugrue, "Structure of Urban Poverty," p. 87.

18. Sugrue, "Structure of Urban Poverty," pp. 88–91.

fever pitch in the United States early in the twentieth century. Workers in many manufacturing industries tried unionizing to bring about higher wages and better working conditions, and they were bitterly opposed by business owners.

Reformers such as Theodore Roosevelt were dismayed by the concentration of wealth and power among prominent industrialists and giant corporations and favored a more equitable distribution of resources among the population. While World War I shifted the focus of politics to other issues, these basic tensions between capital and labor simmered through the first half of the twentieth century. Slowly, however, labor unions gathered wider acceptance, and membership grew.[19] In addition, most segments of the population shared in the economic boom that followed World War II.[20]

By the early 1970s, the situation had changed once again. In addition to the slowing of economic growth, inequality began to increase. Figure 4.2 compares the annual percentage change in family income across the income distribution for the two time periods of 1947 to 1973 and 1973 to 1995. All groups experienced income increases in the earlier, 1947–1973 period, with the poorest fifth experiencing the greatest growth—a 3.0 percent annual rate. In contrast, after 1973, overall GDP growth rates slowed, so that no group did better than in the earlier period. Moreover, while the richest 20 percent saw their incomes rise by an average of 1.3 percent a year in this period, the poorest 20 percent experienced a 0.6 percent annual decline.[21] One estimate has it that for every 1 percent increase in income inequality (measured by the ratio of median income to income in the lowest quintile), poverty increases by 0.26 percentage points.[22]

19. Sugrue, "Structure of Urban Poverty," pp. 95–97.
20. Bluestone and Harrison, *Growing Prosperity,* p. 183.
21. Bluestone and Harrison, *Growing Prosperity,* pp. 183, 185.
22. Freeman, "Rising Tide," pp. 27–31.

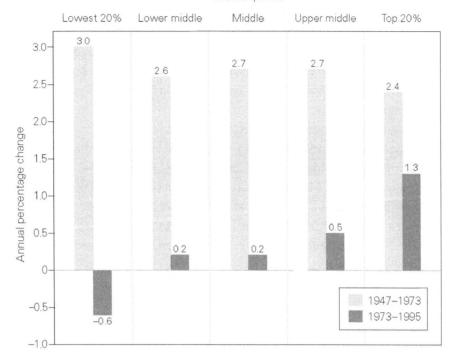

Income quintile

FIGURE 4.2   The Growth of Family Income: 1947–1973 versus 1973–1995

Barry Bluestone and Bennett Harrison, Growing Prosperity: The Battle for Growth with Equity in the Twenty-First Century (Boston: Houghton Mifflin, 2000), pp. 183, 185.

Why, after decades of decreasing inequality throughout the middle of the twentieth century, did inequality then rise in the last quarter of the century? Changes in the structure of the economy were clearly important.[23] Some believe that the declining demand for workers at the lower end of the economic ladder vis-à-vis the supply contributed to inequality. In other words, there were shifts in the demand for labor among firms to which labor supply (workers) was slow to adjust. This line of thinking has been referred to as the "skills mismatch" hypothesis. The result was that the level of education or other skills needed for employment was rising more quickly than the level of education of the workforce. A much higher proportion of jobs required, or were most suitably filled by, college graduates than before.[24]

Much of the evidence for this hypothesis comes from the growing inequality in wages by level of

---

23. Changes in family structure and the demographic composition of the population have likely played a role (see Sara McLanahan and Lynne Casper, "Growing Diversity and Inequality in the American Family," in *State of the Union: America in the 1990s*, vol. 2, ed. Reynolds Farley [New York: Russell Sage Foundation, 1995]); the effect of family structure on poverty is discussed later in this chapter and in chapter 6.

24. For a more detailed description of the skills mismatch hypothesis, see Harry J. Holzer and Wayne Vroman, "Mismatches and the Urban Labor Market," in *Urban Labor Markets and Job Opportunity*, ed. George Peterson and Wayne Vroman (Washington, DC: Urban Institute Press, 1992), pp. 81–112; George E. Peterson and Wayne Vroman, "Urban Labor Markets and Economic Opportunity," in *Urban Labor Markets and Job Opportunity*, pp. 1–29; Harry J. Holzer, *What Employers Want: Job Prospects for Less-Educated Workers* (New York: Russell Sage Foundation, 1996).

education.[25] While average weekly wages rose by 9.8 percent among men who held a college degree between 1979 and 1993, the wages for male high school dropouts fell by 22.5 percent.[26] The distribution of earnings also widened among women over the period, though it was mainly because of higher earnings among more highly educated women rather than declines among others. African Americans were perhaps the most affected by skills mismatches. It has been argued that, while the educational attainment of black city residents improved in the 1970s and 1980s, it was not sufficient to keep pace with even faster rises in the educational attainment of those persons being employed by city industries.[27]

What produced these skills mismatches, and declining wages for less educated workers more generally? Four common explanations are deindustrialization, technological change, globalization, and declining unionism. The premise of the deindustrialization hypothesis is that the shift of employment in the economy from manufacturing to services resulted in the destruction of a disproportionate number of higher-wage jobs, especially those whose primary requirement is manual skill. In their place, the service and retail trade sectors of the economy generated millions of new jobs, but these tend to be associated with a polarized earnings distribution and poverty.[28] Yet not all evidence indicates that deindustrialization is solely to blame for persisting high levels of poverty, as wage inequality has also increased within industries.[29]

Technological changes in the economy also played a role in increasing inequality by raising the demand for highly skilled workers relative to those with lower skills. For example, computerization increased the demand for engineers and programmers, while it reduced the demand for typists and already lower-paid secretaries. Yet while technological shifts likely explain some of the rising inequality, there is much it also does not explain. For example, real earnings have increased more for some less technically oriented professions, such as among lawyers, brokers, and managers, than among science technicians.[30]

Globalization of the market economy affected inequality because U.S. workers increasingly compete with workers around the world. Highly skilled U.S. workers tend to have a comparative advantage in the global economy because of both the high quality of postsecondary education in the United States and because the headquarters of many multinational corporations, to which profits flow, are located in U.S. cities. Conversely, many less educated American workers are at a disadvantage given the lower costs of living and low wage levels in other parts of the globe.[31]

The decline of unions also likely contributed to inequality. The proportion of the workforce that is

25. See, for example, Richard Murnane, "Education and the Well-Being of the Next Generation," in *Confronting Poverty*, pp. 289–307; Barry Bluestone, "The Inequality Express," *The American Prospect* 20 (winter 1994): 81–93; Sheldon Danziger and Daniel H. Weinberg, "The Historical Record: Trends in Family Income, Inequality, and Poverty," in *Confronting Poverty*, pp. 18–50.

26. Blank, *It Takes a Nation*, p. 61.

27. See John Kasarda, "Caught in the Web of Change," *Society* (November–December 1983): 41–47; John Kasarda, "Urban Industrial Transition and the Underclass," *Annals of the American Academy* 501 (January 1989): 26–47.

28. John Iceland, "Urban Labor Markets and Individual Transitions out of Poverty," *Demography* 34, 3 (1997): 429–41; Bennet Harrison and Barry Blue-stone, *The Great U-Turn: Corporate Restructuring and the Polarizing of America* (New York: Basic Books, 1990).

29. Danziger and Gottschalk, *America Unequal*, p. 137.

30. Danziger and Gottschalk, *America Unequal*, pp. 140–43; Bluestone and Harrison, *Growing Prosperity*, pp. 190–97.

31. Bluestone and Harrison, *Growing Prosperity*, pp. 190–97.

unionized has been falling since the 1950s, but it accelerated after the mid-1970s.[32] The proportion of workers in unions declined from 29 percent in 1975 to 14 percent in 1997.[33] Nonunionized workers typically are paid lower wages and have less job security.[34]

Inequality leads to poverty because many low-wage jobs simply do not pay enough to keep families from falling into poverty, even when using the current official (absolute) measure. In 1997, when the minimum wage was $5.15 an hour, the income of a full-time worker (forty hours, fifty weeks) making minimum wage would be $10,300—about $2,500 below the average 1997 poverty line for a three-person family and $6,100 under the average poverty line for a four-person family (though none of these figures takes into account government transfers these low-income families may receive). A family of four in which one person worked full-time and the other half-time at minimum wage would still produce earnings falling $950 below the poverty line for such a family ($16,400).

A majority of the poor do in fact have a family member with some attachment to the labor market. Figure 4.3 shows that, among poor families with children in 1997, 37 percent were in full-time working families, another 35 percent were in part-time working families, and only 28 percent were in nonworking families.[35] When using the National Academy of Sciences (NAS) measure, less than a quarter (24 percent) were in nonworking families. People in full-time working families were particularly more likely to be poor under the NAS measure because their expenses, such as Social Security taxes and other work-related expenses, are higher (these elements are not taken into account in the official poverty measure).[36] Since 1973, both the number and share of the poor who are employed full-time and year-round has risen.[37]

32. Danziger and Gottschalk, *America Unequal,* pp. 130–31.

33. Jared Bernstein, Elizabeth C. McNichol, Lawrence Mishel, and Robert Zahradnik, "Pulling Apart: A State-by-State Analysis of Income Trends," Center on Budget and Policy Priorities and Economic Policy Institute Report, January 2000.

34. See Paul Osterman, *Securing Prosperity* (Princeton, NJ: Princeton University Press, 1999).

35. Iceland and Kim, "Poverty among Working Families." A "full-time working family" is defined as one in which family members work at least 1,750 hours in total over the previous year. The 1,750 figure is equivalent to a work effort of 35 hours a week for fifty weeks. A "part-time working family" is defined here as one in which the total number of hours worked by family members ranges from 50 to 1,749 hours in the previous year.

36. See chapter 3 for more details about the two measures.

37. See Linda Barrington, "Does a Rising Tide Lift All Boats?" The Conference Board, research report 1271-00-RR, 2000.

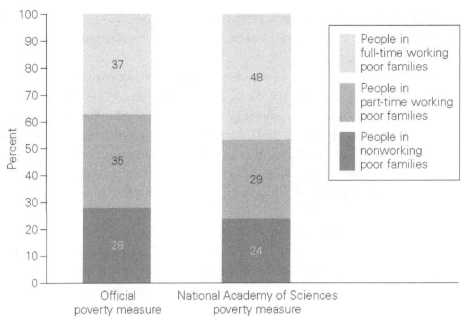

FIGURE 4.3   Distribution of People in Poor Families with Children, by Working Status and Poverty Measure, 1997

John Iceland and Josh Kim, "Poverty among Working Families: Insights from an Improved Measure," Social Science Quarterly 82, 2 (June 2001): 253–67.

Social Stratification—Race, Ethnicity, Gender, and Culture

While the economic forces described above determine overall levels of economic growth and inequality, social stratification across social ("status") groups determine, in a world of finite resources, who becomes poor. The main status groups in today's society are defined by the intersection of ethnic, gender, and class affiliations.[38]

Social stratification across status groups occurs when social groups seek to maximize their rewards by restricting others' access to resources and opportunities. Weber noted that usually one social group "takes some externally identifiable characteristic of another group—[such as] race, language, religion, local or social origin, descent, residence, etc.—as a pretext for attempting their exclusion."[39] Caste systems are an extreme form of closed stratification systems; this system prevailed in parts of the United States until the middle of the twentieth century.

Monopolization of social and economic goods and institutions can occur through a number of ways. Discrimination in the form of legal barriers is one mechanism, as described below. Other exclusionary devices include restricting access to people with sufficient wealth or with certain credentials.[40] For example, wealth enables families to obtain high-quality education in private schools and in that way retain their elevated

38. Interested readers should refer to Grusky's edited volume, *Social Stratification in Sociological Perspective,* for an in-depth discussion of these perspectives.

39. Max Weber, "Open and Closed Relationships," in *Social Stratification in Sociological Perspective*, p. 128.

40. Frank Parkin, "Marxism and Class Theory: A Bourgeois Critique," in *Social Stratification in Sociological Perspective*, pp. 141–54.

economic and social standing. Obtaining official credentials—such as a degree from a prestigious university, or union membership—is another way access to certain opportunities is controlled and institutionalized.

The process of stratification is usually a cumulative one. A person may begin life at a disadvantage, and disadvantages may be augmented at each stage of the life cycle, such as through the restriction of educational opportunities, then job opportunities, and so on.[41] When stratification is so deeply ingrained in society, ameliorating its effects becomes very difficult. The analysis of trends in poverty that follows indicates that, while social stratification across racial, ethnic, and gender lines inhibits opportunities and serves to increase poverty among some groups, the degree of stratification across these groups clearly diminished over the last half of the twentieth century in the United States.

Racial and Ethnic Stratification

In the U.S. context, several minority groups fare worse than whites according to a number of social and economic indicators. On average, minorities are more likely than whites to have low levels of education, lower levels of employment, lower wages, and have chronic health problems—all characteristics associated with higher poverty rates.[42]

Discrimination against minority group members has historically played a role in producing social inequalities. Discrimination arises out of competition for scarce resources and serves to protect group solidarity.[43] In the educational system, discrimination has contributed to school segregation, classroom segregation, and access to unequal facilities.[44]

Societies characterized by high levels of discrimination also usually have highly segregated labor markets where the price of labor, and therefore wages, for the same work typically differs across groups. In other words, the wages of minority group members are artificially devalued because the labor market is neither fully free nor fully competitive.[45] Disadvantaged group members may be excluded altogether from many better-paying jobs and may thus have to settle for less desirable jobs, whose wages are in turn driven lower by higher levels of competition from others in a similar situation.[46]

A less overt but perhaps more common type of bias in the labor market is "statistical discrimination," which refers to the tendency of employers to use generalizations in their hiring practices. Employers basically lower their search costs for employees by using easily identifiable characteristics, such as sex or race, to predict job performance instead of determining actual individual skill. This reliance on stereotypes is inherently unfair because individuals are judged not by their ability but by their appearance. Shelly Lundberg and Richard Startz

41. Peter M. Blau, Otis Dudley Duncan, and Andrea Tyree, "The Process of Stratification," in *Social Stratification in Sociological Perspective,* pp. 317–29.

42. O'Hare, "A New Look at Poverty in America."

43. C. Price, "The Study of Assimilation," in *Sociological Studies: Migration,* ed. J. A. Jackson (Cambridge, UK: Cambridge University Press, 1969).

44. Schiller, *Economics of Poverty and Discrimination,* pp. 159–66.

45. See E. Bonacich, "A Theory of Ethnic Antagonism: The Split Labor Market," *American Sociological Review* 37 (October 1972): 547–59; Gary S. Becker, *The Economics of Discrimination* (Chicago: University of Chicago Press, 1971).

46. Dennis P. Hogan and M. Pazul, "The Occupational and Earnings Returns to Education among Black Men in the North," *American Journal of Sociology* 90 (1982): 584–607; Michael J. Piore, "The Dual Labor Market: Theory and Implications," in *Social Stratification in Sociological Perspective*, pp. 359–61.

note that this can lead to actual differentials in skills and productivity if minority group members invest less in their education or training because they feel this type of investment would not be rewarded.[47]

Racial and ethnic minority groups in the United States, and indeed in multicultural nations around the globe, often struggle to obtain equal access to resources, such as jobs, education, and health services. In the American context, these conflicts have a long history, though their scope and nature have evolved. African Americans, Asian Americans, Hispanics, and Native Americans and even many white ethnic groups, such as the Irish, have all had to cope with limited opportunities, though their experiences have qualitatively differed.

African American Poverty

The official poverty rate among African Americans in 2003 was 24.4 percent. Although this was near the historic low achieved in 2000, it was still almost double the national poverty rate of 12.5 percent (see Figure 4.4). African Americans, who comprised about 13 percent of the U.S. population as of 2000, have long had to contend with acute forms of discrimination and inequality, including a severely constrained labor market throughout the nineteenth century and into the twentieth. After the abolition of slavery during the Civil War, blacks in the South often worked as sharecroppers, mainly because they were barred by law or custom from almost all other full-time jobs. In addition, under the system of Jim Crow, most blacks who lived in cities were employed as common laborers or as domestic and personal servants. Opportunities for promotion and advancement were uncommon, if not impossible, for African Americans in these and other occupations.[48]

William Julius Wilson, among others, has argued that more recently the traditional patterns of interaction between African Americans and whites in the labor market have fundamentally changed, where economic class position is now more important in determining success among African Americans than their daily encounters with whites.[49] From the antebellum period through the first half of the twentieth century, racial oppression was deliberate, overt, and easily observable—ranging from slavery to segregation. By the latter half of the twentieth century, many traditional barriers were dismantled as a result of political, social, and economic changes of the civil rights era. Wilson emphasizes that it is not so much that racial segregation and discrimination have been eliminated as that they have become less rampant, whereas economic conditions play an increasingly important role in determining black disadvantage. He argues that deindustrialization and class segregation in particular have hampered the economic mobility of less skilled blacks in the labor market.[50]

47. Shelly J. Lundberg and Richard Startz, "Inequality and Race: Models and Policy," in *Meritocracy and Economic Inequality*, ed. Kenneth Arrow, Samuel Bowles, and Steven Durlauf (Princeton, NJ: Princeton University Press, 2000), p. 273.
48. Jones, "Southern Diaspora" p. 31; Trotter, "Blacks in the Urban North," p. 60.
49. William Julius Wilson, *The Declining Significance of Race: Blacks and Changing American Institutions* (Chicago: University of Chicago Press, 1978).
50. Wilson, *The Truly Disadvantaged.*

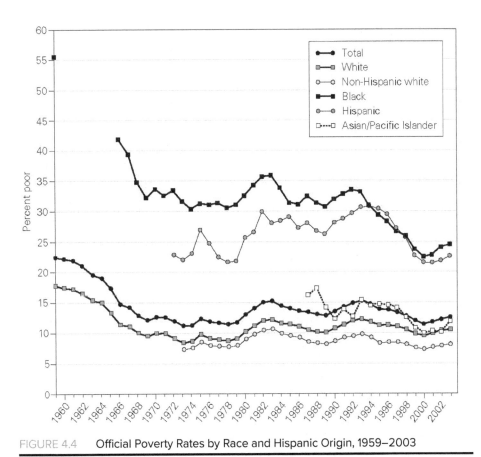

FIGURE 4.4   Official Poverty Rates by Race and Hispanic Origin, 1959–2003

U.S. Census Bureau, "Poverty Status of People, by Family Relationship, Race, and His-panic Origin: 1959 to 2003." Historical Poverty People Tables, table 2, Internet release data

Glenn Loury asserts that, while "discrimination in contract"—the unequal treatment of otherwise like persons based on race in the execution of formal transactions—has declined drastically in the period since 1965, "discrimination in contact" remains more prevalent. Discrimination in contact refers to the unequal treatment of persons on the basis of race in the associations and relationships that are formed among individuals in social life. It involves discrimination in the informal, private sphere. Loury argues that economic achievement depends on the nature of social interactions in both spheres because people obtain resources by both formal and informal, by contractual and noncontractual, social relations.[51]

Empirical studies tend to show that the economic penalty of race—of being African American in particular—has declined since the 1960s. Occupational mobility has increased, as has wage parity.[52] Arthur

51. Glenn C. Loury, "What's Next? Some Reflections on the Poverty Conference," *Focus* 21, 2 (fall 2000): 60.
52. Michael Hout, "Occupational Mobility of Black Men, 1962 to 1973," in *Social Stratification in Sociological Perspective,* pp. 531–42; Reynolds Farley, *Blacks and Whites: Narrowing the Gap?* (Cambridge, MA: Harvard University Press, 1984); Arthur Sakamoto, Huei-Hsia Wu, and Jessie M. Tzeng, "The Declining Significance of Race among American Men during the Latter Half of the Twentieth Century," *Demography* 37, 1 (2000): 41–51; G. Farkas and K. Vicknair, "Appropriate Tests of Racial Wage Discrimination Require Controls for Cognitive Skill: Comment on Cancio, Evans, and Maume," *American Sociological Review* 1 (1996): 557–60.

Sakamoto and his coauthors, in their study of declining wage differentials between 1950 and 1990, find that "the net disadvantage of being black was reduced by more than half over this period," even after taking into account changing group educational levels and other factors.[53]

Because the extent of employment discrimination is difficult to measure and quantify, it is difficult to say precisely to what extent discrimination still directly contributes to income disparities and poverty. Studies tend to indicate that discrimination persists in labor markets and other areas. For example, "paired-test studies" in which minority job applicants were paired with white applicants with similar backgrounds and trained to be as similar as possible in behavior, have shown that minorities, particularly African Americans and foreign-sounding Latinos, were less likely to receive job interviews and offers.[54] Racism therefore continues to contribute to a social hierarchy that puts African Americans at an economic disadvantage.

Other factors have also contributed to relatively high levels of African American poverty, some based on social stratification and related to race and others more nonracial in origin. For one, continued high levels of black-white segregation affect individual economic opportunities.[55] Douglas Massey and Nancy Denton, in American Apartheid, argued that segregation, interacting with economic forces, reinforces minority poverty by limiting access to the potentially broad range of metropolitan area employment opportunities.[56] The deconcentration of employment from central cities to the surrounding suburbs has also reduced the number of employment opportunities for inner-city blacks.[57]

High levels of residential segregation may contribute to patterns of unequal schooling, perpetuate ethnic stereotypes that give rise to discrimination in employers' hiring patterns, and reproduce segregated job referral networks.[58] In places segregated by both race and class, the poor also often face high rent burdens, lack of access to housing wealth, and housing health risks.[59] These all contribute to feelings of alienation, discouragement, and pessimism, which can in turn reproduce negative economic outcomes.[60]

Deindustrialization and the decline in the strength of unions also appear to contribute to the continued wage and poverty gap between African Americans and whites,[61] as Wilson also argued. Black women have

53. Sakamoto, Wu, and Tzeng, "Declining Significance of Race," pp. 8–9.

54. See Harry Cross, Genevieve Kenney, Jane Mell, and Wendy Zimmermann, *Employer Hiring Practices* (Washington, DC: Urban Institute Press, 1990); Margery Turner, Michael Fix, and Raymond Struyk, *Opportunities Denied, Opportunities Diminished: Discrimination in Hiring* (Washington, DC: Urban Institute Press, 1991).

55. Reynolds Farley and William H. Frey, "Changes in the Segregation of Whites from Blacks during the 1980s: Small Steps toward a More Integrated Society," *American Sociological Review* 59, 1 (February 1994): 23–45; Michael J. White, *American Neighborhoods and Residential Differentiation* (New York: Russell Sage Foundation, 1987).

56. Massey and Denton, *American Apartheid,* pp. 2–3.

57. Keith R. Ihlanfeldt and David L. Sjoquist, "The Impact of Job Decentralization on the Economic Welfare of Central City Blacks," *Journal of Urban Economics* 26 (1989): 110–30.

58. See, for example, James H. Johnson and Melvin L. Oliver, "Structural Changes in the U.S. Economy and Black Male Joblessness: A Reassessment," in *Urban Labor Markets and Job Opportunity,* pp. 113–47; Massey and Denton, *American Apartheid,* pp. 2–3; Ted Mouw, "Job Relocation and the Racial Gap in Unemployment in Detroit and Chicago, 1980 to 1990," *American Sociological Review* 65, 5 (2000): 730–53.

59. John Yinger, "Housing Discrimination and Residential Segregation as Causes of Poverty," *Focus* 21, 2 (fall 2000): 51–55.

60. George C. Galster, "A Cumulative Causation Model of the Underclass: Implications for Urban Economic Development Policy," in *The Metropolis in Black and White: Place, Power, and Polarization*, ed. George Galster and Edward W. Hill (New Brunswick, NJ: Center for Urban Policy Research, Rutgers University, 1992).

61. John Bound and Richard Freeman, "What Went Wrong? The Erosion of Relative Earnings and Employment among

benefited from public sector unionism in particular, and black men benefited from industrial unionism.[62] African Americans have been especially affected by deindustrialization because, as late as the 1968–1970 period, more than 70 percent of all blacks working in metropolitan areas held blue-collar jobs at the same time that more than 50 percent of all metropolitan workers held white-collar jobs.[63]

Another factor that contributes to higher poverty rates among African Americans is human-capital skills differentials. This refers to differences in average levels of education, quality of educational opportunities, and subsequent work experience. The gap in average levels of education has declined over the past few decades. Nevertheless, the quality of schooling received by children varies widely, and African Americans are more likely to attend inferior schools with fewer resources. Lower employment levels among young African Americans subsequently contribute to earnings differentials. Some research has indicated that school achievement, as measured by Armed Forces Qualifications Test (AFQT) scores, and work experience explain a significant portion of the earnings difference between African American and white men under the age of thirty,[64] though these findings are more suggestive than definitive.

Poverty among Other Minority Groups

Some of the processes that have hampered African American economic well-being, such as discrimination, segregation, and human capital differentials, have also affected other minority groups—Latinos, Asian Americans, and Native Americans. Yet the experiences of each group differ considerably because of its regional concentration, population size, and labor market niche and the white population's reaction to its presence in, or immigration to, America.

Hispanics have a long history in the United States, dating at least as far back as the annexation of territory in Florida and, in 1848, huge swaths of land from Mexico extending from Texas westward to California. Asians historically suffered discriminatory treatment in immigration policies limiting their arrival. The 1882 Chinese Exclusion Act barred the immigration of Chinese laborers, and immigration from Japan was completely halted in 1924. By the early decades of the twentieth century, Japanese and Chinese immigrants were denied citizenship and voting rights and were prevented from joining most labor unions. Through intimidation and discrimination, whites limited the economic achievement of Asian Americans.[65]

Young Black Men in the 1980s," *Quarterly Journal of Economics* 107 (1992): 201–32; John Bound and Harry J. Holzer, "Industrial Shifts, Skills Levels, and the Labor Market for White and Black Males," *Review of Economics and Statistics* 75, 3 (1993): 387–96; Leslie McCall, "Sources of Racial Inequality in Metropolitan Labor Markets: Racial, Ethnic, and Gender Differences," *American Sociological Review* 66, 4 (2001): 520–41; Iceland, "Urban Labor Markets and Individual Transitions out of Poverty."

62. John Bound and Laura Dresser, "Losing Ground: The Erosion of the Relative Earnings of African American Women during the 1980s," in *Latinas and African American Women at Work*, ed. Irene Browne (New York: Russell Sage Foundation, 1999), pp. 61–104.

63. John Kasarda, "Industrial Restructuring and the Changing Location of Jobs," in *State of the Union: America in the 1990s*, vol. 1, ed. Reynolds Farley (New York: Russell Sage Foundation, 1995), pp. 215–67.

64. June O'Neill, "The Role of Human Capital in Earnings Differentials between Black and White Men," *Journal of Economic Perspectives* 4, 4 (1990): 25–46; Farkas and Vicknair, "Appropriate Tests of Racial Wage Discrimination," pp. 557–60.

65. Arthur Sakamoto and Satomi Furuichi, "Wages among White and Japanese-American Male Workers," *Research in Stratification and Mobility* 15 (1997): 177–206.

Latinos and Asian Americans share certain commonalities: they both have historically been discriminated against, have recently experienced increases in their population due to immigration, and are very heterogeneous in terms of their national origins and educational skills. The 1965 Immigration Act, which dropped the bias in favor of immigrants from Europe and set more equitable immigration quotas across global regions, led to immediate, striking, and unexpected shifts in immigration flows. The number of immigrants from Latin America and Asia exploded.[66] In the 1980s, for example, 85 percent of immigrants to the United States were from those two regions.[67]

Despite these similar experiences, poverty rates vary considerably. While the Asian poverty rate in 2003 was 11.8 percent, the Latino poverty rate was about twice as high, at 22.5 percent. While poverty rates among both groups declined significantly in the period of economic expansion in the 1990s, Hispanic rates increased over the 1970s and 1980s (see Figure 4.4).[68] Differences in the characteristics of the immigrants coming to the United States and in the levels of education of immigrants and native-born people of each of the two groups, explain many of these differences.

In general, immigrants often have different labor force outcomes than natives. On one hand, immigrants are often a "select" group of people—they often possess qualities such as ambition and eagerness to learn that are helpful in achieving economic success. On the other hand, limited language proficiency and unfamiliarity with American customs and the labor market considerably hinder immigrant economic mobility, especially in the short run. Overall, immigrant families are at greater risk of poverty than nonimmigrant families. Yet over time and subsequent generations, labor market barriers become less important.[69] Immigrants become more similar to the native-born population in terms of their employment, earnings, English-language fluency, fertility, and poverty the longer they have been in the United States. Some studies show, however, that an increasing number and proportion of immigrants have been arriving with very low levels of skills, contributing to higher overall immigrant poverty rates.[70] In places with many immigrants, the competition for low-wage jobs also appears to drive down wages for these immigrants.[71]

Data from the Current Population survey bear these arguments out. Table 4.1 shows that poverty rates

66. Roderick J. Harrison and Claudette Bennett, "Racial and Ethnic Diversity," in *State of the Union,* vol. 2, pp. 141–210.

67. Barry R. Chiswick and Teresa A. Sullivan, "The New Immigrants," in *State of the Union,* vol. 2, pp. 211–70.

68. U.S. Census Bureau, "Poverty Status of People, by Family Relationship, Race, and Hispanic Origin: 1959 to 2003." Historical Poverty People Tables, table 2. Internet release data (http://www.census.gov/hhes/www/poverty/histpov/hstpov2.html), last revised May 13, 2005.

69. See George J. Borjas, "Assimilation, Changes in Cohort Quality, and the Earnings of Immigrants," *Journal of Labor Economics* 3 (1987), 463–89; George J. Borjas, *Friends or Strangers: The Impact of Immigrants on the U.S. Economy* (New York: Basic Books, 1990); Nancy S. Landale and Avery M. Guest, "Generation, Ethnicity, and Occupational Opportunity in Late 19th Century America," *American Sociological Review* 55 (April 1990): 280–96; Victor Nee and Jimy Sanders, "The Road to Parity: Determinants of the Socioeconomic Achievements of Asian Americans," *Ethnic and Racial Studies* 8, 1 (January 1985): 75–93; Barry R. Chiswick, "The Effect of Americanization on the Earnings of Foreign-Born Men," *Journal of Political Economy* 86, 5 (1978): 897–921; Sharon M. Lee and Barry Edmonston, "The Socioeconomic Status and Integration of Asian Immigrants," in *Immigration and Ethnicity: The Integration of America's Newest Arrivals,* ed. Barry Edmonston and Jeffrey S. Passel (Washington, DC: Urban Institute Press, 1994); Chiswick and Sullivan, "The New Immigrants."

70. See Borjas, "Assimilation, Changes in Cohort Quality, and the Earnings of Immigrants"; Borjas, *Friends or Strangers;* Chiswick and Sullivan, "The New Immigrants."

71. McCall, "Sources of Racial Inequality in Metropolitan Labor Markets," pp. 520–41.

were highest among recent immigrants, particularly among recent immigrants from Mexico. Mexican immigrant households had an overall poverty rate of 33.3 percent, higher than the 25.4 percent poverty rate among immigrant households from Central America. The Asian immigrant household poverty rate, at 15.2 percent, was lower than the Mexican and Central American ones, though still higher than the poverty rate among immigrant households from Europe. Pre-1970 immigrants from Europe and Asia had poverty rates that were quite similar (close to 8 percent). In general, immigrants who have been in the United States longer had considerably lower poverty rates than recent arrivals.[72]

Table 4.1. Poverty rates for people in immigrant households by selected region of origin and year of entry, 1997

Years of entry	Europe	Mexico	Central America	Asia	Africa	All Immigrants
1990s	19.9	46.3	33.0	21.1	31.1	30.7
1980s	11.1	35.1	26.7	18.1	18.1	25.4
1970s	6.5	26.5	17.2	7.7	13.9	16.1
Pre-1970s	8.0	20.9	14.9	7.6	17.5	11.4
Total	11.0	33.3	25.4	15.2	18.5	21.8

Source: Steven A. Camarota, Importing Poverty: Immigration's Impact on the Size and Growth of the Poor Population in the United States, Center for Immigration Studies Paper 15, September 1999, p. 23.

Note: Native-born poverty rate: 12.0 percent.

These figures suggest that immigrants from Asia tend to comprise a more "select" group than those from Latin America. Indeed, other evidence indicates that newer immigrants from Korea, India, and the Philippines exhibit higher average levels of education than both Latinos and native-born whites.[73] One factor explaining these differences is that, while many immigrants from Asia become eligible to migrate to the United States because of their work-related skills, a larger proportion of immigrants from Latin America immigrate because they have relatives who are U.S. citizens.[74]

Even among the native-born, Asian Americans tend to have high levels of education, which translate into better jobs, higher incomes, and less poverty. Japanese Americans have achieved a level of education similar to that of whites since the early 1940s, as have Chinese Americans since 1960. Asian Americans have also gained

72. Steven A. Camarota, *Importing Poverty: Immigration's Impact on the Size and Growth of the Poor Population in the United States,* Center for Immigration Studies Paper #15, September 1999: 23.
73. H. R. Barringer, R. W. Gardner, and M. J. Levin, *Asian and Pacific Islanders in the United States* (New York: Russell Sage Foundation, 1993).
74. See Chiswick and Sullivan, "The New Immigrants."

greater access to ·high-tier technical and professional occupations.[75] Latinos are less likely to have a college degree and tend to work in lower-skill, lower-wage jobs.

It is once again difficult to separate the effects of discrimination from those of immigration and human capital in determining why Latinos have higher poverty rates than Asians and why both groups have higher poverty rates than whites. The available evidence tends to suggest that native-born Asian Americans' wages, returns to occupational status, and poverty resembles that of otherwise similar whites, though immigrants' economic well-being still lags.[76] The evidence for Latinos suggests the persistence of some racial/ethnic effect on wages and earnings.[77]

The experience of Native Americans differs from all other groups. In addition to being forcibly removed from their land to reservations, Native Americans have had to overcome a dearth of job opportunities in and around reservations and also low levels of educational attainment. The poverty rate among Native Americans in the 1998–2000 period was 25.9 percent, similar to African American and Latino poverty rates. Some evidence indicates a decline (but not elimination) of the net negative effect of being Native American on wages over the last half of the twentieth century.[78] Quantitative research on Native Americans tends to be more limited than that of other groups, in part due to the relatively small Native American population. Additional research on Native Americans, not to mention the other groups, would help shed further light on the complex interrelationship between race and poverty.

Gender, Family Structure, and Poverty

The term feminization of poverty was coined by Diana Pearce in a 1978 article in which she argued that poverty was "rapidly becoming a female problem."[79] The term gained further currency in the 1980s and early 1990s. While it originally referred to the process by which the poverty population in the United States became increasingly female, it is currently more often used to refer to the growing number of poor people living in female-headed families (which of course include both male and female children). In 1970, 42 percent of families included an employed father, a homemaker mother, and children; now, only 16 percent of families fit this model, and half of all children will spend some portion of their childhood living with only one parent.[80] Family arrangements today are much more diverse than they were fifty years ago.[81]

75. Gillian Stevens and Joo Hyun Cho, "Socioeconomic Indexes and the New 1980 Census Occupational Classification Scheme," *Social Science Research* 14, 2 (1985): 142–68.

76. John Iceland, "Earnings Returns to Occupational Status: Are Asian Americans Disadvantaged?" *Social Science Research* 28 (1999): 45–65; Sharon M. Lee, "Poverty and the U.S. Asian Population," *Social Science Quarterly* 75 (September 1994): 541–59; Sakamoto, Wu, and Tzeng, "Declining Significance of Race."

77. C. W. Reimers, "A Comparative Analysis of the Wages of Hispanics, Blacks, and Non-Hispanic Whites," in *Hispanics in the U.S. Economy*, ed. George Borjas and Marta Tienda (New York: Academic Press, 1985); Sakamoto, Wu, and Tzeng, "Declining Significance of Race."

78. Gary Sandefur and W. J. Scott, "Minority Group Status and the Wages of Indian and Black Males," *Social Science Research* 12 (1983): 44–68; Sakamoto, Wu, and Tzeng, "Declining Significance of Race."

79. Diana Pearce, "The Feminization of Poverty: Women, Work, and Welfare," *Urban Sociological Change* 11 (1978): 128–36.

80. Larry Bumpass and R. Raley, "Redefining Single-Parent Families: Cohabitation and Changing Family Reality," *Demography* 32 (1995): 97–109.

81. McLanahan and Casper, "Growing Diversity and Inequality in the American Family."

Women's poverty rates were 55 percent higher than men's in 1968, then peaked at 72 percent higher in 1978, before declining to 47 percent by the end of the 1980s.[82] In 2000 the female poverty rate (12.5 percent) was 26 percent higher than the male poverty rate (9.9 percent). Women comprise about 57 percent of the poverty population; this figure has changed little since the mid-1970s.[83] Trends differ by age. The gap in poverty rates between working-age women and men has narrowed since 1980, while increasing among young women (those under age twenty-five) and among elderly women (over age sixty-five). Overall, the empirical claims for an accelerating "feminization of poverty" are weak, though female poverty rates do remain disproportionately high.[84]

Women tend to have higher poverty rates than men for two main reasons: (1) they have fewer economic resources than men, and (2) they are more likely to be the heads of single-parent families.[85] Minority women are further overrepresented among the poor because of both their minority status and higher rates of single parenthood.[86] Elderly women are also more likely to be poor than elderly men because of fewer economic resources—such as less Social Security income—but also because of higher female life expectancies, which make elderly women more likely to live alone than men.[87]

Many argue that women's lower economic status reflects the unequal distribution of power in society.[88] It is asserted that men have long maintained control over women's labor power by excluding women from access to some essential productive resources and by limiting women's social roles more generally.[89] Labor market discrimination is a manifestation of unequal power. First, discrimination occurs when men are paid more than women for the same work. Second, discrimination contributes to occupational sex segregation—where men and women are highly concentrated in different types of jobs. The result is that women's work is typically accorded both lower status and lower earnings than occupations with high concentrations of men.[90]

Inequality in the labor market may also occur due to bias or discrimination prior to a person's entrance into the labor market, such as in the education system or in the family.[91] For example, girls are more typically socialized into family-oriented roles, while boys and young men are encouraged to enter careers that

82. Suzanne Bianchi, "Feminization and Juvenilization of Poverty: Trends, Relative Risks, Causes, and Consequences," *Annual Review of Sociology* 25 (1999): 307–33.

83. U.S. Census Bureau, "Poverty of People, by Sex: 1966 to 2000," Historical Poverty Tables, Table 7, Internet release data (www.census.gov/hhes/poverty/histpov/hstpov7.html), 13 February 2002.

84. Lichter and Crowley, "Poverty in America: Beyond Welfare Reform," 7.

85. Devine, Plunkett, and Wright, "The Chronicity of Poverty"; Majorie Starrels, Sally Bould, and Leon J. Nicholas, "The Feminization of Poverty in the United States," *Journal of Family Issues* 15, 4 (December 1994): 590–607; Stevens, "Dynamics of Poverty Spells"; Stevens, "Climbing Out of Poverty."

86. Starrels, Bould, and Nicholas, "Feminization of Poverty in the United States."

87. Bianchi, "Feminization and Juvenilization of Poverty," pp. 307–33.

88. Paula England, "Wage Appreciation and Depreciation: A Test of Neoclassical Economic Explanations of Occupational Sex Segregation," in *Social Stratification in Sociological Perspective,* pp. 590–603; Heidi Hartmann, "The Unhappy Marriage of Marxism and Feminism: Towards a More Progressive Union," in *Social Stratification in Sociological Perspective,* pp. 570–76.

89. Hartmann, "Unhappy Marriage of Marxism and Feminism," p. 570.

90. England, "Wage Appreciation and Depreciation," p. 599.

91. Solomon W. Polachek and W. Stanley Siebert, "Gender in the Labour Market," in *Social Stratification in Sociological Perspective,* pp. 583–89.

emphasize making money and becoming leaders.[92] Women may be more likely to take jobs that are easier to reenter after an interruption in employment, such as for pregnancy and raising young children, and that therefore do not offer as much upward mobility.

Because of the sexual revolution of the 1960s and the high visibility of the women's rights movement, commentators through the 1980s puzzled over why there had been so little accompanying change in the ratio of women's to men's earnings in the labor market. After all, between World War II and 1980, the gap between women's and men's labor force participation rates narrowed steadily, and their college enrollment rates were virtually identical. Between 1970 and 1980, women increased their share of law, medical, and dental school degrees and moved into managerial positions in record numbers. Yet women's earnings hovered around 60 percent of men's throughout the 1955 to 1980 period.[93] Beginning in the 1980s, however, the trend began to change rapidly.

Figure 4.5 shows the change in the female-male ratio of earnings since 1960, using the most commonly used indicator of the gender wage gap—the median earnings of full-time, year-round workers. After 1980, the earnings gap declined rapidly for the next decade or so, before stabilizing. As of 2003, the median annual earnings of full-time, year-round women workers was 75.5 percent of men's.[94] The mean earnings ratio among young workers (age twenty-five to thirty-four) in 1995, at 78 percent, was considerably greater than the ratio among women thirty-five to forty-four years old (65 percent) and women forty-five to fifty-four (58 percent).[95] Sociologist Suzanne Bianchi has described how much of the movement toward gender inequality has been the result of a gradual process of "cohort replacement," where younger women have been taking on new roles and earning more in the labor market than their mothers. Because of the increase in women's employment and earnings, the relative risk of poverty among working-age women actually declined in the early 1980s.[96]

92. T. Daymont and P. Andrisani, "Job Preferences, College Major, and the Gender Gap in Earnings," *Journal of Human Resources* 19 (1984): 408–28.

93. Suzanne Bianchi, "Changing Economic Roles of Women and Men," in *State of the Union,* vol. 1, pp. 107–54.

94. U.S. Census Bureau, "Women's Earnings as a Percentage of Men's Earnings by Race and Hispanic Origin: 1960 to 2003," Historical Income Tables, table P-40, Internet release data (www.census.gov/hhes/income/histinc/p40.html), last revised May 18, 2005.

95. Francine D. Blau, Marianne A. Ferber, and Anne E. Winkler, *The Economics of Women, Men, and Work* (Upper Saddle River, NJ: Prentice Hall, 1998), p. 137.

96. See Bianchi, "Changing Economic Roles of Women and Men."

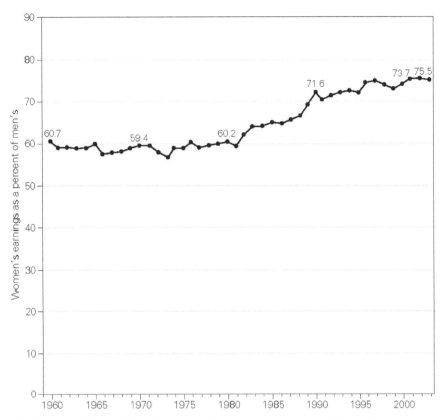

FIGURE 4.5   Women's Median Annual Earnings as a Percent of Men's Earnings for Full-Time, Year-Round Workers, 1960–2003

U.S. Census Bureau, "Women's Earnings as a Percentage of Men's Earnings by Race and Hispanic Origin: 1960–2003," Historical Income People Tables, table P-40. Internet release data

Nevertheless, despite these improvements, the earnings gap persists. A 1997 study by Francine Blau and Lawrence Kahn of the wage gap in the 1980s found that some of the gap was due to differences in education and amount of work experience. Once they accounted for these, the authors estimated that women earned about 80.5 percent of what men did (rather than about 72 percent). When yet more factors were taken into account, such as the industry, occupation, and union status differences in the jobs men and women occupy, then women were estimated to earn about 88.2 percent of similar men. They therefore concluded that gender discrimination in the labor market still plays a role in depressing women's earnings, though the exact causes of the differential is not yet fully understood.[97] Some of the narrowing of the earnings gap in the 1980s was due not only to gradual increases in women's earnings but also men's losses in employment and wages, particularly among those with less education.[98]

Changes in family structure have also contributed to higher rates of poverty among women. The percent

97. Francine D. Blau and Lawrence M. Kahn, "Swimming Upstream: Trends in the Gender Wage Differential in the 1980s," *Journal of Labor Economics* 15, 1, part 1 (1997): 1–42.

98. Jane Waldfogel and Susan Mayer, "Differences between Men and Women in the Low-Wage Labor Market," *Focus* 20, 1 (winter 1998–1999): 11–16.

of families with children headed by single women rose rapidly over the last few decades of the twentieth century, from 11.5 percent of all families with children in 1970 to 26.5 percent in 1995 (see Figure 4.6), with higher rates for blacks and His-panics. After 1995, however, trends leveled for all race groups, and even declined for blacks and Hispanics. As of 2003, 26.1 percent of all families with children were headed by women. For whites the figure in that year was 21.1 percent, and for blacks it was 55.8 percent.

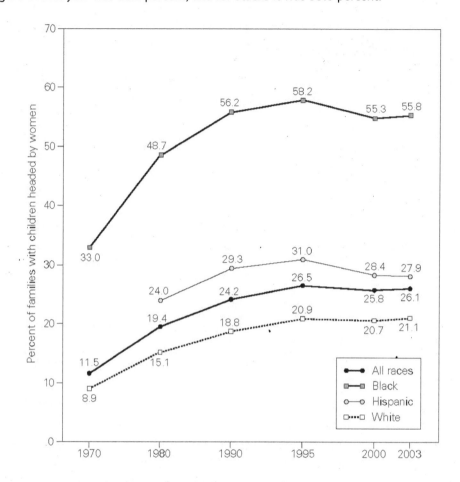

FIGURE 4.6   Trends in Female-Headship, 1970–2003

U.S. Census Bureau, "All Parent/Child Situation, By Type, Race, and Hispanic Origin of Householder of Reference Person: 1970 to Present." Historical Time Series Tables on Families, table FM-2. Internet release data

The contribution of single parenthood to higher levels of poverty, particularly among African American families, was discussed by, among others, E. Franklin Frazier in 1932 and 1939, Gunnar Myrdal in 1944, Daniel

Patrick Moynihan in 1965, and many others since.[99] Numerous reasons have been offered for changing family formation patterns, including changes in social norms and the declining economic fortunes of men.

The crux of the problem with this trend is that single-parent families headed by women are considerably more likely to be poor. While the poverty rate among married-couple families with children was 7.0 percent in 2003, it was 35.5 percent among female-headed families with children (see Figure 4.7). Poverty rates also vary by race and ethnicity, ranging from 6.6 percent among white married-couple families with children to close to 43 percent for both African American and Hispanic female-headed families with children. Yet it should be noted that the poverty rate for female-headed families with children has declined—from 59.9 percent in 1959 to 43.8 percent in 1970 to 35.5 percent in 2003.[100]

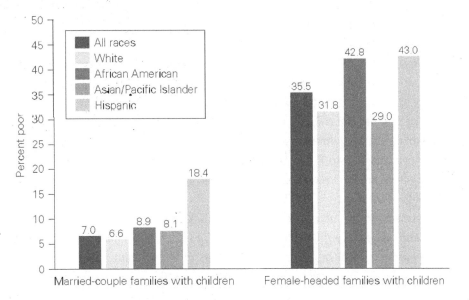

FIGURE 4.7   Poverty Rates of Families with Children by Marital Status and Race/ Ethnicity, 2003. Note: People of Hispanic origin may be of any race.

U.S. Census Bureau, "Poverty Status of Families, by Type of Family, Presence of Related Children, and Hispanic Origin: 1959 to 2003." Family Historical Poverty Tables, table 4. Internet release data

Poverty is high among female-headed families for several reasons. Single mothers (and fathers) often face the challenge of supporting a family on one income, as well as finding and paying for child care while they work and running a household alone when they do not. Children add to living costs but usually do not contribute to

99. E. Franklin Frazier, *The Negro Family in the United States* (Chicago: University of Chicago Press, 1939); E. Franklin Frazier, *The Negro Family in Chicago* (Chicago: University of Chicago Press, 1932); Gunnar Myrdal, *An American Dilemma* (New York: Harper and Row, 1944); Daniel Patrick Moynihan, *The Negro Family: The Case for National Action* (Washington, DC: U.S. Department of Labor, 1965); Suzanne Bianchi, "America's Children: Mixed Prospects," *Population Bulletin* 45 (1990): 1–43; Dennis Hogan and Daniel Lichter, "Children and Youth: Living Arrangements and Welfare," in *State of the Union,* pp. 93–139; Daniel T. Lichter, "Poverty and Inequality among Children," *Annual Review of Sociology* 23 (1997): 121–45.

100. U.S. Census Bureau, "Poverty Status of Families, by Type of Family, Presence of Related Children, Race, and Hispanic Origin: 1959 to 2003." Family Historical Poverty Tables, table 4. Internet release data (http://www.census.gov/hhes/www/poverty/ histpov/hstpov4.html), last revised May 13, 2005.

family income. Lower levels of education among women who head such families also contributes to their lower earnings.[101]

Furthermore, as discussed above, women tend to earn considerably less than men with comparable qualifications, and mothers tend to accumulate less experience than other workers.[102] Finally, many such families do not receive sufficient (or any) child support from the children's absent fathers.[103] However, research tends to show that, even if all families received the full amount of child support due them, poverty rates would decline only a little. While many fathers deliberately evade their child support obligations, others simply earn too little to pay much.[104]

Poverty is most feminized among African American and some His-panic (particularly Puerto Rican) families, mainly because these women are more likely to become single-parent householders and to be out of the labor force, live in low-income neighborhoods, have low levels of education, and face labor market discrimination than other women.[105]

Some studies suggest that changes in family structure played a major role in growing child poverty rates from the early 1970s through the mid-1990s.[106] In 1972, 86 percent of children lived in married-couple families, while in 1999 only 71 percent did. White and Asian children are more likely to be living in married-couple families, and African American children are least likely.[107] It has been estimated that the high proportion of children living in female-headed families accounts for just over half of the difference in child poverty rates between African American and Puerto Rican children on one hand and non-Hispanic white children on the other.[108] Declining real wages among less skilled young adults have also contributed to high child poverty rates and to group differentials.[109]

Yet the poverty rate among female-headed families declined in the 1990s, mainly because of increases in women's employment and wages. The greatest rise in employment among single mothers was concentrated in the mid-1990s. In 1999, employment rates for single mothers of young children were 79, 75, and 59 percent for whites, African Americans, and Hispanics, respectively. Among African American mothers of young children, there was a 22 percentage point increase in employment over the 1990 to 1999 period.[110] The employment

101. O'Hare, "A New Look at Poverty in America," pp. 18, 21.

102. Blau, Ferber, and Winkler, *Economics of Women, Men, and Work,* p. 169.

103. Bianchi, "Feminization and Juvenilization of Poverty."

104. Elaine Sorenson, "Noncustodial Fathers: Can They Afford to Pay More Child Support?" Urban Institute working paper, December 1994; O'Hare, "A New Look at Poverty in America," pp. 21–23.

105. Daniel T. Lichter and Nancy S. Landale, "Parental Work, Family Structure, and Poverty among Latino Children," *Journal of Marriage and the Family* 57 (1995): 346–54; Starrels, Bould, and Nicholas, "Feminization of Poverty in the United States."

106. See Maria Cancian and Deborah Reed, "Changes in Family Structure: Implications for Poverty and Related Policy," *Focus* 21, 2 (2000): 21–26; David J. Eggebeen and Daniel T. Lichter, "Race, Family Structure, and Changing Poverty among American Children," *American Sociological Review* 56 (1991): 801–17; Robert I. Lerman, "The Impact of the Changing U.S. Family Structure on Poverty and Income Inequality," *Economica* 63 (1996): S119–S139; Donald J. Hernandez, *America's Children: Resources from Family, Government, and the Economy* (New York: Russell Sage Foundation, 1993); Bianchi, "America's Children: Mixed Prospects"; Lichter, "Poverty and Inequality among Children."

107. Cancian and Reed, "Changes in Family Structure."

108. Lichter and Landale, "Parental Work, Family Structure, and Poverty among Latino Children."

109. Danziger and Gottschalk, *America Unequal,* pp. 67–92; Lichter, "Poverty and Inequality among Children."

110. Cancian and Reed, "Changes in Family Structure."

rate of never-married mothers, who are the most likely to have little education or job experience and long stays on welfare, rose from 43 percent in 1992 to 65 percent in 1999.[111]

Evidence from other countries also suggests that, while poverty tends to be more common among female-headed families, the poverty rates are not inherently high. Using a relative poverty line equaling 50 percent of the national median income, the poverty rate in 1995 for children in lone-parent families in Sweden (a majority of which are female headed), for example, was 6.7 percent. For children in other family types it was 1.5 percent. In Finland rates were even closer—7.1 percent for children in lone-parent families and 3.9 percent for children in other families. The poverty rates for children in the United States, using that relative measure, were 55.4 in single-parent families and 15.8 percent in other families. Notably, Sweden also has a slightly higher proportion of its children living in lone-parent families than in the United States. High employment rates among women, lower general wage inequality in the labor market, and generous government transfer policies help explain these low poverty rates in single-parent families in Sweden and Finland.[112]

Based on this analysis of child poverty rates across industrialized countries, the UNICEF Innocenti Research Centre argues that reducing poverty in female-headed families would therefore do more to reduce child poverty than reducing the incidence of female headship itself. That is, if the poverty rates of married-couple and female-headed families were more similar, then trends in headship would make little difference.[113]

[...]

Culture and Poverty

Because culture has become a politically loaded term in poverty discussions, it is a thorny issue often broached with caution by researchers. Culture is also a complex concept, hard to define and challenging to discern in its effects. Today, the view that cultural behavior contributes to poverty differentials tends to be associated with conservative commentators, though this has not always been the case.

In the 1920s, a number of sociologists from the University of Chicago and their students began to focus more systematically on the effect of social disorganization on the poor. Poverty was thought to result from temporary "cultural breakdown" that occurred in many immigrant and (in the case of African Americans) migrant communities in urban and industrial cities. The breakdown of social controls and customs led to increased crime, sexual promiscuity, family breakup, and economic dependency.[114]

Following the lead of Booker T. Washington (in 1902), sociologists such as Gunnar Myrdal (1944) and E. Franklin Frazier (1932, 1939), in adopting these arguments, were debunking the idea that the poor—and poor African Americans in particular—were genetically inferior.[115] They traced the roots of racial inequality to a wide range of factors, including racism and discrimination, which helped produce a deviant cultural response. Frazier, for example, saw "Negro matriarchy" as an accommodation to slavery and black male joblessness, and therefore

---

111. Ron Haskins, "Giving Is Not Enough," *Brookings Review* 19, 3 (summer 2001): 13–15.

112. UNICEF Innocenti Research Centre, "Child Poverty in Rich Nations," p. 8.

113. UNICEF Innocenti Research Centre, "Child Poverty in Rich Nations," pp. 11–13.

114. For an extended discussion, see O'Connor, *Poverty Knowledge,* pp. 74–123.

115. Booker T. Washington, *The Future of the American Negro* (New York, 1902); Myrdal, *An American Dilemma;* Frazier, *The Negro Family in the United States;* Frazier, *The Negro Family in Chicago.*

a common feature of lower-class culture and poverty.[116] Similarly, other progressives at the beginning of the twentieth century de-emphasized the notion that southern and eastern European immigrants were genetically inferior by arguing that immigrants needed to be Americanized and adapt to mainstream American values and culture.[117]

In the two decades after World War II, however, there was greater discussion of a culture of poverty without reference to other social and economic conditions. These arguments echoed nineteenth-century beliefs about the "undeserving" poor. Oscar Lewis, quoted at the beginning of this chapter, was a strong promoter of the culture of poverty thesis. Lewis believed that the poor contribute to their own impoverishment and identified seventy behavioral traits that distinguish the poor.[118] Similarly, in the late 1950s, Edward Banfield asserted: "The lower-class person lives from moment to moment, he is either unable or unwilling to take into account the future or to control his impulses ... being improvident and irresponsible, he is likely also to be unskilled, to move frequently from one dead-end job to another, to be a poor husband and father."[119]

Recent observers who have adopted this view—that the poor are essentially different, governed by their own code of values and behavior—tend to emphasize that the poor, or wayward government policies aimed at helping the poor, are often responsible for their degraded position. The argument goes that in the post–Great Society era, high welfare benefit levels provided work disincentives and encouraged dependency. The resulting culture of poverty consists of an eroded work ethic, dependency on government programs, lack of educational aspiration and achievement, increased single parenthood and illegitimacy, criminal activity, and drug and alcohol abuse.[120] Policy did not reward good behavior and did little to penalize harmful behavior. All of these problems in turn have an adverse effect on patterns of income and poverty, producing a vicious cycle of multigenerational dependency, primarily in high poverty areas in many central cities.

While it is likely that "culture" plays some role in reproducing poverty, social and economic structures are probably more important than culture. After all, as described in the previous chapter, many poor people are poor for only a short time, and those living in underclass neighborhoods make up only a small proportion (about 8 percent) of the poor.[121] Even among people who have been poor for a long time and, moreover, live in high poverty areas, differences are likely less rooted in aberrant values and more a result of functional adaptations to a difficult environment.[122] Overall, studies examining cultural differences do not provide overwhelming evidence that most of the poor people adhere to very different value systems than nonpoor people.[123]

116. O'Connor, *Poverty Knowledge*, p. 81.
117. Robert Cherry, "The Culture-of-Poverty Thesis and African Americans: The Work of Gunnar Myrdal and Other Institutionalists," *Journal of Economic Issues* 29, 4 (December 1995): 1119–32.
118. Schiller, *Economics of Poverty and Discrimination*, p. 127.
119. Edward C. Banfield, *The Unheavenly City* (Boston: Little, Brown, 1958), quoted in Michael B. Katz, *The Undeserving Poor: From the War on Poverty to the War on Welfare* (New York: Pantheon, 1989), pp. 31–32.
120. See Murray, *Losing Ground*; Robert Rector, "Welfare Reform, Dependency Reduction, and Labor Market Entry," *Journal of Labor Research* 14, 3 (summer 1993): 283–97.
121. Ronald Mincy, "The Underclass: Concept, Controversy, Evidence," in *Confronting Poverty*, pp. 108–46.
122. Michael B. Teitz and Karen Chapple, "The Causes of Inner-City Poverty: Eight Hypotheses in Search of Reality," *Cityscape* 3, 3 (1998): 33–70; Lee Rainwater, *Behind Ghetto Walls: Black Families in a Federal Slum* (Chicago: Aldine, 1970).
123. Rachel K. Jones and Ye Luo, "The Culture of Poverty and African-American Culture: An Empirical Assessment," *Sociological Perspectives* 42, 3 (1999): 439–58; Carole Marks, "The Urban Underclass," *American Review of Sociology* 17 (1991): 445–66.

Conclusion

All too often people assume that personal traits are the sole determinants of economic well-being, and they overlook the impact of environment. This is not surprising given that it is often difficult to recognize how structural forces affect our daily lives. Sociological concepts such as "class," "status" (social group differences), and "party" (policy) are helpful for understanding how stratification systems evolve. This chapter focused on the first two concepts [...] by examining how economic and social factors determine levels and patterns of poverty in the United States.

Economic growth tends to drive down absolute poverty rates. As standards of living rise, more and more people earn incomes above the unchanging (absolute) poverty line. However, income inequality, resulting from the ordinary workings of the market system in which the accumulation of assets (profit) is the goal and also from economic shifts and instability, may impede the positive impact of economic growth. If only the rich benefit from growth, then growth will have little impact on poverty. Increasing inequality since the 1970s contributed to stagnant absolute poverty rates in the 1970s and 1980s.

Social stratification by race and gender helps explain why some groups of people are more likely to be poor than others. Notably, however, the effect of social stratification along these group lines on poverty declined significantly over the last half of the twentieth century, likely due in large part to a decline in discrimination—especially in its overt, legal forms. Today, past poverty, economic dislocation, wealth differentials, and family instability are barriers at least as important as racism and discrimination in producing the exclusion of African Americans, Hispanics, American Indians, and some Asian Americans from full and equal participation in American society.[124] Nevertheless, despite this progress, racial and ethnic antipathy and discrimination have not disappeared. Moreover, the simple lifting of many barriers does not mean that equality is immediate or automatic.

Changing patterns of family formation also affected trends in poverty in the United States, though the impact is more pronounced among some racial and ethnic groups. Female-headed families are particularly more likely to be poor because women householders face the challenge of supporting a family on one income and often paying for child care while they work. Lower levels of education among women who head such families also contributes to their lower earnings. Furthermore, women tend to earn considerably less than men with comparable qualifications, and mothers tend to accumulate less experience than other workers. Finally, many such families do not receive sufficient child support from the children's absent fathers. Despite these obstacles, poverty rates among single-parent families, while still significantly higher than poverty rates among others, declined over much of the 1990s, largely because of greater employment and earnings among single parents.

References

Banfield, Edward C. 1958. *The Unheavenly City.* Boston: Little, Brown.
Barringer, H. R., R. W. Gardner, and M. J. Levin. 1993. *Asian and Pacific Islanders in the United States.* New York: Russell Sage Foundation.
Barrington, Linda. 2000. "Does a Rising Tide Lift All Boats?" The Conference Board. Research Report no. 1271-00-RR.
Becker, Gary S. 1971. *The Economics of Discrimination.* Chicago: University of Chicago Press.

124. Harrison and Bennett, "Racial and Ethnic Diversity."

Bernstein, Jared, Elizabeth C. McNichol, Lawrence Mishel, and Robert Zahradnik. 2000, January. "Pulling Apart: A State-by-State Analysis of Income Trends." Center on Budget and Policy Priorities and Economic Policy Institute Report.

Bianchi, Suzanne. 1990. "America's Children: Mixed Prospects." *Population Bulletin* 45: 1–43.

———. 1995. "Changing Economic Roles of Women and Men." In *State of the Union: America in the 1990s*, vol. 1, edited by Reynolds Farley. New York: Russell Sage Foundation.

———. 1999. "Feminization and Juvenilization of Poverty: Trends, Relative Risks, Causes, and Consequences." *Annual Review of Sociology* 25: 307–33.

Blank, Rebecca. 1997. "Why Has Economic Growth Been Such an Ineffective Tool Against Poverty in Recent Years?" In *Poverty and Inequality: The Political Economy of Redistribution*, edited by Jon Neil. Kalamazoo, MI: W. E. Upjohn Institute for Employment Research.

———. 1997. *It Takes a Nation: A New Agenda for Fighting Poverty*. Prince-ton, NJ: Princeton University Press.

Blau, Francine D., and Lawrence M. Kahn. 1997. "Swimming Upstream: Trends in the Gender Wage Differential in the 1980s." *Journal of Labor Economics* 15, 1, part 1 (January): 1–42.

Blau, Francine D., Marianne A. Ferber, and Anne E. Winkler. 1998. *The Economics of Women, Men, and Work*. Upper Saddle River, NJ: Prentice Hall.

Blau, Peter M., Otis Dudley Duncan, and Andrea Tyree. 1994. "The Process of Stratification." In *Social Stratification in Sociological Perspective*, edited by David B. Grusky. Boulder, CO: Westview Press.

Bluestone, Barry. 1994. "The Inequality Express." *The American Prospect* 20 (winter): 81–93.

Bluestone, Barry, and Bennett Harrison. 2000. *Growing Prosperity: The Battle for Growth with Equity in the Twenty-First Century*. Boston: Houghton Mifflin.

Bonacich, E. 1972. "A Theory of Ethnic Antagonism: The Split Labor Market." *American Sociological Review* 37 (October): 547–59.

Borjas, George J. 1987. "Assimilation, Changes in Cohort Quality, and the Earnings of Immigrants." *Journal of Labor Economics* 3: 463–89.

———. 1990. *Friends or Strangers: The Impact of Immigrants on the U.S. Economy*. New York: Basic Books.

Bound, John, and Harry J. Holzer. 1993. "Industrial Shifts, Skills Levels, and the Labor Market for White and Black Males." *The Review of Economics and Statistics* 75, 3 (August): 387–96.

Bound, John, and Laura Dresser. 1999. "Losing Ground: The Erosion of the Relative Earnings of African American Women during the 1980s." In *Latinas and African American Women at Work*, edited by Irene Browne. New York: Russell Sage Foundation.

Bound, John, and Richard Freeman. 1992. "What Went Wrong? The Erosion of Relative Earnings and Employment among Young Black Men in the 1980s." *Quarterly Journal of Economics* 107: 201–32.

Bumpass, Larry, and R. Raley. 1995. "Redefining Single-Parent Families: Cohabitation and Changing Family Reality." *Demography* 32: 97–109. Bureau of Economic Analysis. 2002. "Gross Domestic Product, in Current Dollars and in Chained (1996) Dollars." *National Accounts Data*, Times Series Estimates of Gross Domestic Product (http://www.bea.doc.gov/bea/dn1.htm).

Camarota, Steven A. 1999. *Importing Poverty: Immigration's Impact on the Size and Growth of the Poor Population in the United States,* Center for Immigration Studies Paper #15, September.

Cancian, Maria, and Deborah Reed. 2000. "Changes in Family Structure: Implications for Poverty and Related Policy." *Focus* 21, 2 (fall): 21–26.

Cherry, Robert. 1995. "The Culture-of-Poverty Thesis and African Americans: The Work of Gunnar Myrdal and Other Institutionalists." *Journal of Economic Issues* 29, 4 (December): 1119–32.

Chiswick, Barry R. 1978. "The Effect of Americanization on the Earnings of Foreign-Born Men." *Journal of Political Economy* 86, 5: 897–921.

Chiswick, Barry R., and Teresa A. Sullivan. 1995. "The New Immigrants." In *State of the Union America in the 1990s*, vol. 2, edited by Reynolds Farley. New York: Russell Sage Foundation.

Cross, Harry, Genevieve Kenney, Jane Mell, and Wendy Zimmermann. 1990. *Employer Hiring Practices*. Washington, DC: Urban Institute Press.

Dalaker, Joseph. 2001. "Poverty in the United States: 2000." U.S. Census Bureau, Current Population Reports, series P60-214. Washington, DC: U.S. Government Printing Office.

Danziger, Sheldon, and Daniel H. Weinberg. 1994. "The Historical Record: Trends in Family Income, Inequality, and Poverty." In *Confronting Poverty*, edited by Sheldon Danziger, Gary Sandefur, and Daniel Weinberg. Cambridge, MA: Harvard University Press.

Danziger, Sheldon H., and Peter Gottschalk. 1995. *America Unequal*. Cambridge, MA: Harvard University Press.

Daymont, T., and P. Andrisani. 1984. "Job Preferences, College Major, and the Gender Gap in Earnings." *Journal of Human Resources* 19: 408–28.

Devine, Joel A., Mark Plunkett, and James D. Wright. 1992. "The Chronicity of Poverty: Evidence from the PSID, 1968–1987." *Social Forces* 70, 3 (March): 787–812.

Eggebeen, David J., and Daniel T. Lichter. 1991. "Race, Family Structure, and Changing Poverty among American Children." *American Sociological Review* 56: 801–17.

England, Paula. 1994. "Wage Appreciation and Depreciation: A Test of Neoclassical Economic Explanations of Occupational Sex Segregation." In *Social Stratification in Sociological Perspective,* edited by David B. Grusky. Boulder, CO: Westview Press.

Farkas, G., and K. Vicknair. 1996. "Appropriate Tests of Racial Wage Discrimination Require Controls for Cognitive Skill: Comment on Cancio, Evans, and Maume." *American Sociological Review* 1: 557–60.

Farley, Reynolds. 1984. *Blacks and Whites: Narrowing the Gap?* Cambridge, MA: Harvard University Press.

Farley, Reynolds, and William H. Frey. 1994. "Changes in the Segregation of Whites from Blacks during the 1980s: Small Steps toward a More Integrated Society." *American Sociological Review* 59, 1 (February): 23–45.

Fisher, Gordon M. 1986. "Estimates of the Poverty Population under the Current Official Definition for Years before 1959." Mimeo, Office of the Assistant Secretary for Planning and Evaluation: U.S. Department of Health and Human Services.

Frazier, E. Franklin. 1939. *The Negro Family in the United States*. Chicago: University of Chicago Press.

———. 1932. *The Negro Family in Chicago*. Chicago: University of Chicago Press.

Freeman, Richard. 2000. "The Rising Tide Lifts … " *Focus* 21, 2 (fall): 27–31.

Galster, George C. 1992. "A Cumulative Causation Model of the Underclass: Implications for Urban Economic Development Policy." In *The Metropolis in Black and White: Place, Power, and Polarization*, edited by George Galster and Edward W. Hill. New Brunswick, NJ: Center for Urban Policy Research, Rutgers University.

Grusky, David. 1994. "The Contours of Social Stratification." In *Social Stratification in Sociological Perspective*, edited by David B. Grusky. Boulder, CO: Westview Press.

Harrison, Bennett, and Barry Bluestone. 1990. *The Great U-Turn: Corporate Restructuring and the Polarizing of America*. New York: Basic Books.

Harrison, Roderick J., and Claudette Bennett. 1995. "Racial and Ethnic Diversity." In *State of the Union America in the 1990s*, vol. 2, edited by Reynolds Farley. New York: Russell Sage Foundation.

Hartmann, Heidi. 1994. "The Unhappy Marriage of Marxism and Feminism: Towards a More Progressive Union." In *Social Stratification in Sociological Perspective*, edited by David B. Grusky. Boulder, CO: Westview Press.

Haskins, Ron. 2001. "Giving Is Not Enough." *Brookings Review* 19, 3 (summer): 13–15.

Haveman, Robert, and Jonathan Schwabish. 1999. "Economic Growth and Poverty: A Return to Normalcy?" *Focus* 20, 2 (spring): 1–7.

Hernandez, Donald J. 1993. *America's Children: Resources from Family, Government, and the Economy*. New York: Russell Sage Foundation.

Hogan, Dennis, and Daniel Lichter. 1995. "Children and Youth: Living Arrangements and Welfare." In *State of the Union: America in the 1990s*, vol. 2, edited by Reynolds Farley. New York: Russell Sage Foundation.

Hogan, Dennis P., and M. Pazul. 1982. "The Occupational and Earnings Returns to Education among Black Men in the North." *American Journal of Sociology* 90: 584–607.

Holzer, Harry J. 1996. *What Employers Want: Job Prospects for Less-Educated Workers*. New York: Russell Sage Foundation.

Holzer, Harry J., and Wayne Vroman. 1992. "Mismatches and the Urban Labor Market." In *Urban Labor Markets and Job Opportunity*, edited by George Peterson and Wayne Vroman. Washington, DC: Urban Institute Press.

Hout, Michael. 1994. "Occupational Mobility of Black Men: 1962 to 1973." In *Social Stratification in Sociological Perspective*, edited by David B. Grusky. Boulder, CO: Westview Press.

Iceland, John. 1999. "Earnings Returns to Occupational Status: Are Asian Americans Disadvantaged?" *Social Science Research* 28: 45–65.

———. 1997 "Urban Labor Markets and Individual Transitions out of Poverty." *Demography* 34, 3 (August): 429–41.

Iceland, John, and Josh Kim. 2001. "Poverty among Working Families: Insights from an Improved Measure." *Social Science Quarterly* 82, 2 (June): 253–67.

Ihlanfeldt, Keith R., and David L. Sjoquist. 1989. "The Impact of Job Decentralization on the Economic welfare of Central City Blacks." *Journal of Urban Economics* 26: 110–30.

Johnson, James H., and Melvin L. Oliver. 1992. "Structural Changes in the U.S. Economy and Black Male Joblessness: A Reassessment." In *Urban Labor Markets and Job Opportunity*, edited by George Peterson and Wayne Vroman. Washington, DC: Urban Institute Press.

Jones, Jacqueline. 1993. "Southern Diaspora: Origins of the Northern 'Underclass.'" In *The "Underclass" Debate: Views from History*, edited by Michael B. Katz. Princeton, NJ: Princeton University Press.

Jones, Rachel K., and Ye Luo. 1999. "The Culture of Poverty and African-American Culture: An Empirical Assessment." *Sociological Perspectives* 42, 3 (fall): 439–58.

Kasarda, John. 1995. "Industrial Restructuring and the Changing Location of Jobs." In *State of the Union: America in the 1990s*, vol. 1, edited by Reynolds Farley. New York: Russell Sage Foundation.

———. 1989. "Urban Industrial Transition and the Underclass." *The Annals of the American Academy* 501 (January): 26–47.

———. 1983. "Caught in the Web of Change." *Society* (November–December): 41–47.

Katz, Michael B. 1989. *The Undeserving Poor: From the War on Poverty to the War on Welfare*. New York: Pantheon.

Landale, Nancy S., and Avery M. Guest. 1990. "Generation, Ethnicity, and Occupational Opportunity in Late 19th Century America." *American Sociological Review* 55 (April): 280–96.

Lee, Sharon M. 1994. "Poverty and the U.S. Asian Population." *Social Science Quarterly* 75 (September): 541–59.

Lee, Sharon M., and Barry Edmonston. 1994. "The Socioeconomic Status and Integration of Asian Immigrants." In *Immigration and Ethnicity: The Integration of America's Newest Arrivals*, edited by Barry Edmonston and Jeffrey S. Passel. Washington, DC: Urban Institute Press.

Lerman, Robert I. 1996. "The Impact of the Changing U.S. Family Structure on Poverty and Income Inequality." *Economica* 63: S119–S139.

Lewis, Oscar. 1966. *La Vida*. New York: Random House.

Lichter, Daniel T., and Martha L. Crowley. 2002. "Poverty in America: Beyond Welfare Reform." *Population Bulletin* 57, 2 (June): 1–36.

Lichter, Daniel T., and Nancy S. Landale. 1995. "Parental Work, Family Structure, and Poverty among Latino Children." *Journal of Marriage and the Family* 57 (May): 346–54.

Lichter, Daniel T. 1997. "Poverty and Inequality among Children." *Annual Review of Sociology* 23: 121–45.

Loury, Glenn C. 2000. "What's Next? Some Reflections on the Poverty Conference." *Focus* 21, 2 (fall): 58–60.

Lundberg, Shelly J., and Richard Startz. 2000. "Inequality and Race: Models and Policy." In *Meritocracy and Economic Inequality*, edited by Kenneth Arrow, Samuel Bowles, and Steven Durlauf. Princeton, NJ: Princeton University Press.

Marx, Karl. 1994. "Classes in Capitalism and Pre-Capitalism." Reprinted from *The Communist Manifesto* in *Social Stratification in Sociological Perspective*, edited by David B. Grusky. Boulder, CO: Westview Press.

Marx, Karl. 1994. "Value and Surplus Value." Reprinted in *Social Stratification in Sociological Perspective*, edited by David B. Grusky. Boulder, CO: Westview Press.

Massey, Douglas S., and Nancy Denton. 1993. *American Apartheid*. Cambridge, MA: Harvard University Press.

McCall, Leslie. 2001 "Sources of Racial Inequality in Metropolitan Labor Markets: Racial, Ethnic, and Gender Differences." *American Sociological Review* 66, 4 (August): 520–41.

McLanahan, Sara, and Lynne Casper. 1995. "Growing Diversity and Inequality in the American Family." In *State of the Union America in the 1990s*, vol. 2, edited by Reynolds Farley. New York: Russell Sage Foundation.

Mincy, Ronald. 1994. "The Underclass: Concept, Controversy, Evidence." In *Confronting Poverty*, edited by Sheldon Danziger, Gary Sandefur, and Daniel Weinberg. Cambridge, MA: Harvard University Press.

Mouw, Ted. 2000. "Job Relocation and the Racial Gap in Unemployment in Detroit and Chicago, 1980 to 1990." *American Sociological Review* 65, 5 (October): 730–53.

Moynihan, Daniel Patrick. 1965. *The Negro Family: The Case for National Action*. Washington, DC: U.S. Department of Labor.

Murnane, Richard. 1994. "Education and the Well-Being of the Next Generation." In *Confronting Poverty*, edited by Sheldon Danziger, Gary Sandefur, and Daniel Weinberg. Cambridge, MA: Harvard University Press.

Murray, Charles. 1984. *Losing Ground: American Social Policy, 1950–1980*. New York: Basic Books.

Myrdal, Gunnar. 1944. *An American Dilemma*. 2 vols. New York: Harper and Row.

Nee, Victor, and Jimy Sanders. 1985. "The Road to Parity: Determinants of the Socioeconomic Achievements of Asian Americans." *Ethnic and Racial Studies* 8, 1 (January): 75–93.

O'Connor, Alice. 2001. *Poverty Knowledge: Social Science, Social Policy, and the Poor in Twentieth-Century U.S. History*. Princeton, NJ: Princeton University Press.

O'Hare, William P. 1996. "A New Look at Poverty in America." *Population Bulletin* 51, 2: 1–48.

O'Neill, June. 1990. "The Role of Human Capital in Earnings Differentials between Black and White Men." *Journal of Economic Perspectives* 4, 4: 25–46.

Orshansky, Mollie. 1965. "Counting the Poor: Another Look at the Poverty Profile." *Social Security Bulletin* 28, 1 (January): 3–29.

Osterman, Paul. 1999. *Securing Prosperity*. Princeton, NJ: Princeton University Press.

Parkin, Frank. 1994. "Marxism and Class Theory: A Bourgeois Critique." In *Social Stratification in Sociological Perspective*, edited by David B. Grusky. Boulder, CO: Westview Press.

Pearce, Diana. 1978. "The Feminization of Poverty: Women, Work, and Welfare." *Urban Sociological Change* 11: 128–36.

Peterson, George E., and Wayne Vroman. 1992. "Urban Labor Markets and Economic Opportunity." In *Urban Labor Markets and Job Opportunity*, edited by George E. Peterson and Wayne Vroman. Washington, DC: Urban Institute Press.

Piore, Michael J. 1994. "The Dual Labor Market: Theory and Implications." In *Social Stratification in Sociological Perspective*, edited by David B. Grusky. Boulder, CO: Westview Press.

Plotnick, Robert D., Eugene Smolensky, Eirik Evenhouse, and Siobhan Reilly. 1998, August 23–29. "The Twentieth Century Record of Inequality and Poverty in the United States." Paper presented at the General Conference of the International Association for Research on Income and Wealth. Cambridge, UK.

Polachek, Solomon W., and W. Stanley Siebert. 1994. "Gender in the Labour Market." In *Social Stratification in Sociological Perspective*, edited by David B. Grusky. Boulder, CO: Westview Press.

Price, C. 1969. "The Study of Assimilation." In *Sociological Studies: Migration*, edited by J. A. Jackson. Cambridge, UK: Cambridge University Press.

Rainwater, Lee. 1970. *Behind Ghetto Walls: Black Families in a Federal Slum*. Chicago: Aldine.

Rector, Robert. 1993. "Welfare Reform, Dependency Reduction, and Labor Market Entry." *Journal of Labor Research* 14, 3 (summer): 283–97.

Reimers, C. W. 1985. "A Comparative Analysis of the Wages of Hispanics, Blacks, and Non-Hispanic Whites." In *Hispanics in the U.S. Economy*, edited by George Borjas and Marta Tienda. New York: Academic Press.

Sakamoto, Arthur, and Satomi Furuichi. 1997. "Wages among White and Japanese-American Male Workers." *Research in Stratification and Mobility* 15: 177–206.

Sakamoto, Arthur, Huei-Hsia Wu, and Jessie M. Tzeng. 2000. "The Declining Significance of Race among American Men during the Latter Half of the Twentieth Century." *Demography* 37, 1: 41–51.

Sandefur, Gary, and W. J. Scott. 1983. "Minority Group Status and the Wages of Indian and Black Males." *Social Science Research* 12: 44–68.

Schiller, Bradly R. 2001. *The Economics of Poverty and Discrimination*, 8th ed. Upper Saddle River, NJ: Prentice Hall.

Sorenson, Elaine. 1994, December. "Noncustodial Fathers: Can They Afford to Pay More Child Support?" Urban Institute working paper.

Starrels, Marjorie E., Sally Bould, and Leon J. Nicholas. 1994. "The Feminization of Poverty in the United States." *Journal of Family Issues* 15, 4 (December): 590–607.

Stevens, Ann Huff. 1999. "Climbing out of Poverty, Falling Back In: Measuring the Persistence of Poverty over Multiple Spells." *Journal of Human Resources* 34, 3 (summer): 557–88.

– – –. 1994. "The Dynamics of Poverty Spells: Updating Bane and Ellwood." *AEA Papers and Proceedings* 84, 2 (May): 34–37.

Stevens, Gillian, and Joo Hyun Cho. 1985. "Socioeconomic Indexes and the New 1980 Census Occupational Classification Scheme." *Social Science Research* 14, 2: 142–68.

Sugrue, Thomas J. 1993. "The Structure of Urban Poverty: The Reorganization of Space and Work in Three Periods of American History." In *The "Underclass" Debate: Views from History*, edited by Michael B. Katz. Princeton: Princeton University Press.

Teitz, Michael B., and Karen Chapple. 1998. "The Causes of Inner-City Poverty: Eight Hypotheses in Search of Reality." *Cityscape* 3, 3: 33–70.

Trotter, Joe William, Jr. 1993. "Blacks in the Urban North: The 'Underclass Question' in Historical Perspective." In *The "Underclass" Debate: Views from History*, edited by Michael B. Katz. Princeton: Princeton University Press.

Turner, Margery, Michael Fix, and Raymond Struyk. 1991. *Opportunities Denied, Opportunities Diminished: Discrimination in Hiring*. Washington, DC: Urban Institute Press.

UNICEF Innocenti Research Centre. 2000. "Child Poverty in Rich Nations." *Innocenti Report Card*, no. 1 (June): 1–28.

U.S. Census Bureau. 1993. "Population and Housing Counts: 1790–1990." Selected Historical Census Data, Population and Housing Counts Internet report, CPH-2-1, table 16 (www.census.gov/population/www/censusdata/pop-hc.html).

– – –. 2000. "DP-1. Profile of General Demographic Characteristics: 2000." Census 2000 summary file 1 (SF 1), 100-Percent Data Quick Table (American FactFinder tabulation available at: factfinder.census.gov).

– – –. 2000, September 15. "Percent of People 25 Years Old and Over Who Have Completed High School or College, by Race, Hispanic Origin and Sex: Selected Years 1940 to 1999." Educational Attainment Historical Tables, table A-2. Internet release data (www.census.gov/population/socdemo/education/tableA-2.txt).

−−−. 2002, February 13. "Poverty of People, by Sex: 1966 to 2000." Historical Poverty Tables, table 7. Internet release data (www.census.gov/hhes/poverty/histpov/hstpov7.html).

U.S. Census Bureau. 2004, September 14. "All Parent/Child Situation, By Type, Race, and Hispanic Origin of Householder or Reference Person: 1970 to Present." Historical Time Series Tables on Families, table FM-2. Internet release data (http://www.census.gov/population/socdemo/hh-fam/tabFM-2.pdf).

U.S. Census Bureau. 2005, May 13. "Poverty Status of People, by Family Relationship, Race, and Hispanic Origin: 1959 to 2003." Historical Poverty Tables, table 2. Internet release data (http://www.census.gov/hhes/www/poverty/histpov/hstpov2.html).

U.S. Census Bureau. 2005, May 13. "Poverty Status of Families, by Type of Family, Presence of Related Chldren, Race, and Hispanic Origin: 1959 to 2003." Family Historical Poverty Tables, table 4. Internet release data (http://www.census.gov/hhes/www/poverty/histpov/hstpov4.html).

U.S. Census Bureau. 2005, May 18. "Women's Earnings as a Percentage of Men's Earnings by Race and Hispanic Origin: 1960–2003." Historical Income People Tables, table P-40. Internet release data (http://www.census.gov/hhes/www/income/histinc/p40.html).

Waldfogel, Jane, and Susan Mayer. 1998–1999. "Differences between Men and Women in the Low-Wage Labor Market." *Focus* 20, 1 (winter): 11–16. Washington, Booker T. 1902. *The Future of the American Negro.* New York: Metro Books, 1969.

Weber, Max. 1994. "Class, Status, Party." In *Social Stratification in Sociological Perspective,* edited by David B. Grusky. Boulder, CO: Westview Press.

−−−. 1994. "Open and Closed Relationships." In *Social Stratification in Sociological Perspective,* edited by David B. Grusky. Boulder, CO: Westview Press.

White, Michael J. 1987. *American Neighborhoods and Residential Differentiation.* New York: Russell Sage Foundation.

Wilson, William Julius. 1978. *The Declining Significance of Race: Blacks and Changing American Institutions.* Chicago: University of Chicago Press.

−−−. 1987. *The Truly Disadvantaged: The Inner City, the Underclass, and Public Policy.* Chicago: University of Chicago Press.

World Bank. 2001. *World Development Report, 2000/2001: Attacking Poverty.* Oxford, UK: Oxford University Press.

Yinger, John. 2000. "Housing Discrimination and Residential Segregation as Causes of Poverty." *Focus* 21, 2 (fall): 51–55.

Discussion Topics

1. Explain the statement: Poor are poor because they "are not doing enough."
2. Discuss the challenges minority groups face in the United States when it comes to economic well-being.
3. Explain the relationship between race and poverty in the United States.
4. What is meant by the concept of "feminization of poverty"?

Gender Inequality

Philip N. Cohen

Philip N. Cohen, "Gender Inequality," *Enduring Bonds: Inequality, Marriage, Parenting, and Everything Else That Makes Families Great and Terrible,* pp. 127-155, 219-222, 227-248. Copyright © 2018 by University of California Press. Reprinted with permission.

Editor's Introduction

This article titled "Gender Inequality" by Philip Cohen is focused on the economic dimension of gender inequality. This article was included in this text because it discusses in some depth three main themes associated with gender economic inequality, including job, income, and wealth inequality. After reading this article, you will have a better understanding of the gender gap, gender paid gap, and gender gap theory, and approaches to solutions to gender paid gap.

Difference is a precondition of inequality between groups. The condition of inequality requires a referent—one group has more or less of something than another. With regard to gender inequality, it is not the case that men have more of everything desirable than women, or that all men have more of anything desirable than all women do, or that gender inequality results from a single, coherent set of sexist motivations or the actions they inspire. Yet it is reasonable for practical—or political—purposes to refer to gender inequality as a systemic property of contemporary US society (and all other societies). To do so responsibly, however, requires grappling with a complicated set of facts that change over time according to patterns that are linked but not synchronized. Retreating behind the gauzy haze of terms like *nuance* and *complexity* is not a solution to this problem; rather, we need to name and measure the quantities we hope to understand and to explain them in both specific and systemic terms, quantitatively and qualitatively. We need facts and theory, and intelligible descriptions of both.[1]

This [reading] deals mostly with economic inequality—jobs and incomes and wealth. That's partly because economic inequality is very important and partly because it's easier to measure than a lot of other things, like sexual assault, mansplaining, childhood socialization, and other kinds of inequality that I discuss in other essays. Because I often come at gender inequality through critiques of media accounts, I start here with what the news people call a "deep dive" into one highly influential publication: the *New York Times*.

Gender Segregation at the New York Times

The Women's Media Center (WMC) reported in 2015 that women wrote 37 percent of print news stories in major newspapers. Levels ranged from a low of 31 percent female at the *New York Daily News* to a high of 54 percent at the *Chicago Sun-Times*. The *New York Times* is near the bottom of the major newspapers, with just 32 percent female bylines in the last quarter of 2014.[2]

The WMC report focused on the front section of each newspaper. Thanks to a data collection by my colleague Neal Caren, we can do better (Figure 5.1).[3] Neal extracted everything the *Times* published online from October 23, 2013, to February 25, 2014—a total of 29,880 items, including online-only as well as print items. After eliminating the 7,669 pieces that had no author listed (mostly wire stories), we tried to determine the gender of the first author of each piece. Neal identified the gender for all first names that were more than 90 percent male or female in the Social Security name database in the years 1945–70. That covered 97 percent of the bylines. For the remainder, I investigated the gender of all writers who had published ten pieces or more during the period (attempting to find both images and gendered pronouns). That resolved all but 255 pieces, leaving me with a sample of 21,440.[4]

This analysis showed:

1. Women were the first or only author on 34 percent of the articles.
2. Women wrote the majority of stories in five out of twenty-one major sections, from Fashion (52 percent women), to Dining, Home, Travel, and Health (76 percent women). Those five sections, however, account for only 11 percent of the total.
3. Men wrote the majority of stories in the seven largest sections. Two sections were more than three-

---

1. On the pitfalls of the "unconstrained" search for ever more explanatory factors, see Healy (2017).
2. Women's Media Center (2015).
3. Neal Caren has posted training materials and code for his data extraction and analysis work, including details on working with Python, at "Resources for Learning Python," http://nealcaren.github.io/.
4. This is a count of stories by the gender of their authors, not a count of authors. If men or women write more stories per person, then the figures will differ from those for the gender composition of authors. So it's not a workplace study but a content study. It asks: When you see something in the *Times,* what is the chance it was written by a woman versus a man? I combined Sunday Review (which was small) with Opinion, since they have the same editor and are the same on Sundays. I combined Style (which was small) into Fashion, since they're "Fashion and Style" in the paper. I combined *T Magazine* (which was small) into *T:Style*, since they seem to be the same thing. Also, I coded Reed Abelson's articles as female because I know she's a woman even though "Reed" is male more than 90 percent of the time.

fourths male: Sports (89 percent) and Opinion (76 percent). US, World, and Business were between 66 and 73 percent male.

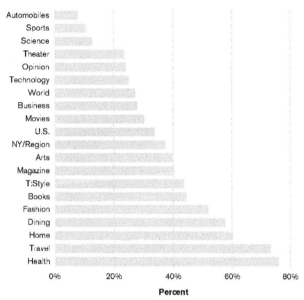

FIGURE 5.1   Percentage of stories with female first or only author, by section, for 21,440 *New York Times* articles, October 23, 2013, to February 25, 2014.

Since we have all this text, we can go a little beyond the section breakdown in the *Times*. What are men and women writing about? Using the words in the headlines, I compiled a list of those headline words with the biggest gender difference in rates of appearance. To get that, I calculated the frequency of occurrence of each headline word, as a fraction of all headline words in female-authored versus male-authored stories. For example, *children* occurred thirty-six times in women's headlines and twenty-four times in men's headlines. Since men used more than twice as many headline words as women, this produced a very big gender spread in favor of women for the word *children*. On the other hand, women's headlines had ten instances of *Iran*, versus eighty-five for men. Repeating this comparison for every headline word, I generated the ranked lists in table 5.1, with the most gender-tilted words at the top of each list.

TABLE 5.1. New York Times headline words used disproportionately in stories written by women versus men, October 23, 2013, to February 25, 2014

Women	Men
Scene	US
Israel	Deal
London	Business
Hotel	Iran

Her	Game
Beauty	Knicks
Children	Court
Home	NFL
Women	Billion
Holiday	Nets
Food	Music
Sales	Case
Wedding	Test
Museum	His
Cover	Games
Quiz	Bitcoin
Work	Jets
Christie	Chief
German	Firm
Menu	Nuclear
Commercial	Talks
Fall	Egypt
Shoe	Bowl
Israeli	Broadway
Family	Oil
Restaurant	Shows
Variety	Super
Cancer	Football
Artists	Hits
Shopping	UN
Breakfast	Face
Loans	Russia
Google	Ukraine

Living	Yankees
Party	Milan
Vows	Mets
Clothes	Kerry
Life	Gas
Child	Investors
Credit	Plans
Health	Calls
Chinese	Fans
India	Model
France	Fed
Park	Protesters
Doctors	Team
Hunting	Texas
Christmas	Play

What Does It Mean?

With some exceptions, the list of words gives the impression that men cover the important geopolitical questions of the day (*Iran, nuclear*), the economy (*deal, billion, oil*), and the masculine world of sports while more women spend their days writing about *hotels, beauty, children, weddings, shoes,* and *Christmas*. However, this doesn't mean most women write about hotels and most men write about Iran. It means these are the words with the biggest gender disparities, so they show where the extreme differences lie—it's an indicator of segregation. Surely this segregation reflects the influence of diverse factors, including editor and reader expectations, gender socialization, and women's ways of adapting to work in a male-dominated industry. But the bottom line of male domination is clearly evident.

This is just one newspaper, but it matters a lot. According to the Alexa Web traffic analysts, NYTimes.com is the 32nd most popular website in the United States and the 117th most popular in the world—and the most popular website of a printed newspaper in the United States.[5] By my count, in the JSTOR database of academic scholarship, the *Times* was mentioned almost four times more frequently than the next most frequently mentioned newspaper, the *Washington Post*.

5. The rankings are updated regularly. See Alexa's rankings at "nytimes.com Traffic Statistics," accessed July 23, 2017, www.alexa.com/siteinfo/nytimes.com.

A growing body of research (some by me and Matt Huffman, among others) suggests that having women in charge produces better average outcomes for women below them in the organizational hierarchy.[6] Jill Abramson, the *Times*'s executive editor for the period I studied here, was listed as the nineteenth most powerful woman in the world by *Forbes,* behind only Sheryl Sandberg and Oprah Winfrey among media executives. Abramson was aware of the gender issue and proudly told the Women's Media Center that she had reached the "significant milestone" of having a half-female news masthead. So why are women underrepresented in such prominent sections? Under Abramson the *Times* didn't even do as well as the national average: 39 percent of the 61,500 news reporters working full time, year round in 2014 were women, according to the American Community Survey.[7]

Organizational research finds that large companies are less likely to discriminate against women, and we suspect three main reasons: greater visibility to the public, which leads to complaints about bias; greater visibility to the government, which may enforce antidiscrimination laws; and greater use of formal personnel procedures, which limits managerial discretion and weakens old-boy networks. Among writers, however, an informal, back-channel norm still apparently prevails in hiring decisions—at least according to recent personal accounts.[8] Maybe the *Times*'s big-company, formalized practices apply more to departments other than those that select and hire writers, where subjective assessment remains the dominant mode of assessing performance—perhaps even more in this most elite of journalism workplaces. Several weeks after I posted this analysis on my blog, Abramson was fired by the *Times*'s publisher, Arthur Sulzberger, who said she had lost the confidence of her staff (reports described her as abrasive and alienating); her allies said she had recently complained about being paid less than the previous (male) executive editor.[9] After her replacement by a (Black) man, she is no longer on the *Forbes* list of most powerful women.

The Gender Gap Gets It from All Sides

The "gender gap" is a regular feature of public debate over gender inequality. This hardworking statistic is as often abused and attacked by antifeminists as it is misused and misunderstood by those sympathetic to feminism. But it is good for one thing: information.

The statistic is released each year with the US Census Bureau's income and poverty report. The Current Population Survey (CPS) reports annual incomes from 2015: the median earnings of full-time, year-round working women ($40,742) was 80 percent of men's ($51,212).[10] That is the source of (accurate, at the time) statements such as Barack Obama's "Women still earn only 79 cents to every dollar that men make."[11]

This statistic has the undeniable advantage of being relatively easy to calculate and comparable over time, so we can use it to assess one trend in gender inequality. The Institute for Women's Policy Research

6. See, e.g., Huffman, Cohen, and Pearlman (2010); Stainback, Kleiner, and Skaggs (2016). However, some evidence supports the contrary view, e.g., Srivastava and Sherman (2015).

7. These figures are from my use of American Community Survey data at IPUMS.org.

8. A. Friedman (2014).

9. Auletta (2014).

10. Proctor, Semega, and Kollar (2016).

11. Barack Obama Facebook status update, April 12, 2016, https://www.facebook.com/barackobama/posts/10153800980901749.

(IWPR), for example, informs us that "if change continues at the same slow pace as it has done for the past 50 years, it will take 44 years—or until 2059—for women to finally reach pay parity."[12] The trend that forms the basis for that prediction is shown in Figure 5.2.

FIGURE 5.2   Female-to-male earnings ratio, 1960–2015. Median earnings of full-time, year-round workers.

Current Population Survey via IPUMS.org.

There is no reason to think the future will follow a linear trend established by this distinctly nonlinear history. If you did want to fit a line to the trend, the bad news is that a third-order polynomial fits very well—that is, an S-shaped line fits almost perfectly, and predicts the gap will never narrow further. Fortunately, this kind of math doesn't actually tell us what will happen in the social world. But it does caution against resting on our laurels and simply waiting for equality.

Some defenders of equal pay for women misstate the statistic, as President Bill Clinton did when he said: "How would you like to show up for work every day, but only get to take home three out of every four paychecks? ... If you get paid 75 percent for the same kind of work, it's as if you were only picking up three paychecks, instead of four, in four pay periods. The average woman has to work, therefore, an extra 17 weeks a year to earn what a similarly-qualified man in the same kind of job makes."[13]

The mistake here is that he said "same kind of work" and "similarly-qualified man." This statistic is not designed to identify that sort of close-up discrimination. It's a broad indicator of earnings inequality, not a measure of employer discrimination. Clinton's comment led to a screaming headline on the American Enterprise

12. Institute for Women's Policy Research (2015).
13. Clinton (2000).

Institute website, "Still Hyping the Phony Pay Gap."[14] But Clinton also went on to say: "Yes, some of this can be explained—by differences in education, experience and occupation." So he belatedly acknowledged the complexities. Oh, and that exchange occurred in 2000. How far we've come.

When Bill Clinton, ever a repository for handy statistics, essentially repeated his statement in 2013, he played right into the screaming headlines of today's antifeminists, including Hanna Rosin, who declared, "I feel the need to set the record straight" in a piece she titled "The Gender Gap Lie."[15] Kay Hymowitz also has written extensively to debunk the gender gap, arguing that it mostly results from women's choices—the educations and occupations they choose, the hours they choose, the "mommy track" they prefer.[16]

There is no single number that can tell us the true state of gender inequality. But if you had to pick one, this one is actually pretty good. That's because it reflects a combination of factors that affect gender inequality. Men and women have different employment levels, work experience, and occupational distributions, some of which reflect employer discrimination; many people aren't in the job of their "choice," maybe because someone decided not to hire or promote them to a better job. And there is pay discrimination, too, though it's almost impossible to measure in a survey. This single statistic ends up giving a sense of the place of the typical worker after all those factors come into play. As long as pay is not equal, there is a gender inequality problem to discuss, whether it results from socialization, family demands, educational sorting and tracking, hiring and promotion discrimination, or pay discrimination.

Consider the case of Angelica Valencia, whose story was told in 2014 by one of the women writing at the *New York Times*, Rachel Swarns.[17] Valencia was fired from her $8.70-an-hour job packing produce after her doctor said she couldn't work overtime because she was three months into a risky pregnancy. The state actually had a new law against pregnancy discrimination on her side, but her employer somehow didn't get around to notifying her of her right to a reasonable accommodation.[18] It's important to keep cases like this in mind when critics complain that the gender gap statistic doesn't account for occupational choice, time out of the labor force, women's reduced hours, and so on.

Such critics include Ruth Davis Konigsberg, who had a piece in *Time* with the sneering subtitle "Women don't make 77 cents to a man's dollar. They make more like 93 cents, as long as they don't major in art history."[19] I guess Angelica Valencia should have thought of that, although it's really only something that the 29 percent of adults with bachelor's degrees need to lose sleep over. Hanna Rosin offered a similarly helpful explanation: "Women congregate in different professions than men do, and the largely male professions tend to be higher-paying."[20]

So what does the story of Angelica Valencia's pregnancy tell us, besides the pitfalls of majoring in art history or congregating in the wrong profession? I don't know what happened in her case, but let's assume that she, or someone in a situation like hers, took a while to find a new job and then ended up in a lower-paying job as a result of that discrimination. If we insist on statistically controlling for occupation, hours, job tenure,

14. Furchtgott-Roth (2000).
15. The Clinton quote is from ABC News (2013). See Rosin (2013).
16. Hymowitz (2011).
17. Swarns (2014).
18. New York City Commission on Human Rights (n.d).
19. Konigsberg (2013).
20. Rosin (2013).

and time out of the labor force in order to see the "real" wage gap, someone like her may not show up as underpaid—if they're paid the same as men in the same jobs, working the same hours, for the same length of time, and so on. So the very thing that makes Valencia earn less—being fired for getting pregnant—disappears from the wage gap analysis. Instead, the data shows that women take more time off work, work fewer hours, change jobs more often, and "choose" less lucrative occupations. Of course, a lot of women choose to get pregnant (and a lot of men choose to become fathers). But getting fired and ending up in a lower-paid job as a result is not part of that choice (and it rarely happens to fathers). That's why the overall difference in pay between men and women, which reflects a complicated mix of factors, is a good indicator of inequality.

Segregation

But let's look more closely at those college graduates that journalists often assume represent all workers. The ACS asks college graduates what their major was. In Figure 5.3 I've taken full-time, full-year workers who have a bachelor's degree and no further education (to remove the influence of later degrees), by college major, and arranged them from most to least male dominated. The level of gender segregation itself is remarkable, as the majors range from construction services, at 6 percent female, to family and consumer sciences, which is 87 percent female. The figure shows the average earnings as well as the spread between men's and women's average earnings. The male-dominated majors do pay more than the female-dominated ones, as engineering majors earn the most, while education majors earn the least. But there is also a male advantage within every group. Women's earnings range from a low of 75 percent of men's for area studies majors at the worst, all the way up to 92 percent for engineering technologies majors at the best. Seeing the gap within each major is especially useful for those who think the gender gap results from women choosing less lucrative majors.

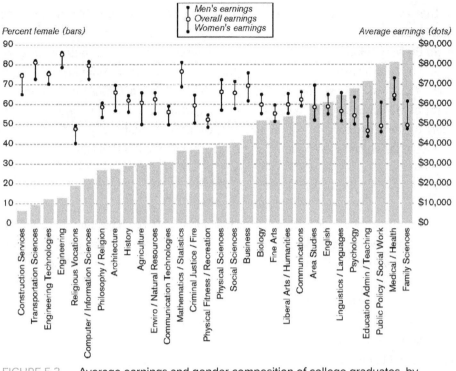

FIGURE 5.3   Average earnings and gender composition of college graduates, by college major.

Author calculations from the 2014 American Community Survey via IPUMS.org. Includes only full-time, year-round workers, ages twenty-five to fifty-four, with a bachelor's degree and no further degrees.

College majors, of course, are closely related to the jobs people have (if they've graduated from college), so the sorting of people into majors—like the sorting of workers into jobs more generally, is a key issue. One way to look at that is by breaking occupations down by education level, as I have done with the twenty-five largest occupations in Figure 5.3. This illustrates how much segregation there is at every education level. A separate analysis (not shown) confirms that within each group of occupations, the female-dominated jobs have lower average earnings than those dominated by men—a finding consistent with decades of research.[21]

Job segregation lies behind much of the gender gap in pay—representing the culmination of historical and contemporary processes of allocating people to tasks. If women earn less than men on average, than the jobs in which they are crowded will tend to have lower pay. And then discrimination pushes, or pulls, women into those lower-paying jobs. In fact, there is evidence that the presence of women in an occupation itself leads to lower average pay, as a result of what we call gender devaluation.

21. For a review, see Cohen (2013j).

Carpenters — Low education:
Construction laborers — 3-8% have BA or more
Sales and truck drivers
Laborers
Janitors
Cooks
Food service managers
Cashiers
Nurse aides

Non-retail sales supervisors — Medium education:
Wholesale sales reps — 19-40% have BA or more
Miscellaneous managers
Retail sales
Retail supervisors
Customer service reps
Office supervisors
Secretaries

Software engineers — High education:
Lawyers — 59+% have BA or more
Sales managers
Financial managers
Accountants
Secondary teachers
Elementary/middle teachers
Registered nurses

0   50   100
Percent female

FIGURE 5.4   Percentage female in twenty-five largest occupations, by education level.

Author analysis of 2015 March Current Population Survey data from IPUMS.org. Full-time, full-year workers (excluding chief executives).

I developed one comparison to illustrate this devaluation process—the process of rewarding "male" work more than "female" work. Consider two of the occupations in the low-education group: sales workers and truck drivers versus nursing aides. These are narrowly defined occupations, but they include millions of workers: in 2014 there were 2 million nursing aides and 3.2 million sales workers and truck drivers (I'll call them truck drivers for short, but this category excludes big industrial trucks).[22] The nursing aides are 88 percent female, the truck drivers are 94 percent male. Drawn from Census Bureau data, and information from the US Department of Labor's O*Net job classification system, here are some other facts:

- The nursing assistants are better educated on average, with only 50 percent having no education beyond high school, compared with 67 percent of the light truck drivers.
- But in terms of job skills, they are both in the O*Net "Job Zone Two," meaning three months to one year of training is "required by a typical worker to learn the techniques, acquire the information, and develop the facility needed for average performance in a specific job-worker situation."
- The O*Net reported median wage for 2012 was $11.74 for nursing assistants, compared with $14.13 for light truck drivers, so nursing assistants earn 83 percent of light truck drivers' hourly earnings.

To make a stricter apples-to-apples comparison, I took just those workers from the two occupations who

22. The full comparison is at Cohen (2013d). The full titles of the occupations are "Nursing, Psychiatric, and Home Health Aides," and "Driver/Sales Workers and Truck Drivers." The 2014 estimate is from the Current Population Survey. For the rest of this comparison I drew on the 2009–11 American Community Survey data at IPUMS.org. For a more in-depth analysis of the nursing aides and their occupational mobility, see Ribas, Dill, and Cohen (2012).

fit these narrow criteria: age twenty to twenty-nine, high school graduate with no further education, employed fifty to fifty-two weeks in the previous year, with usual hours of forty per week, never married, no children. In the 2009–11 ACS, this gave me a sample of 748 light truck drivers and 693 nursing assistants, with median annual earnings of $22,564 and $20,000, respectively—the light truck drivers earn 13 percent more. Why?

The typical argument for heavy truck drivers' higher pay is that they spend a lot of time on the road away from home. But that's not the case with these light truck drivers, and I restricted this comparison to forty-hour workers only. The O*Net database includes a long list of abilities and working conditions for people to evaluate jobs and the workers who do them. There are clues in here about why men and women with similar skill and education levels are separated across these two occupations, but not much to explain why the truck drivers earn more. In terms of abilities, the nursing aide job requires more explosive strength and trunk strength, but less dynamic strength and static strength. The nursing aides have more language skills while the truck drivers have more coordination and dexterity. In terms of working conditions, the nursing aides face disease and infection, spend more time on their feet as well as stooping, crouching, bending, and twisting—and dealing with physically aggressive people. The truck drivers, on the other hand, spend more time exposed to the weather and experience more loud sounds and lights that are too bright or not bright enough.

You can stare at these lists and try to figure out which skills should be rewarded more, or which conditions compensated more. Or you could derive some formula based on the pay of the hundreds of occupations, to see which skills or conditions "the market" values more. But the problem for understanding gender inequality is that you will not be able to divine a fair market value for these differences that doesn't already have gender composition baked into it. By *baked in*, I mean: things men do—have always done—are more valuable in our market system than things women do. It's hard to pin down, because "the market" doesn't make this comparison directly, because nursing aides and light truck drivers generally don't work for the same employers or get hired from the same labor pools. Sociologists who have studied these patterns over time conclude that gender composition itself is a strong independent driver of pay differences, with inequalities derived more from the traditional division of labor than from individual actions of today's employers.[23]

The only solution I know of to the problem of unequal pay according to gender composition is government wage scales according to a "comparable worth" scheme. That was the subject of an extensive debate several decades ago, but such radical state intervention is not high on the current political agenda, despite repeated promises by Democratic leaders (including Barack Obama and Hillary Clinton) that they would address the gender gap.[24] Under our current legal regime it is virtually impossible for one woman, or even a class of women, to successfully bring a suit to challenge this kind of disparity—because it does not entail individuals being paid unequally for the same work. That means occupational integration might be the best way to reduce the pay gap.[25]

23. Levanon, England, and Allison (2009).
24. For the comparable-worth debates, see Acker (1991); P. England (1992). Neither the Lilly Ledbetter Fair Pay Act, signed by Obama in 2009, nor the Paycheck Fairness Act, backed by Clinton, would have imposed a comparable worth scheme, although the latter law would have narrowed the scope of justifications allowed for disparities in pay between different jobs.
25. One exception is the public sector in Minnesota, which has something like comparable worth, in which local jurisdictions have their pay structures reviewed at regular intervals for evidence of gender bias, based on the required conditions and abilities of their jobs. See Legislative Office on the Economic Status of Women (2016).

Each of these comparisons tells us something different. We must be careful not to read into these numbers more than they can tell us. None of the numbers I've shown can fully distinguish occupational choice from employer discrimination, for example, or the cumulative effects of family time out of the labor force versus discrimination in previous jobs. But the gender gap numbers are measures of inequality. And as long as we are accurate and responsible in our use of these numbers, that's useful information about the state of gender inequality.

Gender Shifts in Families

Breadwinner women are all over the news, but the simple story in most versions is not good enough, and in some cases, as we will see, it's very wrong. The promotional materials for Farnoosh Torabi's book *When She Makes More* rely on a single, dramatic statistic: "The number of married couples with top-earning wives is *four* times greater than it was in the 1960s."[26] A Pew Research Center report carried the banner statistic, "Mothers are the sole or primary provider in four-in-ten households with children."[27] These numbers are quite slippery, and those without a firm grasp are likely to overreact. On cue, *Fox and Friends* host Clayton Morris expressed his concern: "Are female breadwinners a problem? Isn't there some sort of biological, innate need for men to be the caveman? Go out and bring home the dinner—is it emasculating if we don't do it?"[28]

Here are three central facts to keep in mind, illustrated in Figure 5.5, which shows the distribution of income within married couples in 1970, 1990, and 2014. From this we can see:

1. *Yes, the balance of income within married couples has shifted toward women since the 1950s.* There is a dramatic drop in the percentage of couples in which the husband earns all the income—from 45 percent in 1970 to 20 percent in 2014. That is the plummet of the "traditional" male breadwinner.
2. *But the pace of change slowed dramatically after the 1990s.* The vast majority of that change had happened already by 1990—a generation ago. The shift since 1990 has mostly been a decline in couples where the wife earns 1 to 20 percent, and a rise in those where the wife earns 50 to 70 percent, but it's modest compared with what happened before 1990.
3. *Today's female "breadwinners" are not much like the men who filled that role a half century ago.* As of 2014, only 2 percent of couples have a wife that earned all the income in the previous year. That's more than it used to be, but it's not a role reversal.

26. Torabi (2015).
27. Wang, Parker, and Taylor (2013).
28. Luscombe (2014).

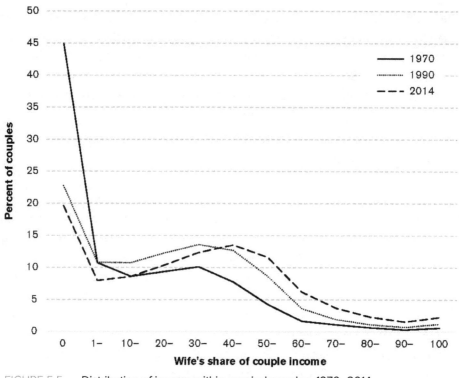

FIGURE 5.5   Distribution of income within married couples, 1970–2014.

Author calculations from Decennial Censuses and the American Community Survey data via IPUMS.org. Restricted to different-sex couples with positive total incomes in which the wife is age eighteen to sixty-four.

These three facts are essential to understanding the nature of changing gender inequality within families. There may be something psychologically triggering for some people who experience a wife earning anything more than her husband does, but we do nothing to help that situation by exaggerating the extent of women's dominance. Consider that, on average, in 2014 wives who earned more than their husbands brought in 68 percent of the couple's income. On the other hand, the average husband who earned more brought in 82 percent of the total. A male "breadwinner" is three times more likely to earn all the income in the couple than a female "breadwinner." In addition, those analyses, like Pew's above, that report the highest prevalence of female providers are including single mothers—who are of course primary providers for their families, but their prevalence is not a good indicator of declining gender inequality.

Actually, this triplet pattern fits a lot of trends regarding gender inequality: *yes,* lots of change, *but* most of it decades ago, *and* not quite as fundamental as it looks. Consider stay-at-home fathers—the complement to the female breadwinner.

A *New York Times* Style section piece featured a picture of a "Daddy and me" class in Central Park and reported on the rapid growth of the population of stay-at-home fathers. "Until recently, stay-at-home fathers made up a tiny sliver of the American family spectrum," wrote Alex Williams, describing the new trend as "a lifestyle choice—one that makes sense in an era in which women's surging salaries have thrown the old family hierarchy into flux."[29] The cover of the *New Yorker* on Mother's Day of that year (May 7, 2012) showed a lone mother with her toddler in a stroller, standing at the edge of a playground full of dads and children.

The data in that article were accurate. Gretchen Livingston wrote a report for Pew Social Trends on fathers staying at home with their kids. She defined stay-at-home fathers as any father age eighteen to sixty-nine living with his children who did not work for pay in the previous year. Her analysis showed a doubling of stay-at-home fathers from 1989 to 2012. There are especially pronounced spikes during recessions, which highlights the economic context of the trend, but even without the recessions the trend is upward.[30]

As with breadwinners, we also need to understand the definition. In Livingston's analysis, 21 percent of the stay-at-home fathers reported that their reason for not working was caring for their home and family; 23 percent couldn't find work, 35 percent couldn't work because of health problems, and 22 percent were in school or retired. It is reasonable to call a father "stay-at-home" regardless of his reason (after all, we never needed stay-at-home mothers to fulfill motive-based criteria before we gave them that label). And yet there is a tendency to read into this a bigger change in gender dynamics than it justifies. The Census Bureau has for years calculated a much more narrow definition that applies only to married parents of kids under fifteen: those out of the labor force all year, whose spouse was in the labor force all year, and who specified their reason as taking care of home and family.[31] You can think of people in this category as the *hardcore* stay-at-home parents, the ones who do it long term and have a carework motivation for doing it. When you define them that way, stay-at-home mothers outnumber fathers 100 to 1.

In Figure 5.6 I show trends in two simple measures. The first, which I calculate from 1976 through 2014, includes all married parents (living with children under age fifteen) who reported no employment in the previous year. This is the broadest category of stay-at-home parents, not dependent on their reason for not working or on what anyone else in the household is doing. By this measure, the prevalence of stay-at-home mothers fell markedly from 1970s until 2000, but it has since rebounded back up over 30 percent. In the figure I also show the percentage of parents who did not work in the previous year who reported that their reason for nonemployment was "caring for home and family." This doesn't change the trend for mothers much, as the great majority of nonemployed mothers gave this as their reason. For fathers, however, only 23 percent of those who didn't work said the reason was caring for home and family. So even though the percentage of fathers in this role has more than doubled, it's never surpassed 1.5 percent of all married fathers—maybe still a "tiny sliver of the American family spectrum." As in the case of female breadwinners, then, although there has been a pronounced change in the pattern of stay-at-home parents compared with the period of extreme gender division epitomized by the 1950s, it mostly occurred decades ago. And the trend shows something more like a role shift than a revolution or role reversal.

29. Williams (2012).
30. Livingston (2014).
31. US Census Bureau (2015b).

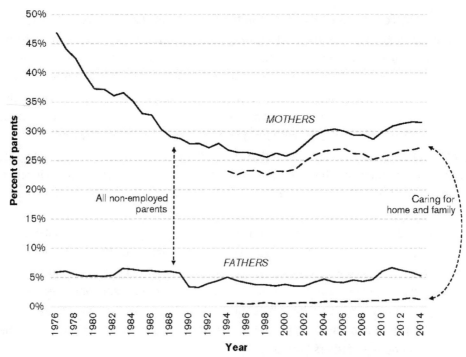

FIGURE 5.6   Stay-at-home parents as percentage of married parents living with children ages zero through fourteen.

Author calculations from Current Population Survey data via IPUMS.org.

Exaggerating Change

In the last few years, on this and other questions, I've spent a lot of time trying to combat the tendency to exaggerate the extent of change toward gender equality. My basic concern is that if we don't understand the trends we won't be able to see what remains to be done—and the obstacles to inequality that remain. Maybe it's uniquely American, but we have a strong urge to see equality approaching as an inevitable evolution of impartial social forces. Somewhere between our natural inclination toward egalitarianism and against injustice on the one hand, and technological advances on the other, men and women are presumed to be heading toward equality in the foreseeable and not-too-distant future. Failure to see that most change toward gender equality happened decades ago also distorts our view of the importance of explicit feminist politics as a crucial factor in that change. And it prevents us from understanding how contemporary policies and practices—especially around the work-family intersection—are blocking further progress.[32]

Exaggerations of the gender equality trend also may be a natural product of the perceived need in journalism to tell a linear story with clear implications for the future. This tendency was apparent in the book by journalist Liza Mundy, *The Richer Sex,* with the wishful-thinking subtitle "How the New Majority of Female Breadwinners Is Transforming Sex, Love and Family." A more aggressive mischaracterization of reality appeared

32. I made this case in an op-ed (Cohen 2013f). For the general stalling of progress on gender equality, see Cotter, Hermsen, and Vanneman (2011). On stalled progress toward equality in the division of labor, see Sayer (2015).

in Hanna Rosin's TED talk, *Atlantic* article, and eventually book *The End of Men*.[33] She opened the TED talk by declaring that "in many of the places where it counts the most, women are in fact taking control of everything." Unlike the feminist surges in the 1920s and 1960s, however, she added, "This time it's not about passion and it's not about any kind of movement. This is really just about the facts of this economic moment that we live in. The 200,000-year period in which men have been top dog is truly coming to an end, believe it or not, and that's why I talk about 'the end of men.' "

In the months that followed, I chronicled the amazing collection of errors and distortions that Rosin made in her articles and the book. She claimed that the majority of "managers" are now women (it's actually "managers and professionals," which includes nurses and teachers); that "young women are earning more than young men" (this is true only for single, childless women under thirty in urban areas); that "70% of fertility clinic patients" prefer to have a female child (there's just no evidence for that); that Auburn, Alabama, is "a town dominated by women" (it has the same male dominance as most US cities); that "rates [of sexual assault] are so low in parts of the country … that criminologists can't plot the numbers on a chart" (that's just ridiculous); that the average age of marriage for women "in Asia" is thirty-two (it's much lower); and that "the recent rise in plastic surgeries is fueled by men" (there is no rise, and men account for only 13 percent of plastic surgeries).[34]

Rosin illustrated the problem of assuming that gender trends map onto a linear progress story when, after the 2012 election, she somehow thought women made up one-third of Congress and wrote: "A record number of women were elected to Congress, bringing their number to a third of the membership, the level many sociologists cite as a tipping point when a minority becomes normalized and starts to enter the mainstream. In other words, it's no longer big news when a woman gets elected; it's expected."

This one-third tipping point theory Rosin attributes (without citation) to "many sociologists" is, not surprisingly, a myth; if there's one thing we have learned about minority representation and its effects on inequality, it's that we can't apply a simple numerical rule to the many patterns observed in the research literature. And even if her facts on the number of women in Congress were correct, the suggestion that the United States has reached the point where women's representation at the top is no longer news is obviously not true in the simplest sense. When informed that women held only 18 percent of seats in Congress, *Slate* deleted the whole passage. (The article was as clear an illustration as you could ask for of sloppy writers' tendency to advance a theory on the basis of cherry-picked facts and to distort or omit any evidence that doesn't fit.)

I eventually concluded that Rosin's story of women sweeping into dominance without the impetus of "passion" or "any kind of movement" was misleading to the point of being corrosive—it harms our ability not just to understand but to mobilize people to address gender inequality. She essentially turned several broad facts—that women are earning more degrees in higher education than men and that the service economy is growing—and manufactured around them a story of technological change (the shift from brawn to brains) tipping the power balance from male to female. This is not complete fiction, as the changing composition of the economy through the mid-twentieth century did produce rapid growth in occupations that

---

33. See Mundy (2012a); Rosin (2012a). I reviewed Mundy and Rosin's books together in Cohen (2013k). My full-length critique
    of Rosin was published in a law review article (Cohen 2013c).
34. I detailed these specific errors in Cohen (2013b).

were female dominated, such as medical, educational, and administrative occupations.[35] But the part about women becoming socially dominant remains purely hypothetical—albeit theoretically plausible.[36]

In the *New York Times* magazine excerpt from her book, Rosin wrote: "As the usual path to the middle class disappears, what's emerging in its place is a nascent middle-class matriarchy, in which women like Patsy [one of her interviewees] pay the mortgage and the cable bills while the men try to find their place."[37] This is completely inaccurate. There has of course been movement toward gender equality (with the caveats I noted above), but the evidence simply does not support anything like a "matriarchy" or female dominance in families or in the economy generally. The idea that women are inevitably rising to power in politics and the economy, replacing men in the pants-wearing driver's seat, is both disempowering to feminists and enraging to sexists. With careful attention to the actual trends, we can understand the necessity of further efforts toward equality and can illuminate the ways forward, while also disarming the militant purveyors of antifeminist backlash.

That Feminist Viral Statistic Meme

Exaggerating the progress and promise of equality is disempowering because it undermines the urgency of calls for concerted action to address gender inequality. But exaggerating the extent of patriarchal domination is also disempowering because it presents the problem as hopelessly unchanging. In the last few years I have been fortunate to be on the receiving end of feminist criticism (and also feminist support) for criticizing both of these disempowering tendencies.

The one-hundredth anniversary of International Women's Day, in 2011, came at an auspicious time for statistical infographic memes. The coming wave of "data journalism" was as yet only nascent, but social media were already demonstrating the potential for a statistic-based meme to have outsized influence in the political arena: not just a political statement, not just an empirical fact, but a single fact (or a few of them) propelling a perspective, making it visually as well as verbally memorable, and anchoring it in a base of credibility.

That year I was reminded of something that had been nagging at me for at least ten years, since I read it in Judith Lorber's excellent 1994 book, *Paradoxes of Gender*. She wrote: "An often-cited United Nations Report (1980) claims that women do two-thirds of the world's work, receive 10 percent of the income, and own 1 percent of the property."[38] The reference wasn't helpful (a 1980 report I couldn't access), but those facts had never seemed plausible to me.

Then, in 2011, as International Women's Day approached, we were treated to a barrage of mainstream, corporate-backed liberal feminism, including a collaboration between Google and a nonprofit called Women for Women, which encouraged women to march across bridges around the world on March 8. To promote the effort, they produced a video, which has now been viewed almost a million times, that includes this in the

---

35. Cotter, Hermsen, and Vanneman (2001).
36. For an extended version of this theory, see Jackson (1998).
37. The cover of the magazine showed a man with no pants, and the subtitle for the article was "Welcome to the New Middle-Class Matriarchy" (Rosin 2012c).
38. Lorber (1994, 288).

narration: "Did you know that women perform two-thirds of the world's work and produce half the world's food, but earn just 10 percent of the income and own just one percent of the property?"[39]

The inequality described in that video is easily understood as outrageously immoral. But why would a 2011 infographic include a statistic from a 1995 book that cited a 1980 report? As memes travel from mind to mind, like viruses, such questions are lost. A statistical meme just needs a plausible link or citation to make the leap from one host to another and—unlike a virus—can be transmitted from one person to millions more instantly, without the need for face-to-face contact.

For example, *Wall Street Journal* writer Sudeep Reddy (later an economics editor) wrote a blog post titled "New Facts on the Gender Gap from the World Bank." The first of his bullet point facts was dramatic: "Women represent 40 percent of the world's labor force but hold just one percent of the world's wealth." The labor force statistic was in the World Bank report (in the first paragraph, actually, giving some hint of the depth of his research), but the wealth statistic, which isn't true, was not. The *Journal*'s Twitter account fit that fact into a tweet, and by the next day it was being reported on ThinkProgress as a "newsflash," which got repeated by *Ms.*, and then became the "number of the day" on the feminist site Shakesville.[40] And so on.

On the Trail

Because I'm concerned about both kinds of disempowering errors—the optimistic and pessimistic overstatements—and generally want to promote the responsible use of social statistics, I wanted to find out where the meme came from and then repair or retire it. It really only took a few hours of research, and some interlibrary loan requests, to track it down.

That 2011 International Women's Day version—which gave the meme new global momentum—was more or less verbatim how it had appeared in Lorber's book and a decade earlier, on page 1 of Robin Morgan's introduction to the classic collection called *Sisterhood Is Global: The International Women's Movement Anthology*.[41] Beyond that, I quickly found three sources offered by bona fide scholars. The first was the footnote from Morgan's book, which says: "Statistics from Development Issue Paper No. 12, UNDP." Produced as part of the UN's Decade for Women (1975–85), this report was titled "Women and the New International Economic Order" and was probably published in 1980. That document is fascinating reading, but on the key point it is just a restatement of the meme, without documentation.[42] It is not the true source. The second was a report called "World Conference of the United Nations Decade for Women: Equality, Development and Peace" (UN document buffs might call it A/Conf. 94/20), or the "Programme of Action" that emerged from that 1980 meeting, which was in Copenhagen. That document was released under the name of Kurt Waldheim, who (before his Nazi past was revealed) was secretary general to the UN at the start of the Decade for Women.[43] This was Lorber's source, but it is not the true source.

Finally, the Copenhagen report contains a footnote to a 1978 edition of a Decade for Women–inspired journal published by the International Labour Organization, called *Women at Work*. This, I eventually discovered,

39. Women for Women (2011).
40. The chain of links is detailed in Cohen (2011).
41. R. Morgan (1984).
42. I have placed a copy of this document online at philipncohen.com/working/WNIEO.pdf
43. Zinsser (2002).

is the true source.[44] It occurs in the editor's introduction to the journal. Unfortunately, the sum total of what it provides is this: "A world profile on women, using selected economic and social indicators, reveals that women constitute one half of the world population and one third of the official labour force; perform nearly two-thirds of work hours; but according to some estimates receive only one-tenth of the world income and possess less than one-hundredth of world property."

There is no information on the indicators used or their sources, or what is meant by "some estimates." That is where the trail went cold, until I found the testimonial of Krishna Ahooja-Patel, who took credit for the passage. In 2007, Ahooja-Patel, the editor over whose initials that editorial appeared, published a book called *Development Has a Woman's Face: Insights from within the U.N.*, in which she offers an unsourced sketch of the methods she used to derive the famous statement. "Several assumptions had to be made," she concedes, "based on some available global data and others derived by use of fragmentary indicators at the time, in the late 1970s."[45]

The figures used were crude estimates at best. Women were 33 percent of the world's formal workforce, and they were "only on the low income level in the pyramid of employment," where (on the basis of data from "several countries") they earned 10 to 30 percent of men's income. Therefore, "One could assume that women's income is only one-third of the average income of men." Since women were one-third of the workforce and earned one-third as much as men, their total income was .33 × .33, or 11 percent (which she rounded down to 10 percent). In short, the statistic was a guess based on an extrapolation wrapped round an estimate.

What about the dramatic conclusion, that women "possess less than one-hundredth of world property"? Ahooja-Patel offers only this explanation: "If the average wage of women is so low, it can be assumed that they do not normally have any surplus to invest in reproducible or non-reproducible assets." Hence, their share of those assets is less than 1 percent. That's it. In fact, she adds, "In reality the figure may be much lower" (than 1 percent). Her source? "Various UN Statistics."

The Inequality Between Women

These things are hard to measure, hard to know, and hard to explain. Setting aside the problem that the data didn't (and still don't, completely) exist to fill in the true numbers in this famous sequence of facts—the first and perhaps greatest problem is that we can't easily define the concepts, which is part of a larger feminist problem. Defining work as a quantity is fraught, as is property. Even in 1970, how could women own only 1 percent of property, when most women were married and in many countries had at least some legal claim to their families' property? Similarly, what claim did women who worked without pay in private homes and fields have to their husbands' cash incomes? And what about socialist countries (which were a big deal back then), where a lot of payment was in the form of in-kind transfers, and where various forms of collective ownership were pervasive? Did "women" own state or commune land in socialist China? Was their food ration "income"? So it's too simple to say the famous facts are wrong.

44. International Labour Office (1978).

45. Ahooja-Patel (2007, 367). In 2015, in response to a *Washington Post* reporter who got her name from my post, she wrote, reasonably: "Please understand that the knowledge of statistics we have now in 2015 is not the same as what we knew earlier, especially in the 1970s and 80s. Some of the statistics we were looking at in that period were estimates and the national statistical offices of the period did not cover women's issues or data" (Kessler 2015).

One of the complaints I have heard often from feminists (of which, to repeat, I am one) is that debunking this meme without offering the true statistics is harmful to the movement. This complaint reflects the common conflation of data and argument—the belief that citing a fact is making an argument, so that debunking the fact undermines the argument. Angry with my apparent attack on feminism, one commenter on my blog wrote, "I'm sorry but in order to claim something is false you have to be able to prove it by showing the truth." But the burden of proof is not on us (me) to show it is wrong. My responsibility is rather to point out that it was never demonstrably true, which is enough to conclude we shouldn't use it.

One of the potential negative consequences of this meme is also one of its attractions: the claim that, despite all the work women do, they own virtually nothing the world over, supports a call to global unity for women. But it is undermined by the fact that a large number of women are, of course, rich. The meme doesn't just represent a failure of education in the areas of ballpark demography and statistical critical thinking. People who fall for it also aren't realizing how rich the rich countries are—including the women in them—in the global scheme of things. If global feminist unity is to be had, it simply won't be built from a shared experience of poverty. We need to understand that so we can move on to a more fruitful approach. I eventually decided to give up on the argument that the meme needs no refuting and instead tried to show how it couldn't be true, that it must be off by orders of magnitude. Debunking this is a good exercise for statistical and demographic literacy and helps drive home the extent of global inequality *between women,* which is what's missing from the appeals that employ the meme.

So let's consider some facts. Start with the statement that women earn only 10 percent of the world's income. With a combination of arithmetic and basic knowledge of a few demographic orders of magnitude, it's straightforward to identify and conduct a simple test of the claim.

In the United States in 2015, the 112.6 million adult women reported average incomes in the previous year of $32,588 each. That is a total of $3.67 trillion. The whole world's gross domestic product—a rough measure of total income—is $77.96 trillion. So, US women *alone* earn 4.7 percent of world income today.[46] Unless the rest of the world's women combined earn less than US women (they don't), it's impossible that women earn less than 10 percent of global income. Ballpark, but you see the point. We needed only five minutes to prove the income statistic isn't true.

What about property? Recall that Ahooja-Patel described her original 1 percent estimate as referring to women's "reproducible or non-reproducible assets," which she wrote as "property." (Since then people have changed it to "land," or even "titled land," changing the words to make the claim seem more plausible without doing any real research.) My strategy for debunking this, similar to the one I used for income, is to find a small group of women who themselves own more than 1 percent of all world wealth and let that set the matter to rest.

For practical reasons, I decided to figure out the wealth owned by single women in the United States. That's because US data are pretty good, the women are pretty rich (in the scheme of things) so they're likely to satisfy the goal, and single women are simpler because you don't have to worry about defining or identifying shared wealth. (If married men and women jointly own their wealth, the "Women own 1 percent" claim is obviously implausible from the start.)

46. US women's income is from US Census Bureau (2015a); global gross domestic product figures are from World Bank (2016).

The Credit Suisse Research Institute estimated global household wealth at $243.1 trillion in 2013.[47] To estimate the share of global household wealth held by single women in the United States, I compared this with data from the 2013 Survey of Consumer Finances (SCF).[48] By my calculations, the SCF shows a total household net worth of $65.2 trillion. That works out to about $294,000 per adult (the average is so high because rich people are really rich)—a figure pretty close to the CSRI estimate of $348,000 per US adult, which is good for confidence in making this comparison.

The SCF is useful because it includes a breakdown of households by sex and marital status. Using that, I calculate that US single women (not married or living with a partner, in their own households), have a total net worth of $6.2 trillion. So single women in the United States are not doing well by US standards. They are 28 percent of the households but have only 9.5 percent of the wealth. But by global standards they look much better. They are just 0.7 percent of the world's adult population but have 2.6 percent of the global household wealth. That means that no matter how much property the billions of other women in the world own—including all married women in the United States, all single and married women in every other country—the women of the world own more than 2.6 percent of total, and the meme is wrong.

As an aside, what about extremely rich women? Sample surveys like the SCF are unlikely to call on the tiny sliver of people who are super-rich (and if they did, those people probably wouldn't talk). But when outsiders, such as Forbes, estimate the wealth of the wealthy, they can give us some clue of the share owned by women at the very top. I looked at the 2016 Forbes list of billionaire women, led by the ninety-four-year-old L'Oreal heir Liliane Bettencourt ($36 billion in 2016) and the Wal-Mart heir Alice Walton ($32 billion), all the way down to the barely billionaires such as tech executive Meg Whitman.[49] These lists bounce around a lot, so the estimates will vary, but they are good for a ballpark figure. By my count, the 108 women billionaires on the list have a combined net worth at $536 billion, which is about one-fifth of 1 percent of global household wealth. There are very few women among the richest rich (if you don't count wives), but so vast is their wealth that alone they do a lot to push "all women" up toward the 1 percent threshold needed to debunk the meme.

A final empirical point about this meme concerns geography and land. Although Ahooja-Patel was guesstimating wealth, as I noted, some people have turned this into a statement about land ownership. This is the case even when their own evidence provides enough data to refute the meme. For example, in a post on the *Ms.* magazine blog, Jessica Mack describes the problem of women's land ownership in China. Land ownership has been a big problem there ever since the breakup of the collective ownership system in the 1980s, with massive land-grabbing and the migration of tens of millions of people to the cities. She writes: "In China, women have equal rights to inherit and own land, yet rarely do. A recent survey in 17 Chinese provinces, undertaken by the global land rights group Landesa, found that only 17.1 percent of existing land contracts and 38.2 percent of existing land certificates include women's names."[50]

I don't doubt there is a serious gender inequality problem. But what does it mean that "17.1 percent of existing land contracts and 38.2 percent of existing land certificates include women's names"? Does it mean women "own" that land? Are they part owners? That's a question she should have considered before writing,

47. Credit Suisse AG (2014).
48. Data are from Board of Governors of the Federal Reserve System (2014).
49. Forbes (2016).
50. Mack (2012).

later in the post: "Yet women globally own only one to two percent of all titled land." This was really a rhetorical flourish, though, not a fact. For a source she reached into the meme's giant grab bag and came up with a blog post from World Food Program USA, which says that women "own less than 2 percent of the world's titled land."[51] That fact in turn is sourced to someone just repeating the classic meme.[52]

Anyway, the good news is that the seeds of the meme's undoing are in Jessica Mack's own post. You just to have a sense of the size of the world, and China within it. If women "own" either 17 percent or 38 percent of land in China, could they really own just 1 percent of land in the world? No. China has 7 percent of the world's total land area and 20 percent of the world's harvested land area.[53] Assuming all land parcels are the same size (not a safe assumption, but we have nothing else to go on), if women in China have their names on 17 percent of land contracts and 38 percent of land certificates, that represents 1 to 3 percent of the total land, or 3 to 8 percent of the harvested land. That's in China alone, so the meme is killed again.[54]

Why?

Despite being included in antifeminist Christina Hoff Sommers's list of "five feminist myths that will not die," this meme may in fact finally be dying.[55] I didn't see it used at all around the most recent International Women's Day. The old online references by the UN and international development organizations have all been revised or taken down. The fact-checking sites PolitiFact and Washington Post Fact Checker eventually did debunking pieces, relying in part on my research (the *Post* gave Oxfam four "Pinocchios" for using it in 2015).[56]

But why did this thing, which never had many legs to stand on, ever become so pervasive even decades after it was devised? I have seen it used by legislators in South Africa, international universities, feminist organizations, journalists, humanitarians, activists, sociologists, economists—and, amazingly, UN organizations speaking in the present tense in the 2010s. There is a great, much longer story here, which is beyond my capacity to tell, having to do with statistical memes in general as well as this one in particular. The story involves access to information and deference to, and cynicism about, statistical authorities—in the context of statistical and demographic (sorry to say) illiteracy; the relationship between feminism and science; and even the role of social media in social movements. I can't explain why it happened, but I'm quite sure that debunking it hasn't hurt feminism.

Gender inequality is not simple, one-dimensional, or universal. And it's not always easy to measure. But that must not deter us from trying to understand and act upon it. As Alan Alda likes to say in his science communication workshops, we need to "surf uncertainty rather than avoiding it."[57] We can know enough to

51. World Food Program USA (2010).

52. Hanstad (2009).

53. Food and Agriculture Organization of the United Nations (2016).

54. Others have investigated the land question also, finding that while of course women own less land than men, there's no way it's as low as 1 percent. For example, an analysis of sub-Saharan African countries found that women owned anywhere from a few percent to almost half of the privately held land. See Doss et al. (2013).

55. Sommers (2014).

56. Greenberg (2014); Kessler (2015).

57. See the promotion video at Alan Alda Center for Communicating Science, Facebook page, December 24, 2014, https://www.facebook.com/aldacenter/posts/764774310245069.

make sound generalizations, and to inform our social interventions, even while our knowledge remains partial. Of course, the risk of being wrong is real, but so are the potential consequences of inaction. This is what makes the social science of inequality important (and also sometimes fun). When we turn, in the next chapter, to the intersections of different kinds of inequality, it will be especially helpful to maintain a perspective that is empirically rigorous while also avoiding the fatalistic surrender to uncertainty.

References

ABC News. 2013. "This Week: Bill Clinton on CGI." September 29.

Acker, Joan. 1991. *Doing Comparable Worth: Gender, Class, and Pay Equity.* Philadelphia: Temple University Press.

Ahooja-Patel, Krishna. 2007. *Development Has a Woman's Face: Insights from within the U.N.* New Delhi: APH Publishing.

Auletta, Ken. 2014. "Why Jill Abramson Was Fired." *New Yorker,* May 14.

Board of Governors of the Federal Reserve System. 2014. "Survey of Consumer Finances." www.federalreserve.gov/econresdata/scf/scfindex.htm.

Clinton, Bill. 2000. "Remarks by the President in Statement on Equal Pay Day." National Archives and Records Administration, January 24. http://clinton6.nara.gov/2000/01/2000-01-24-remarks-by-the-president-in-statement-onequal-pay.html.

Cohen, Philip N. 2011. "Follow the Bouncing 1% Meme…." *Family Inequality*, September 21. https://familyinequality.wordpress.com/2011/09/20/follow-the-bouncing-1-meme/.

– – –. 2013b. "Correct That Error, Hanna Rosin Edition." *Family Inequality*, September 12. https://familyinequality.wordpress.com/2013/09/12/correct-that-error-hanna-rosin-edition/.

– – –. 2013c. "The 'End of Men' Is Not True: What Is Not and What Might Be on the Road toward Gender Equality." *Boston University Law Review* 93 (3): 1159–84.

– – –. 2013d. "Gender Devaluation, in One Comparison." *Family Inequality*, December 5. https://familyinequality.wordpress.com/2013/12/05/gender-devaluation/.

– – –. 2013f. "Jump-Starting the Struggle for Equality." *New York Times,* November 24, SR9.

– – –. 2013j. "The Persistence of Workplace Gender Segregation in the US." *Sociology Compass* 7 (11): 889–99.

– – –. 2013k. "Still a Man's World: The Myth of Female Ascendance." *Boston Review* 38 (1): 54–58.

Cotter, David A., Joan M. Hermsen, and Reeve Vanneman. 2001. "Women's Work and Working Women: The Demand for Female Labor." *Gender and Society* 15 (3): 429–52.

– – –. 2011. "The End of the Gender Revolution? Gender Role Attitudes from 1977 to 2008." *American Journal of Sociology* 117 (1): 259–89.

Credit Suisse AG. 2014. "Credit Suisse: Global Household Wealth Increases by 8.3% to USD 263 Trillion, Driven by Wealth Growth in the United States and Europe." PR Newswire, October 14.

Doss, Cheryl, Chiara Kovarik, Amber Peterman, Agnes R. Quisumbing, and Mara van den Bold. 2013. "Gender Inequalities in Ownership and Control of Land in Africa: Myths versus Reality." IFPRI Discussion Paper 1308.

England, Paula. 1992. *Comparable Worth: Theories and Evidence.* New Brunswick, NJ: Transaction.

Food and Agriculture Organization of the United Nations. 2016. *Statistical Yearbook 2016.* Rome: FAO Publications.

Forbes. 2016. "The World's Billionaires: 2016 Ranking." *Forbes*, March 21.

Friedman, Ann. 2014. "Journalism's Hiring Transparency Problem." *Columbia Journalism Review,* April 24.

Furchtgott-Roth, Diana. 2000. "Still Hyping the Phony Pay Gap." AEI Online, January 31. American Enterprise Institute.

Greenberg, Jon. 2014. "Do Women Own 1% of the World's Land? No." *Politifact*, August 5.

Hanstad, Tim. 2009. "Access to Land Improves Women's Lives around the World." *Seattle Times,* March 10.

Healy, Kieran. 2017. "Fuck Nuance." *Sociological Theory* 35(2): 118–127.

Huffman, Matt L., Philip N. Cohen, and Jessica Pearlman. 2010. "Engendering Change: Organizational Dynamics and Workplace Gender Desegregation, 1975–2005." *Administrative Science Quarterly* 55 (2): 255–77.

Institute for Women's Policy Research. 2015. "Pay Equity and Discrimination." www.iwpr.org/initiatives/pay-equity-and-discrimination.

International Labour Office. 1978. *Women at Work.* No. 1. Geneva: ILO.

Jackson, Robert Max. 1998. *Destined for Equality: The Inevitable Rise of Women's Status.* Cambridge, MA: Harvard University Press.

Kessler, Glenn. 2015. "The Zombie Statistic about Women's Share of Income and Property." *Washington Post,* March 3.

Legislative Office on the Economic Status of Women. 2016. "Pay Equity: The Minnesota Experience (6th Edition)." www.oesw.leg.mn/PDFdocs/Pay_Equity_Report2016.pdf.

Levanon, Asaf, Paula England, and Paul Allison. 2009. "Occupational Feminization and Pay: Assessing Causal Dynamics Using 1950–2000 U.S. Census Data." *Social Forces* 88 (2): 865–91.

Livingston, Gretchen. 2014. "Growing Number of Dads Home with the Kids." Pew Research Center's Social and Demographic Trends Project, June 5. www.pewsocialtrends.org/2014/06/05/growing-number-of-dads-home-withthe-kids/.

Lorber, Judith. 1994. *Paradoxes of Gender.* New Haven, CT: Yale University Press.

Luscombe, Belinda. 2014. "The Real Problem with Women as the Family Breadwinner." *Time,* May 5.

Mack, Jessica. 2012. "Women Losing Land Rights in China." *Ms. Magazine Blog*, March 8. http://msmagazine.com/blog/2012/03/08/women-losing-landrights-in-china/.

Morgan, Robin. 1984. *Sisterhood Is Global: The International Women's Movement Anthology.* New York: Feminist Press at CUNY.

Mundy, Liza. 2012a. *The Richer Sex: How the New Majority of Female Breadwinners Is Transforming Sex, Love and Family*. New York: Simon and Schuster.

Proctor, Bernadette D., Jessica L. Semega, and Melissas A. Kollar. 2016. *Income and Poverty in the United States: 2015*. P60–256. Washington, DC: US Census Bureau.

Ribas, Vanesa, Janette S. Dill, and Philip N. Cohen. 2012. "Mobility for Care Workers: Job Changes and Wages for Nurse Aides." *Social Science and Medicine* 75 (12): 2183–90.

Rosin, Hanna. 2012a. *The End of Men: And the Rise of Women*. New York: Riverhead Books.

– – –. 2012c. "Who Wears the Pants in This Economy?" *New York Times Magazine,* August 30.

– – –. 2013. "The Gender Wage Gap Lie." *Slate*, August 30.

Sayer, Liana C. 2015. "Trends in Women's and Men's Time Use, 1965–2012: Back to the Future?" In *Gender and Couple Relationships,* edited by Susan M. McHale, Valarie King, Jennifer Van Hook, and Alan Booth, 43–77. New York: Springer.

Sommers, Christina Hoff. 2014. *The Top Five Feminist Myths of All Time*. American Enterprise Institute. YouTube, uploaded September 8. https://www.youtube.com/watch?v=3TR_YuDFIFI.

Srivastava, Sameer B., and Eliot L. Sherman. 2015. "Agents of Change or Cogs in the Machine? Reexamining the Influence of Female Managers on the Gender Wage Gap." *American Journal of Sociology* 120 (6): 1778–1808.

Stainback, Kevin, Sibyl Kleiner, and Sheryl Skaggs. 2016. "Women in Power: Undoing or Redoing the Gendered Organization?" *Gender and Society* 30 (1): 109–35.

Torabi, Farnoosh. 2015. *When She Makes More: The Truth about Navigating Love and Life for a New Generation of Women*. New York: Plume.

US Census Bureau. 2015a. Annual Social and Economic Supplement, 2014 Person Income, Table PINC-09. https://www.census.gov/data/tables/time-series/demo/income-poverty/cps-pinc/pinc-09.2014.html.

– – –. 2015b. "Parents and Children in Stay at Home Parent Family Groups: 1994 to Present." https://www.census.gov/population/socdemo/hh-fam/shp1.xls.

Wang, Wendy, Kim Parker, and Paul Taylor. 2013. "Breadwinner Moms." Pew Research Center's Social and Demographic Trends Project. May 29. www.pewsocialtrends.org/2013/05/29/breadwinner-moms/.

Williams, Alex. 2012. "Dads Are Taking Over as Full-Time Parents (Just Wait Till Your Mother Gets Home)." *New York Times,* August 10.

Women for Women. 2011. "Join Us on the Bridge on March 8th." *YouTube*, uploaded February 24. https://www.youtube.com/watch?v=hUF65dRO8ic.

Women's Media Center. 2015. "The Status of Women in the U.S. Media 2015." http://wmc.3cdn.net/83bf6082a319460eb1_hsrm680x2.pdf.

World Bank. 2016. "World Development Indicators, Table 4.2." http://wdi.worldbank.org/table/4.2.

World Food Program USA. 2010. "Women's Greater Access to Land Can Increase Food Security." March 5. http://wfpusa.org/blog/womens-greateraccess-land-can-increase-food-security.

Zinsser, Judith P. 2002. "From Mexico to Copenhagen to Nairobi: The United Nations Decade for Women, 1975–1985." *Journal of World History* 13 (1): 139–68.

Discussion Topics

1. What is the main idea of this article?
2. What does "gender gap" refer to? Use examples from the text to substantiate your answer.
3. What are the arguments advanced by feminist critics against the "gender gap" theory?
4. Explain the "exaggerating change" dilemma.

CONCLUSION

This article explains the important role that sociology plays in the investigation of social problems. The contribution of sociology to social problems is unique through its perspective, which is sociological imagination. Coined by C. Wright Mills, the concept of sociological imagination refers to the ability to establish a link between "biography" and "history." That is, sociological imagination enables us to understand that our personal troubles are connected to public issues. In a sense, this unique perspective of sociology allows uncovering or discovering the influential effects of social structure on social problems, which leads to theory formulation: theorizing. A social theory can be defined as a systematic, disciplined, and logical explanation of social phenomena, such as social problems. The process of theorizing occurs in three major steps: (1) Identify a problem ("the something ain't right"); (2) Describe the nature of the problem, its manifestation, and implications; and (3) Provide a description of how the problem can be solved and the impact of the solution on society.

UNIT 3

DEVIANCE, SEXUALITY, AND CRIME

Introduction

The central point of this unit is deviance. From a sociological perspective, the concept of deviance refers to a departure from societal norms. In this unit, the concept will be applied to sexuality and crime. In "*Conformity and Deviance: Advantages and Disadvantages*," Narváez argues that most people in society have a tendency to conform to social norms. To substantiate this claim, he points to the results of an experiment conducted by Asch in 1951. According to this experiment, most people follow the law and regulations established in society, while a small portion of the population deviates from societal norms. Consequently, society has a panoply of sanctions reserved for infractions, such as raised eyebrows, cold shoulders, ostracism, etc., even death in the case of authoritarian societies.

An example of deviance studied at some length in the unit is crime, defined as a violation of formal norms or laws. As such, crimes are serious, compared to violations of other societal norms, and therefore carry heavy sanctions or punishments. In "*Crime, the Emotions and Social Psychology*," Carrabine, Cox, Lee, Plummer, and South argue that the existing literature on crime fails to investigate the relationship between emotions and crime. They subscribe to the idea that most crimes can be traceable to emotions. There are two type of emotions: primary and secondary emotions. Examples of primary emotions include happiness, fear, anger, and depression. These are basic emotions shared by all human beings. Besides these four primordial, are secondary emotions, such as hate, shame, guilt, pride, wonder, resentment, nostalgia, and dread. This set of emotions is secondary because they are socially constructed. That is, they vary by society. In a sense, what is viewed as an object of pride in the United States might not be the same in China, for example. The authors uncovered the link between fear of crime-anxiety, thrill-shame-respect and crime, humiliation-rage-edgework and crime, risk-excitement-routine and crime. Other topics covered in this article are reintegrative shaming as a way to restore justice and the concept of hate crime.

Sexuality and deviance is also discussed in this unit. Butler, in her article titled "*Undiagnosing Gender*," argues that gender identity along with sexual implications, such as homosexuality or heterosexuality, are important social problems. Heterosexuality, which is the most common sexual practice in society, is considered to be the normal or standard sexuality, while homosexuality is the deviating type. Also discussed in this article is the concept of gender identity. Conceived as "the perception of enduring gendered traits of the opposite sex," gender identity disorder has a dialectic nature according to Butler. For Butler, pathologizing gender identity as a disorder in the Diagnostic and Statistical Manual of Mental Disorders (DSM-IV) is oppressing, as doing so comes with labels as well as ensuing stigma. However, the exclusion of gender identity disorder from DSM will make it virtually impossible for individuals experiencing gender identity crisis, especially poor ones, to be covered by insurance for their gender reassignment surgeries. A solution to this dilemma is to fundamentally change the norms governing our understanding of the relation between gender identity and mental health.

Undiagnosing Gender

Judith Butler

Judith Butler, "Undiagnosing Gender," *Undoing Gender*, pp. 75-101, 253-255, 261-267. Copyright © 2004 by Taylor & Francis Group. Reprinted with permission.

Editor's Introduction

This article titled "Undiagnosing Gender" by Judith Butler explores problems associated with gender identity. This article is included in the text because it discusses the link between deviance and sexual orientation (homosexuality and heterosexuality). After reading this article, you will have a better understanding of the polemic around pathologizing gender identity and possible approach to solution to problems related to gender identity.

I n recent years there have been debates about the status of the *Diagnostic and Statistical Manual of Mental Disorders'* (*DSM-IV*) diagnosis of gender identity disorder and, in particular, whether there are good reasons to keep the diagnosis on the books, or whether there are no longer very many good reasons. On the one hand, those within the GLBQTI community who want to keep the diagnosis argue that it offers certification for a condition, and facilitates access to a variety of medical and technological means for transitioning. Moreover, some insurance companies will only absorb some of the very high costs of sex change if they first can establish that the change is "medically necessitated." It is important, for these reasons, not to understand sex change surgery or hormonal usage as "elective surgery." Although one might want to say that it is a choice, even a choice of a dramatic and profound kind, for the purpose of the insurance allocation it has to be a medically conditioned choice. We can surely think for quite some time about what a medically conditioned choice actually is, but for the purpose of this argument it's important to distinguish between a choice conditioned by a diagnosis and one that is not. In the latter case, the choice to transition can include some or all of the following: the choice to live as another gender, to take hormonal surgery, to find and declare a name, to secure new legal status for one's gender, and to undergo surgery. If it is determined by psychological or medical professionals to be necessitated, that is, if it is determined that not undergoing this transition produces distress, maladaptation, and other forms of suffering, then it would seem to follow that the choice to transition is conceived as one that is embraced and condoned by medical professionals who have the person's ultimate well-being at issue. The "diagnosis" can operate in several ways, but one way it can and does operate, especially in the hands of those who are transphobic, is as an instrument of pathologization.

To be diagnosed with gender identity disorder (GID) is to be found, in some way, to be ill, sick, wrong, out of order, abnormal, and to suffer a certain stigmatization as a consequence of the diagnosis being given at all. As a result, some activist psychiatrists and trans people have argued that the diagnosis should be eliminated altogether, that transsexuality is not a disorder, and ought not to be conceived of as one, and that trans people ought to be understood as engaged in a practice of self-determination, an exercise of autonomy. Thus, on the one hand, the diagnosis continues to be valued because it facilitates an economically feasible way of transitioning. On the other hand, the diagnosis is adamantly opposed because it continues to pathologize as a mental disorder what ought to be understood instead as one among many human possibilities of determining one's gender for oneself.

One can see from the above sketch that there is a tension in this debate between those who are, for the purposes of the debate, trying to gain entitlement and financial assistance, and those who seek to ground the practice of transsexuality in a notion of autonomy. We might well hesitate at once and ask whether these two views are actually in opposition to one another. After all, one might argue, and people surely have, that the way that the diagnosis facilitates certain entitlements to insurance benefits,[1] to medical treatment, and to legal status, actually works in the service of what we might call transautonomy. After all, if I want to transition, I may well need the diagnosis to help me achieve my goal, and achieving my goal is precisely an exercise of my autonomy. Indeed, we can argue that no one achieves autonomy without the assistance or support of a community, especially if one is making a brave and difficult choice such as transitioning. But then we have to ask whether the diagnosis is unambiguously part of the "support" that individuals need in order to exercise self-determination with respect to gender. After all, the diagnosis makes many assumptions that undercut transautonomy. It subscribes to forms of psychological assessment which assume that the diagnosed person is affected by forces he or she does not understand. It assumes that there is delusion or dysphoria in such people. It assumes that certain gender norms have not been properly embodied, and that an error and a failure have taken place. It makes assumptions about fathers and mothers, and what normal family life is, and should have been. It assumes the language of correction, adaptation, and normalization. It seeks to uphold the gender norms of the world as it is currently constituted and tends to pathologize any effort to produce gender in ways that fail to conform to existing norms (or, fails to conform to a certain dominant fantasy of what existing norms actually are). It is a diagnosis that has been given to people against their will, and it is a diagnosis that has effectively broken the will of many people, especially queer and trans youth.

So, it would seem that the debate is a very complex one, and that, in a way, those who want to keep the

---

1. See Richard Friedman, "Gender Identity." This viewpoint, however, maintains that the diagnosis describes a pathology; so in his view the diagnosis should not be kept only for instrumental reasons.

diagnosis want to do so because it helps them achieve their aims and, in that sense, realize their autonomy. And those who want to do away with the diagnosis want to do so because it might make for a world in which they might be regarded and treated in non-pathological ways, therefore enhancing their autonomy in important ways. I think we see here the concrete limits to any notion of autonomy that establishes the individual as alone, free of social conditions, without dependency on social instruments of various kinds. Autonomy is a socially conditioned way of living in the world. Those instruments, such as the diagnosis, can be enabling, but they can also be restrictive and often they can function as both at the same time.

On the face of it, it would seem that there are two different approaches to autonomy, but it is important to note that this is not only a philosophical problem to be answered in the abstract. To understand the difference between these views, we have to ask how the diagnosis is actually lived. What does it mean to live with it?[2] Does it help some people to live, to achieve a life that feels worth living? Does it hinder some people from living, make them feel stigmatized, and, in some cases, contribute to a suicidal conclusion? On the one hand, we ought not to underestimate the benefits that the diagnosis has brought, especially to trans people of limited economic means who, without the assistance of medical insurance, could not have achieved their goals. On the other hand, we ought not to underestimate the pathologizing force of the diagnosis, especially on young people who may not have the critical resources to resist this force. In these cases, the diagnosis can be debilitating, if not murderous. And sometimes it murders the soul, and sometimes it becomes a contributing factor in suicide. So, the stakes of this debate are high since it would seem, in the end, to be a matter of life and death, and for some the diagnosis seems to mean life, and for others, the diagnosis seems to mean death. For others too, it may well seem to be an ambivalent blessing or, indeed, an ambivalent curse.

In order to understand how these two understandable positions have emerged, let's consider first what the diagnosis consists of in the United States and, second, its history and present usages. A diagnosis of gender disorder has to conform to the sway of the *DSM-IV*'s definition of gender dysphoria.[3]

For more information, see http://trans-health.com, Issue 4, Volume 1, spring 2002; see the same journal on-line, Issue 1, Volume 1, summer 2001 for an important critique titled "The Medicalization of

2. See Robert Pela, "Boys in the Dollhouse, Girls with Toy Trucks," 55. He argues that "the American Psychiatric Association has invented mental health categories—specifically, gender identity disorder—that are meant to pathologize homosexuality and to continue the abuse of gay youth." He also cites Shannon Minter to the effect that "GID is just another way to express homophobia." See also, Katherine Rachlin, "Transgender Individuals' Experiences of Psychotherapy." She notes that "individuals may resent having to spend time and money for psychological services in order to obtain medical services. They may also have fears concerning speaking to someone who holds the power to grant or deny them access to the interventions they feel they need. This fear and resentment creates a dynamic between therapist and client which may have an impact on the process and outcome of treatment." See also A. Vitale, "The Therapist Versus the Client."

3. It is important to note that transsexualism was first diagnosed in 1980 in *DSMIII*. In *DSM-IV*, published in 1994, transsexualism does not appear but is treated instead under the rubric of gender identity disorder (GID). The diagnosis as it currently stands requires that applicants for transsexual surgery and treatment show "evidence of a strong and persistent cross-gender identification, which is the desire to be, or the insistence that one is the other sex." Moreover, "this cross-identification must not be merely the desire for any perceived cultural advantages of being the other sex," but "there must also be evidence of persistent discomfort about one's assigned sex or a sense of inappropriateness in the gender role of that sex." The diagnosis "is not made if the individual has a concurrent physical intersex condition," and "to make the diagnosis, there must be evidence of clinically significant distress or impairment in social, occupational, or other important areas of functioning."

Transgenderism," a five-part work by Whitney Barnes (published in successive issues), which very thoroughly and trenchantly covers a range of pertinent issues related to the diagnostic category. The last revision to that set of definitions was instituted in 1994. For a diagnosis to be complete, however, psychological tests are needed along with "letters" from therapists providing a diagnosis and vouching that the individual in question can live and thrive in the new sexed identity. The 1994 definition is the result of several revisions, and probably needs to be understood as well in light of the American Psychiatric Association's (APA) decision in 1973 to get rid of the diagnosis of homosexuality as a disorder and its 1987 decision to delete "ego dystonic homosexuality," a remaining vestige from the earlier definition. Some have argued that the GID diagnosis took over some of the work that the earlier homosexuality diagnosis performed, and that GID became an indirect way of diagnosing homosexuality as a gender identity problem. In this way, the GID continued the APA's tradition of homophobia, but in a less explicit way. In fact, conservative groups that seek to "correct" homosexuality, such as the National Association of Research and Therapy of Homosexuality, argue that if you can identify GID in a child, there's a 75 percent chance that you can predict homosexuality in that person as an adult, a result which, for them, is a clear abnormality and tragedy. Thus, the diagnosis of GID is in most cases a diagnosis of homosexuality, and the disorder attached to the diagnosis implies that homosexuality remains a disorder as well.

The very way that groups such as these conceptualize the relationship between GID and homosexuality is very problematic. If we are to understand GID as based on the perception of enduring gendered traits of the opposite sex, that is, boys with "feminine" attributes, and girls with "masculine" attributes, then the assumption remains that boy traits will lead to a desire for women, and girl traits will lead to a desire for men. In both of these cases, heterosexual desire is presumed, where presumably opposites attract. But this is to argue, effectively, that homosexuality is to be understood as gender inversion, and that the "sexual" part remains heterosexual, although inverted. It is apparently rare, according to this conceptualization, that boy traits in a boy lead to desire for other boys, and that girl traits in a girl lead to desire for other girls. So the 75 percent of those diagnosed with GID are considered homosexual only if we understand homosexuality under the model of gender inversion, and sexuality under the model of heterosexual desire. Boys are still always desiring girls, and girls are still always desiring boys. If 25 percent of those diagnosed with GID do not become homosexual, that would seem to mean that they do not conform to the gender inversion model. But because the gender inversion model can only understand sexuality as heterosexuality, it would seem that the remaining 25 percent would be homosexual, that is, nonconforming to the model of homosexuality as inverted heterosexuality. Thus, we could argue, somewhat facetiously, that 100 percent of those diagnosed with GID turn out to be homosexual!

Although the joke is irresistible to me only because it would so alarm the National Association of Research and Therapy of Homosexuality, it is important to consider, more seriously, how the map of sexuality and gender is radically misdescribed by those who think within these terms. Indeed, the correlations between gender identity and sexual orientation are murky at best: we cannot predict on the basis of what gender a person is what kind of gender identity the person will have, and what direction(s) of desire he or she will ultimately entertain and pursue. Although John Money and other so-called transpositionalists think that sexual orientation tends to follow from gender identity, it would be a huge mistake to assume that gender identity causes sexual orientation or that sexuality references in some necessary way a prior gender identity. As I'll try to show, even if one could accept as unproblematic what "feminine" traits are, and what "masculine" traits are, it would not follow that the "feminine" is attracted to the masculine, and the "masculine" to the feminine. That would only follow if we used an exclusively heterosexual matrix to understand desire. And actually, that matrix would misrepresent some of the queer crossings in heterosexuality, when for instance a feminized heterosexual man wants a feminized woman, in order that the two might well be "girls together." Or when masculine heterosexual women want their boys to be both girls and boys for them. The same queer crossings happen in lesbian and gay life, when butch on butch produces a specifically lesbian mode of male homosexuality. Moreover, bisexuality, as I've said before, can't be reducible to two heterosexual desires, understood as a feminine side wanting a masculine object, or a masculine side wanting a feminine one. Those crossings are as complex as anything that happens within heterosexuality or homosexuality. These kinds of crossings occur more often than is generally noted, and it makes a mockery of the transpositionalist claim that gender identity is a predictor of sexual orientation. Indeed, sometimes it is the very disjunction between gender identity and sexual orientation—the disorientation of the transpositionalist model itself—that constitutes for some people what is most erotic and exciting.

The way that the disorder has been taken up by researchers with homophobic aims presupposes the tacit thesis that homosexuality is the damage that will follow from such a sex change, but it is most important to argue that it is not a disorder and that there is a whole range of complex relations to cross-gendered life, some of them may involve dressing in another gender, some of them may involve living in another gender, some of them may involve hormones, and surgery, and most of them involve one or more of the above. Sometimes this implies a change in so-called object choice, but sometimes not. One can become a transman and want boys (and become a male homosexual), or one can become a transman and want girls (and become a heterosexual), or one can become a transman and undergo a set of shifts in sexual orientation that constitute a very specific life history and narrative. That narrative is not capturable by a category, or it may only be capturable by a category for a time. Life histories are histories of becoming, and categories can sometimes act to freeze that process of becoming. Shifts in sexual persuasion can be in response to particular partners, so that lives, trans or no, don't always emerge as coherently heterosexual or homosexual, and the very meaning and lived experience of bisexuality can also shift through time, forming a particular history that reflects certain kinds of experiences rather than others.

The diagnosis of gender dysphoria requires that a life takes on a more or less definite shape over time; a gender can only be diagnosed if it meets the test of time.[4] You have to show that you have wanted for a long time to live life as the other gender; it also requires that you prove that you have a practical and livable plan to live life for a long time as the other gender. The diagnosis, in this way, wants to establish that gender is a relatively permanent phenomenon. It won't do, for instance, to walk into a clinic and say that it was only after you read a book by Kate Bornstein that you realized what you wanted to do, but that it wasn't really conscious for you until that time. It can't be that cultural life changed, that words were written and exchanged, that you went to events and to clubs, and saw that certain ways of living were really possible and desirable, and that something about your own possibilities became clear to you in ways that they had not been before. You would be ill-advised to say that you believe that the norms that govern what is a recognizable and livable life are changeable, and that within your lifetime, new cultural efforts were made to broaden those norms, so that people like yourself might well live within supportive communities as a transsexual, and that it was

4. For a discussion on changes of nomenclature within the history of the diagnosis to differentiate those who are considered to be "gender dysphoric" from the start from those who arrive at this conclusion in time, see "The Development of a Nomenclature," in the Harry Benjamin International Gender Dysphoria Association's *The Standards of Care for Gender Identity Disorders*.

precisely this shift in the public norms, and the presence of a supportive community, that allowed you to feel that transitioning had become possible and desirable. In this sense, you cannot explicitly subscribe to a view that changes in gendered experience follow upon changes in social norms, since that would not suffice to satisfy the Harry Benjamin standard rules for the care of gender identity disorder. Indeed, those rules presume, as does the GID diagnosis, that we all more or less "know" already what the norms for gender—"masculine" and "feminine"—are and that all we really need to do is figure out whether they are being embodied in this instance or some other. But what if those terms no longer do the descriptive work that we need them to do? What if they only operate in unwieldy ways to describe the experience of gender that someone has? And if the norms for care and the measures for the diagnosis assume that we are permanently constituted in one way or another, what happens to gender as a mode of becoming? Are we stopped in time, made more regular and coherent than we necessarily want to be, when we submit to the norms in order to achieve the entitlements one needs, and the status one desires?

Although there are strong criticisms to be made of the diagnosis—and I will detail some of them below when I turn to the text itself—it would be wrong to call for its eradication without first putting into place a set of structures through which transitioning can be paid for and legal status attained. In other words, if the diagnosis is now the instrument through which benefits and status can be achieved, it cannot be simply disposed of without finding other, durable ways to achieve those same results.

One obvious response to this dilemma is to argue that one should approach the diagnosis *strategically*. One could then reject the truth claims that the diagnosis makes, that is, reject the description it offers of transsexuality but nevertheless make use of the diagnosis as a pure instrument, a vehicle for achieving one's goals. One would, then, ironically or facetiously or half-heartedly submit to the diagnosis, even as one inwardly maintains that there is nothing "pathological" about the desire to transition or the resolve to realize that desire. But here we have to ask whether submitting to the diagnosis does not involve, more or less consciously, a certain subjection to the diagnosis such that one does end up internalizing some aspect of the diagnosis, conceiving of oneself as mentally ill or "failing" in normality, or both, even as one seeks to take a purely instrumental attitude toward these terms.

The more important point in support of this last argument has to do with children and young adults, since when we ask who it is who would be able to sustain a purely instrumental relation to the diagnosis, it tends to be shrewd and savvy adults, ones who have other discourses available for understanding who they are and want to be. But are children and teens always capable of effecting the distance necessary to sustain a purely instrumental approach to being subjected to a diagnosis?

Dr. Richard Isay gives as the primary reason to get rid of the diagnosis altogether its effect on children. The diagnosis itself, he writes, "may cause emotional damage by injuring the self-esteem of a child who has no mental disorder."[5] Isay accepts the claim that many young gay boys prefer so-called feminine behavior as children, playing with their mother's clothes, refusing rough and tumble activities, but he argues that the problem here is not with the traits but with "parental admonitions ... aimed at modifying this behavior [which] deleteriously affect[s] these boys' self-regard." His solution is for parents to learn to be supportive of what he calls "gender atypical traits." Isay's contribution is important in many respects, but one clear contribution it makes is that it calls for a reconceptualization of the phenomenon that refuses pathologizing language: he

5. Richard Isay, "Remove Gender Identity Disorder from *DSM*."

refuses to elevate typical gender attributes to a standard of psychological normality or to relegate atypical traits to abnormality. Instead, he substitutes the language of typicality for normality altogether. Physicians who argue against Isay not only insist that the disorder *is* a disorder, and that the presentation of persistently atypical gender traits in children is a "psychopathology,"[6] but they couple this insistence on pathologization with a paternalistic concern for the afflicted, citing how the diagnosis is necessary for insurance benefits and other entitlements. Indeed, they exploit the clear and indisputable need that poor, working class, and middle class trans-aspirants have for medical insurance and legal support to argue not only in favor of keeping the diagnosis on the books but in favor of their view that this is a pathology that must be corrected. So even if the diagnosis is approached as an instrument or vehicle for accomplishing the end goal of transitioning, the diagnosis can still (a) instill a sense of mental disorder on those whom it diagnoses, (b) entrench the power of the diagnosis to conceptualize transsexuality as a pathology, and (c) be used as a rationale by those who are in well-funded research institutes whose aim is to keep transsexuality within the sphere of mental pathology.

Some other solutions have been proposed that seek to ameliorate the pathological effects of the diagnosis by taking it out of the hands of the mental health profession altogether. Jacob Hale argues that this matter should not be mediated by psychologists and psychiatrists; the question of whether and how to gain access to medical and technological resources should be a matter between client and medical doctor exclusively.[7] His view is that one goes to the doctor for other kinds of reconstructive surgeries or on other occasions where taking hormones may prove felicitous, and no one asks you a host of questions about your earliest fantasies or childhood practices of play. The certification of stable mental health is not required for breast reduction or menopausal ingestion of estrogen. The required intervention of a mental health professional on the occasion in which one wants to transition inserts a paternalistic structure into the process and undermines the very autonomy that is the basis for the claim of entitlement to begin with. A therapist is asked to worry about whether you will be able, psychologically, to integrate into an established social world characterized by large-scale conformity to accepted gender norms, but the therapist is not asked to say whether you are brave enough or have enough community support to live a transgendered life when the threat of violence and discrimination against you will be heightened. The therapist is not asked whether your way of living gender will help to produce a world of fewer constrictions on gender, or whether you are up to that important task. The therapist is asked to predict whether your choice will lead to postoperative regret, and here your desire is examined for its persistence and tenacity, but little attention is given to what happens to one's persistent and tenacious desires when the social world, and the diagnosis itself, demeans them as psychic disorders.[8]

6. See, for example, Friedman, "Gender Identity."

7. Jacob Hale, "Medical Ethics and Transsexuality." See also Richard Green: "Should sex change be available on demand?" That was hardly the issue in 1969, as the nearly insurmountable hurdle then was professionally endorsed reassignment. If gender patients can procure surgeons who do not require psychiatric or psychological referral, research should address outcome for those who are professionally referred versus the self-referred. Then an ethical issue could be, if success is less (or failure greater) among the self-referred, should otherwise competent adults have that autonomy of self-determination? Later he asks, "should there be a limit to a person's autonomy over body?" ("Transsexualism and Sex Reassignment, 1966–1999"). Green also applauds the fact that some transgendered individuals have now entered into the profession, so that they are the ones making the diagnosis and also electing the medical benefits.

8. For a discussion of the etiology of the diagnosis that covers recent psychological findings about postoperative regret

I began this essay by suggesting that the view one takes on keeping or opposing the diagnosis depends in part on how one conceives the conditions for autonomy. In the arguments of Isay, we see an argument that claims that the diagnosis not only undermines the autonomy of children but mistakes their autonomy for pathology. In the argument that Hale offers, we see that the diagnosis itself takes on a different meaning if it is no longer used by mental health professionals. The question remains, though, whether medical practitioners with no particular background in mental health will nevertheless use mental health criteria to make decisions that could be no less favorable than those made by mental health practitioners. If Hale is arguing, though, that it ought to be shifted to medical doctors as part of a drive to redefine the diagnosis so that it no longer contains mental health criteria in it, then he is also proposing a new diagnosis or no diagnosis, since the *DSM-IV* rendition cannot be voided of its mental health criteria. To answer the question of whether the shift to medical doctors would be propitious, we would have to ask whether the inclinations of medical practitioners are generally to be trusted with this responsibility, or whether the world of progressive therapists offers a better chance for humane and successful passage through the process of diagnosis. Although I do not have a sociologically grounded answer to this question, I consider that it has to be pursued before one can judge the appropriateness of Hale's recommendation. The great benefit of his view is that it treats the patient as a client who is exercising consumer autonomy within the medical domain. That autonomy is assumed, and it is also posited as the ultimate goal and meaning of the process of transitioning itself.

But this raises the question of how autonomy ought to be conceived in this debate, and whether revisions in the diagnosis itself might provide a way around the apparent stand-off between those who wish to have the diagnosis deleted and those who wish to keep it for the instrumental value it provides, especially for those in financial need. There are two different conceptions of autonomy at work in this debate. The view that opposes the diagnosis altogether tends to be individualist, if not libertarian, and the views that argue in favor of keeping the diagnosis tend to acknowledge that there are material conditions for the exercise of liberty. The view which worries that the diagnosis may well be internalized or damaging suggests that the psychological conditions for autonomy can be undermined, and have been undermined, and that youth are at higher risk for this compromised and damaged sense of self.

Autonomy, liberty, and freedom are all related terms, and they also imply certain kinds of legal protections and entitlements. After all, the U.S. Constitution guarantees the pursuit of liberty. It could be argued that restrictive conditions imposed upon transsexual and transgendered individuals to exercise a liberty proper to that identity and practice is discriminatory. Paradoxically, the insurance companies demean the notion of liberty when they distinguish, say, between mastectomies that are "medically necessitated" and those that constitute "elective surgery." The former are conceived as operations that no one readily chooses, that are imposed upon individuals by medical circumstance, usually cancer. But even that conceptualization misrepresents the kinds of choices that informed patients can make about how to approach cancer, when possible treatments include radiation, chemotherapy, Arimidex, lumpectomy, partial and full mastectomy. Women will make different choices about treatment depending on how they feel about their breasts and the prospects of further cancer, and the range of choices made is significantly broad. Some women will struggle to keep their breasts no matter

and sex reassignment surgery's "success rates," see P. T. Cohen-Kettenis and L. J. G. Gooren, "Transsexualism: A Review of Etiology, Diagnosis, and Treatment."

what, and others let them go without much difficulty. Some will choose reconstruction and make some choices about prospective breasts, and others choose not to.

A rather butch lesbian in San Francisco recently had cancer in one breast, and decided, in consultation with her doctor, to have a full mastectomy. She thought it was a good idea to have the other breast removed as well, since she wanted to minimize the chances of a recurrence. This choice was made easier for her because she had no strong emotional attachment to her breasts: they did not form an important part of her gendered or sexual self-understanding. Whereas her insurance company agreed to pay for the first mastectomy, they worried that the second breast was "elective surgery" and that, if they paid for that, it would be setting a precedent for covering elective transsexual surgery. The insurance company thus wanted to limit both consumer autonomy in medical decision making (understanding the woman as someone who wanted for medical reasons to have the second breast removed), and to dismiss autonomy as the basis for a transsexual operation (understanding the woman as a possible transitioner). At the same time, a friend of mine recovering from a mastectomy sought to understand what possibilities existed for her for reconstructive surgery. She was referred by her doctor to transsexual clients who could introduce her to various technologies and the relative aesthetic merits of those options. Although I'm not aware of coalitions of breast-cancer survivors and transsexuals, I can see how a movement could easily emerge whose main demand would be to petition insurance companies to recognize the role of autonomy in producing and maintaining primary and secondary sex characteristics. All this seems less strange, I would suggest, when we understand cosmetic surgery on a continuum with all the other practices that humans engage in order to maintain and cultivate primary and secondary sex characteristics for cultural and social reasons. I gather that men who want penile augmentation or women who want breast augmentation and reduction are not sent to psychiatrists for certification. It is, of course, interesting to consider in light of current gender norms why a woman who wants breast reduction requires no psychological certification, but a man who wants penile reduction may well. There is no presumption of mental malfunctioning for women who take estrogen or men who take Viagra. This is, I presume, because they are operating within the norm to the extent that they are seeking to enhance the "natural," making readjustments within acceptable norms, and sometimes even confirming and strengthening traditional gender norms.

The butch, nearly trans, person who wanted both her cancerous and noncancerous breasts removed understood that the only way she could gain the benefits of a mastectomy was to get cancer in her other breast or to subject her own gender desires to medical and psychiatric review. Although she didn't consider herself trans, she understood that she could present as trans in order to qualify for the GID and insurance benefits. Sometimes reconstructive breast surgery is covered by medical insurance, even if done for elective reasons, but mastectomy is not included as elective surgeries covered by insurance. In the world of insurance, it appears to make sense that a woman might want less breast, but no sense that she would want no breast. Wanting no breast puts into question whether she still wants to be a woman. It is as if the butch's desire to have the breast removed is not quite plausible as a healthy option unless it is the sign of a gender disorder or some other medical urgency.

But why is it that we do accept these other choices as choices, regardless of what we take their social meaning to be? Society doesn't consider itself to have a right to stop a woman from enlarging or diminishing her breasts, and we don't consider penile enhancement to be a problem, unless it is being done by an illegitimate doctor who botches the results. No one gets sent to a psychiatrist for announcing a plan to cut or grow his or her hair or to go on a diet, unless one is at risk for anorexia. Yet these practices are part of the daily habits of cultivating secondary sex characteristics, if that category is taken to mean all the various bodily indicators of sex. If the bodily traits "indicate" sex, then sex is not quite the same as the means by which it is indicated. Sex is made understandable through the signs that indicate how it should be read or understood. These bodily indicators are the cultural means by which the sexed body is read. They are themselves bodily, and they operate as signs, so there is no easy way to distinguish between what is "materially" true, and what is "culturally" true about a sexed body. I don't mean to suggest that purely cultural signs produce a material body, but only that the body does not become sexually readable without those signs, and that those signs are irreducibly cultural and material at once.

So what are the versions of autonomy at work in these various approaches to the *DSM* diagnosis of Gender Identity Disorder? And how might we conceive of autonomy in such a way that we might find a way of thinking through the very reasonable disagreements that have emerged regarding whether to preserve or eradicate the diagnosis? Although it is obvious that not all individuals diagnosed with GID are or wish to become transsexual, they are nevertheless affected by the use of the diagnosis to further the aims of transsexuals, since to use the diagnosis is to strengthen its status as a useful instrument. This is no reason not to use it, but it does imply a certain risk, and certain implications. A strengthened diagnosis can have effects that its users do not intend or condone. And though it may well serve an individual's important needs to secure status and funding for a transition, it may well be used by the medical and psychiatric establishments to extend its pathologizing influence on populations of transsexuals, trans youth, and lesbian, bi-, and gay youth as well. From the point of view of the individual, the diagnosis can be regarded as an instrument by which to further one's self-expression and self-determination. Indeed, it can be counted among the very fundamental instruments one needs in order to make a transition that makes life livable, and that provides the grounds for one's flourishing as an embodied subject. On the other hand, the instrument takes on a life of its own, and it can work to make life harder for those who suffer by being pathologized, and who lose certain rights and liberties, including child custody, employment, and housing, by virtue of the stigma attached to the diagnosis or, more precisely, by virtue of the stigma that the diagnosis strengthens and furthers. Whereas it would no doubt be best to live in a world in which there was no such stigma, and no such diagnosis, we do no yet live in such a world. Moreover, the profound suspicion about the mental health of those who transgress gender norms structures the majority of psychological discourses and institutions, medical approaches to gender, and legal and financial institutions that regulate questions of status and possibilities for financial assistance and medical benefits.

There is an important argument to be made from the perspective of freedom, however. It is important to remember that the specific forms which freedom takes depend upon the social conditions and social institutions that govern human options at this time. Those who claim that transsexuality is, and should be, a matter of choice, an exercise of freedom, are surely right, and they are right as well to point out that the various obstacles posed by the psychological and psychiatric professions are paternalistic forms of power by which a basic human freedom is being suppressed. Underlying some of these positions is a libertarian approach to sex transformation. Richard Green, president of the Harry Benjamin International Gender Dysphoria Association, and a strong advocate for transsexual rights, including the rights of transsexual parents, argues on behalf of this issue as a matter of personal freedom and of privacy. He cites John Stuart Mill, writing that he "argued forcefully that adults should be able to do with their bodies as they wish providing that it did not bring harm to another. Therefore, if the third gender, the transsexual, or the would-be limb amputee can continue to shoulder social responsibilities post-surgery, then the surgical requests are not society's business."[9] Although Green makes this claim, one he himself calls "philosophical," he notes that it comes into conflict with the question of who will pay, and whether society has an obligation to pay for a procedure which is being defended as a matter of personal liberty.

I don't find many people writing in this area, except from within the discourse of the Christian Right, whose response to the GID is to embrace it wholeheartedly and say, "Don't take this diagnosis away from me! Pathologize me, please!" There are, surely, many psychiatrists and psychologists who insist upon gender identity disorder as a pathology. And there is a well-funded and impossibly prolific professor of neuropsychiatry and behavioral science at the University of South Carolina, George Rekers, who combines a polemical political conservatism with an effort to intensify and extend the use of this diagnosis.[10] His main concern seems to be about boys, boys becoming men, and men becoming strong fathers in the context of heterosexual marriage. He also traces the rise of GID to the breakdown of the family, the loss of strong father figures for boys, and the subsequent "disturbance" that it is said to cause. His manifest concern about the emergence of homosexuality in boys is clear from his discussion as well, citing as he does the 1994 *DSM* conclusion that 75 percent of GID youth turn out to be homosexual as adults. Rekers has published loads of studies strewn with "data" presented within the context of empirical research protocols. Although intensely polemical, he understands himself as a scientist and an empiricist, and he attributes ideological bias to his opponents. He writes that "in a generation confused by radical ideologies on male and female roles, we need solid research on men and women who are well-adjusted examples of a secure male identity and a secure female identity."[11] His "solid research" is intended to show the benefits of distinguishing clearly between gender norms and their pathologies "for family life and the larger culture." In this vein, Rekers also notes that "preliminary findings have been published in the literature which report on the positive therapeutic effects of religious conversion for curing transsexualism ... and on the positive therapeutic effect of a church ministry to repentant homosexuals."[12] He seems to be relatively unconcerned with girls, which impresses me as entirely symptomatic of his preoccupation with patriarchal authority, and his inability to see the threat that women of all kinds might pose to the presumptions he makes about male power. The fate of masculinity absorbs this study because masculinity, a fragile and fallible construct, needs the social support of marriage and stable family life in order to find its right path. Indeed, masculinity by itself tends to falter, in his view, and needs to be housed and propped up by various social supports, suggesting that masculinity is itself a function of these social organizations, and has no intrinsic meaning outside of them. In any case, there are people like Rekers who make an adamant and highly polemical case, not only for retaining the diagnosis, but for strengthening it, and they give highly conservative political reasons for strengthening the diagnosis so that the structures that support normalcy can be strengthened.

9. Richard Green, "Transsexualism and Sex Reassignment."
10. See, for example, George A. Rekers, "Gender Identity Disorder," in *The Journal of Family and Culture*, later revised for the *Journal of Human Sexuality*, a Christian Leadership Ministries publication in 1996, www.leaderu.com\jhs\rekers. He proposes conversion to Christianity as a "cure" for transsexuality and provides a psychological guide for those "afflicted" with and "repentant" of this condition in his *Handbook of Child and Adolescent Sexual Problems*.
11. Rekers, "Gender Identity Disorder."
12. Ibid.

Ironically, it is these very structures that support normalcy that compel the need for the diagnosis to begin with, including its benefits for those who need it in order to effect a transition.

It is with some irony, then, that those who suffer under the diagnosis also find that there is not much hope for doing without it. The fact is that under current conditions a number of people have reason to worry about the consequences of having their diagnosis taken away or failing to establish eligibility for the diagnosis. Perhaps the rich will be able to shell out the tens of thousands of dollars that an FTM transformation entails, including double mastectomy and a very good phalloplasty, but most people, especially poor and working-class transsexuals, will not be able to foot the bill. At least in the United States where socialized medicine is largely understood as a communist plot, it won't be an option to have the state or insurance companies pay for these procedures without first establishing that there are serious and enduring medical and psychiatric reasons for doing so. A conflict has to be established; there has to be enormous suffering; there has to be persistent ideation of oneself in the other gender; there has to be a trial period of cross-dressing throughout the day to see if adaptation can be predicted; and there have to be therapy sessions and letters attesting to the balanced state of the person's mind. In other words, one must be subjected to a regulatory apparatus, as Foucault would have called it, in order to get to the point where something like an exercise in freedom becomes possible. One has to submit to labels and names, to incursions, to invasions; one has to be gauged against measures of normalcy; and one has to pass the test. Sometimes what this means is that one needs to become very savvy about these standards, and know how to present oneself in such a way that one comes across as a plausible candidate. Sometimes therapists find themselves in a bind, being asked to supply a letter for someone they want to help but abhorring the very fact that they have to write this letter, in the language of diagnosis, in order to help produce the life that their client wants to have.

In a sense, the regulatory discourse surrounding the diagnosis takes on a life of its own: it may not actually describe the patient who uses the language to get what he or she wants; it may not reflect the beliefs of the therapist who nevertheless signs her name to the diagnosis and passes it along. Approaching the diagnosis strategically involves a series of individuals not quite believing what they say, signing on to language that does not represent what the reality is or should be. The price of using the diagnosis to get what one wants is that one cannot use language to say what one really thinks is true. One pays for one's freedom, as it were, by sacrificing one's claim to use language truthfully. In other words, one purchases one sort of freedom only by giving up another.

Perhaps this brings us closer to understanding the quandary of autonomy that the diagnosis introduces and the specific problem of how freedom is to be understood as conditioned and articulated through specific social means. The only way to secure the means by which to start this transformation is by learning how to present yourself in a discourse that is not yours, a discourse that effaces you in the act of representing you, a discourse that denies the language you might want to use to describe who you are, how you got here, and what you want from this life. Such a discourse denies all this at the same time that it holds out the promise, if not the blackmail, that you stand a chance of getting your life, the body and the gender you want, if you agree to falsify yourself, and in so doing support and ratify the power of this diagnosis over many more people in the future. If one comes out in favor of choice, and against diagnosis, it would seem that one has to deal with the enormous financial consequences of this decision for those who cannot pay for the resources at hand, and whose insurance, if there is insurance, will not honor this choice as one that is to be included as a covered elective treatment. And even when local laws are passed, offering insurance to city workers who seek such treatments, as is the case now in San Francisco, there are still diagnostic tests to pass, so choice is clearly bought at a price, sometimes at the price of truth itself.

The way things are set up, if we want to support the poor and the uninsured in this area, it would seem that we have to support efforts to extend insurance coverage and to work within the diagnostic categories accepted by the AMA and the APA, codified in the *DSM-IV*. The call to have matters of gender identity depathologized and for elective surgery and hormone treatment to be covered as a legitimate set of elective procedures seems bound to fail, only because most medical, insurance, and legal practitioners are only committed to supporting access to sex change technologies if we are talking about a disorder. Arguments to the effect that there is an overwhelming and legitimate human demand here are bound to prove inadequate. Examples of the kinds of justifications that ideally would make sense and should have a claim on insurance companies include: this transition will allow someone to realize certain human possibilities that will help this life to flourish, or this will allow someone to emerge from fear and shame and paralysis into a situation of enhanced self-esteem and the ability to form close ties with others, or that this transition will help to alleviate a source of enormous suffering, or give reality to a fundamental human desire to assume a bodily form that expresses a fundamental sense of selfhood. However, some gender identity clinics, like the one at the University of Minnesota run by Dr. Walter Bockting, do make such arguments and do provide supportive therapeutic contexts for people disposed to make a choice on this issue, whether it be to live as transgendered or transsexual, whether to be third sex, whether to consider the process as one of a becoming whose end is not in sight, and may never be.[13] But even that clinic has to supply materials to insurance companies that comply with *DSM-IV*.[14]

The exercise of freedom that is performed through a strategic approach to the diagnosis involves one in a measure of unfreedom, since the diagnosis itself demeans the self-determining capacities of those it diagnoses, but whose self-determination, paradoxically, it sometimes furthers. When the diagnosis can be used strategically, and when it undermines its own presumption that the individual diagnosed is afflicted with a condition over which no choice can be exercised, the use of the diagnosis can subvert the aims of the diagnosis. On the other hand, in order to pass the test, one must submit to the language of the diagnosis. Although the stated aim of the diagnosis is that it wants to know whether an individual can successfully conform to living according to the norms of another gender, it seems that the real test that the GID poses is whether one can conform to the language of the diagnosis. In other words, it may not be a matter of whether you can conform to the norms that govern life as another gender, but whether you can conform to the *psychological discourse* that stipulates what these norms are.

Let's take a look at that language. The GID section of the *DSM* starts by making clear that there are two parts of this diagnosis. The first is that "there must be strong and persistent cross-gender identification." This would be difficult to ascertain, I would think, since identifications do not always appear as such: they can remain aspects of hidden fantasy, or parts of dreams, or inchoate structures of behavior. But the *DSM* asks us

13. See Walter O. Bockting and Charles Cesaretti, "Spirituality, Transgender Identity, and Coming Out," and Walter O. Bockting, "From Construction to Context: Gender Through the Eyes of the Transgendered."

14. For an impressive account of how that clinic works to provide a supportive environment for its clients at the same time that it seeks to secure benefits through use of the diagnosis, see Walter O. Bockting, "The Assessment and Treatment of Gender Dysphoria." For another impressive account, see Richard Green, "Transsexualism and Sex Reassignment, 1966–1999."

to be a bit more positivist in our approach to identification, assuming that we can read from behavior what identifications are at work in any given person's psychic life. Cross-gender identification is defined as "the desire to be" the other sex, "or the insistence that one is." The "or" in this phrase is significant, since it implies that one might desire to be the other sex—we have to suspend for the moment what "the other sex" is and, by the way, in my mind, it is not quite clear—without necessarily insisting upon it. These are two separate criteria. They do not have to emerge in tandem. So if there is a way to determine that someone has this "desire to be" even though he or she does not insist upon it, that would seem to be satisfactory grounds for concluding that cross-gender identification is happening. And if there is "an insistence that one is" the other sex, then that would function as a separate criterion which, if fulfilled, would warrant the conclusion that cross-gender identification is happening. In the second instance, an act of speech is required in which someone insists that one *is* the other sex; this insistence is understood as a way of laying claim to the other sex in one's own speech and of attributing that other sex to oneself. So certain expressions of this "desire to be" and "insistence that I am" are precluded as viable evidence for the claim. "This must not merely be a desire for any perceived cultural advantages of being the other sex." Now, this is a moment for pause, since the diagnosis assumes that we can have an experience of sex without considering what the cultural advantages of being a given sex are. Is this, in fact, possible? If sex is experienced by us within a cultural matrix of meanings, if it comes to have its significance and meaning in reference to a wider social world, then can we separate the experience of "sex" from its social meanings, including the way in which power functions throughout those meanings? "Sex" is a term that applies to people across the board, so that it is difficult to refer to my "sex" as if it were radically singular. If it is, generally speaking, then, never only "my sex" or "your sex" that is at issue but a way in which the category of "sex" exceeds the personal appropriations of it, then it would seem to be impossible to perceive sex outside of this cultural matrix and to understand this cultural matrix outside of the possible advantages it may afford. Indeed, when we think about cultural advantages, whether we are doing something—anything—for the cultural advantage it affords, we have to ask whether what we do is advantageous for me, that is, whether it furthers or satisfies my desires and my aspirations.

There are crude analyses that suggest that FTM happens only because it is easier to be a man in society than a woman. But those analyses don't ask whether it is easier to be *trans* than to be in a perceived bio-gender, that is, a gender that seems to "follow" from natal sex. If social advantage were ruling all these decisions unilaterally, then the forces in favor of social conformity would probably win the day. On the other hand, there are arguments that could be made that it is more advantageous to be a woman if you want to wear fabulous red scarves and tight skirts on the street at night. In some places in the world, that is obviously true, although bio-women, those in drag, transgendered, and transwomen, all share certain risks on the street, especially if any of them are perceived as prostitutes. Similarly, one might say, it is generally more culturally advantageous to be a man if you want to be taken seriously in a philosophy seminar. But some men are at no advantage at all, if they cannot talk the talk; being a man is not a sufficient condition for being able to talk that talk. So I wonder whether it is possible to consider becoming one sex or the other without considering the cultural advantage it might afford, since the cultural advantage it might afford will be the advantage it affords to someone who has certain kinds of desires and who wants to be in a position to take advantage of certain cultural opportunities.

If the GID insists that the desire to be another sex or the insistence that one is the other sex has to be evaluated without reference to cultural advantage, it may be that the GID misundertands some of the cultural forces that go into making and sustaining certain desires of this sort. And then the GID would also have to respond to the epistemological question of whether sex can be perceived *at all* outside the cultural matrix of power relations in which relative advantage and disadvantage would be part and parcel of that matrix.

The diagnosis also requires that there be "persistent discomfort" about one's assigned sex or "inappropriateness," and here is where the discourse of "not getting it right" comes in. The assumption is that there is an appropriate sense that people can and do have, a sense that this gender is appropriate for me, to me. And that there is a comfort that I would have, could have, and that it could be had if it were the right norm. In an important sense, the diagnosis assumes that gender norms are relatively fixed, and that the problem is making sure that you find the right one, the one that will allow you to feel appropriate where you are, comfortable in the gender that you are. There must be evidence of "distress"—yes, certainly, distress. And if there is not "distress," then there should be "impairment." Here it makes sense to ask where all this comes from: the distress and the impairment, the not being able to function well at the workplace or in handling certain daily chores. The diagnosis presumes that one feels distress and discomfort and inappropriateness because one is in the wrong gender, and that conforming to a different gender norm, if viable for the person in question, will make one feel much better. But the diagnosis does not ask whether there is a problem with the gender norms that it takes as fixed and intransigent, whether these norms produce distress and discomfort, whether they impede one's ability to function, or whether they generate sources of suffering for some people or for many people. Nor do they ask what the conditions are in which they provide a sense of comfort, or belonging, or even become the site for the realization for certain human possibilities that let a person feel futurity, life, and well-being.

The diagnosis seeks to establish criteria by which a cross-gendered person might be identified, but the diagnosis, in articulating criteria, articulates a very rigid version of gender norms. It offers the following account of gender norms (the emphases are mine) in the language of simple description: "In boys, cross-gendered identification is manifested by a marked preoccupation with traditionally feminine activities. They may have a preference for dressing in girls' or women's clothes *or may improvise such items from available materials* when genuine materials are unavailable. Towels, aprons, and scarves are often used to represent long hair or skirts." The description seems to be based on a history of collected and summarized observations; someone has seen boys doing this, and reported it, and others have done the same, and those reports are collected, and generalizations are derived from the observable data. But who is observing, and through what grid of observation? This we do not know. And though we are told that in boys this identification is "marked" by a preoccupation with "traditionally feminine activities," we are not told what this mark consists of. But it seems important, since the "mark" will be what selects the observation as evidence for the thesis at hand.

In fact, what follows from this claim seems to undermine the claim itself, since what the boys are said to do is to engage in a series of substitutions and improvisations. We are told that they may have a preference for dressing in girls' or women's clothes, but we're not told whether the preference manifests itself in actually dressing in them. We are left with a vague notion of "preference" that could simply describe a supposed mental state, or internal disposition, or it may be inferred by practice. This last seems open to interpretation. We are told that one practice they do engage in is improvisation, taking items that are available and making them work as feminine clothing. Feminine clothing is called "genuine clothing," which leaves us to conclude that the materials with which these boys are improvising is less than genuine, other than genuine, if not ungenuine and "false." "Towels, aprons, scarves are often used to represent long hair or skirts." So there is a certain imaginary play, and a capacity to transfigure one item into another through a process of improvisation and substitution. In other words, there is an art practice at work here, one that would be difficult to name, simply, as the simple act of conforming to a norm. Something is being made, something is being made from something else, something is being tried out. And if it is an improvisation, it is not fully scripted in advance.

Although the description goes on to insist on the fascination of these boys with "stereotypical female-type dolls"—"Barbie" is mentioned by name—as well as "female fantasy figures," we are not really given an account of the place that dolls and fantasy have in the formulation of gender identification. For a given gender to be a site of fascination, or indeed, for a so-called stereotype to be a source of fascination, may well involve several kinds of relations to the stereotype. It may be that the stereotype is fascinating because it is overdetermined, that it has become the site for a number of conflicting desires. The *DSM* assumes that the doll you play with is the one you want to be, but maybe you want to be her friend, her rival, her lover. Maybe you want all this at once. Maybe you do some switching with her. Maybe playing with the doll, too, is a scene of improvisation that articulates a complex set of dispositions. Maybe something else is going on in this play besides a simple act of conforming to a norm. Perhaps the norm itself is being played, explored, even busted. We would need to take play as a more complex phenomenon than does the *DSM* if we were to begin to pose and pursue these kinds of questions.

The way you can tell that girls are having cross-gendered identification according to the *DSM-IV* is that they argue with their parents about wearing certain kinds of clothes. They prefer boys clothing and short hair, apparently, and they have mainly boy friends, express a desire to become a boy, but also, oddly, "they are often misidentified by strangers as boys." I am trying to think through how it could be that evidence of one's cross-gendered identification is confirmed by being identified as a boy by a stranger. It would seem that random social assignment functions as evidence, as if the stranger *knows* something about the psychological make-up of that girl, or as if the girl has solicited that interpellation from the stranger. The *DSM* goes on to say that the girl "may ask to be called by a boy's name." But even there, it seems, she is first addressed as a boy, and only after being addressed, wants to take on a name that will confirm the rightness of the address itself. Here again, the very language that the *DSM* provides seems to undercut its own arguments, since it wants to be able to claim cross-gendered identification as part of gender identity disorder, and so as a psychological problem that can be addressed through treatment. It imagines that each individual has a relation to its "assigned sex" and that this relation is either one of discomfort and distress or a sense of comfort and being at peace. But even this notion of "assigned sex"—sex "assigned" at birth—implies that sex is socially produced and relayed, and that it comes to us not merely as a private reflection that each of us makes about ourselves but as a critical interrogation that each of us makes of a social category that is assigned to us that exceeds us in its generality and power, but that also, consequentially, instances itself at the site of our bodies. It is interesting that the *DSM* seeks to establish gender as a set of more or less fixed and conventional norms, even as it keeps giving us evidence to the contrary, almost as if it is at cross purposes with its own aims. Just as the boys who were improvising and substituting were doing something other than conforming to preestablished norms, so the girls seem to be understanding something about social assignment, about what might happen if someone starts to address them as a boy, and what that might make possible. I'm not sure that the girl who seizes upon this stray and felicitous interpellation is giving evidence to a preestablished "disorder" of any kind. Rather she is noting that the very means by which sex comes to be, through assignment, open up possibilities for reassignment that excite her sense of agency, play, and possibility. Just as the boys who are playing with scarves as if they were something else are already versing themselves in the world of props and improvisation, so the girls, seizing upon the possibility of being called by another name, are exploring the possibilities of naming themselves in the context of that social world. They are not simply giving evidence to internal states, but performing certain kinds of actions, and even engaging practices, practices that turn out to be essential to the making of gender itself.

The *DSM* offers a certain discourse of compassion, as many psychiatrists do, suggesting that life with such a disorder is a cause of distress and unhappiness. The *DSM* has its own antipoetry on this subject: "in young children, distress is manifested by the stated unhappiness about their assigned sex." And here it seems that the only unhappiness is one that is created by an internal desire, not by the fact that there is no social support for such children, that the adults to whom they express their unhappiness are diagnosing and pathologizing them, that the norm of gender frames the conversation in which the expression of unhappiness takes place. At the same time that the *DSM* understands itself as diagnosing a distress which then becomes a candidate for alleviation as a result of the diagnosis, it also understands that "social pressure" can lead to "extreme isolation for such a child." The *DSM* does not talk about suicide, even though we know that the cruelty of adolescent peer pressure on transgendered youth can lead to suicide. The *DSM* does not talk about risks of death, generally, or murder, something that happened only miles from my home in California in 2002 when transgendered Gwen Araujo arrived at a teen party in a dress, and her body was found dead from beating and strangulation in the Sierra foothills.

Apparently, the "distress" that comes from living in a world in which suicide and death by violence remain real issues is not part of the diagnosis of GID. Consider that the *DSM* remarks, after a brief discussion of the euphemistically called "peer teasing and rejection," that "children may refuse to attend school because of teasing or pressure to dress in attire stereotypical of their assigned sex." Here the language of the text seems to understand that there may be an impairment of ordinary functioning caused by the pressure of social norms. But then, in the next sentence, it domesticates the distress caused by social norms, by claiming that it is the person's own preoccupation with cross-gender wishes that often "interferes with ordinary activities" and ends up in situations of social isolation. In a way, the fact of social violence against transgendered youth is euphemized as teasing and pressure, and then the distress caused by that is recast as an internal problem, a sign of preoccupation, self-involvement, which seems to follow from the wishes themselves. Indeed, is the "isolation" noted here real, or are the communities of support eclipsed from the observation? And when there is isolation, is it, therefore, a sign of a pathology? Or is it, for some, the cost of expressing certain kinds of desires in public?

What is most worrisome, however, is how the diagnosis works as its own social pressure, causing distress, establishing wishes as pathological, intensifying the regulation and control of those who express them in institutional settings. Indeed, one has to ask whether the diagnosis of transgendered youth does not act precisely as peer pressure, as an elevated form of teasing, as a euphemized form of social violence. And if we conclude that it does act in such a way, standing for gender norms, seeking to produce adaptation to existing norms, then how do we return to the vexed issue of what the diagnosis also offers? If part of what the diagnosis offers is a form of social recognition, and if that is the form that social recognition takes, and if it is only through this kind of social recognition that third parties, including medical insurance, will be willing to pay for the medical and technological changes that are sometimes desired, is it really possible to do away with the diagnosis altogether? In a way, the dilemma with which we are faced in the end has to do with the terms by which social recognition is constrained. Since even if we are tempted by the civil libertarian position in which this is understood as a personal right, the fact is that personal rights are only protected and can only be exercised through social and political means. To assert a right is not the same as being empowered to exercise it, and in this case, the only recognizable right at hand is the "right to be treated for a disorder and to take advantage of medical and legal benefits that seek its rectification." One exercises this right only by submitting to a pathologizing discourse, and in submitting to the discourse, one also gains a certain power, a certain freedom.

It is possible to say, and necessary to say, that the diagnosis leads the way to the alleviation of suffering; and it is possible, and necessary, to say that the diagnosis intensifies the very suffering that requires alleviation. Under present and entrenched social conditions in which gender norms are still articulated in conventional ways, and departures from the norm regarded as suspect, autonomy remains a paradox.[15] Of course, it is possible to move to a country where the state will pay for sex reassignment surgery, to apply to a "transgender fund" that a broader community supplies to help those who cannot pay the high costs, or indeed to apply for a "grant" to individuals that cover "cosmetic surgery." The movement for trans people to become the therapists and diagnosticians has and will surely help matters. These are all ways around the bind, until the bind goes away. But if the bind is to go away for the long run, the norms that govern the way in which we understand the relation between gender identity and mental health would have to change radically, so that economic and legal institutions would recognize how essential becoming a gender is to one's very sense of personhood, one's sense of well-being, one's possibility to flourish as a bodily being. Not only does one need the social world to be a certain way in order to lay claim to what is one's own, but it turns out that what is one's own is always from the start dependent upon what is not one's own, the social conditions by which autonomy is, strangely, dispossessed and undone.

In this sense, we must be undone in order to do ourselves: we must be part of a larger social fabric of existence in order to create who we are. This is surely the paradox of autonomy, a paradox that is heightened when gender regulations work to paralyze gendered agency at various levels. Until those social conditions are radically changed, freedom will require unfreedom, and autonomy is implicated in subjection. If the social world—a sign of our constitutive heteronomy—must change for autonomy to become possible, then individual choice will prove to be dependent from the start on conditions that none of us author at will, and no individual will be able to choose outside the context of a radically altered social world. That alteration comes from an increment of acts, collective and diffuse, belonging to no single subject, and yet one effect of these alterations is to make acting like a subject possible.

Works Cited

American Psychiatric Association. *Diagnostic and Statistical Manual of Mental Disorders DSM-IV*. Rev. ed. Washington, D.C.: American Psychiatric Association, 2000.

Barnes, Whitney. "The Medicalization of Transgenderism." http://trans-health.com Serialized in five parts beginning issue 1, vol. 1 (Summer 2001).

Bockting, Walter O. "From Construction to Context: Gender through the Eyes of the Transgendered." *Siecus Report* (October/November 1999).

———. "The Assessment and Treatment of Gender Dysphoria." *Direction in Clinical and Counseling Psychology*, 7, lesson 11 (1997): 11.3–11.22.

Bockting, Walter O. and Charles Cesaretti. "Spirituality, Transgender Identity, and Coming Out." *Journal of Sex Education and Therapy* 26, no. 4 (2001): 291–300.

Cohen-Kettenis, P. T. and L. J. G. Gooren. "Transsexualism: A Review of Etiology, Diagnosis, and Treatment." *Journal of Psychosomatic Research* 46, no. 4 (April 1999). 315–33.

Friedman, Richard. "Gender Identity." *Psychiatric News*, January 1, 1998.

15. Richard Green in the lecture cited above suggests that the paradox is not between autonomy and subjection but is implied by the fact that transsexualism is self-diagnosed. He writes, "it is difficult to find another psychiatric or medical condition in which the patient makes the diagnosis and prescribes the treatment."

Green, Richard. "Transsexualism and Sex Reassignment, 1966–1999." Presidential Address to the Harry Benjamin International Gender Dysphoria Association. http://www.symposion.com/ijt/greenpresidential/green00.htm/

Hale, Jacob. "Medical Ethics and Transsexuality." Paper presented at the 2001 Harry Benjamin International Symposium on Gender Dysphoria.

Harry Benjamin International Gender Dysphoria Association. *The Standards of Care for Gender Identity Disorders*, 6th ed. Düsseldorf: Symposion Publishing, 2001.

Isay, Richard. "Remove Gender Identity Disorder from DSM." *Psychiatric News*. November 21, 1997.

Pela, Robert. "Boys in the Dollhouse, Girls with Toy Trucks." *The Advocate*. November 11, 1997.

Rachlin, Katherine. "Transgender Individuals' Experience of Psychotherapy." Paper presented at the American Psychological Association meeting in August 2001. http://www.symposion.com/ijt/ijtvo06no01_03.htm/

Rekers, George A. "Gender Identity Disorder." *The Journal of Family and Culture* 2, no. 3, 1986. Revised for the *Journal of Human Sexuality* 1, no. 1 (1996): 11–20.

– – –. *Handbook of Child and Adolescent Sexual Problems*. Lexington: Simon and Schuster, 1995.

Vitale, A. "The Therapist Versus the Client: How the Conflict Started and Some Thoughts on How to Resolve It." In *Transgender Care*, edited by G. Israel and E. Tarver. Philadelphia: Temple University Press, 1997.

Discussion Topics

1. Why is it problematic to establish a relationship between gender identity disorder and homosexuality?
2. Discuss the difference between the phrases "sexual orientation" and "sexual preference."
3. What are the major points advanced by G. Rekers in support for the diagnosis argument?
4. What are the characteristics of cross-gendered identification?

Conformity and Deviance

Advantages and Disadvantages

Rufael F. Narváez

Rafael F. Narváez, "Conformity and Deviance," *Reading the World: An Introduction to Sociological Critique and Analysis*, pp. 75-86, 127-137. Copyright © 2019 by Cognella, Inc. Reprinted with permission.

Editor's Introduction

This article titled "Conformity and Deviance: Advantages and Disadvantages" by Rafael Narváez focuses on deviance and sanctions. This current article was selected to be included in this text because it discusses deviance, its impacts, and social mechanisms to control it. After reading this article you will have a better understanding of several concepts related to deviance such as individualistic cultures, collectivistic cultures, sanctions, social norms, conformity, norms violation, and social isolation.

Human Beings Tend to Adapt to Social Circumstances

Even the most democratic societies constantly nudge people to conform to certain standards, ideas, values, fashion styles, and appropriate emotional styles (e.g., "boys don't cry"), often regardless of whether these habits are good or bad for us, or for our society, or for the future. In this [reading], we study why people tend to comply, in different ways and by different degrees, with the broader demands of culture. We will examine important studies pertaining to how and why our decisions and aspects of our lifestyles may become manufactured *by the broader array of social and cultural forces*, not only by the market. And, relatedly, we will also see why we say in sociology that, unlike any other animal species, human beings are, in fact, largely created by culture and history.

Let us begin by discussing some of the classic studies pertaining to the phenomena of conformity, studies that let us see why we generally tend to follow the will of a group. Solomon Asch (1951), one of the prominent social psychologists of the 20th century, was the person who pioneered research pertaining, precisely, to how and why people conform to the norms and expectations of groups. Let us outline one of his most illustrative experiments, which took place in the 1950s. Asch recruited 123 male study participants who were told that they were going to participate in an experiment about visual acuity. One by one, these subjects entered a room where they encountered five or seven males who also seemed to be participants in the experiment, although in reality, they were confederates working for Asch. The experimenter showed the participant and the confederates two large cards, A and B, and asked the group to compare the contents of these cards. Card A had three perpendicular and parallel lines, marked as lines 1, 2, and 3. And card B featured only one perpendicular line, which was the exact size one of the lines on card A. All A and B cards in a stack were designed so as to make it immediately and unambiguously obvious that the single line on the B cards matched in length *only with one* of the three lines on the A cards.

One by one, the confederates and the real study participants were shown pairs of A and B cards drawn from the stack, and they were asked to state which of the three lines on card A matched in length with the line on card B. For the first couple of trials, the confederates gave the obviously correct answer, but after the fourth trial, the confederates began to give obviously incorrect answers. Let us say that the single line on card B matched in length with line *two* on card A, and yet the confederates were all in agreement that the line on card B matched with line *three* on card A. At this point, something interesting began to happen. Save some exceptions, the actual participants also began to provide the obviously incorrect answers, following the cue of the confederates, even if the confederates were wrong. Some participants went along with the wrong assessments of the group simply because they didn't want to rock the boat; they didn't want to stand out. Asch called this "normative conformity to the group." But others, importantly, went along with the group *by first denying the visual evidence provided by their own eyes*. It was easier for them to think that their own eyes were conveying the wrong information, rather than thinking that *the group* was conveying the wrong information. Solomon Asch called this phenomenon "informational conformity." This means that participants became blind to obvious aspects of reality merely to go along with a group of strangers.

Asch's research suggests that human beings are, in general, strongly motivated by a will to conform. Human beings generally avoid transgressing the norms that govern their social surroundings. Although we are a predatory species (responsible, in fact, for the massive disappearance of other species), we also often act like members of a herd species and bow to the will of the group. Asch and many others have shown that individuals, in fact, often strive to dissolve themselves within the group, even if in doing so these individuals may be causing at least some harm to themselves (examples will be provided soon).

Cultures That Encourage Individualism

All societies and all social groups elicit a degree of conformity from most social actors (save young children or people with socialization deficits, such as sociopaths). Indeed, without a minimal degree of conformity, no society can exist, as we will also see next.

Yet the idea that individuals normally tend to adapt to external demands is difficult to accept for many people, particularly for members of cultures that outwardly encourage self-reliance, self-determination, and a sense of uniqueness in citizens. So, beyond the laboratory conditions that frame Asch's research, let us presently consider everyday examples pertaining to the phenomena of conformity and adaptation. Consider such occasions as weddings, funerals, parties, church functions, classrooms, your place of work, elevators—circumstances that demand a degree of conformity from all of us. It is clear that, in these environments, people generally tend to abide by the expectations of the group; for example, dress codes, codes of conduct, and rules of speech, as noted. As many researchers have shown, we dress, behave, speak, and even gesture in ways that are more or less appropriate for the particular occasion. We tend to carry ourselves so as to signal a degree of agreement with the norms governing the interaction. In an elevator, for instance, people typically try to avoid displays of emotion and speak with an "appropriate" tone of voice, with appropriate manners and gestures. At a funeral, we generally broadcast appropriate signals; at a job interview, as we saw when we discussed the work of Goffman, we tend to act and behave in a manner that befits the expectations of interviewers; when meeting acquaintances for the first time, we yet again tend to display the version of ourselves that facilitates and eases the encounter, etc.

To be sure, even members of groups who profess nonconformity—for instance, those who defy mainstream standards, values, or tastes—also tend to conform to the standards that govern their particular subcultures. Punks, hippies, gang members, the Amish, and many other communities contest mainstream social norms. But members of these groups very much adhere to a subset of expectations and codes that govern their own subcultures. In fact, these groups tend to abide by compulsory and minute codes of conduct that, in their minuteness and forcefulness, resemble those of institutions such as monasteries, corporations, or the military. This is similar to members of highly individualistic cultures—that is to say, cultures that encourage individuals to see themselves as unique, independent, self-reliant, and self-directed, cultures that value individual determination and perseverance. We also tend to conform to social requirements. The mainstream American culture, for example, is arguably the most individualistic in the world (Suh et al., 1998), and yet Americans also tend to conform and to adapt to the requirements of the social system. Bear in mind, first, that economic growth in the United States has historically hinged on consumption (among other factors), which means that, as suggested, the personal desires and motives of consumers have to reflect, at least minimally, the needs of the market itself and the ideas and values engineered by it.

But, second, and more importantly, Americans undergo, much as members of any other society, a process of *socialization* whereby the person, from birth on, learns the social and cultural codes, how to display them, and what to expect if he or she violates them. Which teaches him or her how to fit in, which allows him or her to partake from the social order and to become part of a larger and stronger (social) organism, a family, a church, a country, a nation, etc. Hence, like any member of any other society, Americans also undergo, and typically comply with, various mechanisms of *social control* and *behavior modification*: precisely, the social mechanisms that enforce collectively relevant beliefs, norms, and values, mechanisms that not only reward conformity but also punish those who overstep these social norms. If you go to a wedding wearing the normative, expected attire and display the normative behavior, you will be welcomed and thus rewarded. On the other hand, if you go wearing a T-shirt, for example, and thus infringe upon the codes, you will likely receive raised eyebrows, cold shoulders, be subjected to gossip, etc., which are, of course, punishments and, more generally, mechanisms of social control that keep people from going against the norm. (The law is a mechanism of social control organized and enforced by the government itself.)

Perhaps, as some researchers have argued, Americans, much as the members of other individualistic cultures, conform less if compared to members of collectivistic cultures—cultures that encourage individuals to see themselves *not* as unique but as active members of a larger social order, cultures that value group accomplishment over individualistic perseverance, cultures that underscore the notion that fate is, above all, a collective accomplishment. Nevertheless, the point to keep in mind is that all human beings, regardless of their culture, *must* conform to at least a minimum of social demands and must *accept* social norms and values. And our conformity, for this reason, legitimizes these norms and values, and helps society to sustain, enforce, and maintain a certain civic order, certain societal rules, a tradition. Conformity thus facilitates social interconnection, cohesiveness, stability, and continuity. And in this particular sense, conformity—and attendant mechanisms of behavior modification and social control—are not only helpful but also necessary for any society. In fact, no society can survive without them. But on the other hand, these same mechanisms also have the potential to harm and defeat individuals and groups, as we discuss next.

The Risks of Noncompliance

Again, just as some people conform more readily than others, others resist social injunctions and demands more readily and frequently than others. But anyone who resists is likely to face retaliation from society itself. At a minimal level, these involve raised eyebrows and cold shoulders, as noted, but retaliation may also involve degrees of ostracism that can be injurious, psychologically, physically, socially, economically, and legally.

Here is a telling example: In 2017, a Saudi woman named Manal al-Sharif was imprisoned and endlessly harassed by Saudi authorities *and* by fellow citizens merely because she dared to drive a car, which meant going against the social rules in that country. As she noted, "[T]he secret police took me from my home in Saudi Arabia in the middle of the night, while my 5-year-old son was sleeping. I might have disappeared without a trace—if it wasn't for one brave witness […] who took the risk of live-tweeting the details of the incident" (2018). Her son was bullied and bruised at school on account of the "unfeminine" behavior of his mother. Her brother was detained twice for giving her the keys to his car and was subsequently harassed to the point of having to quit his professional job and having to leave the country with his wife and children. Her father had to endure sermons from the local imam, who equated women who drive with prostitutes. (Another woman, Loujain al-Jatoul, who also campaigned for the right to drive, had to flee to the Emirates where she was reportedly kidnapped by Saudi agents, taken back to Saudi Arabia, imprisoned, "held in solitary confinement, beaten, waterboarded, given electric shocks, sexually harassed and threatened with rape and murder," as recounted by the *New York Times* [Kristof, 2019].) And yet, despite these risks, Manal al-Sharif insisted on defending her elemental right to drive a car. And, for this reason, concerned Saudi citizens further retaliated and used social media to demand, among other things, that she be flogged in public.

As this courageous woman said, *fighting against oppressive societal norms is often harder than fighting against openly oppressive and tyrannical laws* (paraphrasing).

This idea is important. Explicitly oppressive laws, precisely because they are explicit and thus visible, can be easily identified and therefore resisted. Oppressive social *norms*, on the other hand, pass themselves off as, precisely, *normal*. They are often seen as simple common sense. And hence they tend to be invisible—*as mere norms*: People generally do not see them as the arbitrary societal rules that they are but, again, as mere, commonsensical standards of normality. These kinds of rules of conduct seem commonsensical *not* because they, in fact, make sense, but because the people who see them as such grew up with them and were socialized to think of them as okay, as something expected. As Thomas Paine, the 18th-century English-

American revolutionary, argued, sometimes the will to follow "common sense" does not stem from the power of "commonsensical" ideas themselves, or from their intrinsic goodness, but simply from the fact that people tend to get used to inherited ideas, often unthinkingly and mechanically abiding by the imaginations and by the rules of the dead generations. The Saudi folks who demanded that their neighbor be flogged in public—because she wanted to drive a car—had a life-long mental training that simply marked their hearts and minds with the preposterous notion that it is not normal, and that it is indeed immoral, for women to drive a car.

Note as well that, for this reason, social norms may also pass themselves off as morally correct—even when they are morally repellent. So when citizens such as Manal al-Sharif defend a basic and simple right, and thus go against these preposterous manifestations of "common sense" and "morality," their actions are naturally resisted. And these actions are resisted not by dictatorial institutions that uphold dictatorial laws but also by citizens who see themselves as reasonable and virtuous—citizens who see the actions of these "traitors," as Manal al-Sharif was often labeled, as threats to reason and virtue themselves. The larger idea is that, throughout history, oppression and evil have often stemmed from collectively relevant (and warped) standards of normality, from malevolent nonsense that passes itself off as virtue and reason, and from people who mechanically conform to such standards.

The foregoing example is perhaps too obvious in any context outside Saudi Arabia. Less obviously and closer to home, let us consider persons who transgress the codes of gender that apply not only in Saudi Arabia but also in the United States. Persons who, for example, choose *not* to deploy the gestures, the sign language, the dress codes that American men and women are expected to deploy so that others can identify them as men and women "proper." These transgressors are also likely to endure more than just disapproving looks. Hate crimes against gay men and lesbians—indeed the murdering of members of these communities—tragically illustrate this idea. And, more generally, those who transgress the codes of gender may suffer a disproportionate burden of mental health problems, such as stress and depression, as data pertaining to the health status of gay men and women clearly show (Meyer, 2003).

To be sure, sometimes noncompliers become cultural heroes, as the example of Manal al-Sharif suggests, or as the civil rights movement or the feminist movement illustrate. But more often than not, people who transgress dominant norms, rather than becoming cultural heroes, tend to become handicapped: socially, they are often ostracized or scorned rather than celebrated; politically, they may become disenfranchised; economically, they may carry disproportionate burdens; psychologically, they may experience extra fear, anxiety, and depression. Transsexual men and women, for example, have a much harder time finding adequate employment, adequate housing, adequate education, and adequate health care, regardless of their skills and of their character. Even the noncompliers who eventually emerge as cultural heroes also tend to first pay the price of noncompliance. Some of the artists who opened entire new fields of aesthetic expression and experience—from the painter Vincent van Gogh to the poet Charles Baudelaire—also experienced the sort of little daily miseries that often punctuate the existence of *true* outsiders (who are not merely fashionable eccentrics). Many of such artistic pioneers in fact died forsaken, even despised. The case of Nelson Mandela, who spent 27 years in prison, also illustrates this idea in the most sobering manner. Or consider Nobel Laureate Malala Yousafzai, who, as noted, was shot in the head when she was 12 years old for the crime of wanting to attend school.

Compliance with Absurd or Belittling Social Norms

The everyday existence of noncompliers is likely to be burdened, *even if the social codes that noncompliers violate are arbitrary and absurd, and even if these codes aim to dehumanize them or other citizens in general.* The example of Manal al-Sharif suggests that most Saudi women, save daring exceptions, had internalized the bizarre notion that driving was somehow unfeminine, immoral, and embarrassing, and they were thus ready to comply with it. This idea, the idea that people often comply with absurd or dehumanizing norms or with norms that damage their own existence, counterintuitive as it might be, warrants a full theoretical explanation, which I will provide subsequently. But for now, let us consider a couple of additional examples closer to home and closer, perhaps, to your own immediate world.

Let us go back to the 1950s. American girls and women of this generation were socialized, in general and save exceptions, to believe that they would find fulfillment primarily, or even exclusively, in their God-given role as nurturers (Friedan, 2001). This particular belief system, which Betty Friedan, the leader of the second wave of feminism, termed the "feminine mystique," postulated that women's natures had been intended for nurturing. Men and women often thought that women could, therefore, fulfill their biological fate primarily in the domestic sphere, nurturing the family, the children, the garden, the pets, taking care of the meals, the cleaning, etc. Naturally, in principle, there is nothing wrong with these activities, which can enhance the life of a family. But what is indeed problematic is the idea that women, as the mainstream culture maintained, may not find fulfillment through other means, through any other life paths. This belief system postulated that women should exclude themselves from the public sphere and from any life path that would drive them away from their role as nurturers. Hence, from a young age, women were discouraged from pursuing careers, businesses, and occupations with higher levels of responsibility, as these were seen as not feminine and indeed as unfeminine. And, hence, women were discouraged from being financially, intellectually, and socially independent. Noncompliers (i.e., "nonfeminine" women who strove to attain education and positions of power) often faced daily petty retaliation from both men and women, from strangers and from kin. These outsiders brooked much ill-treatment precisely because they went against the *arbitrary, absurdly limiting and belittling* social codes that governed femininity.

More contemporarily, the work of Michael Kimmel, an American sociologist who has devoted most of his career to studying masculinity in the United States, can help us understand how gender codes might have, perhaps, marked the life of some of our friends and kin. If Friedan showed that gender norms had diminished the lives of women, Kimmel has similarly shown that gender codes are damaging the lives of millions of young American men today. Men who often find themselves, much as their grandmothers in the '50s, unable to go against the codes of their gender, *however absurd and belittling these codes of masculinity might be.* Let us consider initially an obvious example: "bro codes" about drinking. Kimmel (2008) describes the following scene pertaining to drinking rituals:

> Nick starts his night by ingesting some vile concoction invented solely for the enjoyment of the onlookers. Tonight the drink of choice is a 'Three Wise Men,' a shot composed of equal parts Jim Beam, Jack Daniels, and Johnnie Walker. Other variations include the more ethnically diverse (substitute Jose Cuervo for the Johnnie Walker), or the truly vomit-inducing (add a little half-and-half and just a splash of Tabasco). The next drink comes at him fast, a Mind Eraser, another classic of the power hour [the time that Nick and buddies reserve for fun]. It's like a Long Island Iced Tea except more potent, and it is drunk through a straw as

quickly as possible. Shot after shot after shot is taken, the guys become all the more loud and obnoxious, and the bar manager brings a trashcan over to Nick's side, just in case. [...] Not surprisingly, the trashcan comes in handy. Nick's body finally relents as closing time approaches. He spews out a stream of vomit and the other guys know it's time to go. Fun was had, memories were made, but most importantly ... he puked. His friends can rest easy: a job well done. (Kimmel, 2008, pp. 95–96)

For many of the Nicks who inhabit Guyland, getting sick in such a manner is clearly preferable to breaking the norms that govern their world. As Kimmel reports, doing fraternity pledges that involve, for example, cleaning vomit, walking around grabbing the penises of other pledges while being mocked and insulted, or, in fact, risking being killed in hazing rituals is also seen as preferable to breaking these norms. Every year, Kimmel notes, about 1,400 college students aged 18 to 24, almost four students per day, are in fact "killed as a result of drinking [and] nearly half a million suffer some sort of injury" (Kimmel, 2008, p. 106). Andrew Coffey was a student at Florida State University. He died after drinking an entire bottle of bourbon, simply because his peers asked him to do so to join their fraternity. Coffey could have said, "No, I don't want to drink an entire bottle of hard alcohol." But it was seemingly easier for him to drink it and to thus fatally poison himself. Or consider another case (not a fatal one this time): "Nicholas Mauricio arrived at Tallahassee's Memorial Hospital on April 9, the 20-year-old Florida State University student was going in and out of consciousness. Blood from a cracked tooth tricked out of his mouth. There was a lump the size of a golf ball on the back of his head. Doctors quickly discovered that his skull had been fractured and he was suffering from multiple brain bleeds," as reported by the *Washington Post* (Farzan, 2018). Mauricio, the *Post* notes, had been named Scumbag of the Week by the "brothers" he wanted to join, had accepted this nomination, and had also *accepted to be beaten by them*, which caused the massive brain injuries, which resulted in a sequel of problems, including impaired cognitive function, paranoia, and panic attacks. He could have said "no" as well. One would think that it would be very easy for anyone to say, "No, I don't want to be beaten." Yet it was seemingly preferable for him to be treated the way he was treated, in accordance to the given normative order, the symbolic universe within which folks can very well accept the job of Scumbag of the Week.

The tragic deaths mentioned in the foregoing are deaths by conformity. They help us see that sometimes it is good, when not literally vital, to go against certain social codes (in this case against "bro codes"). They also help us see that supine obedience to norms, codes, and traditions can be bad when not literally fatal.

Note also that, much as their grandmothers, the guys in the foregoing examples did not invent these norms—the rules that often guide their behavior. They merely inherited them without thinking too much, it would seem, about whether they made sense or whether, all things considered, they were good or bad for them. Had they closely considered these norms, they would have seen that they were not that great. Beyond the humiliation and harm described earlier, a pile of data shows that young American men, particularly the Nicks described by Kimmel, are failing in unprecedented ways in virtually every area of achievement that is important at their age. This includes succeeding in school, moving away from the parental house, becoming financially independent, and finishing school when they are supposed to. In comparison with women of their age, young American men are nearly twice as likely to live with their parents. In comparison to the previous generation, they are more likely to depend on parental money. The list is long. Chances are that you can look around and see for yourself. Philip Zimbardo, one of the most prominent contemporary social psychologists, has in fact described this scenario as the "demise of guys." Guys who are, in this sense, the victims of a form of oppression that they do not see as oppressive at all. And why do we call it "oppression"? From the Latin *premere,* the same origin of the words *press* and *depression, oppression* refers to the action of keeping something down—for example, keeping these guys from reaching their potential. The idea is not that Guyland is governed by a dictatorial bro regime and its oppressive laws, of course. But that it is largely governed by *norms* that are hindering, when not handicapping, these guys; norms that are sometimes literally killing them. And bear in mind that norms, as Manal al-Sharif noted, can be far more effectively oppressive than dictatorial laws. Norms can be far more effective than laws when it comes to preventing individuals or groups or generations from reaching their potential.

Of course, many young men are succeeding, and some of them come from Guyland. But many of those who are failing are the blind victims of a particular, and particularly damaging, narrative about masculinity. This is a story that no longer emphasizes, as it did for previous generations, the idea that "real men" are, above all, providers. And that, therefore, "real men" have to assume the responsibilities inherent to being providers—namely, having a steady job, being financially independent, and so on. Instead, the new narrative that governs Guyland emphasizes other widespread ideas and values, such as "real men drink real beer." Relatedly, this narrative also provides justification for young men to further extend their adolescence, as Kimmel has shown, so, save all the exceptions, the transition between childhood and adulthood is today no longer a transition. Instead, it is often a separate phase of development, which some psychologists have termed "kidulthood": a cross between being nominally an adult, while still clinging to a kid-like worldview. A worldview that, as noted, tends to reject responsibility and to embrace "fun" instead (and let us clarify: fun is, of course, good, by definition, but when it actually means *failing in areas of achievement that are developmentally appropriate, this* kind of "fun" is oppressive, when not fatal sometimes). If you look around, you will likely find guys who, for example, still cling to digital versions of toys, say, to combat games that, closely examined, are digital versions of old GI Joe. These digital games, which the industry designs for "kidults," the main target audience, fulfill similar child-like fantasies: karate chopping, killing bad guys, shooting enemies.

The current narrative about masculinity, in any case, combined with structural economic factors beyond their control, such as an economic shift toward service industries that cater to stereotypically feminine jobs, is making the lives of many young men more difficult than they have to be. This narrative is decreasing their focus; it is making them poorer and more dependent, not to mention less reflective and less introspective. And yet, as noted, many of these men see it as normal and even as desirable. Which is why this story about masculinity is binding them to behaviors that are negatively affecting their lives.

"The Life Others Expected of Me"

Sociologist Talcott Parsons has shown (1968) that social codes tend to be enforced not only by groups or organizations with the authority to enforce them but also, more generally, by social actors themselves. As suggested, if people grow up with certain social norms and see that certain behaviors are simply expected in certain social groups or situations, they will likely internalize the norms in question and will hence see and judge the world and others from that vantage point—the vantage point of the only normative order that they know. When this happens, such persons will also become the enforcers of these norms. And, indeed, they will likely tell themselves that they should abide by the norms in question. They may very well become their own censors or critics, often judging their own actions, behaviors, ideas, clothes, hair, body, choices in life, not by standards invented by them but by the ready-made standards given to them by society or by a certain group: a fraternity, a church, a group of peers, etc. Let's return to George Herbert Mead (1934). He helped us understand that we, in fact, often *see ourselves through the eyes of others* and that we, therefore, conduct ourselves according to their standards. There are legitimate reasons for, and advantages associated with, adhering to collectively relevant norms, to traditions, to the views of others, as we will discuss soon; however, as noted, there are also important risks. Beyond those risks previously discussed, let us consider the following story.

Bronnie Ware, an Australian nurse who spent several years attending terminally ill patients, has reported that the number one regret of those facing death is not having had the "courage to live a life true to myself" and living, instead, "the life others expected of me" (2012, p. 37). The risk of unreflectively complying with social norms, and thus *capitulating to the words and the gaze of others*, is living, like some of Ware's patients, guided only by inherited standards, by a given and unchosen list of ideas, and thus experiencing life as the absence of a life. Ware narrates the moving story of Grace, a woman in her 80s, tormented not only by a painful and humiliating terminal condition but also by the regret of having lived a life under the gaze of a tyrannical husband. "Why didn't I just do what I wanted? Why did I let him rule me?" These were Grace's final regrets. But she also reflected, in a sociological key, about the fact that this was not merely her own personal failure. Grace saw that this was the failure of many women of her generation. Her predicament was not simply an *individual* failure but, above all, a *societal* failure. Society itself had to be reformed and repaired. Important aspects of her troubled existence were done to her and to women of her generation. And yet, of course, she was also an accomplice in this process. Grace ruefully realized that such a life had been chosen for her, not by her, while also seeing that it had been her own individual choice.

Conformity, to be sure, does not mean that we merely succumb to external pressures against our will, or against our better judgment. It means that we often *choose* to abide by such social codes and thus come to live the lives we do—the sort of lives that may, perhaps, elicit regret when we see them in a retrospective fashion, or when we come to face our final hour. And, as also follows from the example of Saudi Arabia earlier, conformity means that people may become spokespersons for the social narrative—regardless, it is important to insist, of whether it makes sense or not. Grace picked up absurd and indeed belittling ideas *from other women* who were undergoing a similar predicament—women who had, nevertheless, became enlisted and deputized by these ideas, by the narrative that befell their generation.

"Imagine Saying This to Our Children"

The earlier examples illustrate the idea that men and women often fall prey to their own instincts, natural and useful as they sometimes are, to follow the will of a larger (social) organism (e.g., groups of peers), even when doing so does not make rational sense. This aspect of human nature is important for the life of a social species, but it also accounts for many of our troubles, much of our suffering, and many of our delusions and humiliations. And it is, therefore, important for democratic societies to understand and to intervene in this aspect of social life. Doris Lessing has argued the following:

> Imagine saying to our children: "in the last fifty or so years, the human race has become aware of a great deal of information about its mechanisms [information provided particularly by sociologists and social psychologists]; how it behaves, how it must behave under certain circumstances. If this is to be useful, you must learn to contemplate these [social] rules calmly, dispassionately, disinterestedly, without emotion. It is information that will set

people free from blind loyalties, obedience to slogans, rhetoric, leaders, group emotions." (1987, p. 61)

Although Lessing imagines a society where schoolchildren are encouraged to learn this sort of lesson, she also realizes that no government and no political party will actually design curricula to teach children "to become individuals able to resist group pressure" (1987, p. 62). Why? Because such institutions and organizations often depend on group members who follow group thinking. Thus, she suggests, it is up to us. It is up to parents, teachers, and friends. It is up to the civil society to nurse these ideas, to encourage *not* fashionable eccentricity or potentially dangerous deviance but an ongoing process of psychological decolonization.

Why Do People Go to Extremes Merely to Conform?

As noted, human beings are an exquisitely social species and therefore the feeling that we belong in a social environment, or to a clan, tribe, fraternity, church, etc., is very important for us. This is why we have, in various ways and degrees, a tendency to follow norms—a tendency that helps us become part of the groups that abide by the norms in question. Let us now add the perhaps strange idea that this sense of belonging, the feeling that we partake from a group and that we follow its norms, can be literally vital, as we will see in this second part of the chapter.

Let us start this discussion by going back to Emile Durkheim (2007), who showed that people are more likely to commit suicide when they fail to find, and conform to, social norms. He called these "anomic suicides." ("Anomic" means "normless": Anomic societies revolve around rules and norms that are either very weak or that have ceased to elicit compliance from citizens. These societies are thus poorly organized, poorly integrated, and rather anarchical.) Durkheim, that is to say, has shown that people who do not have enough norms to follow, or people who face social norms that have become irrelevant or unimportant, *are more likely to kill themselves*. He has shown that a minimum necessary of adherence to, and respect for, norms can be literally vital (an important issue that we will discuss subsequently).

On the other hand, he also shows that people who have to follow too many and too strict norms are also more likely to find their existence unbearable. Hence, Durkheim also speaks of "altruistic suicides," the opposite of anomic suicides. Altruistic suicides involve oppressive and ultimately crushing morals, crushing social rules and norms: Suicide bombers provide examples of "altruistic" suicides, not because their ideals are in fact altruistic but because terrorists often feel that their actions, murderous such as they are, are actually guided by higher moral principles—principles that, in their minds, are in fact so superlative and so morally correct as to justify the sacrifice of human lives, including the lives of those who abide by these supposed values.

But why would weak or inexistent norms lead to suicide? Why is it that not being able to follow norms can be psychologically damaging and even physically damaging? Let us further elucidate these questions by first considering death spells.

Death Spells

Imagine the following scenario: A member of a tribal community breaks a social taboo and is therefore judged and found guilty. To be sentenced and punished, the infractor will be brought before a sorcerer who will invoke the spirits, recite an incantation, perhaps point a dirty bone toward the accused person, and, having thus secured powers over life and death, will finally cast a death spell against this person. Now that the absurd ceremony is over,

> a consensus is reached among all concerned that the end [of the infractor] is near, and the victim's friends and family retreat as from the smell of death. They return, but only to wail and chant over the body of a person whom they consider already dead. Physically the victim still lives; psychologically he or she is dying; socially he or she is already dead (Wade, 1988, p. 206).

Death spells, primitive and scientifically inept as they are, are often effective, nonetheless. Researchers are not sure exactly what physiological mechanisms precipitate these demises, but there are strong indications that they are "psychogenic," anteceded by psychological disturbances, such as depression, as well as "sociogenic," having their origins in social factors. As I have suggested elsewhere, the victim of death spells must remain within the community, but he "is existentially removed from it; divested of his social roles, status, removed from normal contact with others" (Narváez, 2012). Socially, he or she is dead, which "often gives way to supralethal psychological disturbances [e.g., depression] that can antecede physical death" (Narváez, 2012). Researchers working on the absorbing, truly fascinating field of death spells have shown that the breakdown of the social ties that connect the individual to the world can be literally fatal for intensely social creatures like human beings. Hence, returning to Durkheim, the breakdown of social norms that sustain these social interactions and social ties may lead to the feeling of isolation, depression, and, thus, higher rates of suicide. For some individuals, the breakdown of social norms can work like a death spell.

Isolation Experienced as the Collapse of Reality

Relatedly, let us consider phenomena pertaining to physical isolation to further illustrate how vital it is for us to partake in a social environment and, for this reason, how eager we can be to comply with social requirements, which allows us to fit in and to partake from a group.

Years ago, a colleague and I took students to a penitentiary in West Texas. For my part, I was interested in showing these students the solitary confinement cell, in particular, so as to impress upon them precisely the importance that social interaction has for human beings. The cell was a small, padded, entirely white room with no furniture at all (even light switches were on the outside). This eerie box, which closely resembled the cells of psychiatric wards, had a hole in the middle, "the bathroom," the sheriff explained. The cell was padded to prevent inmates from injuring themselves. The sheriff also noted that sometimes, after removing the inmate, guards had to enter the room armed with high-pressure hoses, as some prisoners, presumably experiencing symptoms of psychosis, besmirched the walls and themselves with their own feces. (Modern solitary confinement cells, a criminal justice professor has told me, are already equipped with internal hosing mechanisms that serve this purpose.)

Some people withstand solitary confinement more stoically than others. But typically, "the experience is disorienting, unsettling, and no less acute than the hunger and the thirst that come from a prolonged fast" (Alter, 2013, p. 82). Psychiatrist Stuart Grassian (2006) has reported that inmates in solitary confinement often experience hallucinations, perceptual distortion, loss of "perceptual constancy" (e.g., some objects may be perceived as changing sizes, same noises may become softer and then louder); memory loss; impulsive self-mutilation; difficulty with thinking, which may lead to acute psychotic states; fearfulness; agitation; paranoia; and hypersensitivity to sensory stimuli (e.g., some inmates may scream in response to noises from water pipes). Grassian's research, as well as many other studies (e.g., Liederman, 1962), have helped us see that isolation often leads, in fact, to a specific kind of disease characterized by a breakdown of the person's sense of reality. Charles Dickens visited a Philadelphia prison and described the sight of a sailor in solitary confinement in the following way: "Why does he stare at his hands and pick the flesh open, upon the fingers, and raise his eyes for an instant [...] to those bare walls?" (in Grassian, 2006).

Beyond helping us understand the importance of social interaction, this kind of research has also allowed us to understand that the reality that human beings experience is largely socially constructed, the product precisely of social interaction, and that it cannot be a purely individual construction. We shower, get dressed in the morning, choose certain clothes to put on, etc., not *only* because these things make sense in our heads but also because they *make sense in the presence of others* within a social context. These activities make sense, above all, as social norms. So in isolation, a situation where social norms do not exist, these everyday behaviors will eventually cease to be fully meaningful or meaningful at all. Isolation progressively diminishes meaning; it can, in fact, erase the meaning that everyday life has for us; and this progressive absence of meaning can lead to psychological breakdown. In this particular sense, isolation can work like a death spell as well.

Other people thus help us confirm that some things "make sense" and others do not. The presence of others, the gaze of others, the viewpoints of others, largely sustain our meanings. Meaning is, in this sense, largely othered, collectively sustained (and collectively constructed, as we will soon see). The experience of reality is likewise othered, sustained by a social context. And, therefore, the absence of others is often experienced as the absence of reality, a strange predicament that closely resembles madness. It is not a coincidence that the experience of solitary confinement—"no-touch torture," as human rights activists have named it—is often characterized by the same symptoms that characterize psychosis.

José Mujica, former president of Uruguay, was imprisoned in his youth for political reasons and spent two years confined to the bottom of a well. Some of his comrades who were also imprisoned lost their reason to similar conditions of existence, and it appears that the goal of their jailers was, in fact, to fracture the prisoners' very sense of self, their grasp of reality. But Mujica managed to retain his sanity, in part by "befriending" a frog and some rats, that, in such circumstances, provided the illusion of a social link. Michel Siffre was a French explorer who volunteered to participate in a research study about solitary confinement, spending six months in a cave in Texas. By day 79, he descended into a severe bout of depression and considered suicide. Much as Mujica, however, Siffre also clung to a newfound "friend": a mouse that helped him regain his will to live. When he accidentally killed the mouse, he sunk again into depression, which became, as he later wrote, "overwhelming."

Such is the need for social contact among human beings. Some speculative theologians have defined Hell not as a place of eternal flames, but as a state of complete and eternal isolation, accompanied by deafening silence and total darkness—a state of "nonbeing."

Hospitalism

Let us discuss a final example that also bespeaks the vital importance that human contact has for us. During the Second World War, England was virtually devastated. Children were orphaned in disproportionate numbers, and nurses were overworked, attending to soldiers near battlefields as well as wounded civilians in the cities. Orphanages were, therefore, severely overcrowded and severely understaffed. But the English managed to secure the basic necessities for the survival of the children: food, warm rooms, clean diapers, safe cribs, medicine. Yet these infants and children eventually began to show noticeable deficits: Many of them were not developing normal cognitive abilities and indeed their physical growth was sometimes stunted. Some of them in fact died. How was this possible given that they had their necessities covered? Rene Spitz, a now famous English pediatrician, studied the problem and discovered a stunning and truly sobering fact about human development. These children failed to develop normally *not* because they lacked food, or warmth, or medicine but because they lacked human contact. The overworked nurses did not have time to hold them, to caress them, to return their gaze. The children's brains were not developing properly because of this tragic fact. Their brains needed social contact. Stunningly, their bones were not properly growing either—*not because they lacked milk and calcium but because the children lacked the company of other human beings*. Such symptoms were originally characterized under the label "hospitalism," a pediatric failure to thrive that has origins in *social*, not originally physiological, deficits.

To summarize, because we are social animals incapable of initially surviving and growing without the presence of others, we may easily feel that social groups and networks around us are like shelters of sorts. And for this reason, we can also easily sense that the norms that govern the lives of these networks are like keys to these shelters, links that allow us to partake from the lives of these groups. Bear in mind that noncompliance with these norms will automatically make us outsiders. And precisely because a social context is so important for us, societies, groups of peers, tribes, clans, fraternities, churches, monasteries, military institutions, etc., often elicit a genuine desire, an almost instinctive readiness to follow social norms that, in the end, can affect or indeed determine our biography, our life, and, as the example of Grace suggests, even how we die.

References

Alter, Adam. 2013. *Drunk tank pink: And Other Unexpected Forces That Shape How We Think, Feel, and Behave.* New York: Penguin Books.

Asch, Solomon. 1951. "Effects of Group Pressure upon the Modification and Distortion of Judgment" In *Groups, Leadership and Men*, edited by H. Guetzkow, 1951. Pittsburgh, PA: Carnegie Press.

Durkheim, Emile. 2007. *On Suicide.* Translated by Robin Buss. New York: Penguin.

Friedan, Betty. 2001. *The Feminine Mystique.* New York: W. W. Norton

Grassian, Stuart. 2006. "*Psychiatric Effects of Solitary Confinement*" Washington University Journal of Law & Policy (22): 325 http://digitalcommons.law.wustl.edu/wujlp/vol22/iss1/24.

Kimmel, Michael. 2008. *Guyland: The Perilous World Where Boys Become Men.* New York: Harper Collins

Lessing, Doris. 1987. *Prisons We Choose to Live Inside.* New York: Harper Collins

Liederman, Herbert. 1962. "Man Alone: Sensory Deprivation and Behavioral Change" *Correctional Psychiatry & Soc. Therapy (8): 64, 66.*

Mead, George Herbert. 1934. *Mind, Self, and Society.* Edited by Charles W. Morris. Chicago: University of Chicago Press.

Meyer, Ilan. 2003. "Prejudice, Social Stress and Mental Health in Lesbian, Gay, and Bisexual Populations." *Psychological Bulletin* 129: 674–97.

Narváez, Rafael. 2012. *Embodied Collective Memory: The Making and Unmaking of Human Nature.* Maryland: University Press of America.

Parsons, Talcott. 1968. *The Structure of Social Action.* New York: The Free Press

Suh, Eunkook, et al. 1998. "The Shifting Basis of Life Satisfaction Judgments Across Cultures: Emotions Versus Norms." *Journal of Personality and Social Psychology* 74 (2): 482–493.

Wade, Davis. 1988. *Passage of Darkness: The Ethnobiology of the Haitian Zombie.* Chapel Hill: The University of North Carolina Press.

Ware, Bronnie. 2012. *The Top Five Regrets of the Dying: A Life Transformed by the Dearly Departing.* Carlsbad, CA: Hay House.

Discussion Topics

1. Compare individualistic cultures to collectivistic cultures.
2. Discuss the advantages and weaknesses of individualistic cultures and collectivistic cultures.
3. Discuss the effectiveness of mechanisms of social control to discourage individuals from deviating. Use examples from the text to support your answer.
4. Discuss the relationship between suicide and social norms.

Crime, the Emotions and Social Psychology

Eamonn Carrabine, Pam Cox, Maggy Lee, Ken Plummer, and Nigel South

Eamonn Carrabine, et al., "Crime, the Emotions and Social Psychology," *Criminology: A Sociological Introduction*, pp. 217-235, 464-507. Copyright © 2009 by Taylor & Francis Group. Reprinted with permission.

Editor's Introduction

This article titled "Crime, the Emotions, and Social Psychology" by Carrabine, Cox, Lee, Plummer, and South explores the importance of social psychology in investigating the relationship between crime and emotions. This article was selected to be included in the text because it documents crime which is an important topic in social problems. Additionally, the influence of emotion on crime is not well documented in the extant literature. After reading this article, you will understand why emotions have been absent in the literature about crime, thrill-seeking-crime, self-esteem-shame-crime relations. Also, you have a working definition of some concepts such as fear of crime, hate crime, primary emotions, and secondary emotions.

Key Issues

- Why have the emotions been neglected in criminology?
- Is crime seductive?
- What is meant by 'fear of crime'?
- How does resentment structure 'hate' crime?
- What role does 'respect' play in violent encounters?
- Does 'shaming' restore the balance of justice between offenders, victims and the

community?

Introduction

It might seem obvious that human emotions play a significant part in the commission of crime, in punishment and in social control. Indeed, the relationship between emotion and crime has fuelled the creative imagination. To take an intense emotion—passion, for instance—*la crime passionel* has inspired great works of literature, theatre, art, symphonies and the opera. It is perhaps the tragedy of crimes of passion that has inspired the artistic imagination; they are offences committed by wretched but ordinary people, not otherwise inclined to transgress. Fuelled by one or more of a myriad of emotions—the wounds of betrayal, the hurt of infidelity, broken hearts, wounded pride, spoiled virtue, jealousy, envy, and many more—they are criminalized by their acts. Passion comes to overrule reason—usually with dire consequences for the offender and the victim.

In Shakespeare's tragic tale *Othello*, the enraged Othello 'the Moor' murders his wife, Desdemona, on account of her alleged adultery, and then kills himself in deep remorse when he realizes he has been deceived into believing in her infidelity. In Bizet's *Carmen*, the smitten soldier Don José kills his love, Carmen, after she has an affair with the handsome Escamillo. In 2002, the tragic story was recast as a 'Hiphopera' by MTV and New Line Television, starring the singer Beyonce Knowles. While in the world of popular music, crimes of passion have been acted out in numerous songs. 'Delilah', the hit by Tom Jones, is a classic example of betrayal with fatal consequences and more recently Nick Cave released an entire album of 'Murder Ballads'. In this [reading] we will examine how the emotions figure in criminology. We begin with describing how the emotions have been marginalized in much intellectual work, but have recently become a focal point across the humanities and social sciences.

Rediscovering the Emotions

Although crimes of passion have inspired great artistic works and enthralled audiences for centuries, the subject of emotion, it has recently been argued, has been only a peripheral interest within criminological inquiry and theory.Willem de Haan and Ian Loader, for instance, suggest that

> Many established and thriving modes of criminological reflection and research continue to proceed in ways that ignore entirely, or at best gesture towards, the impact of human emotions on their subject matter—if you doubt this, take a quick glance at almost any criminology textbook, whether of a conventional, radical or integrating bent.

(2002: 243)

FIGURE 8.1   Nick Cave's collection of murder ballads reveals the enduring popularity of blood, sex, melodrama and crime as themes in popular culture.

Murder Ballads by Nick Cave and The Bad Seeds front cover image reproduced courtesy of Nick Cave & Mute Records.

However, while the impact of human emotion on crime appears to be in the process of rediscovery in theoretical criminology, it has hardly been neglected in the past by research on crime and deviance. Many of these texts are among the foundational texts of social psychology, which can be defined as the systematic study of people's thoughts, feelings and conduct in social contexts. On this reckoning the emotions should not be reduced to psychological states, but as social and cultural practices that both come from within ourselves and from without—in larger structural processes that ritually shape how we feel and act.

Historically, indeed, a defining feature of Western thought is the way that emotion and reason have been regarded as opposing forces, with the emotional often seen as beneath the rational, as a sign of the lowly, primitive, natural and feminine. It has only been since the late 1970s that the sociology of emotions has become an established field within the discipline. Since then there appeared several major perspectives on the emotions and social life (Hochschild, 1983; Kemper, 1978; Scheff, 1979), as well as the repositioning of the emotions in classical and contemporary social theory (Barbalet, 1998; Williams, 2001; Shilling, 2002), while feminists have explained how the marginalization of emotion has worked to subordinate the feminine, the body and intimate desires (Spelman, 1989; Jaggar, 1989; Ahmed, 2004).Taken together these developments suggest that criminology has much to gain from engaging with this resurgence of interest in the emotions across the humanities and social sciences. Nor should this be a one-way conversation. Criminological work has a crucial place in revealing the importance of emotions in shaping our inner worlds as well as broader social and cultural practices.

Status, Stigma and Seduction

The contemporary interest in crime and the emotions can usefully be traced back to Albert Cohen's study (1955:

17) of delinquent boys, which sought to demonstrate how 'psychogenic and subcultural factors' combined to produce delinquency through the humiliating 'status frustrations' experienced by working-class boys and the alienating differences of class-based value systems. In a series of insightful pieces Erving Goffman described how all encounters are guided by certain cultural scripts that establish the ground rules for interaction. His work captures how perceptions of social worth regulate human conduct. Famously, he argued that mental patients 'suffer not from mental illness, but from contingencies' (Goffman, 1961: 135)—people who may or may not have been experiencing some degree of mental distress, but have had the misfortune to end up in an asylum and then had to adjust their self-identities in line with the 'heavy machinery of mental-hospital servicing'. In *Stigma*, Goffman (1963) examined how people managed 'spoiled identity', the pain and shame associated with being considered less than human. Crucially, he emphasized that we all move between normal and troubled worlds, and each of us falls short some of the time, such that embarrassment (and the anxious expectation of it) clouds every social interaction.

In important ways, Goffman exposed in *Stigma* the very inappropriateness of the term deviance to describe physical handicap, ethnic difference and numerous forms of social disaffiliation. Likewise, the sharp distinction drawn between deviant and conventional values in subcultural theory was also criticized by David Matza (1964) who pointed out that juveniles intermittently drift into and out of delinquency. His focus on motivational will manages to grasp something of the immediate, intoxicating and alluring spell that delinquency casts, which he would later describe as the 'invitational edge' that deviancy offers (Matza, 1969: 111). It is this dizzying edge that Jack Katz (1988) attempts to capture in his seminal *Seductions of Crime* through concentrating on the experiential foreground of crime across a diverse range of acts that include juvenile 'sneaky thrills', armed robbery and cold-blooded, 'senseless' murder.

Each specific crime offers distinctive ways of overcoming the mundane routines of everyday life through presenting unique emotional attractions that provide 'a dialectic process through which a person empowers the world to seduce him to criminality' (Katz, 1988: 7). While Katz's work has been influential (especially in cultural criminology) it has not escaped criticism on the grounds that it

- disregards the wider social context in which all action takes place (O'Malley and Mugford, 1994; Young, 2007a);
- fails to secure 'serious distance' (implying that offending stories are taken at face value); and
- lacks any 'systematic explanation' of the various 'motivational' accounts (I. Taylor, 1999: 224).

Yet, as Hayward (2002: 83) suggests, these objections ignore 'the failure of "background" structural theories of crime to address the fundamental question of why (under shared social conditions) one person rather than another commits crime'. It is by exploring the relationships between crime, emotion and social psychology that some of these answers are to be found.

Conceptualizing Emotions

Although there are ongoing debates over how to define exactly what are emotions, what they do and how they should best be studied (Williams, 2001; Strongman, 2003), there is now much agreement that *happiness, fear, anger* and *depression* are universal to all humans and are even said to be hardwired into human neuroanatomy (Kemper, 1987). Importantly, three of the four emotions are negatively tuned (Turner and Stets, 2005: 11) and we will be exploring how these primary emotions shape and colour other emotions like hate, shame, guilt, pride, wonder, resentment, nostalgia and dread among the many feelings encountered in our daily experiences. In his influential article Theodore Kemper (1987) argues that these secondary emotions are more socially constructed and arise from specific contexts where experiences are learnt. Guilt, for example, is derived from the primary emotion of fear and the social organization of punishment, religion or nationhood inducing some experience of shame, regret and sorrow. Table 8.1 summarizes his characterization of primary and secondary emotions, which provides a useful taxonomy of the emotions. Of course, it is important to recognize that there is considerable cultural and social variation in how these emotions are experienced, expressed and practised. We now turn from these broad conceptual issues to that emotional state which has received considerable criminological attention—fear. Indeed, it has become a well-worn observation that the problems posed by the fear of crime are potentially greater than crime itself and as we will see it was this discovery that prompted the plethora of studies on the topic.

TABLE 8.1 Kemper's primary and secondary emotions

Primary emotions	Fear	Anger	Depression	Happiness
Emotions attached to primary emotions	Guilt	Shame	Ennui, sadness, resignation	Pride, loving, gratitude
Some combinations of primary emotions	Fear-anger: hate, jealousy, envy	Fear-happiness: wonder, awe, hope, shyness	Anger-happiness: vengeance, snobbery, contempt	Depression-happiness: nostalgia, yearning

Source: Adapted from Kemper, 1987; and Turner and Stets, 2005: 18.

Fear of Crime

Fear is a complex human emotion. While fear is ubiquitous and felt by every living creature, the actual sources of dread are socially distributed. Different societies have developed different ways of living with the dangers that haunt them. Yet contemporary terms like the 'politics of fear', 'fear of crime', 'age of anxiety', 'risk society' and most recently 'liquid fear' (Bauman, 2006; see also Box 1) each suggest that we are living in times of such heightened insecurity that danger lurks everywhere. A number of important social changes are said to herald this new era and break with the past—the mass media now provide us with round-the-clock news of crisis, disaster and trauma; rising social mobility brings a greater range of experiences, expectations and troubles; technological innovations have brought with them immense global dangers; and since 9/11 'new' forms of terrorism further contribute to the cultural climate of fear (Carrabine, 2008).

Although research on the fear of crime was established in the late 1960s—paralleling the growth in more general criminological interest and policy concerns over victims of crime—it had moved to the centre of intense empirical, political and theoretical disputes by the 1980s. Today, the 'fear of crime' is an area of criminological inquiry that constitutes a 'sub-discipline in itself' (Lee, 2001: 468) and 'is probably the main legacy of endless, and endlessly repeated, national crime surveys which have consistently identified it as a social problem of striking dimensions' (Ditton et al., 1999: 83). Few issues trouble the public in Europe and the United States more than crime. Surveys have repeatedly shown that worries over victimization surpass losing a job, ill-health, road accidents and indebtedness as issues of major concern (Farall and Gadd, 2004: 127).

From the late 1960s, in the United States initially but later elsewhere around the world, interviewing citizens about their personal experiences of crime became commonplace. In addition to trying to obtain a more accurate view of victimization levels these national household crime surveys provide information on the public's beliefs and attitudes towards crime, policing, punishment and prevention. The British Crime Survey was first carried out in 1982 and has been repeated at regular intervals since. Accompanying national surveys have been an increasing number of local crime surveys, which in the UK have been carried out in various places like Bristol, Sheffield, Merseyside, Islington and Edinburgh (Hale, 1996: 79).Typically fear of crime is often measured by responses to the question 'How safe do you feel walking alone in this area after dark?', or similar formulations, to which respondents are invited to reply by saying they feel 'very safe', 'fairly safe', 'a bit unsafe' or 'very unsafe'. The use of this question to uncover 'fear of crime' has been widely criticized, as it

- fails to explicitly mention crime (Garafalo, 1979);
- cannot do justice to the emotional complexity of fear (Box et al., 1988);
- ignores the fluidity of lived experiences (Goodey, 2005: 69);
- and through questionnaires respondents are 'forced to use the same language to express very different feelings' (O'Mahony and Quinn, 1999: 232–3).

BOX 1 FEARS IN MOTION

The trade in safety and security is highly lucrative. To take one example, there is the quite extraordinary phenomenon of the 'Sports Utility Vehicle' (SUV) in the United States. This massive petrol-guzzling, quasi-military vehicle had at one point reached 45 per cent of all car sales in the United States and is sold as a 'defensive capsule'. It is portrayed in advertisements as offering immunity against the dangerously unpredictable urban life outside the protective armoured shell (Bauman, 2006: 143–4). According to Josh Lauer (2005) the SUV first emerged as a status symbol in the early 1980s with the introduction of the military Humvee (which stands for High Mobility Multipurpose Wheeled Vehicle) which was commissioned by the army to replace the jeep, and came to popular attention during the first Gulf War. This prompted the development of a civilian version and the continuing occupation of Iraq has only heightened their popularity.

The massive civilian Hummer was embraced as an ultra macho novelty vehicle and quickly became one of the most fashionable and popular vehicles in America, with more than a third of its sales to women drivers. Indeed, a recent television ad features a woman driving a Hummer through city streets, with the tagline, 'Slip into something more metal'. Clearly there is something more going on here than an increased fear consciousness, as the SUV is an expensive piece of 'high-end automotive jewellery' in which risk management is transformed into a symbol of conspicuous consumption (Lauer, 2005: 163–5). It is significant however that in the UK similar oversized, four-wheel-drive vehicles are frequently derided as 'Chelsea Tractors', which indicates their almost ridiculous remove from their original use among working farmers and the rural gentry (Carrabine, 2008).

As Evi Girling and her colleagues (Girling et al., 2000: 13) emphasize, these studies tend to 'discover a lack of "fit" between expert knowledge and "lay" opinion' that have come to revolve around the question of whether fear is rational or irrational in an effort to distinguish between 'warranted' estimates of risks as opposed to debilitating misperceptions of threats by particular groups of the public. Home Office research continued to find that both women and the elderly were particularly 'irrational' given the distance between their high levels of expressed fear and their low levels of actual risk. The conclusion was that women and the aged were incapable of making rational sense of the risks they faced.

Feminists quickly challenged the gendered stereotypes of women as fearful and men as fearless in much of these approaches (see, *inter alia*, Goodey, 1997; Stanko, 1997; Gilchrist et al., 1998; Sutton and Farrall, 2005). Betsy Stanko (1987, 1988) was an early critic and argued that this work could not adequately grasp women's experiences and fears of sexual danger. By using alternative research methodologies (like ethnographic studies, life histories and individual interviews) significant empirical evidence was unearthed that debunked 'the myth of the safe home' (Stanko, 1988) to reveal the extent of 'ordinary violence' women regularly face and manage across public and private domains (Stanko, 1990). Such work raises 'fundamental questions of whose standards are used as markers of a reasonable or rational fear' (Walklate, 1998: 409) and suggests there are some dubious conceptual assumptions behind conventional approaches to researching fear. In any case, the debate over whether the 'fear of crime' is rational or irrational is one that can never really be resolved, as it is difficult to see what a rational fear would look like (Sparks, 1992: 10). For women fear of sexual danger is a normal condition—a 'governing of the soul' (Stanko, 1997)—such that much criminological attention has now shifted to the issue of 'ontological security' (Giddens, 1991) in an effort to grasp how inner anxieties are structured in social space.

Urbanism, Anxiety and the Human Condition

A rich seam of work has attempted to understand the ways fears and anxieties are locally constructed. Ian Taylor (1996, 1997) has argued that the fear of crime has become a condensed metaphor, which attempts to capture broader concerns over the pace of socio-economic change. As he explains, the rise of defensive middle-class suburban social movements organized around crime prevention

> are activated not just by immediately presenting sets of problems in the specific locality (stories of aggressive young people and actual violence on the hitherto peaceful local High Street) but by deeper fears about joblessness and house prices, and (in the case of parents with suburban children) schooling 'for success', child safety, moral socialization ... and a host of other increasingly agitated concerns. (Taylor, 1997: 66)

On this account, worries about crime are intimately bound up with the less easily grasped or articulated troubles generated by changes in economic, moral and social life. It is a 'fear of falling' that is the defining condition of the suburban middle class in contemporary England (Taylor and Jamieson, 1998).

A point further explored by Girling et al. (2000) in their study of public perceptions of crime in a prosperous English market town is that

> people's responses to crime (in its association with other matters of concern to them) are both informed by, and in turn inform, their *sense of place*; their sense, that is, of both *the*

place they inhabit (its histories, divisions, trajectories and so forth), and of *their place* within a wider world of hierarchies, troubles, opportunities and insecurities. (Girling et al., 2000: 17; emphasis in original)

The importance of this work is that it attempts to situate people's fears in specific everyday contexts and in doing so it chimes with other recent developments that have highlighted how the individual's social location (Walklate, 1998) and inner personal senses of security (Hollway and Jefferson, 2000) shape perceptions of the wider world around them.

The introduction of psychoanalytical theory into the fear of crime debate offers much potential. Wendy Hollway and Tony Jefferson (1997, 2000) draw on the key psychoanalytical insight that anxiety is the price we pay for having a sense of self. Their work emphasizes that anxiety is a universal feature of the human condition and that dynamic 'unconscious defences against anxiety are a commonplace and constructive aspect of response to threats' (Hollway and Jefferson, 2000: 32).The specific unconscious defence mechanisms they focus on are **denial**, **splitting** and **projection** to explore how threats to the self are managed by these displacing activities. Their overall argument is that anxiety, as a pervasive yet inchoate emotion, lies behind much of the contemporary concerns over fear of crime. Drawing on their research with people living on two council estates in northern England their analysis reveals quite varied and diffuse responses to the threat of crime. The differing responses are informed by individual biography, social location and unconscious defence mechanisms. As they put it 'a rampant "fear of crime" discourse which might on the face of it be thought to exacerbate fears, could actually serve unconsciously as a relatively reassuring site for displaced anxieties which otherwise would be too threatening to cope with' (Hollway and Jefferson, 1997: 263–4).

Hollway and Jefferson (2000: 31) have introduced a notion of human subjectivity that recognizes 'the non-rational, unintentional and emotional aspects of people's actions and experience' that had largely been neglected by criminologists. Nevertheless, sympathetic critics have contended that their approach is more about 'feeling than structure' (Walklate, 1998: 411) while others argue that to 'focus only on unconscious displacement tends to ignore both the conscious strategies and various circuits of communication' (Lupton and Tulloch, 1999: 515) adopted by their respondents. But replacing the rational, unitary subject with the anxious, fragmented subject need not dispense with a socially literate understanding of subjectivity. Instead, unconscious processes combine with cognitive choices as well as social structures, like language, so that these aspects of explanation are best seen as complementary rather than alternatives (Carrabine, 2008).

Yet it would be wrong to assume that people are constantly afraid—life would be unbearable if that were so—but rather the emotional intensity varies and we find imaginative ways of ignoring or adapting to precarious environments (Tuan, 1979: 9). As Walklate (2007a: 100) has succinctly put it, fear 'is not an ever present feeling or state of mind but burns differently in different contexts'. These different contexts will include our immediate social relations, broader external forces as well as our own anxious inner worlds, such that calls for a 'psychosocial criminology' (Jefferson, 2002a; Gadd and Jefferson, 2007) will involve a greater attention to emotional life than criminologists have conventionally been prepared to pay.

Hate Crime

Perhaps one of the most explicit connections drawn between crime and a specific emotion in recent years concerns the emergence of the concept of 'hate crime' in the United States. The United States Federal Bureau of

Investigation (FBI) defines hate crimes as offences that are 'motivated in part or singularly by personal prejudice against others because of a diversity—race, sexual orientation, religion, ethnicity/national origin, or disability'. While the term 'hate crime' is institutionalized in law in the United States—as in the Hate Crime Statistics Act 1990—it has gradually become a site of legal intervention in Britain:

- The Crime and Disorder Act 1998 created a number of new racially and religiously aggravated offences;
- The Criminal Justice Act 2003 introduced tougher sentences for offences motivated by hatred of the victim's sexual orientation (this must now be taken into account by the sentencing court as an aggravating factor, in addition to race or religious hate motivation);
- The Racial and Religious Hatred Act 2006 has made it a criminal offence to use threatening words or behaviour with the intention of stirring up hatred against any group of people because of their religious beliefs or their lack of religious beliefs.

The term hate crime has been adopted by the Metropolitan Police Service (MPS), and other police services, as can be seen in Figure 3.3.2, and the media, and has become firmly established in popular discourse. It is contestable, however, whether 'hate crime' does in fact manifest hate.

For many people, the term hate crime arguably conjures up an image of a violent crime committed by extremists, by neo-Nazis, racist skinheads and other committed bigots—in other words, hate-fuelled individuals who subscribe to racist, anti-semitic, homophobic and other bigoted ideologies. It is not surprising that many people think this way about hate crimes, because the media focus on the most extreme incidents—as is the case with crime reporting in general. The murder of Stephen Lawrence in south London in 1993, and the subsequent media coverage of the young men suspected of the murder, and the racist views they expressed, provide a prime example. Other extreme incidents in Britain that quite understandably gained notoriety include the bombing in May 1999 of the Admiral Duncan, a 'gay pub' in Soho, London (Figure 3.3.3), in which three died and scores were injured. The young man convicted, David Copeland, had a history of involvement with racist organizations.

FIGURE 8.2   Campaign poster to combat hate crime.

West Midlands Police.

In the United States the brutality of the murder of James Byrd, an African American—who was beaten unconscious, chained to the back of a pick-up truck and dragged for miles along rural roads outside the town of Jasper, Texas, in June 1998—attracted widespread media coverage. The brutality of the murder and the fact that the two perpetrators were members of a white supremacist organization evoked painful memories of **lynching** (see Box 2) and historical racial violence in the United States. The callousness of the attack on the young gay man Matthew Shepard, who was pistol-whipped and left lashed to a fence in freezing conditions to die later in hospital in Wyoming in October 1998, generated considerable debate about homophobic bigotry. The incident itself and its repercussions have been portrayed in the play and film *The Laramie Project*.

Two dead and 70 injured as Soho is rocked by blast

GAY BAR NAIL BOMB HORROR

By STEPHEN WRIGHT

TWO people died and 70 were injured when a nail bomb demolished a gay pub in Central London last night.

FIGURE 8.3   class="import-Italic">Daily Mail extract, 1 May 1999.

extract © Atlantic Syndication; photo: David Gaywood.

BOX 2 THE POLITICS OF LYNCHING

Lynching is a form of extrajudicial punishment involving public torture revived in the Southern United States as a response to the perceived loss of white male domination in the nineteenth century. The passage of the Thirteenth Amendment (1865) outlawed slavery and with emancipation former slaves became 'African Americans'. It has been argued that it was 'through the process of Reconstruction, the Union attempted to restore relations with the Confederate states' (Messerscmidt, 2007: 81) and it is in this context white male mob violence quickly arose as an attempt to reassert old hierarchies. For example, in May 1866, forty-six African Americans were murdered when their schools and churches were set on fire by a white male mob in Memphis. Two months later, in July, thirty-four African Americans were killed in New Orleans at the hands of a white mob (Ayers, 1984).

The lynchings were explicitly violent and looked to ancient and medieval forms of aggravated death penalty, which included burning, castration, whipping as well as hanging. Indeed, the lynch mob insisted on punishments that were barbaric, and the fact that they would outrage liberal sensibility was all part of their appeal. They were deliberately racialized and the lynch victim was often sought out as retribution for the alleged rape of a white woman by an African-American man. The public lynching has been understood as a carnival critique of official criminal justice and total rejection of the law's commitment to equality while reasserting local understandings of caste superiority. As Garland (2007: 147) explains, public torture lynching communicated 'impassioned sentiments that could no longer be expressed in the official idiom of the criminal law' and inflicted 'a level of suffering that had long since been officially disavowed'. [...]

Paul Iganski (2006) has demonstrated how the New Labour government's specific concerns over racially aggravated offences—influenced to some extent by US legislation and debate—has led to a gradual expansion of British law in this field, from race to religion, and also sexuality and disability. His account describes the many dilemmas surrounding such legislation: from the supporting arguments that crimes motivated by hate cause damage to the victim beyond the crime itself, that this additionally infects a wider community with fear and trauma, and constitutes an assault on the dominant values of society. Opponents criticize the legislation on the grounds that

- legislating against hate is indefensible as it suggests that hurting some kinds of people isn't quite as bad as hurting others (Jacoby, 2002);
- it is a totalitarian response to prejudice as it punishes 'thought crime' in Orwellian fashion (Phillips, 2002); and
- it treats equal crimes unequally, which goes against fundamental legal principles.

The Thrill of It All?

Given the range of victims of hate crimes, the variety of offenders involved and the different social situations in which hate crimes occur, there can obviously be no single explanation, and in any one incident there may be a range of explanations. However, one thing does appear to stand out: many incidents seem to be committed *for the fun of it*, for the kicks, for the excitement, as well as for other reasons. According to Jack Levin and Jack McDevitt:

> Like young men getting together on a Saturday night to play a game of cards, certain hatemongers get together and decide to go out and destroy property or bash minorities. They want to have some fun and stir up a little excitement—at someone else's expense.

The payoff in such 'thrill-seeking hate crime', as Levin and McDevitt famously called it, is psychological as well as social:

> They enjoy the exhilaration and the thrill of making someone suffer. For those with a sadistic streak, inflicting pain and suffering is its own reward. In addition, the youthful perpetrators receive a stamp of approval from their friends who regard hatred and violence as 'hot' or 'cool'. (Levin and McDevitt, 2002: 67)

In a 'pick and mix' of bigotry, the victims of thrill-seeking hate crimes are often interchangeable.

Excitement is not the only emotion involved in so-called hate crime. Levin and McDevitt argue that resentment—to one degree or another—can be found in the personality of most hate crime offenders, and it takes many forms. There are individuals who, perhaps because of some personal misfortune, feel rejected by, estranged from and wronged by society. They look for someone to target in venting their anger.

For others, their bitterness is fuelled by a perceived or real threat to their economic security, and some strike at those they think are to blame: newcomers, immigrants, asylum seekers. Larry Ray and colleagues, drawing on research based in Greater Manchester, argue that much of the violence is related to the sense of shame and failure, resentment and hostility felt by young men who 'are disadvantaged and marginalised economically and culturally, and thus deprived of the material basis for enacting a traditional conception of working-class masculinity'. Such emotions, according to Ray et al., 'readily lead to violence only in the case of young men (and occasionally for young women) for whom resorting to violence is a common approach to settling arguments and conflicts' (2003: 112).

Self-Esteem, Shame and Respect

The significance of self-esteem in violent encounters has been explored by Thomas Scheff and his colleagues. From their perspective, 'self-esteem concerns how we usually feel about ourselves. High self-esteem means that we usually feel justified pride in ourselves, low self-esteem that we often and easily feel ashamed of ourselves or try to avoid feelings of shame' (Scheff et al., 1989: 178). They propose that 'shame' is a primary emotion generated by the constant, incessant but commonly unacknowledged monitoring and negative evaluation of self in the eyes of others. Shame, however, is generally unacknowledged, and as an emotion it is seen to be socially unacceptable.

Self-esteem, in short, is a 'summary concept', representing how well a person overall manages shame. People with high self-esteem have had sufficient experience of pride to outweigh their experience of shame; they can manage shame. However, when a person has had an insufficient experience of pride, then shame becomes a calamity for them. When they experience some form of humiliation, real or imagined, rather than acknowledging it, it is masked with anger. The person is then caught in a 'shame–rage feeling trap'. According to Scheff and colleagues,

> In our theory, rage is used as a defense against threat to self, that is, feeling shame, a feeling of vulnerability of the whole self. Anger can be a protective measure to guard against shame, which is experienced as an attack on self. As humiliation increases, rage and hostility increase proportionally to defend against loss of self-esteem.

In short, violence is the consequence of trapped shame and anger. Crucially, Scheff and colleagues further argue that

> Pride and shame states almost always depend on the level of deference accorded a person: pride arises from deferential treatment by others ('respect'), and shame from lack of deference ('disrespect'). Gestures that imply respect or disrespect, together with the emotional response they generate, make up the deference/emotion system, which exerts a powerful influence on human behavior. (Scheff et al., 1989: 184–5)

These arguments have also proven especially influential on the role of shame in restorative justice practices, where it is argued that the community conferences that lie at the heart of reintegrative shaming (see Box 3) work not so much through the words said but on facial expressions, gestures and physical posture

(Retzinger and Scheff, 1996). We now describe how the emotions are embodied in contemporary street cultures, where crime, hustling and violence have become a defining way of life for the ghetto poor.

BOX 3 REINTEGRATIVE SHAMING

In his classic study *Crime, Shame and Reintegration* (1989), John Braithwaite emphasized the importance of the emotions in the restoration of justice between offenders, victims and the wider community. This work provided a powerful impetus to the 'restorative justice' movement in criminology and challenge to vindictive models of retributive punishment [...]. The book has decisively influenced studies of conflict, reconciliation and 'peace-making' as well as enabling accounts of the place of 'emotional work' in criminal justice institutions to emerge (e.g. Karstedt, 2002). His argument is that shaming the offence, and not the offender, will reintegrate the offender back into the community while giving victims a strong role in these reconciliation processes. Crucially, though, the agents of shaming are not the victims, but the family and friends of the offender so that shame integrates rather than alienates. As he famously put it, the 'best place to see reintegrative shaming at work is in loving families' (Braithwaite, 1989: 56).

Braithwaite's arguments are closely allied to Thomas Scheff's work on shame (which suggests that one of the central features of life is our search for honour and the ways in which shaming plays a role in that search). Shame is linked to taking on the role of 'the other' (cf. Mead, 1934), and links to the pangs of conscience when confronted with the possibility of wrongdoing. We want and need the social approval of others. Shaming involves all social processes expressing disapproval that have the aim of inducing remorse in the offender. For Braithwaite, the shame that matters most is not that coming from officials such as the police, judges, courts or even victims, but that from the people we care most about. It is not stigmatizing in so far as it is aimed not at the offender per se but at the act the offender commits; the ultimate aim must be reintegration and he contends that reintegrative shaming is effective in complex societies as well as more traditional ones.

It is significant that Braithwaite developed his arguments from accounts of indigenous procedures of 'conferencing' in New Zealand and Australia, where he found that these community settings successfully combined shaming and reintegration. Critics worry whether these processes will be used against the most vulnerable groups in society or deployed only for trivial offences while conventional, custodial punishments continue to expand. It has been noted how the model of reintegrative shaming developed in Australia and currently exported around the world is one principally targeted at Aboriginal youth, intensifying police controls over this already marginalized population (Blagg, 1997). More recent Australian research has suggested that 'net-widening' may be a problem, and that more marginalized young people (including non-Aboriginal) are channelled away from youth conferencing into a youth 'justice system more punitive in its sentencing' (Cunneen and White, 2006: 107). The idealization of the family at the heart of the approach has been criticized for its reliance on defining 'others *as* others' (Ahmed, 2004: 199; emphasis in original)—those who have failed to live up to this ideal social bond—like single mothers, queer relationships, and so forth. To be fair, Braithwaite has always recognized that shaming can be used tyrannically against unpopular minorities, but it is difficult to see how the communitarian politics that informs his thinking can oppose hostile collective sentiments when that is the community's will.

Stories from the Street

The issue of 'respect' is a key theme explored by Elijah Anderson in his book *Code of the Streets* (1999). He argues that for many inner-city youths in his study, a street culture has evolved, what he calls a code of the streets—a set of informal rules governing public behaviour and the use of violence. It can be traced to the sense of hopelessness and to the alienation that the youths feel from mainstream society and its institutions, due to the joblessness and the pervasive racism they experience.

'Respect' is 'at the heart of the code', according to Anderson. Respect is about 'being treated "right", or granted the deference one deserves'. But gaining and maintaining respect has to be a constant endeavour:

> In the street culture, especially among young people, respect is viewed as almost an external entity that is hard-won but easily lost, and so must constantly be guarded. The rules of the code in fact provide a framework for negotiating respect. The person whose very appearance—including his clothing, demeanor, and way of moving—deters transgressions, feels that he possesses, and may be considered by others to possess, a measure of respect. With the right amount of respect, for instance, he can avoid 'being bothered' in public. If he is bothered, not only may he be in physical danger but he has been disgraced or 'dissed'. (Anderson, 1994: 82)

One key aspect of a person's demeanour to convey and hold respect is 'having the juice': projecting an image, a willingness to resort to violence, having the nerve to throw the first punch, to pull the trigger and, in the extreme, not being afraid to die, and not being afraid of taking another's life if needs be, if someone 'gets in their face', if disrespected.

Respect is a scarce commodity. Deprived of achieving a sense of self-esteem through participation in the jobs market, and other institutions of mainstream society, 'everyone competes', according to Anderson,

> to get what affirmation he can of the little that is available. The craving for respect that results gives people thin skins. Shows of deference by others can be highly soothing, contributing to a sense of security, comfort, self-confidence, and self-respect. Transgressions by others which go unanswered diminish these feelings and are believed to encourage further transgressions.... Among young people, whose sense of self-esteem is particularly vulnerable, there is an especially heightened concern with being disrespected. Many inner-city young men in particular crave respect to such a degree that they will risk their lives to attain and maintain it. (1994: 89)

Similarly, Philippe Bourgois (1995) describes in his *In Search of Respect* how the street identity cultivated by men from East Harlem, which involved limited social skills, assumed gender arrogance and intimidating physical presence, made them virtually unemployable—often appearing clumsy and illiterate before prospective female supervisors in Manhattan's booming service sector economy.

In an important critique of the underclass thesis, Carl Nightingale's (1993) ethnography of the black Philadelphian ghetto maintains that the culture of the ghetto is not only a product of alienation and isolation but rather a consequence of the desperate embrace of the American Dream:

> Already at five and six, many kids in the neighborhood can recite the whole canon of adult luxury—from Gucci, Evan Piccone, and Pierre Cardin, to Mercedes and BMW ... from the age of ten, kids become thoroughly engrossed in Nike's and Reebok's cult of the sneaker. (Nightingale, 1993:153–4)

In ways that have clear echoes of Albert Cohen's earlier subcultural theory, Nightingale is arguing that structural exclusion is accompanied by an over-identification with mainstream consumer culture. As he explains:

> Inner-city kids' *inclusion* in mainstream America's mass market has been important in determining those kids' responses to the economic and racial *exclusion* they face in other parts of their lives. And, indeed, kids' experiences of exclusion and of the associated painful memories has made their participating in mass culture particularly urgent and enthusiastic, for the culture of consumption has given them a seductive means to compensate for their feelings of failure. (Nightingale, 1993: 135; emphasis in original)

The disturbing ambivalence at the heart of America's race relations is also captured in Naomi Klein's (2000: 76) discussion of companies like Tommy Hilfiger, whose marketing strategy is based on 'selling white youth on their fetishization of black style, and black youth on their fetishization of white wealth'. Jock Young (2007a: 51) has recently argued that these ghetto studies suggest that we need 'to return to the two stigmas which the poor confront, that of relative deprivation (poverty and exclusion from the labour markets) and misrecognition (lower status and lack of respect)'. Both of these are forms of humiliation, each generating powerful dynamics of resentment.

Humiliation, Rage and Edgework

At the beginning of this [reading] it was observed that crimes of passion have fuelled the artistic imagination. We now turn to such crimes and draw from Jack Katz's analysis of the interrelationship of emotion and crime in his book *Seductions of Crime* (1988). In the book Katz covers a range of criminal and deviant behaviour—the ways of the 'badass', the 'hardman', the 'cold-blooded killer' and white-collar criminal—but it is instructive to focus on cases of murder that Katz analyses using a variety of documentary sources. The incidents involving what Katz calls 'Righteous Slaughter' are impassioned acts committed in moments of rage—as is the case with many murders.

In the cases that Katz analyses, the victim-to-be inflicts a humiliation upon the killer-to-be: a wife caught by her husband *in flagrante* with another man; another tortured by her husband's infidelity; a man whose virility is challenged by his partner; a neighbour offended by another neighbour parking in front of their property. In each case, humiliation arises from the violation of a respected social role, such as husband, wife, virile male, property owner. The would-be killer's reaction to the humiliation, according to Katz's analysis, is 'a last stand defence of respectability'. Their mortal act is not calculated in a premeditated sense to restore their self-worth.

It is instead experienced as a compulsion, driven by rage arising from the killer's emotional comprehension of the humiliation they have suffered.

Risk, Excitement and Routine

Jack Katz (1988) is drawing attention to the exciting, pleasurable and transgressive dynamics that are very much at the 'foreground' of criminal activity in an effort to critique the 'sentimental materialism' (as Katz, 1988: 313–17, terms it) of much liberal and radical criminology. British criminologists have also explored these issues. Roger Matthews (2002) in his study of armed robbers, for instance, notes how during his interviews it was usually when his respondents were describing the actual robberies that the attractions of the crime would become all too apparent. Similarly, Mike Collison's (1996) research on masculinities and crimes connects these ideas to cultural consumption, risk-taking and drug use. For example, burgling a house is an activity laced with excitement but it is also riddled with risk. One of the respondents in his study described the dual-edged thrill and danger of getting caught, assault by the homeowner, or the police, or later on the street by failing in front of male friends. As one 20-year-old put it: 'I always used to leave the room they was sleeping in till last … they never used to hear me for some reason … it was scary and exciting' (Collison, 1996: 443). Few stopped to calculate the risks but rather put their faith in a mystical sense of invincibility, or hope for a run of good luck, or sometimes used drugs to ease the risk. It is useful to contrast these accounts though with Tony Kearon and Rebecca Leach's (2000) discussion of burglary where they describe the intense feelings of abjection that many victims of house theft experience.

What seems to be particularly important here, in terms of doing crime, is that this kind of 'edgework' (Lyng, 1990a, 2004) is deeply satisfying and seductive. Edgework has been described as a form of 'experiental anarchy' that is an 'experience that is much more real than the circumstances of everyday experience'. One British 19-year-old explained to Collison (1996: 435) that 'what I really want to do like to occupy my time, I'd like to jump out of planes like that, that's exciting to me, I couldn't afford things like that … so I just pinch cars, get chases, do burglaries and enjoy myself that way'. It is important to recognize that while this edgework is an essential part of street life for underclass male youth, it also has routine features. For what comes across in all the narratives is how surprisingly ordinary this risk-taking is. But, and this is highly significant, these activities are not thought of in this way. They would be impossible to do if they were.

The important question here is why these activities are so exciting and seductive. In answering this question the crucial factor is drugs, not just in the sense of being able to 'get off your face' through Ecstasy, amphetamines and LSD, but that they form a defining part of the irregular economy in poor communities for expendable male youth in Collison's (1996) study. For young underclass men the promised land is on the TV, and it should come as no surprise to learn that their favourite film was *New Jack City*, while real life here 'stinks'. In contrast, the drug economy provides these young men with their only realistic chance of fast living and the high life in Britain. Drug crime, like other forms of street crime, creates a space for acting out predatory forms of masculinity. Street-level drug dealing, whether this is on the corner or watched on film, and the two are frequently conflated, promises action and status success. According to Collison (1996: 441) forms of predatory street crime and excessive lifestyle among some young underclass males are not a simple response to poverty, they are attempts to 'munch' their way through consumer society and fill in the spaces of structure and identity, or in other words, to get a 'reputation as mad'.

Summary

1. Criminology has an important role to play in showing how the emotions shape our inner lives and broader social practices.
2. Fear and anxiety are central characteristics of modern living.
3. Human emotions play a central role in the criminal act.
4. The study of the emotional dynamics of crime illuminates why certain crimes occur.
5. The emotions can restore justice between offenders, victims and the wider community.

Critical Thinking Questions

1. Why have the emotions been marginalized in Western thought?
2. Why is 'fear of crime' an ill-defined term?
3. Why might 'hate crime' legislation be a totalitarian response to prejudice? How could the arguments outlined in this chapter help us understand phenomena like 'road rage', 'lynch mobs' and 'queer bashing'?
4. What are the seductions of crime?
5. How does the 'search for respect' reproduce exclusion in North American ghettoes?

Further Study

Anderson, E. (1999) *Code of the Streets: Decency, Violence and the Moral Life of the Inner City*, New York: W. W. Norton. A highly illuminating ethnographic exploration of the social and cultural dynamics of interpersonal violence in the inner city.

Bauman, Z. (2006) *Liquid Fear*, Cambridge: Polity. One of the most original sociological thinkers casts his eye over the fears and anxieties that haunt our current age.

Gadd, D. and Jefferson, T. (2007) *Psychosocial Criminology: An Introduction*, London: Sage. A lively demonstration of how a psychosocial approach sheds new light on the causes of many crimes, as well as challenging readers to rethink the similarities and differences between themselves and offenders.

Iganski, P. (2008) *'Hate Crime' and the City*, Bristol: Policy Press. A wide-ranging account analysing how we understand and ought to respond to crimes motivated by prejudice in the UK.

Katz, J. (1988) *Seductions of Crime: Moral and Sensual Attractions of Doing Evil*, New York: Basic Books. An indispensable analysis of the sensual and emotional dynamics of crime.

Levin, J. and McDevitt, J. (2002) *Hate Crimes Revisited: America's War on Those Who Are Different*, Boulder, CO: Westview. An invaluable evaluation of the social, cultural, motivational and policy context of hate and crime.

More Information

American Psychological Association: 'Hate Crimes Today: An Age-Old Foe in Modern Dress'
http://www.apa.org/pubinfo/hate/homepage.html
A question-and-answer site shedding some clarification on the hate crime debate.

Hate Crime.org
http://www.hatecrime.org/
Information and links to related news articles concerning current events, political choices, and victims and further information.

National Gay and Lesbian Task Force: information on hate crime laws
http://www.nglft.org/issues/issue.cfm?issueID=12
NGLTF is the national progressive organization working for the civil rights of gay, lesbian, bisexual and transgender people.

Crime reduction
http://www.crimereduction.homeoffice.gov.uk/toolkits/fc00.htm
A typical Home Office site offering advice and information on how to tackle fear and disorder in the community.

Bibliography

Ahmed, S. (2004) *The Cultural Politics of Emotion*, Edinburgh: Edinburgh University Press.

Anderson, E. (1994) 'The Code of Streets', *Atlantic Monthly*, 5: 80–94.

Anderson, E. (1999) *Code of the Streets: Decency, Violence and the Moral Life of the Inner City*, New York: W.W. Norton.

Ayers, E. (1984) *Vengeance and Justice: Crime and Punishment in the Nineteenth-century American South*, New York: Oxford University Press.

Barbalet, J. (1998) *Emotion, Social Theory and Social Structure: A Macrosociological Approach*, Cambridge: Cambridge University Press.

Bauman, Z. (2006) *Liquid Fear*, Cambridge: Polity.

Blagg, H. (1997) 'A Just Measure of Shame: Aboriginal Youth and Conferencing in Australia', *British Journal of Criminology*, 37 (4): 481–501.

Bourgois, P. (1995) *In Search of Respect*, Cambridge: Cambridge University Press.

Box, S., Hale, C. and Andrews, G. (1988) 'Explaining Fear of Crime', *British Journal of Criminology*, 28:340–56.

Braithwaite, J. (1989) *Crime, Shame and Reintegration*, Cambridge: Cambridge University Press.

Carrabine, E. (2008) *Crime, Culture and the Media*, Cambridge: Polity.

Cohen, A. K. (1955) *Delinquent Boys: The Culture of the Gang*, Glencoe, IL: Free Press.

Collison, M. (1996) 'In Search of the High Life: Drugs, Crime, Masculinity and Consumption', *British Journal of Criminology*, 36 (3): 428–44.

Cunneen, C. and White, R. (2006) 'Australia: Control, Containment or Empowerment?', in J. Muncie and B. Goldson (eds) *Comparative Youth Justice*, London: Sage.

de Haan, W. and Loader, I. (2002) 'On the Emotions of Crime, Punishment and Social Control', *Theoretical Criminology*, 6 (3): 243–53.

Ditton, J., Bannister, J., Gilchrist, E. and Farrall, S. (1999) 'Afraid or Angry? Recalibrating the "Fear" of Crime', *International Review of Victimology*, 6: 83–99.

Farrall, S. and Gadd, D. (2004) 'Research Note: The Frequency of the Fear of Crime', *British Journal of Criminology*, 44: 127–32.

Gadd, D. and Jefferson, T. (2007) *Psychosocial Criminology: An Introduction*, London: Sage.

Garafalo, J. (1979) 'Victimisation and the Fear of Crime', *Journal of Research in Crime and Delinquency*,16: 80–97.

Garland, D. (2007) 'Death, Denial, Discourse: On the Forms and Functions of American Capital Punishment', in D. Downes, P. Rock, C. Chinkin and C. Gearty (eds) *Crime, Social Control and Human Rights: From Moral Panics to States of Denial, Essays in Honour of Stanley Cohen*, Cullompton: Willan.

Giddens, A. (1991) *Modernity and Self-Identity*, Cambridge: Polity.

Gilchrist, E., Bannister, J., Ditton, J. and Farrall, S. (1998) 'Women and the "Fear of Crime": Challenging the Accepted Stereotype', *British Journal of Criminology*, 38 (2): 283–98.

Girling, E., Loader, I. and Sparks, R. (2000) *Crime and Social Change in Middle England: Questions of Order in an English Town*, London: Routledge.

Goffman, E. (1961) *Asylums: Essays on the Social Situation of Mental Patients and Other Inmates*, Harmondsworth: Penguin.

Goffman, E. (1963) *Stigma: Notes on the Management of Spoiled Identity*, Harmondsworth: Penguin.

Goodey, J. (1997) 'Boys Don't Cry: Masculinities, Fear of Crime and Fearlessness', *British Journal of Criminology*, 47 (3): 401–18.

Goodey, J. (2005) *Victims and Victimology: Research, Policy and Practice*, Harlow: Longman.

Hale, C. (1996) 'Fear of Crime: A Review of the Literature', *International Review of Victimology*, 4: 79–150.

Hayward, K. (2002) 'The Vilification and Pleasures of Youthful Transgression', in J. Muncie, G. Hughes and E. McLaughlin (eds) *Youth Justice: Critical Readings*, London: Sage.

Hochschild, A. (1983) *The Managed Heart: Commercialization of Human Feeling*, Berkeley: University of California Press.

Hollway, W. and Jefferson, T. (1997) 'The Risk Society in an Age of Anxiety: Situating Fear of Crime', *British Journal of Sociology*, 48 (2): 255–66.

Hollway, W. and Jefferson, T. (2000) 'The Role of Anxiety in Fear of Crime', in T. Hope and R. Sparks (eds) *Crime, Risk and Insecurity*, London: Routledge.

Iganski, P. (2006) 'Free to Speak, Free to Hate?', in L. Morris (ed.) *Rights: Sociological Perspectives*, London: Routledge.

Jacoby, J. (2002) 'Punish Crime, Not Thought Crime', in P. Iganski (ed.) *The Hate Debate*, London: Profile.

Jaggar, A. (1989) 'Love and Knowledge: Emotion in Feminist Epistemology', in S. Bordo and A. Jaggar (eds) *Gender/Body/Knowledge: Feminist Reconstructions of Being and Knowing*, New York: Rutgers University Press.

Jefferson, T. (2002a) 'For a Psychosocial Criminology', in K. Carrington and R. Hogg (eds) *Critical Criminology: Issues, Debates, Challenges*, Cullompton: Willan.

Karstedt, S. (2002) 'Emotions and Criminal Justice', *Theoretical Criminology*, 6 (3): 299–317.

Katz, J. (1988) *Seductions of Crime: Moral and Sensual Attractions of Doing Evil*, New York: Basic Books.

Kearon, A. and Leach, R. (2000) 'Invasion of the "Bodysnatchers": Burglary Reconsidered', *Theoretical Criminology*, 4 (4): 451–72.

Kemper, T. (1978) *A Social Interactional Theory of Emotions*, New York: John Wiley.

Kemper, T. (1987) 'How Many Emotions Are There? Wedding the Social and Automatic Components', *American Journal of Sociology*, 93: 263–89.

Klein, N. (2000) *No Logo*, London: Flamingo.

Lauer, J. (2005) 'Driven to Extremes: Fear of Crime and the Rise of the Sport Utility Vehicle in the United States', *Crime, Media, Culture*, 1 (2): 149–68.

Lee, M. (2001) 'The Genesis of "Fear of Crime"', *Theoretical Criminology*, 5 (4): 467–85.

Levin, J. and McDevitt, J. (2002) *Hate Crimes Revisited: America's War on Those Who Are Different*, Boulder, CO: Westview Press.

Lupton, D. and Tulloch, J. (1999) 'Theorizing Fear of Crime: Beyond the Rational/Irrational Opposition', *British Journal of Sociology*, 50 (3): 507–23.

Lyng, S. (1990) 'Edgework: A Social Psychological Analysis of Voluntary Risk Taking', *American Journal of Sociology*, 95 (4): 851–86.

Lyng, S. (2004) 'Crime, Edgework and Corporeal Transaction', *Theoretical Criminology*, 8 (3): 359–75.

Matthews, R. (2002) *Armed Robbery*, Cullompton: Willan.

Matza, D. (1964) *Delinquency and Drift*, New York: Wiley.

Matza, D. (1969) *Becoming Deviant*, Englewood Cliffs, NJ: Prentice Hall.

Mead, G. H. (1934) *Mind, Self and Society*, Chicago, IL: University of Chicago Press.

Messerschmidt, J. W. (2007) '"We Must Protect Our Southern Women": On Whiteness, Masculinities and Lynching', in M. Bosworth and J. Flavin (eds) *Race, Gender and Punishment: From Colonialism to the War on Terror*, New Brunswick, NJ: Rutgers University Press.

Nightingale, C. (1993) *On the Edge*, New York: Basic Books.

O'Mahony, D. and Quinn, K. (1999) 'Fear of Crime and Locale: The Impact of Community Related Factors upon Fear of Crime', *International Review of Victimology*, 6: 231–51.

O'Malley, P. and Mugford, S. (1994) 'Crime, Excitement and Modernity', in G. Barak (ed.) *Varieties of Criminology: Readings from a Dynamic Discipline*, Westport, CT: Praeger.

Phillips, M. (2002) 'Hate Crime: The Orwellian Response to Prejudice', in P. Iganski (ed.) *The Hate Debate: Should Hate be Punished as a Crime?*, London: Profile.

Ray, L., Smith, D. and Wastell, L. (2003) 'Understanding Racist Violence', in E. A. Stanko (ed.) *The Meanings of Violence*, London: Routledge.

Retzinger, S. and Scheff, T. (1996) 'Strategy for Community Conferences: Emotions and Social Bonds', in B. Galaway and J. Hudson (eds) *Restorative Justice: International Perspectives*, Monsey, NY: Criminal Justice Press.

Scheff, T. J. (1979) *Catharsis in Healing, Ritual, and Drama*, Berkeley: University of California Press.

Scheff, T. J., Retzinger, S. M. and Ryan, M.T. (1989) 'Crime, Violence, and Self-Esteem: Review and Proposals', in A. Mecca, N. J. Smelser and J. Vasconcellos (eds) *The Social Importance of Self-Esteem*, Berkeley: University of California Press.

Shilling, C. (2002) 'The Two Traditions in the Sociology of Emotions', in J. Barbalet (ed.) *Emotions and Sociology*, Oxford: Blackwell.

Sparks, R. (1992) *Television and the Drama of Crime: Moral Tales and the Place of Crime in Public Life*, Milton Keynes: Open University Press.

Spelman, E. (1989) 'Anger and Insubordination', in A. Garry and M. Pearsall (eds) *Women, Knowledge, and Reality: Explorations in Feminist Philosophy*, Boston, MA: Unwin Hyman.

Stanko, B. (1987) 'Typical Violence, Normal Precaution: Men, Women, and Interpersonal Violence in England, Wales and the USA', in J. Hanmer and M. Maynard (eds) *Women, Violence and Social Control*, Basingstoke: Macmillan.

Stanko, B. (1988) 'Fear of Crime and the Myth of the Safe Home: A Feminist Critique of Criminology', in K. Yllo and M. Bograd (eds) *Feminist Perspectives on Wife Abuse*, London: Sage.

Stanko, B. (1997) 'Safety Talk: Conceptualising Women's Risk Assessment as a "Technology of the Soul"', *Theoretical Criminology*, 1 (4): 479–99.

Stanko, E. (1990) *Everyday Violence*, London: Pandora.

Strongman, K. (2003) *The Psychology of Emotion: From Everyday Life to Theory*, Chichester: Wiley.

Sutton, R. and Farrall, S. (2005) 'Gender, Socially Desirable Responding and the Fear of Crime: Are Women Really More Anxious about Crime?', *British Journal of Criminology*, 45 (2): 212–24.

Taylor, I. (1996) 'Fear of Crime, Urban Fortunes and Suburban Social Movements: Some Reflections on Manchester', *Sociology*, 30 (2): 317–37.

Taylor, I. (1997) 'Crime, Anxiety, and Locality: Responding to the Condition of England at the End of the Century', *Theoretical Criminology*, 1 (1): 53–76.

Taylor, I. (1999) *Crime in Context: A Critical Criminology of Market Societies*, Cambridge: Polity.

Taylor, I. and Jamieson, R. (1998) 'Fear of Crime and Fear of Falling: English Anxieties Approaching the Millennium', *Arch. European Journal of Sociology*, 39 (1): 149–75.

Tuan, Y. (1979) *Landscapes of Fear*, New York: Pantheon Books.

Turner, J. and Stets, J. (2005) *The Sociology of Emotions*, Cambridge: Cambridge University Press.

Walklate, S. (1998) 'Excavating the Fear of Crime: Fear, Anxiety or Trust?', *Theoretical Criminology*, 2 (4): 403–18.

Walklate, S. (2007a) *Imagining the Victim of Crime*, Berkshire: Open University Press.

Williams, S. (2001) *Emotion and Social Theory*, London: Sage.

Young, J. (2007a) *The Vertigo of Late Modernity*, London: Sage.

Discussion Topics

1. Discuss the link between fear and crimes.
2. Identify a primary fear and a secondary fear and indicate their relationships with crime.
3. Discuss how fear of crime is linked to anxiety.
4. Describe the concept of "reintegrative shaming" in connection with crime, suggested by J. Braithwaite.

CONCLUSION

This article explains the important role that sociology plays in the investigation of social problems. The contribution of sociology to social problems is unique through its perspective, which is sociological imagination. Coined by C. Wright Mills, the concept of sociological imagination refers to the ability to establish a link between "biography" and "history." That is, sociological imagination enables us to understand that our personal troubles are connected to public issues. In a sense, this unique perspective of sociology allows uncovering or discovering the influential effects of social structure on social problems, which leads to theory formulation: theorizing. A social theory can be defined as a systematic, disciplined, and logical explanation of social phenomena, such as social problems. The process of theorizing occurs in three major steps: (1) Identify a problem ("the something ain't right"); (2) Describe the nature of the problem, its manifestation, and implications; and (3) Provide a description of how the problem can be solved and the impact of the solution on society.

UNIT 4

RACE, ETHNICITY, WHITE PRIVILEGE, AND SOCIAL PROBLEMS

Introduction

This unit discusses race, ethnicity, white privilege, and potential negative impacts for social problems. Most Americans conceive of racial categories as reflecting biological characteristics. This erroneous perception of race according to Buechler in his article, "*The Social Construction of Race*," is reinforced by the difference in skin, hair texture, and facial features between individuals belonging to different racial categories. However, scientific studies have shown that despite these apparent and superficial biological differences, humans share a lot of similarities at the DNA level. Here is the crucial question: If race is not biologically driven, then what explains its existence? Sociologists argue that race is socially constructed, and they develop up to five arguments to substantiate their points. They posit that race is designed for stratification purposes. Using conflict perspective, racial categories can be perceived as artificially created by the dominant group, whites, to put a distance between themselves and others that they consider "inferiors," such as Blacks, Latinos, Asians, Native Americans, etc. While race is an arbitrary construct, ethnicity refers to an individual's cultural heritage. In a sense, ethnicity includes an individual's language, customs, norms, values, and religious beliefs. A problem derived from ethnicity is ethnocentrism, which is the belief in the superiority of one group's way of life compared to another's. Several genocides have been committed in the United States and around the world because of ethnocentrism. A problem associated with race is racism, which refers to unfair treatment of an individual or a group of people based on their race. Racism is a type of discrimination based on race. Stereotypes cause prejudice, which in turn leads to discrimination.

While investigating white privilege, Amico and Gonzales establish a link between racism and the concept of white privilege. As racism, white privilege also refers to a domination. White privilege, according to Amico in *"What Is White Privilege,"* refers to the advantages associated with being white. Even though connected, the two concepts of racism and white privilege are different regarding one major issue. In the case of racism, in most cases, racists know they are being racist. That is not the case with white privilege. White people have a hard time acknowledging that they have advantages unavailable to other races because of their whiteness. The mere existence of white privilege in the United States negates the assertion of meritocracy and underscores the systemic inequality in our society. The concept of white privilege can be useful in explaining the discrimination against minority group members in all sectors of society in the United States, including the job market, housing, environment, health, law enforcement and crime, government policies, and education. Gonzales too, in *"White Privilege"* denounces the systemic inequality which reinforces white privilege to the detriment of other racial groups in the United States. To successfully compete on the global level, it is important for the United States to embrace the diversity of its population.

The Social Construction of Race

Steven M. Buechler

Steven M. Buechler, "The Social Construction of Race," *Critical Sociology*, pp. 131-147, 281-290. Copyright © 2014 by Taylor & Francis Group. Reprinted with permission.

Editor's Introduction

This article titled "The Social Construction of Race" by Steven Buechler discusses race and ethnicity. This article was selected to be included in this reader because it provides a detailed explanation of race as a social construct and its implications on minority group members in the United States. After reading this chapter, you will be able to explain how racial stratification is socially driven instead of biologically. Also, you will be able to describe the connections between racial stratification and some social problems such as ethnocentrism, genocide, and poverty among racial minority groups.

The analysis of social class has been part of sociology from the beginning. Race is different. Although scholars like W. E. B. Du Bois (1903) had crucial insights into race relations more than a hundred years ago, sociology was slow to see race as an important subject in its own right.

This gradually changed after Gunnar Myrdal's *An American Dilemma* (1944) placed racial prejudice at the forefront of public consciousness. Along with other work, it helped establish race and ethnic relations as a major subfield within sociology. Group dynamics, racial conflict, prejudice, and discrimination attracted increasing sociological attention.

What really invigorated the study of race were not academic developments but social conflict. As the civil rights movement overturned the most explicit forms of racial segregation and discrimination in the 1950s and 1960s, race became even more central in public awareness and academic study. As the movement evolved from liberal integration to black power to cultural nationalism, different understandings of race emerged. These movement-inspired analyses revealed how race was embedded in social structure.

Current sociological understandings of race thus have a dual legacy. The slowly developing academic study of race has been infused with critical insights from race-based social movements. As we will see in the next chapter, much the same can be said for the impact of the feminist movement in jump-starting sociology's understanding of gender issues.

What Is Race?

Few things seem more obvious than someone's race. As we interact with others, we unthinkingly place them within familiar racial categories. On rare occasions, someone doesn't easily fit the categories. We might regard them as odd or unusual, but we rarely use such cases to question the categories themselves.

When we "see" race like this, we are also likely to assume race is rooted in biology. The physical differences between races (skin color, facial features, eye shape, hair texture) seem so self-evident as to be beyond question. Everyday consciousness assumes these features reflect well-established biological, physiological, and genetic differences that distinguish races. Well-meaning people might struggle to avoid prejudices and stereotypes, but they are likely to see race as a biologically self-evident reality.

This is a good time to recall Peter Berger's (1963) sociological insight that things are not always what they seem. Beneath the seemingly self-evident biology of race, there are complex social, political, and cultural forces that sustain that appearance. Put differently, race is not biologically determined but rather socially constructed. This implies two seemingly contradictory things. First, racial categories are arbitrary. They have little scientific or biological foundation. They are not "real." Second, these categories nevertheless *become real* through social definitions. As W. I. Thomas noted long ago, if a situation is defined as real, it will be real in its consequences. When the definition is embedded in centuries of institutions and interactions, then race becomes as real as any social phenomenon can be. Race is an illusory biological fiction but a powerful social fact.

There are several reasons to question the biological basis of race. Human beings share almost 99 percent of our genetic composition with higher primates. Put differently, homo sapiens are only 1 to 2 percent genetically different from chimpanzees. If the genetic margin separating two species is so small, the likelihood that there will be consistent genetic differences *within* the category of homo sapiens that sort humans into genetically distinct races is highly implausible.

A second reason to doubt the biological basis of race involves the logic of categories and classification. Such logic makes sense when things fall into mutually exclusive categories based on many relevant traits. It makes less sense if there is a lot of overlap between things in supposedly separate categories. The logic is weakest when there is more individual variation within categories than the average variation between categories. And yet it is this weakest version that applies to race. On any number of physical traits, individual variations within races far exceed average differences between them. When categories persist in such situations, it is because they are based on social definitions rather than on logically compelling reasons or scientifically verifiable data.

A third reason to doubt the biological basis of race involves the history of racial typologies. Systems of racial classification have been proposed for centuries, with none of the logical consistency, cumulative advances, or increasing specificity that define scientific progress. Throughout this history, there has been major disagreement over things as basic as how many races exist. After centuries of work, the only real lesson here is that the very idea of distinguishing races in biological terms is not scientifically feasible.

A fourth reason to question the biological basis of race involves social and legal definitions. When Southern legislators defined people as "Negro" if one thirty-second of their ancestry was African, this was a social definition and not a biological fact. When Native American tribes use similar measures to determine who is a legitimate tribal member, this is also a social definition and not a biological fact. Because racial definitions vary by place, you can change your race by flying to Brazil where an unusually complex set of racial distinctions will define your race differently from the place you just left (Henslin 2005, 327). Racial definitions also change over time; consider "how the Irish became white" (Ignatiev 1995) in nineteenth-century US history.

One final example: People sometimes defend a biological conception of race based on medical conditions. In the United States, sickle-cell anemia is considered a "black disease." In reality, a predisposition to sickle-cell anemia derives from geography and evolution and not race. In places where malaria was a big threat to human health, a few people had a natural immunity. Through natural selection, they reproduced in greater numbers. However, the same factors creating the immunity also made them susceptible to sickle-cell anemia. Thus, some but not all Africans are susceptible, and some non-Africans from Mediterranean regions and South Asia are susceptible. It is difficult to see how this qualifies as a "racial" disease (Adelman 2003).

It is not physical but social facts that make races "real." This social construction of race is a historical process. People have always noted human differences, but a new discourse of race emerged during European exploration, conquest, and colonization typically dated from the "discovery" of the "New World" in 1492. Thus, Columbus's diaries refer to the "savages" he encountered. With each subsequent encounter between European colonizers and indigenous groups, the discourse of race grew to describe these "others" in racial terms (Winant 2004).

This discourse rested on two premises. The first was that races were biological realities. The second was that races existed in a hierarchy of superiority and inferiority. In these hierarchies, whites, Europeans, or some subgroup of Europeans were inevitably located at the top of the hierarchy. Despite many variations, some races (the people doing the classifying) were always superior to others (the people being classified). The very concept of race is *racist*, because beliefs about superiority and inferiority have always been part of the concept.

The reasons are not a big mystery. European colonization was often brutal and inhumane. It contradicted many social norms, religious principles, and moral imperatives of the colonizers. It required some type of legitimation of the contradiction between humane values and inhumane behavior. Thus the invention of race/racism.

Colonialism only poses a moral dilemma if people are seen as equals. The social construction of race/racism defines the colonized group as inferior or subhuman. The more their humanity is denied, the more brutality becomes acceptable. Consider that few people have qualms about the slaughter and consumption of animals because they are seen as a different species. It hardly occurs to us that this requires a justification. Some versions of racism also suggest that "others" are a different species, so the moral code of the dominant group does not apply. The same logic operates in warfare; it is easier to kill people who are seen as less than human. It is no accident that the most extreme versions of racial thinking culminate in genocide, where others are not only seen as subhuman but as a threat that must be eliminated.

The social construction of race links biology, inferiority, and racism in fateful ways. Like race, racism has many variations. It can provide justifications for enslavement and genocide. It can seek to convert others who have not yet had the benefits of "civilization." It can portray "others" as innocent children requiring protection and guidance. In every version, however, a presumption of racial inferiority is central.

The social construction of race and racism was vital in legitimizing European colonization and conquest. The United States followed suit in the exploitation of African slaves, the conquest of Native peoples, and racist relations with Latino/a and Asian populations. The timing and groups were different, but the history of US race relations mirrors the European model quite closely.

Although race is a biological fiction, there is a social logic to why this fiction arose and how it shapes contemporary society. The challenge of seeing race as a social construction is to balance the seeming contradiction that something arbitrary has been socially constructed into something as "real" as any social fact can be.

Race vs. Ethnicity

The social construction of race also becomes evident by contrasting "races" and "ethnic groups." Common sense equates race with biology and ethnicity with culture. Although the link between race and biology is problematic, the equation of ethnicity and culture is sound.

Ethnic groups are distinguished by cultural differences in language, customs, norms, values, and religious beliefs. Although their members might be geographically dispersed, ethnic groups often trace their roots to a distinctive place. Although it is culturally learned, ethnicity "feels" natural to people. Ethnocentrism is a common expression of the "naturalness" or superiority of one's group and way of doing things.

As socially constructed categories, "races" lump together many ethnic groups in the same racial category. Each of the major races typically recognized in the United States (African Americans, European Americans, Latino/a Americans, Native Americans, and Asian Americans) includes multiple ethnicities. The most obvious expression of racism is the blatant division between the dominant racial group of European Americans and all other subordinate racial groups.

A subtler expression of racism is that ethnic variations within the dominant racial group are often recognized, whereas variations within subordinate racial groups are not. Thus, in both popular consciousness and much sociological work, ethnicity really means cultural variations among European Americans (Polish, Swedish, Italian, German, etc.) whereas race lumps others into broad racial categories (blacks, Hispanics, Native Americans, etc.). This practice obscures the fact that "white" is also a socially constructed race and that other races have internal ethnic differences.

A long history of unequal treatment has made these arbitrary distinctions into powerful realities. Consider the following contrasts. Members of white ethnic groups typically entered the United States voluntarily, could sometimes conceal their ethnicity, were seen as variations on a common theme of being white, were eventually pressured to assimilate, and had at least some opportunities for integration and upward mobility. Members of racial minorities, by contrast, became part of the United States involuntarily, could rarely conceal their race, were seen as fundamentally different, were subject to strict segregation, and had few opportunities for integration and upward mobility until quite recently. Such differences suggest different models of ethnic and race relations.

For white ethnic groups, the main story is assimilation. However, the melting pot image of assimilation is misleading by implying that all groups change equally as they are "melted" into something new. In reality, there has always been a hierarchy among white ethnic groups. WASPs, or white Anglo-Saxon Protestants, have been at the top, followed by other Northern Europeans, and then Central and Southern Europeans. Assimilation has not meant blending but rather change by subordinate white ethnic groups. Consider that the United States did not create a new language through assimilation. Assimilating groups gave up native languages and adopted English. Assimilation involved a trade-off in which subordinate white ethnic groups sacrificed ethnic distinctiveness in exchange for admission into mainstream society.

Assimilation involves several stages that begin with cultural assimilation (Gordon 1964). This occurs when a newly arriving white ethnic group learns and adopts the culture of the dominant group. This is the only stage the subordinate group can control. Indeed, they might initially resist this stage, in which case assimilation will not occur. If and when they do initiate the process, control passes to the dominant group.

This is evident in the second stage of structural assimilation. This means acceptance of the subordinate group by the dominant group. Such acceptance initially occurs in secondary groups like the workplace and other public settings. It then involves accepting people as neighbors or in churches and voluntary organizations. It culminates with acceptance into primary groups like friendship networks. At each stage, the subordinate group can initiate contact, but the dominant group retains the power to accept or reject it.

Assimilation then proceeds through other stages that reflect still greater acceptance. Marital assimilation occurs when members of different groups intermarry with increasing frequency and decreasing disapproval. Identificational assimilation occurs when members of the assimilating group switch identities from their original ethnicity to their new nation. This could take generations. Immigrants might retain their Italian identity, while the next generation identifies as Italian American, and subsequent generations identify as American.

Subsequent stages include attitudinal assimilation, indicated by a reduction in prejudicial attitudes about the subordinate group. This often corresponds with behavioral assimilation, evidenced by a reduction in discrimination against members of the group. The process culminates with civic assimilation, signified by the elimination of ethnic conflict.

Although the story of assimilation seems to offer a happy ending, it is shaped by unequal power throughout. The dominant group provides the standard for what assimilation means (becoming like them), and it controls the pace. They retain their dominance because their culture becomes normative for all. The subordinate group pays the cost by relinquishing their ethnic heritage. When the costs seem worth the benefits, groups seek assimilation. Although abstract models oversimplify complex histories, this model accurately describes the assimilation of a number of white ethnic groups in the United States.

Given their different treatment, it is not surprising that the assimilationist model doesn't fit racial groups in the United States. Some insist that with enough time, racial minorities will also assimilate, but this is a dubious claim. The histories of these groups are different, the scope of discrimination is wider, and resistance to assimilation has been substantial. Moreover, the persistence of distinctive racial cultures suggests that many people in these groups would not seek assimilation even if it were possible.

Such differences drew many scholars to the model of internal colonialism to analyze racial dynamics (Omi and Winant 1994, 44–46). This model rests on an analogy between race relations within a single country and colonial relations between countries. In the analogy, the white power structure in a single country is like the colonial power, and racial minorities in that country are like colonies.

Several parallels lend credence to the analogy. Both relationships begin with forced contact, because colonial powers and white power structures use coercion to establish the relationship in the first place.

Coercion might be resisted, but the power imbalance has allowed colonial powers and white power structures to retain dominance for centuries.

A second parallel involves cultural domination. The beliefs and practices of the colonized group or the racial minority are denigrated as primitive or uncivilized. Sometimes there are efforts to convert the subordinate group to the culture of the dominant group, but in all cases the dominant group attempts to undermine the culture of the subordinate group.

Political control is a third parallel. In the colonial situation, extensive staffs of governors and administrators were sent to the colony to run its political affairs on behalf of the colonizing power. With internal colonialism, the dominant group uses both formal and informal political mechanisms to ensure a similar degree of control by the white power structure. The underrepresentation of racial minorities in positions of political power is the tip of the iceberg of political control by the dominant group.

Perhaps the most important parallel involves economic exploitation. This is the driving motive of colonial relations, whether the resources involve cheap labor, raw materials, or commodity markets. With internal colonialism, the role of racial minorities as a secondary labor force with lower pay, fewer benefits, and higher unemployment is merely one indicator of the economic exploitation that is central to this relationship.

Both traditional and internal colonialism create institutional discrimination, as social organizations and practices are built on discriminatory principles. This creates racial inequalities and racially coded practices not just in the economy and polity, but also in housing, education, health care, and criminal justice.

A final parallel is racist legitimation. Systematic beliefs about the inferiority of the subordinate group accompany both forms of colonialism. These beliefs seek to legitimate unequal treatment. At their most powerful, such racist legitimations make colonial domination seem logical, natural, and even beneficial for subordinate groups.

No analogy is perfect, but the history of US race relations more closely approximates internal colonialism than assimilationist integration. What the colonial model underscores is that race relations are rooted in conflicting interests between dominant and subordinate groups. Dominant groups who benefit have a vested interest in maintaining such relations; subordinate groups who pay the price of these relations can be expected to change them if possible.

The question of group interests requires a closer look. The dominant group is really a white power structure of elites who make economic, political, and cultural decisions with far-reaching consequences. This group most clearly benefits from exploitative race relations. The subordinate group refers to racial minorities disproportionately located toward the bottom of class and other hierarchies of inequality. This group most clearly pays the price of racial oppression.

What is less clear are the interests of "ordinary whites." They belong to the dominant racial group but are not in positions of institutional power and do not receive the same material benefits from institutional racism that dominant whites do. This status inconsistency between race and class could lead this group to define its interests in rather different ways.

On one hand, ordinary whites may primarily identify with their race. This links them to dominant whites of the same race but of a different class and distances them from racial minorities with whom they might share similar class positions. Historically, this identification allowed even poor whites to claim status on the basis of race; no matter how economically deprived they were, they were still white in a society where that meant a great deal. Ordinary whites can thus derive a social-psychological benefit from their racial identity regardless of material circumstances. But the benefits are more than psychological. Ordinary whites might also derive material benefits from discrimination against minorities if it expands their opportunities at the expense of minorities. By this logic, ordinary whites might see their interests in alignment with powerful whites despite their class differences.

On the other hand, ordinary whites might primarily identify with their class position, which would distance them from powerful whites and align them more closely with racial minorities. This suggests a class alliance across racial lines in which the material similarities of working-class whites and minorities trump racial differences. Such an alliance could challenge racial discrimination, and there is a logic for doing so. Where racial discrimination is high, it allows employers to use a divide-and-conquer strategy that ultimately undermines living standards for both whites and racial minorities (Reich 1981). Racial discrimination thus hurts minorities directly and ordinary whites indirectly. In this scenario, the collective self-interest of ordinary whites is to align with racial minorities and oppose racial discrimination.

The colonial model remains an imperfect analogy, but it frames important questions about the future of race relations. Even without clear answers, it sensitizes us to how group interests shape the social construction of race.

Forms of Discrimination

The colonial model offers a big picture of race relations that rests on many small episodes of discrimination. It is these practices, enacted on a daily basis, that sustain the social construction of race.

Discrimination ranges across many institutions and social arenas. It obviously includes the economy, employment, and political representation. It also includes differences in health, mortality, and life expectancy as a result of differential access to physical and mental health services. It includes deeply rooted patterns of residential segregation that create other problems like unequal access to education. It includes very different probabilities of becoming caught up in the criminal justice system. The effects of discrimination are cumulative, as initial disadvantages become larger inequities over time. Acts of discrimination are the building blocks of racial inequality.

The traditional view of discrimination is that prejudicial attitudes cause discriminatory behavior (Feagin and Feagin 1978). The term *prejudice* means to "prejudge" people on the basis of their group identity. Such judgments often involve negative stereotypes about an entire category of people that are attributed to all its members.

The discrimination that results from prejudice can be explicit, as when people engage in name-calling, racist behavior, or hate crimes. But it can also be subtle or covert. If someone is advertising a job or an apartment and the "wrong" applicant appears, that applicant might be told that the job has been filled or the apartment rented. When the "right" applicant comes along, the apartment or job suddenly becomes available again. In this case, intentional harm is done to someone who might not be aware that they have been the victim of discrimination. Explicit discrimination grabs headlines, but subtle, covert forms are more common and often go undetected. Indeed, it is impossible to know the full extent of discrimination, because much of it is hidden in this fashion. The common thread is a prejudicial attitude. In the traditional model, discrimination occurs when "evil motives" are translated into action.

This model implies that reducing prejudice reduces discrimination. This was part of the logic behind social policies and court decisions favoring integration. It was thought that, with more social contact between groups, people would rethink their prejudices and treat others as individuals and not stereotypes. If prejudice melted away, discrimination would, too. Although the logic seems plausible, there's a problem. By many measures, prejudice in the United States has declined, but racial discrimination has not shown a corresponding reduction.

This prompted a closer look at the traditional view. It became clear that prejudice alone might not lead to discrimination. Prejudiced people need the power to act on prejudice if it is to become discrimination. It also became more evident that discrimination can occur without prejudice. Thus, an employer might have no prejudice against certain people but still refuse to hire them out of a belief that it would drive customers away.

More generally, discrimination limits opportunities for "others" and increases them for discriminators. In such cases, discrimination simply flows from group interest without prejudice. Such discrimination without an "evil motive" can also be an unintentional by-product of institutional policies. As the limits of the traditional model became more evident, sociologists developed another way of thinking about what causes discrimination.

The result was the institutional model in which organizational practices replace prejudice as the major cause of discrimination (Feagin and Feagin 1978). The idea is that social institutions routinely discriminate against many people. In contrast to the traditional model, the institutional model sees discrimination as a normal, routine, chronic outcome rather than a sporadic one. It recognizes that most discrimination is subtle or covert, although overt institutional discrimination still happens, too. It sees discrimination as something that affects thousands if not millions of people, because it is embedded in major social institutions like the criminal justice system or the labor market. Finally, institutional discrimination can be either intentional or unintentional.

Intentional institutional discrimination occurs when there is a conscious goal of unequal treatment. It might be rooted in prejudice, racism, group interest, or some other motive. As with the traditional model, there is an "evil motive" behind such action. Unlike the traditional model, it is not individuals but large organizations that enact these behaviors. In systems of apartheid or legalized segregation, discriminatory purposes are officially proclaimed.

When segregation becomes illegal, intentions to discriminate might no longer be publicly stated but can continue to shape institutional functioning. The redlining of certain neighborhoods as poor credit risks is one example. The use of racial profiling in police practices is another example. The purging of voter registration lists is a third example of intentional, institutional discrimination (Moore 2001). While rarer hate crimes grab headlines, more routine institutional discrimination affects many more people on a daily basis.

Institutional discrimination can also be unintentional. This is indicated by effects rather than motives. Here, we must work backward from discriminatory outcomes to identify the practice or policy that produced them. An example is "side-effect" discrimination that occurs as an unintended by-product of some other practice. Imagine a university that uses an entrance exam to screen applicants. Assume the exam contains no subtle racial biases. Nonetheless, if applicants have been unequally prepared by previous schooling to perform well on this exam, it will produce discriminatory outcomes despite the best of intentions.

A related example is "past-in-present" discrimination where a current practice unwittingly perpetuates prior discrimination. Consider a layoff policy based on seniority. This is not discriminatory in itself. But to whatever extent racial minorities or women have shorter or more episodic work histories as a result of past discrimination, implementing layoffs by seniority will benefit white males and harm minorities and women despite good intentions.

Unintentional discrimination harms many but remains elusive, because it cannot be traced back to a specific person or group with evil motives. In a final twist, it is also possible for "sophisticated racists" who *do* have evil motives to use practices that do not *appear* to intentionally discriminate, knowing that such practices are difficult to identify (Feagin and Feagin 1978).

According to the traditional model, reducing discrimination requires reducing prejudice. According to the institutional model, reducing discrimination requires changing institutions. Whereas the traditional model is "optimistic" that increased social contact will reduce prejudice and discrimination, the institutional model is "pessimistic" that institutions will not simply evolve into less discriminatory behavior. Indeed, the institutional model suggests that if nothing is done, discrimination will continue indefinitely, because institutions are self-perpetuating and because some groups benefit from discriminatory practices.

This is the logic behind affirmative action. It assumes that discrimination will continue unless affirmative action is taken to change the practices that produce it. As a policy, most affirmative action programs involve voluntary efforts to increase the diversity of a pool of qualified applicants. Such policies target informal practices whereby people tend to recruit, hire, or admit people like themselves. By creating policies that require looking beyond familiar social circles when recruiting applicants, affirmative action programs have made modest contributions to reducing discriminatory outcomes.

The persistence of racial Inequality in the United States has also prompted a rethinking of the traditional focus on individual prejudice. New research has led one analyst to conclude that in the post–civil rights era, we have entered a time of "racism without racists" (Bonilla-Silva 2003). This argument downplays prejudicial attitudes by suggesting that racism rests on a material foundation of group interests and white privilege. Racism persists because whites derive substantial material benefits from it. Thus, even when whites do not have stereotypical views of minorities, they often perpetuate racism in ways that obscure its victims and beneficiaries.

Where traditional prejudice often assumed biological differences, "color-blind racism" is a more complex racial ideology emphasizing cultural differences. Four distinct frames express color-blind racism (Bonilla-Silva 2003). "Abstract liberalism" uses familiar political discourse about individual rights and equal opportunity to subtly deny structural barriers and implicitly blame victims. "Naturalism" suggests that segregation reflects freely chosen preferences of people to associate with others like them. "Cultural racism" identifies supposedly defective values, beliefs, and practices within minority cultures that are responsible for their lack of progress. Finally, "minimizing racism" acknowledges lingering problems of discrimination while emphasizing how much progress has been made. The implication is that such problems no longer require systemic solutions.

None of these frames sound overtly racist. Indeed, they sound quite reasonable by comparison. They still function, however, as an ideology legitimizing racial inequality. Color-blind racism denies or minimizes institutional barriers and uses the rhetoric of individual opportunity and cultural differences to blame minorities and excuse whites for racial inequality. The emergence of "racism without racists" illustrates how racial meanings and definitions change over time. To analyze such changes, we need to revisit the idea that race is socially constructed.

Racial Formation

The theory of racial formation sees the social construction of race as a contested process of ongoing conflict (Omi and Winant 1994; Winant 1994, 2004). "[R]ace can be defined as a *concept that signifies and symbolizes socio-political conflicts and interests in reference to different types of human bodies*" (Winant 2004, 155; italics in original). The theory of racial formation also insists on the "reality" of race despite its origins as a social construction.

The challenge is to understand the simultaneous "arbitrariness" and "reality" of race. It arises once race is decoupled from biology. This has often led social scientists to reduce race to some other kind of group and transpose their experiences onto races. This problematic response implies that if race is not about biology, then it is not about anything real. The theory of racial formation maintains that race is not about biology, but it *is* still about something very real. That reality, moreover, needs to be understood on its own terms and not reduced to something else.

One way mainstream perspectives have denied the reality of race is by equating it with ethnicity and using the ethnicity paradigm to analyze race relations. This inevitably turns the discussion back to assimilation. Despite the different histories of racial minorities and white ethnics in the United States, some maintain that racial minorities will eventually undergo the same assimilation as white ethnic groups in earlier decades and centuries. Rather than analyzing race on its own terms, this substitutes the history of ethnic assimilation as a goal for race relations.

This reduction of race to ethnicity is problematic, because it denies the unique features of racial formation (Omi and Winant 1994). It falsely transposes white experience onto nonwhites. It denies ethnic variations within racial groups by equating broad racial categories ("African American") with specific white ethnicities ("Italian"). The ethnicity paradigm also advocates individualistic solutions like upward mobility. The reduction of race to ethnicity thus obscures the distinctiveness of racial oppression and proposes unachievable or undesirable solutions to racial conflict.

An alternative is the class paradigm. This approach reduces race to class or sees the real meaning of race through a class lens. The class paradigm underscores how members of racial minorities are disproportionately located in the working class or lower socioeconomic levels. The logic is that their fates are determined more by their class position than by their racial identity. Moreover, race has been used to reinforce class exploitation when employers designate racial minorities as a secondary labor force, divide workers along racial lines, and play one group off the other to the detriment of both. In this paradigm, race is important for its role in a more fundamental set of class dynamics.

Although it illuminates intersections of race and class, this paradigm is not sufficient for understanding racial formation on its own terms. It simply assumes class is fundamental and race is secondary. Moreover, the equation of racial minorities with only one class oversimplifies race and implies that middle- or upper-class minorities face no racial barriers. "It would be more accurate to say that race and class are competing modalities by which social actors may be organized" (Omi and Winant 1994, 32). If so, the class model with its reduction of race to class is insufficient.

A third alternative is the nation paradigm or the internal colonialism model discussed earlier. As we saw, this model emphasizes differences between the assimilationist history of white ethnic groups and the quasi-colonial status of racial minorities. The metaphor of colonial relations has much to tell us about the history of race relations within the United States. As a viable model of contemporary racial formation, however, it has serious limitations.

In a postcolonial world of global mobility, equating races with geographically bounded nations is an increasingly implausible way to think about race relations. There is substantially more interracial contact in contemporary, racially diverse societies than in classic colonial relations. The nation paradigm also obscures increasingly important class differences among minorities by reducing them to a homogeneous, cultural nationality. Although more instructive than the ethnicity and class paradigms, this one also falls short as a way to understand racial formation.

The problem is that each paradigm—ethnicity, class, and nation—reduces race to something else. Each fails to see race on its own terms. The solution is to move beyond these paradigms to a model that sees race as an independently constructed social reality.

This means seeing racial formation as a process in which social, economic, and political forces determine the meaning of racial categories in a given historical context. To emphasize the importance of process, the term *racialization* is coined (Omi and Winant 1994) to refer to the extension of racial meanings to relationships that were previously not classified in such terms.

Consider slavery. Although US planters used African Americans as slave labor for centuries, the practice did not originate for racial reasons. It derived from the economic realities of plantation agriculture. In order to be profitable, such agriculture requires the cheapest possible labor. Planters first used white indentured servants from Europe and then captured Native Americans (Geschwender 1978). Neither group worked out well in the long run. Importing African slave labor gradually emerged as a later alternative in the search for cheap labor. Once the practice was institutionalized, slavery was racialized through racist beliefs and legitimations to justify the use of black slave labor by white, "God-fearing" Christians. Slavery became racialized over time. In other words, "we know that racism did not create slavery, but that slavery created racism" (Winant 2004, 84).

Institutions, practices, and beliefs become "raced" when they are shaped and understood through racial categories. Consider how many urban social problems have become "raced," as popular consciousness and media representations link race with poverty, welfare, gangs, drugs, and crime. These issues involve many more whites than nonwhites, but their racialized nature becomes a self-fulfilling prophecy. Thus, people act on racialized beliefs about crime and who commits it, leading to highly disproportionate numbers of racial minorities being suspected, arrested, convicted, and incarcerated for "raced" definitions of crime. The differential penalties for crack cocaine used by minorities and powder cocaine favored by whites is one of the more blatant examples of such racialization.

The most important raced institution is the state. In a racially divided society, the state racializes many social dynamics. "For most of U.S. history, the state's main objective in its racial policy was repression and exclusion" (Omi and Winant 1994, 81). It commenced with the Naturalization Act of 1790 that limited citizenship to free, white immigrants. The pattern continued throughout the nineteenth century as racialized policies of repression and exclusion regulated race relations. A more recent example of state power is the creation of the category "Hispanic" in 1980, racializing a new group of people and embedding the category in state policies, practices, and institutions. States and racial formation are thus closely intertwined.

Racial formation is not just about top-down power. When a collective identity is constructed and used to dominate people, that same identity will eventually become a rallying point for resistance. Whether the identity involves race, ethnicity, gender, nationality, or sexuality, domination provokes resistance. Thus, racial formation is a contested process. People fight back, and even powerful elites cannot completely control racial formation for long. It is more accurate to see racial formation—and the social construction of race more generally—as an ongoing struggle over what race means. Authorities use race to subordinate groups, and racially defined groups use it to resist subordination.

The contested quality of racial formation is evident in recent racial politics. On the eve of the civil rights movement of the 1950s and 1960s, racial formation took the form of domination. White power was the norm, backed up by coercion, segregation, exclusion, and violence. In this period, racial formation was a top-down affair, because of the overwhelming power of whites. Collective resistance appeared futile.

Social changes nevertheless created opportunities to contest racial formation. The disruptions of World War II, the partial integration of the armed forces, the mechanization of Southern agriculture, and migration from the rural South to the urban North all undermined racial domination. When the civil rights movement appeared in the 1950s, it echoed the ethnicity paradigm with themes of individualism, opportunity, and integration. That such a modest agenda provoked such a ferocious backlash is revealing. Simply asking for what whites took for granted amounted to an almost revolutionary challenge to racial domination.

The movement soon transcended the ethnicity paradigm, in part because of the resistance it encountered to its integrationist goals. But the shift was also sparked by "the rearticulation of black collective subjectivity" (Omi and Winant 1994, 98). In other words, black activists made the redefinition of racial identity a central goal. The movement *made* racial formation a two-way street by challenging static notions of race and racial hierarchy. In effect, activists reclaimed the meaning of race from a white power structure and made it their own.

These events transformed the civil rights movement. Activists adopted multiple racial paradigms and diverse political strategies. "Entrists" argued that strategic participation in elections and mainstream institutions could transform the state. Socialists tried to build class alliances across racial lines and link struggles against racism and capitalism. Nationalists encouraged a separatist response of institution building and cultural pride within minority communities. None met with complete success. The entrist, socialist, and nationalist strategies had the same shortcomings as the ethnicity, class, and nation paradigms on which they were based. Each reduced race to something else and missed the complexity of racial formation. This activism nevertheless shattered older understandings of race and put racial formation center stage (Omi and Winant 1994).

As the movement became more complex, so did the response of the raced state. In some instances, it brutally repressed militant leaders and groups that challenged its authority. More broadly, the state shifted from racial domination to racial hegemony. This meant incorporating oppositional challenges in ways that defused their transformative potential. "Under hegemonic conditions, opposition and difference are not repressed, excluded, or silenced (at least not primarily). Rather, they are inserted, often after suitable modification, within a 'modern' (or perhaps 'postmodern') social order" (Winant 1994, 29). Although hegemony might be less violent than outright domination, it amounts to a more complex system of racial control.

Racial hegemony has sparked competing racial projects on both sides. On the reactionary side, the far right still equates race with biology and advocates violence to prevent all forms of "race mixing." The new right translates old-fashioned racism into code words that are not explicitly racist but nonetheless trigger racist attitudes and actions among those who know the code. The neoconservative right uses egalitarian language to advocate individualism and reject group-oriented solutions. They use the rhetoric of a color-blind society while ignoring the historical legacy of being a color-conscious society. This is the most sophisticated defense of the white power structure. It uses familiar, liberal ideas to argue for illiberal ends. It exemplifies "racism without racists" advocating "color-blind racism" (Bonilla-Silva 2003).

On the progressive side, pragmatic liberalism appeals to group identities to mobilize political support for racially progressive policies, including affirmative action. It advocates pluralism and tolerance and attempts a difficult balancing act between advancing minority rights and maintaining social peace. Finally, radical democrats seek full acceptance of racial difference and identities in the name of autonomy. They seek democratization of the state and redistributive policies to foster racial equality (Winant 1994).

Racial formation is thus a dynamic, contested set of social and political meanings. The current diversity of racial politics—consisting of at least five distinct and competing racial projects—testifies to the fluidity of racial formation and the social construction of race.

The Construction of Whiteness

It is intriguing that whites attribute "race" to "people of color" but don't see "white" as a "color." It's as if race applies to people who differ from the norm but not the group that is the norm. Given this, it is important to turn the microscope back on the dominant group and its construction of whiteness.

Like other socially constructed racial categories, whiteness emerged historically. Consider how "the Irish became white" over decades of conflict and eventual assimilation in the United States. More pointedly, this is the story of "how the Catholic Irish, an oppressed race in Ireland, became part of an oppressing race in America" (Ignatiev 1995, 1). When Irish immigrants first arrived in the United States, they were perceived as an inferior race by Anglo-Saxon powers on both sides of the Atlantic. However, rather than joining with other subordinate races, the Irish distanced themselves from minorities and aligned with whites. They pursued the classic assimilationist trade-off: "In becoming white the Irish ceased to be Green" (Ignatiev 1995, 3). This suggests that assimilation means moving toward the dominant group and away from minorities, because the dominant group is defined precisely by its distance from racial minorities. Until a group made both moves, assimilation was unlikely.

The Irish example fits a broader template of how whiteness was created through an amalgamation of initially diverse ethnicities. This history falls into three periods (Jacobson 1998, 13–14). From the founding of the country into the mid-nineteenth century, citizenship was confined to "free white" immigrants, implicitly meaning Anglo-Saxon and sometimes other Northern European peoples. From the mid-nineteenth century to the early twentieth century, immigration from Southern, Central, and Eastern Europe challenged the equation of whiteness and Northern European descent. During this period, a complex racial politics initially defined these immigrants as inferior races at the same time that they sought a broadening of the definition of "white" to include them. It has only been since the 1920s that ethnic differences were downplayed and a more generic white identity was forged. This period "redrew the dominant racial configuration along the strict, binary line of white and black, creating Caucasians where before had been so many Celts, Hebrews, Teutons, Mediterraneans, and Slavs" (Jacobson 1998, 14).

By the mid-twentieth century, whiteness became the dominant racial norm. This proved short-lived, as "it is no longer possible to assume a 'normalized' whiteness, whose invisibility and relatively monolithic character signify immunity from political or cultural challenge" (Winant 2004, 50). As race-based social movements recast their own racial subjectivity, white identity also became more self-conscious.

As white dominance was challenged, it triggered "grievances of the privileged." Some whites claimed they were under attack "simply for their race." Others decried a world in which minorities seemed to get advantages withheld from whites through "reverse discrimination." Still other whites lamented the lack of a distinct and vivid white culture they could identify with just as other races identified with theirs. Such defensive responses imply that although whites are still dominant, such dominance can no longer be taken for granted.

These responses also belie the ongoing privileges of the dominant group. White privilege means that despite recent challenges to the racial order, it continues to be organized in ways that benefit the dominant group. Such privilege is often invisible to those who benefit, while being highly visible to those who pay the price.

This is nicely captured in Peggy McIntosh's (2005) efforts to teach about male privilege in women's studies courses. Her female students quickly grasped the concept and readily supplied examples. Her male students conceded that women faced certain disadvantages but denied their male privilege. To understand this denial, McIntosh examined her own dual status as a white woman. As a woman, she could readily see male privilege. As a white, she had difficulty seeing her racial privilege, just as men had difficulty seeing male privilege. The broader pattern is that privileged groups rarely recognize their own privileges and perceive any challenge to them as victimization. Such complaints are not simply disingenuous; they reflect a real inability to see how whiteness and maleness continue conferring privileges even in a social order undergoing challenge and reformulation.

These privileges come in two categories. "Unearned advantages" are "positive" privileges that should not be abolished but made available to all. The privilege of not being a crime suspect simply on the basis of one's race is an unearned advantage for whites that should ideally be an unearned entitlement for all. "Conferred dominance" involves "negative" privileges that need to be abolished to create racial equality. Discrimination that benefits dominant groups at the expense of subordinate ones fits this type; it should be abolished in any society seeking racial equality (McIntosh 2005).

These are now the goals of a "new abolitionist racial project." Proponents of this movement identify white privilege as the lynchpin of white supremacy and see rejection of privilege by whites as essential to creating a just racial order. Advocates put a positive spin on the epithet "race traitor" by countering that "treason to whiteness is loyalty to humanity" (Winant 2004, 63). As this racial project unfolds alongside others described earlier, it is difficult to deny that we are in a period of highly contested racial formation.

Understanding race requires looking beyond taken-for-granted appearances. It also requires a multilayered analysis of domination. Critical sociology is tailor-made for both tasks. It illuminates both the social construction of race and the challenges seeking to deconstruct racial hierarchies in the name of a more egalitarian society.

References

Adelman, Larry. 2003. *Race: The Power of an Illusion.* Videodisc, California Newsreel.
Berger, Peter. 1963. *Invitation to Sociology.* New York: Doubleday.
Bonilla-Silva, Eduardo. 2003. *Racism without Racists.* Lanham, MD: Rowman & Littlefield.
Du Bois, W. E. B. 1903/1989. *The Souls of Black Folk.* New York: Bantam Books.
Feagin, Joe, and Clairece Booher Feagin. 1978. *Discrimination American Style.* Englewood Cliffs, NJ: Prentice Hall.
Geschwender, James. 1978. *Racial Stratification in America.* Dubuque, IA: Wm. C. Brown.
Gordon, Milton. 1964. *Assimilation in American Life.* New York: Oxford University Press.
Henslin, James. 2005. *Sociology.* 7th ed. Boston: Allyn and Bacon.
Ignatiev, Noel. 1995. *How the Irish Became White.* New York: Routledge.
Jacobson, Matthew. 1998. *Whiteness of a Different Color.* Cambridge, MA: Harvard University Press.
McIntosh, Peggy. 2005. "White Privilege and Male Privilege." In *Great Divides,* ed. Thomas Shapiro, 300–307. New York: McGraw-Hill.
Moore, Michael. 2001. *Stupid White Men.* New York: Regan.
Myrdal, Gunnar. 1944. *An American Dilemma.* New York: Harper and Row.
Omi, Michael, and Howard Winant. 1994. *Racial Formation in the United States.* 2nd ed. New York: Routledge.
Reich, Michael. 1981. *Racial Inequality.* Princeton, NJ: Princeton University Press.
Winant, Howard. 1994. *Racial Conditions.* Minneapolis: University of Minnesota Press.
———. 2004. *The New Politics of Race.* Minneapolis: University of Minnesota Press.

Discussion Topics

1. What does it mean by "race is socially constructed"?
2. What are the five arguments advanced by the author to negate the validity of biological foundation of race?
3. What are the steps of assimilation for white ethnic groups described in the text?
4. What is the main idea of this article?

White Privilege

Richard J. Gonzalez

Richard J. Gonzales, "White Privilege," *Raza Rising: Chicanos in North Texas*, pp. 115-123, 299-300. Copyright © 2016 by University of North Texas Press. Reprinted with permission.

Editor's Introduction

This article titled "White Privilege" by Richard Gonzales focuses on the advantages associated with being white, not available to racial minority group members. This article was included in this reader because it explains the implications of white privileges for both white and other groups such as African Americans, Latinos, Asian Americans, Native Americans, etc. After reading this article, you will understand the relationship between "white privilege" and systemic inequality and explain the importance of promoting racial diversity.

This Mexican transformation for even a short time may be near impossible to discard for those holding white superiority attitudes. This piece stirred the ire of several readers. I find the race question a taboo subject often resulting in hurt feelings, miscommunication, and guilt. Given the pride that many white Southerners have for the Confederacy and the Alamo, any talk about racial oppression roils them to heated defensiveness. History is still with us in today's stringent racial divisions. The 2012 Republican and Democratic Conventions offered stark contrasts of the racial make up of the delegates. What would Abraham Lincoln have said to see his party's nearly all white delegation?

Robert Jensen's book, *The Heart of Whiteness: Confronting Race, Racism and White Privilege*, courageously exposes the minds and hearts of whites benefiting from what he calls a "white-supremacist society." Jensen was not a minority radical spouting Anglo-blue-eyed-devil rhetoric and a call for racial conflict. He described himself as "white as white gets in the United States of America. I am a white-bred, white-bread white boy."[1] He was also an associate professor of journalism at the University of Texas in Austin.

His book addresses white middle-class citizens who deny or ignore the existence of white privilege and disparities in economic, social, and educational levels between whites and ethnic minorities.

Jensen acknowledged that the overt white supremacist activities in America's past—the antics of Klansmen and decades of Jim Crow laws—diminished considerably during the twentieth century. However, he asserted that most whites have never accepted, or have ignored, the historical reality that white supremacy was founded on the killing of millions of Indians, the seizure of their lands, the enslavement of millions of Africans, and wars of expansion into the Third World.

Jensen asked that whites look into their hearts. Like Marlow in Joseph Conrad's *Heart of Darkness*, whites should brave a journey of self-discovery to confront their fears of blacks and Mexican Americans and overcome the evils of racist attitudes and institutions. Otherwise, how can the United States take the high moral ground with dictators and terrorists?

As a personal example, Jensen said that he worked and studied hard to rise from his North Dakota lower-middle-class background to earn his doctorate in journalism and land a job at a prestigious university. He knew that, along the way, he received a significant boost from the fact that he grew up in an almost all-white city, attended all-white schools, had white bosses, and never believed that his failures were because he was white.

He recognized that merit was only part of the reason for his success; his white status in a society that valued whites over ethnic minorities gave him the edge. It was this advantage that he asked his fellow whites to examine and work to eliminate.

Jensen acknowledged that dismantling racism would mean a loss of power, material wealth, and status for whites. An underlying white fear is that with a growing Chicano population and political strength, Mexican Americans will gain governmental and social control. Then a white minority might find that it might receive the same treatment it has doled out over the years.

In a brutally honest story, he talked about a panel presentation he made with Les Payne, a Pulitzer Prize-winner and associate managing editor at *Newsday*. Payne was more experienced, had won more awards, written more serious pieces and spoke publicly better than Jensen. Yet as he sat next to the black journalist, Jensen felt superior. When Payne explained to the audience that he had to struggle to overcome feelings of inferiority from his Southern upbringing to succeed in school and professional life, Jensen felt despair. He had thought that he was one of the "good" whites. He realized that despite his political activism and writings on behalf of racial equality, he hadn't shaken his feelings of superiority.

This attitude of white superiority in history, language, and action forced Payne and other ethnic minorities to feel and act inferior. Jensen's—and other whites'—personal recognition of this ideology is the first step to the white superiority cure. Jensen admitted that he was an angry man who wished more middle-class whites would become indignant. They need to howl at an ideology that forced them to exchange their political souls for material affluence. But not all have sold out.

The League of Women Voters' initiative to persuade the John Peter Smith Health Network board in Fort Worth, Texas, to extend non-emergency healthcare to the undocumented was a noble example of middle-class whites fighting for justice. No doubt they risked the loss of support from white, politically conservative

---

1. Robert Jensen, *The Heart of Whiteness: Confronting Race, Racism and White Privilege* (San Francisco: City Lights, 2007), xiii.

organizations by taking up this cause, but they accepted their moral responsibility to ensure that a healthcare system with a $37.6 million surplus provides care to all sick people in Tarrant County.

As Jensen concluded, the White People's Burden was to civilize themselves and their institutions.

If we are to compete successfully in the global markets, then America must draw on the genius of all of its people. At my last job at Tarrant County Juvenile Services, I tried in vain to motivate the senior managers to instill staff training on cultural and linguistic competency. I had done extensive research in the field, written essays about it, and knew personally the results of insensitive cultural treatment. The senior managers listened with blank looks, engaged in desultory discussions, and never committed to the effort. After I was demoted from the senior management rank for bogus financial reasons, the cultural competency efforts were revitalized. Although I was asked to participate in the development, I was eventually asked not to take a role in the planning committee because of my outspokenness. It seemed that some whites were offended by my directness in explaining that they enjoyed white privilege as a result of historical, institutional racist practices. An elected official in Tarrant County shared that others in the organization treated this office holder with actions reflective of colonialism.

Fortunately, whites like Luke Visconti understand the importance of direct, frank dialogue about race in the work setting. Readers of DiversityInc.com enjoyed a regular dose of Luke Visconti's column, "Ask the White Guy." As co-founder of DiversityInc, he made no excuses for the column title or answering sensitive questions about workplace diversity.

Visconti said he was aware that there were large groups—ethnic minorities, women, the disabled and gays—competing on unlevel playing fields. Visconti exhorted corporations that seek success to find and keep the best talent from a larger pool of candidates.

It worked: The top fifty companies in DiversityInc's 2006 diversity rankings showed superior financial performance. Over a ten-year period, they outperformed the Nasdaq by 28.2 percent, the Standard & Poor's 500 by 24.8 percent and the Dow Jones Industrial Average by 22.4 percent. Verizon Communications/Wireless, Consolidated Edison of New York, and the Coca-Cola Company topped the DiversityInc 2006 ranking.[2]

In 2015, the top ten companies for diversity were Novartis Pharmaceuticals Corporation, Kaiser Permanente, PricewaterhouseCoopers, EY, Sodexo, MasterCard, AT&T, Prudential Financial, Johnson & Johnson, and Procter & Gamble.[3]

If we believe that talent is distributed among all social groups equally, then it follows that education, mentoring, opportunity, and inclusion will foster the skills in minorities, women, gays and the disabled to excel.

The star performers don't necessarily look or sound like the traditional white male executive or manager.

Visconti acknowledged that for some whites, diversity can be disconcerting. He said most whites don't even think about race on a regular basis. Why should they? "Being white means you never have to think about race; you never consider that your application to college will be treated differently; that the police officer stopping you isn't out for anything more than how fast you were going; that your boss didn't really mean to

2. TJ. Degroat, "A Top-Down Approach: 2006 Top 50 Companies For Diversity," *DiversityInc.Magazine,* (June 2006): 34, http://www.diversityinc-digital.com/diversityincmedia/200606#pg34.

3. "DiversityInc Top 50," DiversityInc.com, http://www.diversityinc.com/the-diversityinc-top-50-companies-for-diversity-2015/

insult you to your core when he said 'You're so articulate' or dismiss your entire being by saying 'I don't care if you're Black, Yellow, Brown, Green or Polka-Dot,'" he said.[4]

But some minorities who struggle to live up to an unwritten expectation that they need to perform better than most on the job worry about it. The unspoken fear is that peers and subordinates might believe that the only reason that they landed a managerial job was because of the need to fill an affirmative action quota or to stave off accusations of discrimination. Some grow weary of the photo ops and tagging along to business meetings to smile and nod. Others grow tired of hearing how smart they sound, yet wield no real power. And if they don't make it—well, that proves that they just don't have the right stuff.

As the white workforce ages and a youthful minority workforce grows, especially among Mexican Americans, progressive organizations must examine their inclusion strategies. Customers and employees speaking a variety of languages, with different tastes and cultures, require organizations to reassess their work cultures.

Politicians, conservatives and Horacio Alger Chicanos can bemoan the changes in US culture, but businesses should take a hard look at how they respond to diversity if they hope to compete in a global economy where foreign rivals learn English, Spanish, and any other language and customs to take American customers' bucks.

Is it really any surprise that Toyota will soon surpass General Motors in world car sales? Why was it startling to see Chicano actors speaking Spanish in a Super Bowl commercial in February 2006 advertising the Toyota Camry Hybrid?

Douglas M. West, former senior vice president and chief administrative officer for Toyota Motor Sales USA, said, "at Toyota, our work toward creating a culture of inclusion is in harmony with and supports our vision to become the most successful and respected car company in America."[5] *Se habla dinero* at Toyota.

I look forward to a Chicano entrepreneur driving a Toyota and writing a column called "Ask the Brown Guy."

Another way to spread inclusion is to have our media moguls showcase more Mexican Americans on the wide screen. The paucity of Chicano roles distorts the image of American culture and leaves Chicanos wondering when they became invisible.

Minorities in *Minority Report*, a Steven Spielberg movie set in Washington D.C. in 2054, are African-Americans who mutter a few lines and are props for Tom Cruise, the tragic-hero, in his quest to prevent crimes foretold. In a city currently bursting with African-Americans and Mexican Americans, Spielberg invited us to imagine the future capital populated by witty, hip whites who've invented whiz-bang cars and planes, thought projectors and eye-popping technology. The few minorities of the future were foils for brilliant white scientists, G-men, cops, and genetically engineered seers.

Spielberg portrayed Cruise, Brad Pitt, and Tom Hanks as "everyman" characters whom Americans can easily like and therefore pay to sit watching for hours in the dark. White men admired and white women

---

4. Luke Visconti, "Ask the White Guy," *Diversityinc.Magazine*, http://www.diversityinc.com/ask-the-white-guy/ask-the-white-guydiversity-and-inclusion-apologize.

5. Douglas M. West, Introduction to *The Inclusion Breakthrough: Unleashing the Real Power of Diversity*, by Frederick A. Miller and Judith H. Katz (San Francisco: Berrett-Koehler Publishers, Inc., 2002).

swooned, but I venture that Latinos preferred a Nick Gonzales, Michael Peña, or Andy García to outfight, outclass, and outwit their foes and fates.

Not until the latest Star Wars saga did George Lucas decide to include a Latino, Jimmy Smits, as a minor, costumed character, in his opus of the dark vs. light. Animals, mechanical sharks, dinosaurs, aliens, androids, cartoons, and the Muppets have had more screen and screech time than Chicano/Chicana actors.

In the City of Angels by the Pacific, populated by ethnic minorities who outnumber whites, movie moguls cast an America of the whites, for the whites and by the whites. They spun reels of unrealistic pathos and bathos in which the stars are clever, Aryan-looking men and women and the few Mexican Americans are cooks, cons, crazies, or cowards.

Frances Negrón-Muntaner and others from Columbia University's Center for the Study of Ethnicity and Race published their study "The Latino Media Gap: A Report on the State of Latinos in US Media" in June 2014. Despite the increase in the US Latino population, their presence in the movies and television as actors, writers, directors, producers and CEOs was decreasing. Their findings included: Latino men have disappeared as leading actors while Latina actors have increased their presence slightly; Stereotypes restrict opportunities and perceptions; Latino presence in TV programming and movies is limited; Latino news anchors and producers is low. Negrón-Muntaner wrote "The current data suggests persistent and unchecked job discrimination in a major US industry. The relegation of Latinos similarly deprives media consumers of innovative perspectives at a moment of rapid industry and demographic change."[6]

From a moral viewpoint, perhaps we needed a separate ethnic rating system to prepare the viewer for the depth of ethnic mendacity: "W" for white actors in power roles surrounded by sycophantic minorities; "AA" for movies depicting Ebonics-speaking African-American actors, with whites as cruel oppressors (beware of blaxploitation themes); "L" for Latino actors in Spanglish-speaking roles, mainly associated with drug-dealing, gang-banging, and prisons; "A" for Asian films in which the characters are martial arts experts, extremely polite and wise; "AI" for American Indians, noble warriors of the past with an affinity for white men's scalps, who in the modern era live on reservations and can't handle the firewater.

According to survey research by the Tomás Rivera Policy Institute involving 4,000 Latino actors, all members of the Screen Actors Guild, 73 percent thought a Latino surname was a disadvantage.[7]

Thirty percent responding to the survey said that they were expected to speak poor English or to speak with an accent. Two-thirds said that they lost roles because they didn't fit the Chicano stereotype of a mestizo.[8] Ironically, Mexican casting directors seemed to prefer blond, fair-skinned Latinas in their novelas, or soap operas.

When confronted with the near-invisibility of Chicanos in starring roles, producers and directors respond that economics, not racism, dictated the movies and actors selected. After all, the fair faces of Robert Redford, Julia Roberts, Nicole Kidman, and Russell Crowe generated millions in revenue.

L.A. Chicano activists of a grassroots organization known as the Premiere Weekend Club countered with

6. Frances Negrón-Muntaner, Chelsea Abbas, Luis Figueroa, and Samuel Robson, "The Latino Media Gap: A Report on the State of Latinos in US Media," Center for the Study of Ethnicity and Race, Columbia University, 2014:1-2, http://www.columbia.edu/cu/cser/downloads/Latino_Media_Gap_Report.pdf

7. Harry Pachon, "Still Missing: Latinos In and Out of Hollywood," The Tomas Rivera Policy Institute (May 2000): 4, http://www.trpi.org/PDFs/missing_in_action.pdf

8. Ibid., 5.

their own research showing that movies with positive portrayals of Mexican Americans were profitable. Motion pictures like *La Bamba, McFarland, USA, Spare Parts, Like Water For Chocolate, Mi Familia, El Mariachi, EL Norte, Stand and Deliver,* and *Born in East L.A.* earned millions for investors.[9]

They reported that, based on data from the Motion Picture Association of America, Latinos generated about 15 percent of domestic box office monies, or more than $1 billion in revenue.[10] As the Chicano population swells, so do the movie-attending audiences and revenue. From a strictly economic viewpoint, it's risky business for producers to bypass the Chicano movie market.

Spielberg should have listened to his film's central message: The future may be technologically dazzling, but primal passions still shape our destiny. Before making another movie, Spielberg should exchange his irises for Chicano eyes, walk Olvera Street or East Los Angeles and meet the real people of the future. If so, he'll envision a silver screen of Latino actors performing to the artistic heights of the great performers of the past: Anthony Quinn, Ramón Novarro, Rita Moreno, Dolores Del Río, Katy Jurado, Rita Hayward, and Mario Moreno (Cantinflas).

From a man in brown, that's my minority report.

9. "Latino Films Make Money: Consistently Performing Well at the Box Office," Premiere Weekend Club, http://www.premiereweekend.org/profitsb.html.
10. "Did You Know?" *Premiere Weekend Club*, http://www.premiereweekend.org/didyouknowb.html.

Discussion Topics

1. What is the main idea of this article?
2. What are the implications of white privilege for whites?
3. What are some potential effects of racial diversity on the top fifty companies that Diversity Inc. reported on in this article?
4. Why is it important to have a racially diverse workplace?

What Is White Privilege?

Richard P. Amico

Richard P. Amico, "What Is White Privilege?," *Anti-Racist Teaching*, pp. 1-17. Copyright © 2015 by Taylor & Francis Group. Reprinted with permission.

Editor's Introduction

This article titled "What Is White Privilege?" by Richard Amico explains the concept of "white privilege" and discusses the advantages that white people enjoy. The article was included in this reader because it discusses aspects of white privileges which white have a hard time acknowledging. After reading this article, you will be able to establish a link between "white privilege," racism, discrimination and attendant social problems for minority groups.

White privilege is a form of domination, hence it is a *relational* concept.[1] It positions one person or group over another person or group. It is a concept of racial domination that enables us to see this relationship from the perspective of those who benefit from such domination. Traditionally in the United States, racial domination has been portrayed as discrimination against people of color—that is, from the perspective of those who are disadvantaged by such domination. But you can't have one without the other—you can't have racial domination and disadvantage without racial dominators who are advantaged. This is the insight of Peggy McIntosh's seminal paper "White Privilege and Male Privilege: A Personal Account of Coming to See Correspondences through Work in Women's Studies": "As a white person, I

---

1. Gary R. Howard, *We Can't Teach What We Don't Know: White Teachers, Multiracial Schools,* 2nd ed. (New York: Teachers College Press, 2006), 67.

realized I had been taught about racism as something which puts others at a disadvantage, but had been taught not to see one of its corollary aspects, white privilege, which puts me at an advantage."[2]

As a white male, I know what Peggy McIntosh is talking about. What we are taught to see and not see shapes our view of the world—of what is real. My education through high school, college, and graduate school never included any discussion of white privilege and only discussed racism as a historical phenomenon, something that happened to people of color centuries ago.

Personal Anecdote

I remember watching television with my family in September 1957. I was ten years old and in the fifth grade. President Dwight D. Eisenhower had ordered the 101st Airborne Division of the US Army to Little Rock, Arkansas, to enforce the integration of Central High School and protect the nine black students enrolled that fall. My parents, like many whites at that time, thought that these black students were "troublemakers" who were trying to force themselves on people who didn't want to associate with them. They saw these black students as encroachers on "regular" people's freedom of association. I remember seeing the faces of all the angry white parents standing behind the line of troops and shouting racial epithets at these nine black children. I remember my parents making derogatory comments about African Americans that day and for many years after and telling me that people should "stick to their own kind." They made it clear to me that they did not approve of integration and wanted me to keep my distance from blacks. Three years after the *Brown v. Board of Education* decision, "separate but equal" was the prevailing norm in the world I inhabited. I believed my parents and parroted their views throughout my childhood—their view was my view. And white privilege was not even on the radar.

The natural question that arises from the introduction of the concept of white privilege is, What exactly are these advantages that white people enjoy at the expense and to the detriment of people of color? Since we whites have not been taught to see such advantages, we generally do not. Peggy McIntosh came to see some of her advantages as a white person through first understanding some of her disadvantages as a woman and observing men's inability or unwillingness to recognize their advantages as men: "I have often noticed men's unwillingness to grant that they are over-privileged in the curriculum, even though they may grant that women are disadvantaged. Denials, which amount to taboos, surround the subject of advantages, which men gain from women's disadvantages. These denials protect male privilege from being fully recognized, acknowledged, lessened, or ended."[3]

Again, as a male I know what Peggy McIntosh is talking about. For much of my life I believed that "it's a man's world" because we men deserve to be on top. We are simply better at certain things than women. The idea that we men are privileged was, in my view, "sour grapes" from women who couldn't make the grade. This unwillingness to acknowledge any male privilege is deeply connected to the American myth of meritocracy, which maintains that all advantage in society is based on merit. Some have more than others because they have earned it through hard work, perseverance, and right living. And conversely, those who have less have

2. Peggy McIntosh, "White Privilege and Male Privilege: A Personal Account of Coming to See Correspondences through Work in Women's Studies" (Working Paper 189, Wellesley College, 1988).

3. Ibid., 1.

only themselves to blame. The idea that even some of my advantages are unearned and undeserved and are a function of my status as a male was in my mind, for many years, preposterous and unfounded. But the idea that we live in a meritocracy in the United States is a myth because it has proven to be inconsistent with sociological fact. Structured inequality would be impossible in a meritocracy. Those of every "race," ethnicity, and gender who worked hard, persevered, and lived right would excel in a meritocracy. Yet we have serious structured inequalities along racial, ethnic, and gender lines.[4]

White privilege and male privilege have the common feature that, in both cases, those who are advantaged cannot see their own advantage, although they can see that others are disadvantaged, and those who are privileged tend to fault those who are disadvantaged for their disadvantage. Conversely, those who are disadvantaged can see that they are disadvantaged and that some are advantaged, and they can see that both their disadvantage and the advantages of those who are privileged are unearned and undeserved. Ironically, then, those who enjoy privileges are epistemically disadvantaged, while those who are disadvantaged are epistemically advantaged! Hence, listening to someone who is epistemically advantaged due to her social disadvantage makes sense. The following anecdote illustrates my point.

Personal Anecdote

Many years ago I was settling down with my partner to enjoy a TV movie at home. It was an action-adventure film, and I was excited to watch it. As we began to watch, my partner started to get agitated and said to me, "I am so sick and tired of watching television! Every time I turn it on, all I see is women being victimized, women being brutalized, women being assaulted sexually, women portrayed as stupid, helpless bimbos, as sexual objects! I can't watch another minute!" With that, she left the room. A lot of thoughts went through my mind all at once, and they were all dismissive and condescending: What's the matter with her? Is she having her period? Did she have a bad day? Something must have happened because this is a really good movie. I am embarrassed to reveal those thoughts even now. But although I discounted everything she said, I started to click the remote control (of course, I was always the one to hold the remote, to control the TV) to see what was on other channels. To my surprise I found quite a few programs showing women just the way my partner had described! At that point I could not have admitted this to her, but I did let it sink in. I wondered why I had never noticed it before. I am an educated, observant person; yet I was oblivious to what was obvious to her. That is how I understand epistemic disadvantage and advantage now.

Through comparative analysis with male privilege, Peggy McIntosh reached the following explanation of white privilege: "I have come to see white privilege as an invisible package of unearned assets, which I can count on cashing in each day, but about which I was 'meant' to remain oblivious. White privilege is like an invisible weightless backpack of special provisions, maps, passports, codebooks, visas, clothes, tools and blank checks."[5] After months of reflection McIntosh was able to list forty-six such advantages she enjoys as a white person. They include items like the following:

---

4. See Adalberto Aguirre Jr. and David V. Baker, *Structured Inequality in the United States: Critical Discussions on the Continuing Significance of Race, Ethnicity, and Gender,* 2nd ed. (Upper Saddle River, NJ: Pearson Prentice Hall, 2008).
5. Peggy McIntosh, "White Privilege: Unpacking the Invisible Backpack," *Peace and Freedom* (July/August 1989).

#13. Whether I use checks, credit cards, or cash, I can count on my skin color not to work against the appearance of financial reliability.

#15. I do not have to educate my children to be aware of systemic racism for their own daily physical protection.

#21. I am never asked to speak for all the people of my racial group.

#25. If a traffic cop pulls me over or if the IRS audits my tax return, I can be sure I haven't been singled out because of my race.[6]

For those of us who enjoy one form of privilege or another (e.g., race, gender, sexual orientation, socioeconomic class, ability, age, religion), why don't we feel privileged? As sociologist Allan Johnson explains, privilege attaches itself to social categories, not individuals.[7] So society values whiteness, not a particular person who is white; it values maleness, not a particular person who is male; it values heterosexuality, not any particular person who is heterosexual, and so forth. Hence, the perception that someone is white or male or heterosexual may be sufficient for that person to receive the privilege attached to that social category. And conversely, the perception that someone belongs to a social category that is disvalued in society may cause that person to receive the disadvantages attached to that category. So paradoxically, perception is more important than truth when it comes to who is advantaged and who is disadvantaged in society. How others perceive me may determine whether I am stopped by the police while driving my car, whether I am hired for a job, or whether I am followed in a department store by security. Because privilege does not attach itself to individuals for who they are, I may be privileged without feeling privileged. If I were a king, I would be privileged and feel privileged for who I was. But the kind of privilege we are talking about here is not like that. And the same holds true for disadvantage. Society disvalues certain social categories, and disadvantage attaches to them. Hence, it is possible to be disadvantaged without feeling disadvantaged.

Perception and Truth

Earlier I said that perception is more important than truth, and that may have given the impression that there is a truth to the matter of whether the social category actually applies to a particular individual. Is the individual actually white? Well, the question itself presupposes that there is such a thing as actual whiteness, and there is not. We have learned from biology and history that "race" is a social construction; it is not a biologically real category. There is as much or more genetic variation between any two individuals of the same so-called race as there is between two individuals of two different so-called races.[8] In the late seventeenth century, wealthy, landowning, Christian men who invaded this land created the category of "race" based on

6. McIntosh, "White Privilege and Male Privilege."

7. Allan G. Johnson, *Privilege, Power, and Difference,* 2nd ed. (New York: McGraw-Hill, 2006), 34–37.

8. See Christine Herbes-Sommers, dir., *Race: The Power of an Illusion,* Part 1 (San Francisco: California Newsreel, 2003), for an explanation of the work of evolutionary biologist Richard Lewontin, or see R. C. Lewontin, "The Apportionment of Human Diversity," *Evolutionary Biology* 6 (1972): 381–398.

superficial differences in skin tone and hair texture for the purpose of exploitation and permanent domination.[9] These men created social systems and institutions (e.g., laws, rules, practices, value systems) to reify "racial" difference and continually empower some and disempower others on the basis of this constructed "difference." Hence "race" is a social rather than a biological reality. Many of the social categories surrounding privilege and oppression—gender, sexual orientation, socioeconomic class, ability, and disability—are largely social constructions.

To be sure, there are real differences between people, but we define the social categories, and we assign meaning to those differences. For example, on the face of it, it would seem that nothing is more clear-cut than whether a person is male or female, whether a baby is born a boy or a girl. After all, that is the first question most ask when a baby is born: Is it a boy or a girl? But the experiences of many people born intersexed have led us to understand that whether someone is born a boy or a girl is a matter of definition. Some are born neither. Some are born both. Some simply defy such categorization and force us to realize that this scheme of categorization is a human invention. Some cultures recognize that a binary system of categorization is inadequate and have multiple categories within which to understand gender. Both sex and gender are more complicated than our binary categories allow.[10]

Systemic Privilege: What Does It Look Like?

Understanding the relational nature of white privilege helps us see that white racism and white privilege are two sides of the same coin. Whereas some are undeservedly disadvantaged because they are perceived to be of color, others are undeservedly advantaged because they are perceived to be white. Here are a few examples to illustrate the ubiquity and systemic nature of white privilege.[11]

The Job Market

Tim Wise writes that a 2003 Milwaukee study

> had young black and white male job testers who were otherwise equally qualified apply for jobs in the metropolitan area. Some of the whites and some of the blacks claimed to have criminal records and to have served eighteen months in prison for possession of drugs with intent to distribute, while other whites and blacks presented themselves as having no prior criminal convictions. Whites without records received callbacks for interviews thirty-four percent of the time, compared to only fourteen percent for blacks, and whites with criminal

9. See Ronald Takaki, *A Different Mirror: A History of Multicultural America*, rev. ed. (New York: Little, Brown and Co., 2008); Theodore W. Allen, *The Invention of the White Race*, Vol. 2: *The Origin of Racial Oppression in Anglo-America* (New York: Verso, 1997); Richard Delgado and Jean Stefancic, eds., *Critical White Studies* (Philadelphia: Temple University Press, 1997).

10. See Anne Fausto-Sterling, "The Five Sexes: Why Male and Female Are Not Enough," *Sciences* (March/April 1993): 20–24; Anne Fausto-Sterling, "The Five Sexes Revisited," in *Women's Voices, Feminist Visions,* ed. Susan Shaw and Janet Lee, 5th ed. (New York: McGraw-Hill, 2012), 121–125.

11. In fact I provide my students with a twenty-three-page, single-spaced, documented handout listing hundreds of such examples.

records received callbacks seventeen percent of the time, compared to only five percent for blacks with records. So whites without records were 2.4 times more likely than comparable blacks to receive an interview, and whites with criminal records were 3.4 times more likely to receive a callback than similar blacks. So, at seventeen percent, whites with prior drug convictions were more likely than blacks without records (at fourteen percent) to be called back for an interview, even when all other credentials were equal.[12]

This study reveals the systemic nature of white privilege and white racism. Without the study a person looking for a job would only know that he either did or did not get a callback. From his experience alone, he would have no evidence that he was either privileged or disadvantaged because of his perceived race. The systemic nature of white privilege and white racism explains, in part, why those who receive such privilege are not aware of it and why those who are disadvantaged may not know it. From the outside it simply looks like one person got a callback and another did not. White privilege is embedded in the values, beliefs, and practices of those who are hiring. Even though it is illegal to discriminate in employment on the basis of perceived race, the practice is alive and well, but hidden. Only those explicitly looking for evidence of white privilege will find it.

Housing

In December 2011 Bank of America's Countrywide Financial agreed to pay $335 million to settle a lawsuit claiming it discriminated against black and Latino borrowers. The Justice Department alleged that Countrywide charged a higher interest rate on the mortgages of more than two hundred thousand minority borrowers, despite the fact that their creditworthiness was comparable to whites that received lower rates. The Justice Department called it the "largest residential fair lending settlement in history." According to the Center for Responsible Lending, borrowers of color are twice as likely to receive subprime loans than their white counterparts, and once the housing bubble burst, borrowers of color were more than twice as likely to lose their homes as white households.[13]

Subprime loans are five times more likely in black neighborhoods than in white neighborhoods. In predominantly black neighborhoods, high-cost subprime lending accounted for 51 percent of home loans in 1998—compared with only 9 percent in predominately white areas. Comparable 1993 figures were 8 percent in black neighborhoods and 1 percent in white neighborhoods. Homeowners in high-income black neighborhoods are twice as likely as homeowners in low-income white neighborhoods to have subprime loans. Only 6 percent of homeowners in upper-income white neighborhoods have subprime loans, while 39 percent of homeowners in upper-income black neighborhoods have

12. Tim Wise, *Affirmative Action: Racial Preference in Black and White* (New York: Routledge, 2005), 21, cited in Devah Pager, "The Mark of a Criminal Record," *American Journal of Sociology* 108, no. 5 (March 2003): 937–975.
13. Eyder Peralta, "BofA's Countrywide to Pay $335 Million, Settling Lending Discrimination Case," *The Two-Way*, December 21, 2011, www.npr.org/blogs/thetwo-way/2011/12/21/144083080/bofas-countrywide-will-pay-335-million-in-lending-discrimination-case.

subprime loans, more than twice the 18 percent rate for homeowners in low-income white neighborhoods.[14]

Again, without the studies, lawsuits, and statistics, we would be unable to see the systemic nature of white privilege and white racism. To the individual person pursuing a home mortgage loan, it either seems easy to obtain a prime lending rate or impossible. The white person who receives a prime mortgage loan will have no reason to think she or he is being privileged, and the person of color who receives the subprime rate may or may not understand that she or he is being discriminated against on the basis of perceived race.

Environment

A 1992 study by staff writers for the *National Law Journal* examined the Environmental Protection Agency's response to 1,177 toxic-waste cases and found that polluters of sites near the greatest white population received penalties 500 percent higher than polluters in minority areas—fines averaged $335,566 for white areas contrasted with $55,318 for minority areas. Income did not account for these differences. The penalties for violating all federal environmental laws regulating air, water, and waste pollution were 46 percent lower in minority communities than in white communities.[15]

Race has been found to be an independent factor, not reducible to class, in predicting exposure to a broad range of environmental hazards, including polluted air, contaminated fish, lead poisoning, municipal landfills, incinerators, and toxic-waste dumps.[16]

What white person would feel privileged not to live near toxic-waste dumps, breathe polluted air, or ingest chemicals that make people sick? Who would take the time and energy to investigate where toxic-waste dumps and incinerators are located if those facilities are not near one's neighborhood? As a white person, the first time I heard the term "environmental racism" I had no idea what it meant.

Health

On average white Americans live 5.5 years longer than black Americans do. Blacks die from stroke 41 percent more often than whites, from heart disease 30 percent more often, and from cancer 25 percent more often. Asians, Pacific Islanders, and Hispanics all have lower heart disease rates than whites.

14. US Department of Housing and Urban Development, "Unequal Burden: Income and Racial Disparities in Subprime Lending in America," HUD User, http://www.huduser.org/Publications/pdf/unequal_full.pdf.

15. George Lipsitz, *The Possessive Investment in Whiteness* (Philadelphia: Temple University Press, 1998), 8. Also see John R. Logan and Harvey Molotch, *Urban Fortunes: The Political Economy of Place* (Berkeley: University of California Press, 1987), 113.

16. Lipsitz, *The Possessive Investment,* 9. See also Robert D. Bullard, "Anatomy of Environmental Racism and the Environmental Justice Movement," in *Confronting Environmental Racism: Voices from the Grassroots,* ed. Robert D. Bullard (Boston: South End Press, 1993), 15–39.

During the 1980s federal government researchers came up with a new way to measure "excess deaths" (i.e., deaths that would not have occurred if a minority population's mortality rate had been the same as the white population's). By that standard there were sixty-six thousand "excess deaths" of African Americans in 1940 and roughly one hundred thousand in 1999. That is the equivalent of one plane crash—with no survivors—occurring every day of the year.[17]

One can begin to see how multiple disadvantages compound the effects of each disadvantage and multiple privileges have a synergistic positive effect on those who receive them. It can begin to look like the "natural order" of things, but it is not. It is the result of interlocking systems of privilege and disadvantage in every aspect of life that maintain white supremacy and domination.

Law Enforcement and Crime

In New York City, from 1997 to 1998, the Street Crimes Unit of the New York Police Department (NYPD) stopped and frisked 135,000 people, 85 percent of whom were people of color. Only 4,500 persons were ultimately arrested and prosecuted, meaning that over 95 percent of those harassed were innocent. Interestingly, whites who were stopped were significantly more likely to be found with drugs or other contraband, indicating not only that this policy of racial stops and searches was biased but that it failed the test as valid crime control on its own merits as well.[18]

A federal judge ruled on August 12, 2013, that the NYPD had violated the civil rights of New Yorkers with its broad "stop-and-frisk" policy. US District Court Judge Shira Scheindlin called for an independent monitor to oversee major changes to the policy. She did not end the policy, however, instead saying that an independent monitor would develop an initial set of reforms, as well as provide training, supervision, monitoring, and discipline. "The city's highest officials have turned a blind eye to the evidence that officers are conducting stops in a racially discriminatory manner," she wrote in a lengthy opinion. "In their zeal to defend a policy that they believe to be effective, they have willfully ignored overwhelming proof that the policy of targeting 'the right people' is racially discriminatory." Police brass had received warnings since at least 1999 that officers were violating rights, she said. "Despite this notice, they deliberately maintained and even escalated policies and practices that predictably resulted in even more widespread Fourth Amendment violations."[19]

Criminal Procedure Law § 140.50 (the stop-and-frisk law) became effective on September 1, 1971. That means

17. David R. Williams and James Lardner, "Cold Truths about Class, Race and Health," in *Inequality Matters,* ed. James Lardner and David A. Smith (New York: The New Press, 2005), 105.

18. Tim Wise, "See No Evil," Tim Wise, August 2, 2001, http://www.timwise.org/2001/08/see-no-evil-perception-and-reality-in-black-and-white, originally published as a ZNet Commentary.

19. "Judge Rules NYPD's 'Stop-and-Frisk' Policy Violates Rights," Fox News, August 12, 2013, http://www.foxnews.com/politics/2013/08/12/judge-rules-nypd-stop-and-frisk-policy-violates-rights.

that for more than forty years, it has been the law in New York City. According to the statistic cited above, in one year (1997–1998) NYPD officers stopped 135,000 people, 85 percent of whom were people of color—that is approximately 115,000 people of color stopped in one year. If we multiply that number by forty-three years (as of the time of this writing in 2014) we get just under 5 million people of color! I cannot verify the total number of people of color affected by this policy, but the *New York Times* reported in 2014, "At the height of the program, in the first quarter of 2012, the police stopped people—mostly black and Latino men—on more than 200,000 occasions. A vast majority of those stopped were found to have done nothing wrong."[20] That is at least two hundred thousand people stopped in three months! These policies and practices are known to be ineffective as law enforcement tools to fight crime. What white person living in New York City thinks that not being stopped and frisked on her or his way to work is a privilege? Yet it is.

Government Policies

Beginning in the 1930s the federal government began offering low-interest, taxpayer-guaranteed, underwritten loans through the Federal Housing Administration (FHA). Between the 1930s and the 1960s, more than $100 billion in home equity was loaned through these housing initiatives, boosting the overall rate of home ownership from 44 percent in 1934 to 66 percent in 1969. But loans went almost exclusively to white families. The Home Ownership Lending Corporation made it clear that these preferential loans were off-limits to people who lived in "declining" neighborhoods (every black neighborhood was rated as declining) and that loans were also to be denied to anyone whose receipt of the loan would result in a reduction in a neighborhood's racial homogeneity. The FHA underwriting manual stated to lenders, "If a neighborhood is to retain stability, it is necessary that properties shall continue to be occupied by the same social and racial classes." As a result of these policies, 27 million of the 28 million Americans who moved into suburban areas from 1950 until 1966 were white.[21]

The government, through the FHA, set up a national neighborhood appraisal system, explicitly tying mortgage eligibility to race. Integrated communities were deemed a financial risk ipso facto and made ineligible for home loans, a policy known today as "redlining." Between 1934 and 1962, the federal government backed $120 billion in home loans. More than 98 percent went to whites. Of the 350,000 new homes built with federal support in northern California between 1946 and 1960, fewer than 100 went to African Americans.[22]

20. Benjamin Weiser and Joseph Goldstein, "Mayor Says New York City Will Settle Suits on Stop-and-Frisk Tactics," *New York Times*, January 30, 2014, http://www.nytimes.com/2014/01/31/nyregion/de-blasio-stop-and-frisk.html.

21. Wise, *Affirmative Action*, 31–32. For a detailed analysis of the FHA and Veterans Administration loan programs and how they discriminated racially, see Douglas Massey and Nancy Denton, *American Apartheid: Segregation and the Making of the Underclass* (Cambridge, MA: Harvard University Press, 1993); Melvin L. Oliver and Thomas Shapiro, *Black Wealth, White Wealth: A New Perspective on Racial Inequality* (New York: Routledge, 1997); Michael K. Brown et al., *Whitewashing Race: The Myth of a Color-Blind Society* (Berkeley: University of California Press, 2003); Leonard Steinhorn and Barbara Diggs-Brown, *By the Color of Our Skin: The Illusion of Integration and the Reality of Race* (New York: Dutton, 1999), 95–96.

22. Herbes-Sommers, *Race*.

These governmental policies and practices continue to affect the relative wealth of whites compared to African Americans and Latinos. The privileges of parents and grandparents get passed down to children, grandchildren, and great-grandchildren in the form of inherited wealth, giving each generation an ever-increasing advantage. How many whites today think of the FHA loans their grandparents received as an example of white privilege? Yet they are.

Education

The average black student attends a school with twice as many low-income students as the typical white youth, and schools that are mostly attended by black and Latino students are more than ten times as likely as mostly white schools to have concentrated levels of student poverty. Even black kids with family incomes higher than those of whites are more likely to attend schools with concentrated poverty levels.[23]

High-poverty schools (disproportionately serving a large number of students of color) have, on average, three times as many uncertified teachers or teachers who are teaching outside their field of study as teachers serving low-poverty and mostly white schools.[24]

Even when their prior performance would justify higher placement, students of color are still significantly less likely to be given honors or advanced-placement opportunities than whites, even when white students have lower grades or test scores. While this may be partly due to teacher bias, it is also the result of systematic inequity: schools serving mostly white students offer about three times as many advanced-level courses as schools serving mostly students of color. Thus, even in the total absence of racial bias on the part of school officials, the lack of certain course offerings deprives capable and hardworking students of color of opportunities available to their white counterparts.[25]

Because it is a policy and practice to fund public schools through property taxes, and because white students generally live in more affluent communities due in part to the practice of "redlining" cited above (which is responsible for much of the residential segregation in the United States), white students are again privileged from preschool and kindergarten all the way through their higher education. The educational, legal, housing, health-care, law enforcement, employment, and environmental policy systems all interlock to create a white

23. Judith R. Blau, *Race in the Schools: Perpetuating White Dominance?* (Boulder, CO: Lynne Rienner, 2003), 48; Gary Orfield et al., "Deepening Segregation in American Public Schools: A Special Report from the Harvard Project on School Desegregation," *Equity and Excellence in Education* 30 (1997): 5–24; Gary Orfield and John T. Yun, "Resegregation in American Schools," eScholarship, June 6, 1999, http://escholarship.org/uc/item/6d01084d; Massey and Denton, *American Apartheid,* 153.
24. Deborah L. McKoy and Jeffrey M. Vincent, "Housing and Education: The Inextricable Link," in *Segregation: The Rising Costs for America,* ed. James H. Carr and Nandinee K. Kutty (New York: Routledge, 2008), 128.
25. Rebecca Gordon, *Education and Race* (Oakland, CA: Applied Research Center, 1998), 48–49; Claude S. Fischer et al., *Inequality by Design: Cracking the Bell Curve Myth* (Princeton, NJ: Princeton University Press, 1996), 164–165; Steinhorn and Diggs-Brown, *By the Color of Our Skin,* 47; Gary Orfield and Susan Eaton, *Dismantling Desegregation: The Quiet Reversal of Brown v. Board of Education* (New York: The New Press, 1996), 68.

hegemony in which we live and breathe, without noticing it so long as we are its beneficiaries—so long as we whites are breathing the clean air, drinking the clear water, attending the "good" schools, landing the best jobs, getting the prime loans, not being harassed by police, and living longer with fewer diseases—as long as we are on top! This is what white privilege looks like.

Personal Anecdote

I graduated from the University of Massachusetts, Amherst, in 1970 with a bachelor's degree in philosophy. After graduation I traveled to Los Angeles, California, and took a job in a Danish restaurant as a sandwich preparer. I didn't yet know what I wanted to do as a career, so cooking was a useful way to make money while I figured that out. While I had experience working in restaurants, I'd never worked in a Danish restaurant, and I had a lot to learn about that. I worked alongside two Mexican guys who had been at the restaurant for a couple of years and knew the routine backward and forward. They were incredibly fast and skilled at their job and taught me how to prepare for and keep pace with a very busy luncheon service. I knew nothing about the lived experiences of Mexican people in Los Angeles. I was naive. After a month or two, I sensed that they resented me, and I didn't know why. Had I done something to offend them? There was a clear tension and hostility in our working environment, and I felt that hostility directed at me. The hostility finally came to a head with an argument between them and me. Management stepped in to quell the tempers. Why were they being so critical of my work? Why were they so belligerent? I had improved my speed since I started. Many of their verbal assaults were in Spanish, and I did not understand what they were saying. I only felt their anger. The manager, who was the daughter of the Danish couple who owned the restaurant, asked me if I had told my two coworkers how much I was being paid. I said yes; they had asked me one day, and I had told them. I still didn't get it. She told me not to discuss my salary with anyone. I wasn't being paid a lot, given the experience I had going into the restaurant, but my two Mexican coworkers, I found out, were being paid a lot less than I, even though they were more experienced and more skilled and had been on that job much longer than I had. I was surprised. My first thought was, Why would they work for so little? I wouldn't. And then I thought, Well, that's their problem, not mine! I've got my fair salary! That is white privilege.

Summary

White privilege is a form of domination—it positions one group of people over another group. It is a relational concept that enables us to see clearly that some benefit and others suffer from racial oppression (racism). Both racial oppression and white privilege are two sides of the same coin; you cannot have one without the other. And both racial oppression and white privilege attach to social categories, not individuals. They describe how systems operate to benefit some and disadvantage others on the basis of perceived group membership (white or of color).

This [reading] provides but a few examples of how our American social system manifests systemic white privilege and racial oppression of people of color. Once we begin to look at the extent of this system-wide domination, more and more features appear. As Joe Feagin explains, "Systemic racism encompasses a broad range of white-racist dimensions: racist ideology, attitudes, emotions, habits, actions, and institutions of whites in this society. Systemic racism is far more than a matter of racial prejudice and individual bigotry. It is a material, social and ideological reality that is well-imbedded in major U.S. institutions."[26] As we proceed to the next chapter we should expect to see some of these manifestations of systemic racism and systemic white privilege in the students we teach, the institutions we work in, and indeed in ourselves.

26. Joe R. Feagin, *Systemic Racism: A Theory of Oppression* (New York: Routledge, 2006), 2.

Discussion Topics

1. What does the concept of "white privilege" mean?
2. Compare white privilege to male privilege.
3. What does the author mean in the following statement: "Ironically, then, those ... are epistemically advantaged"?
4. "Why don't we (white people) feel privileged?" Address this inquiry from the author of this article.
5. What are the impacts of systemic privilege in the United States? Use two examples to illustrate your answer.

CONCLUSION

This article explains the important role that sociology plays in the investigation of social problems. The contribution of sociology to social problems is unique through its perspective, which is sociological imagination. Coined by C. Wright Mills, the concept of sociological imagination refers to the ability to establish a link between "biography" and "history." That is, sociological imagination enables us to understand that our personal troubles are connected to public issues. In a sense, this unique perspective of sociology allows uncovering or discovering the influential effects of social structure on social problems, which leads to theory formulation: theorizing. A social theory can be defined as a systematic, disciplined, and logical explanation of social phenomena, such as social problems. The process of theorizing occurs in three major steps: (1) Identify a problem ("the something ain't right"); (2) Describe the nature of the problem, its manifestation, and implications; and (3) Provide a description of how the problem can be solved and the impact of the solution on society.

UNIT 5

HUMAN HEALTH AND ENVIRONMENTAL PROBLEMS

Introduction

Two articles comprise this unit that emphasizes the interrelationship between humans and their natural environment. One of the articles in this unit, titled *"Biodiversity: Society Wouldn't Exist Without It"* by Carolan, discusses the critical roles of biodiversity in human lives. Defined as diversity of species, biodiversity, according to Carolan, is important for four main reasons: 1) It has implications for individual quality of life, 2) It is also important for its medicinal use, 3) It contributes to the reduction of infectious diseases, and 4) It is the source of the resources needed by humans for their survival. Despite all the crucial impacts of the biodiversity on human lives, it is under threat from multiple fronts as a result of the exploding human population. These environmental threats can be curtailed through community conservation and sustainability.

While the article by Carolan superficially discusses the link between biodiversity and human health, the one by Sahagian, titled *"Human Health and the Environment,"* provides some details explaining how both concepts are linked. In this article, Sahagian argues that degradation of the environment affects human health. For example, physical hazards (earthquakes, tsunamis, etc.) and chemical hazards (Dioxin, lead, etc.) can have deleterious effects on human health. The effects of the environment on human lives include poor sleep, autism, cancer, increase in infectious diseases (cholera, dysentery, etc.), and death in some cases.

Human Health and the Environment

Dork Sahagian

Dork Sahagian, "Human Health and the Environment," *A User's Guide for Planet Earth: Fundamentals of Environmental Science*, pp. 131-142. Copyright © 2018 by Cognella, Inc. Reprinted with permission.

Editor's Introduction

This article titled "Human Health and the Environment" by Dork Sahagian deals with the link between environment and human health. This article was selected to be included in this text not only because it discusses the important topic of environment but also and more importantly because it sheds lights on the least-documented aspect of environment-human health relationship, which refers to how the degradation of the environment is affecting human health. After reading this chapter, you will be able describe the different environmental hazards (physical, chemical, and others) and their deleterious effects on human health and explain the concept of biomagnification.

> Our health is important, as mom would insist
> Yet toxins we see would make a long list.
> Mercury and lead
> Can screw with your head
> Exposure to toxins we all should resist.

Environmental Health" can have two meanings; the first, which is the subject of much of this book, is the health of natural ecosystems in terms of functions and sustainability, usually in the context of human perturbations. The second, which is the subject of this chapter, is the impact of environmental degradation of all scales on human health. These scales range from our individual bodies (such as from smoking cigarettes), to our homes (such as from radon), to our cities (such as from water and air pollution), to the entire world (such as from impacts of climate change).

Sources of Environmental Health Hazards

Physical Hazards

Most physical environmental hazards are naturally occurring, with little that humans could do to exacerbate or prevent them. However, some, even at the global scale, have been created by human activities.

Earthquakes occur from the sudden release of elastic strain along a fault in the earth's crust. This strain is caused by differential motion of the tectonic plates, which cause different parts of the crust to move relative to each other, but bend when they get stuck on either side of a fault. When they break free suddenly, it makes an earthquake. People do not create them, nor can we prevent them. We can't even predict when they will occur along the various well-documented faults around the world. The hazard from earthquakes is collapse of buildings and roads leading to immediate injury or death—not the earthquake itself.

Tsunamis are caused by earthquakes that occur at undersea tectonic plate margins (Figure 12.1). The sudden movement makes a long-period wave in the ocean (like the mechanical generation of waves in a wave pool at an amusement park). The wave travels very fast (around 500 mph, or the speed of a commercial jet) and when it reaches shallow water, like any other wave, its wavelength reduces due to interaction with the bottom, and its amplitude increases.

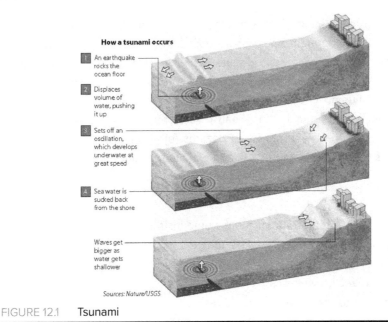

How a tsunami occurs

1. An earthquake rocks the ocean floor
2. Displaces volume of water, pushing it up
3. Sets off an oscillation, which develops underwater at great speed
4. Sea water is sucked back from the shore

Waves get bigger as water gets shallower

Sources: Nature/USGS

FIGURE 12.1   Tsunami

When it washes onto the shore, the sudden flood washes away buildings, roads, boats, and anything else in its path. When a tsunami in the Indian Ocean struck Indonesia and other coastlines in late 2004, hundreds of thousands of people were killed and millions displaced from their homes. A tsunami in 2011 led to a particularly troublesome problem when it washed into the Fukushima Daiichi nuclear power plant in Japan, leading to a meltdown of the reactors, in addition to killing almost 16,000 people directly.

Storms and other extreme weather events all over the world lead to injury and death. Hurricane winds, storm surges, and associated rain are obvious health hazards, even when they do not disable water and sanitation systems, access to medical facilities, heat, electricity, and other critical infrastructure. Whereas storms have occurred since long before human perturbations of the climate system, one manifestation of global change is the intensification of some types of storms, such as hurricanes, in response to warming of sea surface temperatures due to anthropogenic greenhouse gas emissions.

Floods, sometimes associated with storms, but often merely from extreme rainfall events (without excessive winds) in distant regions upstream, are a health hazard from the obvious drowning, but also from transmission of **disease vectors** such as from animal waste from farm feedlots, contamination of domestic water supplies, loss of medical facilities, and other critical infrastructure. Floods are exacerbated by human land use in the upstream regions of a watershed because paved surfaces, and even agricultural land, allow more rapid runoff of rain water into streams, thus raising rivers downstream more rapidly than they would raise if upstream ecosystems were intact.

Volcanic eruptions present a variety of health hazards, ranging from incineration by lava flows at 1200°C or by pyroclastic density currents, to respiratory effects of ash fall, to burial by volcanic mudflows or suffocation from volcanic gases (Cronin et al., 2014). Volcanic ash drawn into modern high-temperature jet engines melts internally, coating turbine surfaces and rendering engines ineffective, which is why flights were grounded and airports closed throughout England and some of northern Europe during the Icelandic eruption of Eyjafjallajökull in 2010. Ash can leach potentially toxic elements into agricultural fields and contaminate water supplies, thus leading to additional health hazards. Ash can also affect the functionality of electrical infrastructure because it is conductive when wet, posing serious implications for the management of healthcare facilities and general public services. There is no human influence on the processes that cause volcanoes to erupt, but increasing population and settlement density in the vicinity of volcanoes increases vulnerability of people and infrastructure to volcanic hazards.

In an unusual volcanic hazard, 1,700 people were found dead, along with their cattle and all other animals, in the vicinity of Lake Nyos, Cameroon, in 1986. Plants were unaffected, yet every animal died. The cause was determined to be the outgassing of CO_2 from volcanic activity beneath the lake. The CO_2 accumulated in bottom water, then when oversaturated, bubbled up and came out all at once into the air. The CO_2 made a blanket of inert gas that asphyxiated all animal life (including human). After this tragedy, a pump was installed to make a fountain bringing bottom water to the surface and spraying into the air to release CO_2 gradually to avoid sudden release in the future.

Ultraviolet Radiation may be the most common physical environmental hazard, as it affects everyone all the time, as well as all ecosystems, both terrestrial and aquatic. With the reduction in stratospheric ozone concentration (Figure 12.2) due to the addition of chlorine from industrially produced **CFCs**, **UVB** reaches the ground at levels not seen since the evolution of land plants and animals (hundreds of millions of years ago). The immediate impact of exposure to UVB on human skin is sunburn, to the point that it is now wise to use sunblock when spending significant amounts of time in direct summer sunlight. This was not the case only a few decades ago, when there was more ozone in the stratosphere to absorb the UVB. [...] Extended exposure to UVB and repeated sunburn cases have been shown to lead to elevated incidence of cataracts in the eye, as well as skin cancer due to disruption of skin cell DNA.

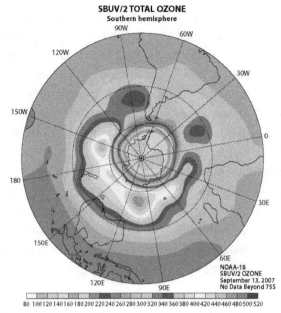

FIGURE 12.2   Ozone Hole

CFCs: (chlorofluorocarbons) were used for decades as refrigerants and propellants for spray cans until it was discovered that they destroy the critical ozone layer in the stratosphere. With the loss of stratospheric ozone, much more ultraviolet light reaches the ground, leading to skin cancer and damage to plant tissue. [...]

UVB: Ultraviolet radiation from the sun between 280 and 315 nanometers (nm). Most solar ultraviolet is in the longer wavelength UVA range (315–400 nm), but it is the UVB that leads to cellular disruption in humans and other organisms.

Endocrine disruptors: Chemicals that interfere with the endocrine system in humans and other animals. The endocrine system consists of the glands that produce and release hormones that control the function of various body organs and functions, including reproduction, growth, cellular metabolism, heart rate, and many other critical functions.

Xenoestrogens: Endocrine disruptors that behave like female sex hormones.

Polychlorinated Biphenyls (PCBs): A class of numerous (209) chlorinated artificial compounds based on attachment of chlorine atoms to a double benzene ring (biphenyl) composed of carbon atoms. The structure is similar to dioxin, another highly toxic substance. PCBs were made between 1929 and 1979 (when they were banned in the U.S.) for many industrial uses, because they were not flammable, were a good electrical insulator, and could be made with a range of consistencies from fluid to almost solid. When ingested, they serve as an endocrine disruptor, impair the reproductive system, and cause cancer.

Chemical Hazards

There is a long list of chemicals released into the environment that adversely affect human health. A few of these are discussed here, but there are many more, some of which may not yet be recognized.

Hormonally Active Agents (HAAs) are a broad class of chemicals that trigger hormonal responses in people (and other animals) (Anwer et al., 2016). These chemicals, when ingested, mimic the role of various hormones in the body, and serve as **endocrine disruptors**. Of considerable concern are those that act like female sex hormones, and are termed **xenoestrogens**. These chemicals are suspected to increase breast cancer rates in women as well as reduce sperm counts in men, in addition to various deformities of wildlife. There are many common chemicals that act as endocrine disruptors, such as bisphenol A (BPA) found in plastic linings of metal cans and in plastic water bottles, **polychlorinated biphenyls (PCBs)** used in electric transformers and other equipment, polybrominated diphenyl ethers (PBDEs) used as fire retardants, and dichlorodiphenyltrichloroethane (DDT) a controversial insecticide famous for reducing the incidence of malaria in Africa.

Methyl Mercury is a compound of mercury $(CH_3Hg)^+$ that interferes with brain function, leading to developmental abnormalities in humans, somewhat like cerebral palsy. It accumulates in animals because it attaches itself to fatty tissue, which is then consumed by other animals, concentrating its way up the food chain. Some high trophic-level fish have elevated levels of methyl mercury (Martinez-Salcido et al., 2018). Elemental mercury is not nearly as toxic as methyl mercury. In order for elemental mercury to convert to methyl mercury, it must first be oxidized, and then bonded to C and H (methylation). The behavioral disorders caused by poisoning by mercuric nitrate used in felt-making for hats in the nineteenth century rendered people "mad as a hatter."

Dioxin may be the most carcinogenic chemical ever known (Figure 12.3). It forms from the oxidation of dichlorobenzene, making 2,3,7,8-tetrachlorodibenzo-p-dioxin (dioxin for short). It was a component of "agent orange" that was used in Vietnam in the 1960s as a defoliant, causing a wide variety of serious health issues for American soldiers and Vietnamese alike. It is also formed inadvertently from the burning of a variety of organic compounds that contain benzene rings. Like methyl mercury, it accumulates in fatty tissue of animals, concentrating its way up the food chain.

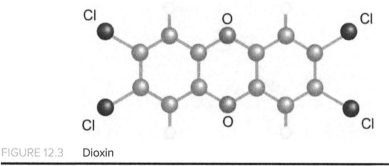

FIGURE 12.3   Dioxin

Hexavalent Chromium $(Cr+6)$ is a carcinogen that is used in the production of paints, stainless steel, metal coatings, and many other applications (McLean et al., 2012). Some industries allowed spills of Hexavalent Chromium to enter surface and groundwater, leading to greatly elevated rates of cancer in local residents. A famous case that occurred in Hinckley, CA, was publicized in the movie "Erin Brockovich."

Ozone (O_3) in the troposphere, at ground level is a lung and eye irritant, being a powerful oxidant. Because the third O atom is loosely bound to the O_2 molecule, it readily combines with other substances, oxidizing (i.e., burning) lung tissues, causing epithelial cells to become disrupted and leak enzymes into the airways. Ozone affects plant leaves in the same manner, leading to the collapse of cells on leaf surfaces (Lefohn et al., 2018). Ozone is formed in chemical reactions with nitrogen oxides, volatile organic compounds, and sunlight, typically in traffic-laden cities in mid-afternoon. [...]

Lead (Pb) is a simple metal element found in minerals and useful for many applications due to its high density and malleability, and low melting point. It had numerous industrial applications in glass, batteries, and paint until 1978; and until 1995 in the U.S., gasoline, in which it served to reduce engine "knock" by enabling smoother burning, and to prevent the microwelding of valves on their seats. By now it is banned in paint and gasoline in most countries due to the neurological impacts of ingesting lead. When ingested (eating, drinking, or breathing), lead preferentially takes the place of other metals, such as iron, that are critical to metabolic function (Cabral et al., 2015). This leads to gene malfunction by the loss of controlling proteins that also affect blood pressure, and most importantly, brain function, especially in developing children, who may have additional exposure by eating lead-containing paint chips from old dwellings. (Crudely put, mercury may make you crazy, but lead makes you "less intelligent.") A recently publicized incident was the case of lead in the public water supply of Flint, Michigan (Figure 12.4) (Zahran et al., 2017).

FIGURE 12.4   Contaminated water protest, Flint, MI

In this case, aging infrastructure involving water pipes made of lead caused high levels of dissolved lead in drinking water throughout a city that was already beleaguered with economic distress since the bursting of the bubble of American car manufacturing. A switch in water source from the Detroit River to the Flint River, followed by management led to public scandal, yet the basic problem remained that an unhealthy amount of lead remained in the public water supply due to supply lines made of lead pipe. In part, this might have been prevented by a standard water treatment technique by orthophosphate, which creates a coating on pipes that prevents the lead from dissolving into the water, but this was not done. The lead pipe will always remain a health threat until they are replaced.

Arsenic is a naturally occurring element that is found in high concentrations in groundwater in some places. It is useful for making semiconductors, especially for lasers. It can be ingested by drinking/cooking with groundwater that contains arsenic and by breathing air with high concentrations of arsenic emitted by fossil fuel burning. Health impacts include skin lesions, stomach pain, nausea, diarrhea, loss of feeling in extremities, paralysis, blindness, and cancer (Bolt, 2012). It is found in particularly high concentrations in the groundwater of Bangladesh, and simple technologies have been engineered to help remove arsenic from the water at well sites.

Other Hazards

It is impossible to even mention all the human health hazards found in the environment, but a few more will be presented here, although this is still an incomplete list.

Particulates serve as irritants to lungs and eyes, and some are particularly damaging in fibrous form. Particulate matter in the 2–10 micron size range (PM2 to PM10) remain suspended for long periods in air (Ding et al., 2005), and are thus available for inhalation (larger particles get stuck in the nose and mouth, so they don't enter the lungs). In the lungs, they lodge in the **alveoli** (tiny air sacs), and are difficult to remove by coughing or other means. They irritate the linings and reduce air-exchange efficiency, leading to asthma and other respiratory conditions as well as cancer. Sources of particulates include burning of all fossil fuels as well as biofuels, and especially smoking cigarettes, which do not limit their effect to the smokers, but to all around them. Some particulates are long and fibrous, the most famous being **asbestos**, widely used as a thermal insulator. The long, sharp shards enter the lungs and irritate the tissues, leading to asbestosis involving scarring of lung tissue, rendering it ineffective at exchanging oxygen for breathing. A special class of particles is **allergens**, usually dust, plant pollen, or pet dander that leads some people to generate **immunoglobulin E** as a defense mechanism against what the body thinks is a parasitic infection. The greatest environmental health hazard involving particulates is the simple act of **smoking cigarettes**. Many consider this a hazard class of its own, because it is optional, expensive, addictive, and deadly.

Alveoli: Tiny "balloons" in the lungs that enable oxygen exchange into the blood (and CO_2 out).

Asbestos: A group of silicate minerals whose crystals form long fibers that have been found to be useful in the production of thermal insulation materials. However, the long thin fibers also irritate and lead to scarring of lung tissue (e.g., alveoli) and reduce lung efficiency (e.g., pulmonary fibrosis) and can lead to uncontrolled cell growth and reproduction (cancer).

Allergens: Anything that is breathed, touched, or ingested that triggers an excessively strong response in the immune system that is "fooled" into perceiving a threat to the body, thus producing lots of immunoglobulin E antibodies, which then produce histamines that make the allergic reaction.

Immunoglobulin E: An antibody produced by our immune systems with the perceived threat of an infection, leading to tissue inflammation, often in response to allergens.

Smoking cigarettes: JUST DON'T DO IT!

Noise pollution does more than disturb the peace. In many people, continued exposure to elevated levels of noise leads to stress-related illnesses, poor sleep, and in extreme cases, loss of hearing.

Electromagnetic fields have been blamed for numerous health problems, including loss of hearing, neurological disorders such as autism, and of course, cancer (Kjellkvist et al., 2016). After years of testing under controlled conditions, studies within various agencies have concluded that there is insufficient evidence for any harmful effects of normal electromagnetic fields. However, research and observation continues. Common fields are created by consumer electronics such as computers, TVs, and cell phones, as well as infrastructure such as cell towers and power transmission lines. However, in extreme cases of powerful fields in microwave frequencies, people exposed can be literally cooked as if they were in a microwave oven. This is theoretically possible, but has never happened as far as anyone knows.

High-Energy Radiation. The highest frequency (energy) forms of electromagnetic radiation, X-rays and Gamma rays, carry sufficient energy to strip electrons off atoms inside the human body (Figure 12.5). When the ionized atoms are in DNA molecules (thus breaking up the DNA) the most serious health impacts are felt, as the cells no longer can replicate properly, leading to cancer, reproductive problems, and other disorders. Other forms of radiation, not in the electromagnetic spectrum, include **alpha** and **beta** radiation, which are merely helium nuclei and electrons, respectively, and they, too, can disrupt DNA and other organic molecules in cells. Radioactivity stems from many natural processes as well as nuclear (fission) power generation and associated waste. Management of these materials is a critical (and controversial) aspect of nuclear power [...]. One natural source of radioactivity is **radon** that accumulates in basements. The alpha radiation that is emitted into lungs when inhaled disrupts DNA and thus cellular function, leading to cancer and lung disease. [...]

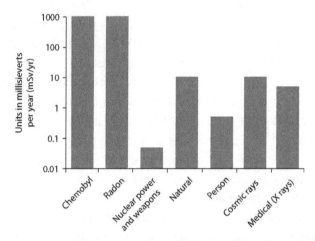

FIGURE 12.5   Sources and range of typical radiation dosage received by people per year. "Natural" includes rocks and soils.

Alpha radiation: Helium nuclei emitted during nuclear decay of radioactive elements.
Beta radiation: Electrons emitted during nuclear decay of radioactive elements.
Radon: A radioactive, invisible, odorless, tasteless gas in the Uranium-238 decay chain that seeps into basements where it decays to Polonium. The Polonium is inhaled into lungs where it quickly decays by alpha decay that shoots a high-energy helium nucleus through tissue, thus disrupting cellular DNA (and leading to cancer). Inhaled radon is commonly exhaled before it decays (half-life of a few days). However, Polonium in the air from Radon decay that is inhaled is more likely to decay in the lungs (half-life of just a few minutes) and lead to cancer.

Infectious diseases are becoming increasingly problematic as human population density increases and greater local and global transportation becomes common. The most common environmental source of disease is surface water that can carry a multitude of pathogens. In parts of the world with little or no sanitation facilities, waterways essentially serve as open sewers, and diseases such as **cholera**, **dysentery**, **typhoid fever**, **polio**, **schistosomiasis**, **cryptosporidiosis**, and many others can be readily transmitted to the human population.

FIGURE 12.6   Deer ticks that carry Lyme disease

Cholera: Bacterial infection of the small intestine leading to diarrhea and vomiting.

Dysentery: Inflammation of the colon by infection by protozoa, bacteria, or parasites, leading to severe diarrhea and blood loss.

Typhoid fever: Debilitating and often deadly bacterial infection caused by ingesting contaminated food or water, leading to high fever, delirium, intestinal hemorrhaging, encephalitis, dehydration, and other symptoms.

Polio: Viral infection of throat and intestines that leads to paralysis but has been essentially eliminated in most of the world by the polio vaccine.

Schistosomiasis: A parasitic tropical disease caused by a group of parasites that live in freshwater snails, travel through the water to enter human skin, and lay eggs that irritate the gastrointestinal and other systems, causing diarrhea, abdominal pain, coughing, fever, and other symptoms.

Cryptosporidiosis: Infection by a protozoan parasite in water that is resistant to usual treatments, such as chlorination, so must be carefully filtered from drinking water. Infection causes diarrhea, stomach pain, fever, vomiting, dehydration and other symptoms, but can be overcome by the human immune system.

Other **disease vectors** include biting insects such as mosquitos that can transmit **malaria** in many tropical regions. Dichlorodiphenyltrichloroethane (DDT) is an insecticide found to be very effective against mosquitos, and reduced the incidence of malaria in Africa for many years, before being banned for its own adverse health effects. The relative harm of malaria vs. DDT is still being discussed, and some African countries are using DDT again to reduce malaria. In the eastern U.S. (and northern California) **Lyme disease** is a bacterial infection carried by ticks who transfer the disease from mice and deer to humans (Figure 12.6). With intensifying encroachment of human settlements on natural ecosystems, infected ticks come into contact with humans more frequently, and the incidence of Lyme disease has been increasing.

Malaria: Infection by a protozoan parasite carried by tropical mosquitos. It infects the blood and liver and leads to high fever, vomiting, muscle pains, and headaches. Control has met limited success by elimination of host mosquitos using DDT, and there is controversy over which is worse for people, DDT or malaria.

Lyme disease: Bacterial infection from tick bites that often makes a bull's-eye rash initially, then leads to fatigue, muscle and joint pain, fever, and swollen lymph nodes. It is easily treated if diagnosed early.

Dose-Response Functions

When something is ingested (be it a toxin or medicine), it is considered a dose, and each individual person has a different response (Figure 12.7). In many cases, there is a **threshold dose**, below which there is no effect, but some toxins, such as dioxin, have a zero-threshold dose. Even a little bit is toxic. Many substances are necessary for the human body, and small doses are needed for metabolic function. An **effective dose** (ED) has a beneficial impact. (TD-50 for 50% of the people) (Figure 12.7). A **toxic dose** (TD) causes health problems for 50% of the people exposed. Because of people's different responses, some remain unaffected, while others are severely impacted. A **lethal dose** (LD) kills 50% of the people.

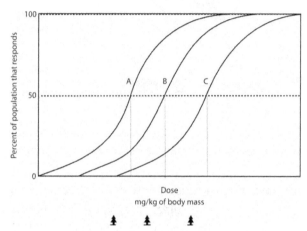

FIGURE 12.7   Dose response-antagonist. Dose Statistical response of a population to a hypothetical toxin. Note that the curves overlap such that what is lethal to one person may not even be toxic to another. A is the dosage that has an impact on 50% of the population. B is the dosage that is toxic to 50%, and C is the dosage that is lethal to 50%.

Disease vectors: Pathways for the pathogens that cause disease to reach humans.
Threshold dose: The amount of a toxin (or medicine) below which there is no response in anyone.
Effective dose (ED-50): The amount of a medicine that has a positive effect on 50% of people that take it.
Toxic dose (TD-50): The amount of a toxin that causes a negative reaction in 50% of people exposed.
Lethal dose (LD-50): The amount of a toxin that kills 50% of people exposed.

Some elements and compounds are necessary for life, yet toxic in overdoses. Fluorine is one such element (found as fluoride, F_2), which is needed for strong teeth and bones, yet in sufficient doses, can cause abdominal pain, convulsions, vomiting, and even heart attack. A corresponding dose response curve shows that insufficient amounts lead to poor health, there is an intermediate range of maximum benefit, and in excessive amounts, can lead to health problems and even death (Figure 12.8).

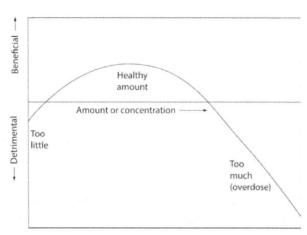

FIGURE 12.8 Hypothetical dose-response curve. If not enough of the substance is ingested, poor health results. An intermediate range provides maximum benefit, while overdose is harmful.

Biomagnification

When toxins are ingested by animals from food (or water, or air), they can be either expelled or absorbed. Many toxins are hydrophobic, meaning that they do not dissolve in or get attracted to water. These toxins bind to fatty tissue in animals, and include substances like methyl mercury, dioxin, and various endocrine disruptors. As such, when animals are eaten by other animals, the toxins are not expelled or metabolized, and remain in the predator (Zenker 2014; Zenker et al. 2014). Recall that only 10% of the energy is retained by the predator, but most of the toxins are transferred to the predator. Thus, the higher up the food chain you go, the more concentrated toxins become in animals. Because the ocean has so many trophic levels, top predators like salmon and swordfish have elevated levels of toxins, with mercury being of special concern.

Risk Assessment

An important aspect of human health is assessing the risk of adverse effects of exposure to various hazards, be they physical, chemical, biological, or otherwise (Ferguson et al., 2017). Risk (R) is normally quantified as the product of probability of occurrence (P) times the severity of impact (I).

In Figure 12.7, Curve "C" represents the response of the population to a "Lethal dose" that kills 50% of the people. At the bottom of the curve shows the dose that kills the first and most sensitive person. What percentage of the population does not even notice this same dosage? Answer: drawing a vertical line up from the start of Curve C, it intersects Curve A at about 35%, so 35% of the population does not even notice the dose that kills the most sensitive people. People respond very differently to toxins, allergens, and other substances.

$R = P \times I$

The usual steps to determine risk are to

1. <u>Identify the hazard</u>. What is the source of concern? Can it be isolated from other hazards?
2. <u>Dose response</u>. What is the dose-response curve of the population exposed?
3. <u>Assessment of exposure</u>. What is the dosage to be received, and by what population?
4. <u>Characterize the risk</u>. With the trivial calculation above, a value, even relative, can be assigned and the nature and severity of the risk can be determined.

Some hazards are very unlikely, yet devastating. The most extreme example of that would be a major asteroid impact on the earth, leading to mass extinction, as apparently occurred at the end of the Cretaceous, about million years ago. It is very unlikely that another of that magnitude will strike in our lifetimes, but if it does, it will be bad. Other hazards are more frequent, but not quite so catastrophic. Tsunamis occur from time to time, volcanoes erupt, and severe droughts and floods occur every few years. Some hazards are very frequent, even constant, with only minor individual impacts. The health hazard of breathing in particulates from diesel engine emissions is ever-present, and most people who live in or near cites are exposed constantly, yet few are particularly afraid of the threat to health it poses. Each of these examples has roughly the same total risk with varying relative contributions of P and I. Public policy and health management seeks to minimize total risk, and when plotting probability against impact (Figure 12.8), one aims to stay as near to the origin (lower left) as possible, where there is little chance of anything happening, but if it does, it will not be so bad anyway. The various areas in Figure 12.9 can be likened to characters in Greek mythology, whose stories are based on various characterizations of risk.

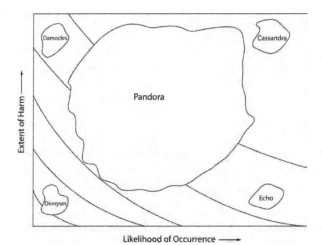

FIGURE 12.9   Characterization of risk in terms of probability versus severity of impact. Lines of "isorisk" have the same risk but in different proportions of probability and impact. One seeks to remain in the realm of Dionysus, the god of poetry and wine, but sometimes one finds one's self with Damocles, who ruled with a large sword dangling over his head. It was unlikely to fall, but if it did, his days were done. Echo was constantly annoying, but posed little immediate threat. The place one never wants to find one's self is with Cassandra, who had foreknowledge that doom was approaching the city, but was cursed by the gods so that no one would ever believe her. Thus destruction was certain, and the impact was severe. In the case of Pandora (and her box), you just don't know what you are going to get, but it will probably be bad.

References

Anwer, F., Chaurasia, S., & Khan, A. A. (2016). Hormonally active agents in the environment: a state-of-the-art review. *Reviews on Environmental Health*, 31(4), 415–433.

Bolt, H. M. (2012). Arsenic: an ancient toxicant of continuous public health impact, from Iceman Otzi until now. Archives of Toxicology, 86(6), 825–830.

Cabral, M., TOure, A., Garcon, G., Diop, C., Bouhsina, S., Dewaele, D., ... & Verdin, A. (2015). Effects of environmental cadmium and lead exposure on adults neighboring a discharge: Evidences of adverse health effects. *Environmental Pollution*, 206, 247–255.

Cronin, S. J., Stewart, C., Zernack, A. V., Brenna, M., Procter, J. N., Pardo, N., ... & Irwin, M.(2014). Volcanic ash leachate compositions and assessment of health and agricultural hazards from 2012 hydrothermal eruptions, Tongariro, New Zealand. *Journal of Volcanology and Geothermal Research*, 286, 233–247.

Ding, G. A., Chan, C. Y., Gao, Z. Q., Miao, Q. J., Li, Y. S., Cheng, X., ... Miao, Q. J. (2005). Vertical structures of PM10 and PM (2.5) and their dynamical character in low atmosphere in Beijingurban areas. *Science in China Series D-Earth Sciences*, 48(2), 38–54.

Ferguson, A., Penney, R., & Solo-Gabriele, H. (2017). A review of the field on children's exposure to environmental contaminants: A risk assessment approach. *International Journal of Environmental Research and Public Health*, 14(3), 265.

Kjellqvist, A., Palmquist, E., & Nordin, S. (2016). Psychological symptoms and health-related quality of life in idiopathic environmental intolerance attributed to electromagnetic fields. *Journal of Psychosomatic Research*, 84, 8–12.

Lefohn, A. S., Malley, C. S., Smith, L., Wells, B., Hazucha, M., Simon, H., ... & Gerosa, G. (2018). Tropospheric ozone assessment report: Global ozone metrics for climate change, human health, and crop/ecosystem research. *Elementa-Science of the Antropocene*, 6(28).

Martinez-Salcido, A. I., Ruelas-Inzunza, J., Gil-Manrique, B., Natares-Ramirez, O., & Amezcua, F. (2018). Mercury levels in fish for human consumption from the Southeast Gulf of California: Tissue distribution and health risk assessment. *Archives of Environmental Contamination and Toxicology*, 74(2), 273–283.

McLean, J. E., McNeill, L. S., Edwards, M. & Parks, J. L. (2012). Hexavalent chromium review, part 1: Health effects, regulations, and analysis. Journal of American Water Works Association, 104(6), 35–36.

Scientific Committee in Emerging Newly Identified Health Risks. (2015). Opinion on potential health effects of exposure to electromagnetic fields. *Bioelectromagnetics*, 36(6), 480–484.

Tuyet-Hanh, T. T., Minh, N. H., Vu-Anh, L., Dunne, M., Toms, L. M. Tenkate, T., ... & Harden, F. (2015). Environmental health risk assessment of dioxin in foods at the two most severe dioxin hot spots in Vietnam. *International Journal of Hygiene and Environmental Health*, 218(5), 471–478.

Zenker, A., Cicero, M. R., Prestinaci, F., Bottoni, P., & Carere, M. (2014). Bioaccumulation and biomagnification potential of pharmaceuticals with a focus to the aquatic environment. *Journal of Environmental Management*, 133, 378–387.

Figure Credits

Fig. 1: Copyright © Sam1353 (CC BY-SA 4.0) at https://commons.wikimedia.org/wiki/Category:Tsunami#/media/File:Tsunami_formation_png

Fig. 2: Source: https://commons.wikimedia.org/wiki/Category:Ozone_layer#/media/File:-Satellite_Image_of_Ozone_Hole_in_2007.jpg

Fig. 3: Copyright © 2011 Depositphotos/natalia2484.

Fig. 4: Copyright © Edward Kimmel (CC BY-SA 2.0) at https://commons.wikimedia.org/wiki/File:Climate_March_1085_(34368550705).jpg.

Fig. 6: Copyright © 2016 Depositphotos/Goldfinch4ever.

Fig. 7: Copyright © Dylan2106 (CC BY-SA 3.0) at: https://commons.wikimedia.org/wiki/File:Dose_response_antagonist.jpg.

Discussion Topics

1. Elaborate on the relationship between the environment and human health.
2. How does the author explain the link between physical hazards and human health?
3. Discuss the dualistic meaning of the title of this article as argued by the author. Select one of the two meanings and discuss its implications.
4. This article describes several environmental hazards. Select two preventable hazards and describe in detail steps that can be adopted to prevent them.
5. What is meant by biomagnification? Use an example discussed in the text to illustrate this concept.

Biodiversity: Society Wouldn't Exist Without It

Michael Carolan

Michael Carolan, "Biodiversity: Society Wouldn't Exist Without It," *Society and the Environment: Pragmatic Solutions to Ecological Issues*, pp. 67-87, 304-328. Copyright © 2016 by Taylor & Francis Group. Reprinted with permission.

Editor's Introduction

This article titled "Biodiversity: Society Wouldn't Exist Without It" by Michael Carolan indicates diversity of species is crucial for human survival. This article was selected to be included in this text because it discusses the threats to the environment. After reading this article you will be able to clearly identify the contributing factors of the declining biodiversity, and its implications on human health, medicine, and quality of life. Also, you should be able to describe an approach to solutions to the declining biodiversity.

It has been my experience that while everyone seems to believe biodiversity ought to be preserved, few can articulate the reasons we value it to the level we do. I discuss the subject every semester in my Global Environmental Issues class. And every semester, when I ask why we ought to preserve biodiversity, I receive in return ... silence. Sure, after an awkward stillness I hear from a few in the audience, but the silence always quickly reappears. It then becomes my turn to speak. I usually begin by making some grand statement pertaining to the value of biodiversity to society, talking about its links to quality of life, therapeutic applications, ability to limit infectious disease, and its role in maintaining "services." In short, biodiversity supports a number of things that lead to happier and healthier humans. Human *health*, as the term is defined here, and as the World Health Organization (WHO) has defined it since 1948, is "a state of complete physical, mental, and social well-being and not merely the absence of disease or infirmity" (WHO 2012c). I will touch briefly on each of the four benefits mentioned above.

Quality of life can be enhanced innumerably by biodiversity, as it boosts mental and spiritual health, provides opportunities for recreation, and enriches human knowledge.

Biodiversity is also responsible for supplying *therapeutic applications*, thanks to medicinal and genetic resources coming from plants and other organisms. The United Nations, for example, recently valued anticancer agents from marine organisms at roughly $1 billion a year, while the global value of herbal medicine has been estimated to be worth more than $80 billion annually (Booker, Johnston, and Heinrich 2015).

Biodiversity places *limits on infectious disease* through biological controls that rein in **disease vectors** (an organism, such as a mosquito or tick, that carries disease-causing microorganisms from one host to another). For instance, when an ecosystem is biologically diverse, predation throughout the food chain is likely to keep populations of all species under control, including those linked to the spread of infectious disease.

The benefits of biodiversity-dependent *services* is incalculable, as many of these values cannot (and should not) be reduced to a monetary figure. This is not to say some haven't tried. Take the concept of **ecosystem services**: the processes by which the environment produces resources that we often take for granted but need for our survival, such as clean air and water, timber, habitat for fisheries, and pollination of native and agricultural plants. A 1997 article published in *Nature* placed the value of seventeen ecosystem services at approximately $33 trillion per year, compared to a gross world product at the time of around $18 trillion (Costanza et al. 1997). More recently, a revised estimate involving updated data was published in 2011 and valued global ecosystem services at between $125 trillion and $145 trillion per year, compared to a gross world product at the time of around $72 trillion (Costanza et al. 2014). From this estimated range, the study's authors calculate the loss of eco-services from 1997 to 2011 as a result of land use change at $4.3 trillion to $20.2 trillion annually. Land use changes include anything from, for example, decreases in coral reef area to deforestation and the draining of wetlands. Yet we can't—nor would we want to—put a price tag on everything that's provided by ecosystems. Right? (See ECOnnection 1.)

Fast Facts

- Approximately 1.2 million species (excluding bacteria) have already been cataloged—just a fraction of the 8.7 million species estimated to exist (Mora et al. 2011).
- We are losing species at an alarming rate, many before even being discovered. Famed biologist Edward O. Wilson ([1992] 1999) has estimated the current rate of species extinction at roughly 27,000 annually, or 74 per day (see Ethical Question 1). A study published in *Science* estimates that current extinction rates are up to a thousand times higher than they would be if we humans were not around (Pimm et al. 2014; see Image 1).
- A recent analysis of ninety-four studies comparing biodiversity under organic and conventional farming methods found that, on average, organic agriculture *increased* species richness by about 30 percent relative to biodiversity levels on conventionally farmed land (Tuck et al. 2014).
- From the more than 1.2 billion hectares of tropical rain forest habitat that originally existed, less than 400 million remain (Spilsbury 2010).

Implications

As detailed in Table 13.1, a great number of events and activities (most of which are human induced) threaten biodiversity. And these threats will only grow in the decades ahead, especially as the world becomes warmer (thanks to climate change), more crowded (as a result of population growth and urbanization trends), and more affluent (particularly in Southeast Asia). Complicating matters further are the ways in which pressures upon biodiversity can act at different temporal and spatial scales. For instance, sediments from deforestation in the headwaters of the Orinoco River along the Venezuelan/Brazilian border negatively affect marine life in the Caribbean more than a thousand miles away by altering the nutrient availability and clarity of the waters (UNEP 2008).

The reasons for biodiversity decline will come up again later, as many of the pressures and drivers discussed in Table 13.1 are subjects of later chapters. What I am most interested in detailing at the moment are impacts. Yet before we look at impacts, there is one small conceptual problem that requires our attention: What precisely does *biodiversity* even mean? Only after working our way through this question can we begin having a conversation about the various consequences associated with biodiversity loss.

ECONNECTION 1: THINKING ABOUT ECOSYSTEM SERVICES CONCEPTUALLY

Ecosystems cannot provide any benefits to humanity without the presence of skilled people (human capital), their communities and social networks (social capital), and their built environment (built capital). This interaction, articulated by Costanza and colleagues (2014), is illustrated in Figure 13.1. The challenge for policies aimed at sustainable development involves understanding how this interaction plays out in enhancing well-being and then taking steps to appropriately enhance all capitals to maximize outcomes.

One thing I appreciate about this figure is that it contextualizes value. Values are not plucked out of thin air. What we value and the degree to which something is valued cannot be abstracted from social context. This is plainly evident in debates over the value of ecosystem services. The $125 trillion to $145 trillion range calculated by Costanza and colleagues (2014) is a lot—an order of magnitude larger than what the global economy produces in a year. And yet our actions indicate that we don't actually value global ecosystem services that much, or anywhere even close to that much (otherwise we wouldn't be trashing them). Why is that? What is it about our political systems, cultures, markets, and social norms and routines that cause us to undervalue ecosystem services to the degree we do?

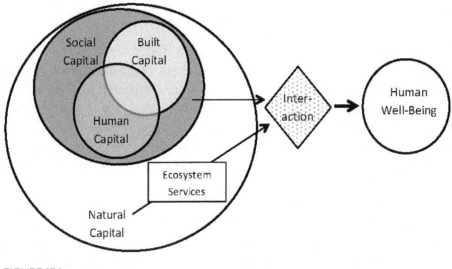

FIGURE 13.1

Adapted from Costanza et al. (2014).

ETHICAL QUESTION 1: SOPHIE'S CHOICE: WHAT IF WE CAN'T SAVE THEM ALL?

Some twenty thousand species are on the cusp of extinction (Dell'Amore 2013). If we had endless resources to commit to saving them all, we wouldn't have to choose which to save. But that's not reality. Ecologists have long argued that how we choose which species live or die is often unscientific, skewed heavily toward preserving cute and fuzzy animals even if those species do little to keep the planet humming by contributing to ecosystem functions (and those ever-important services). For example, ants play a foundational role in most ecosystems: distributing seeds, aerating soils, eating other insects, and providing food for other species. And yet, for every child with a poster of ants in their bedroom there are tens of thousands with posters of pandas, elephants, and polar bears. In the words of Marc Bekoff, an ethologist at the University of Colorado, Boulder, "if we're going to save pandas rather than ants, we need a good reason, and being cute is not a good reason" (Dell'Amore 2013).

Something else to think about: cost. Should the cost of conservation play into our calculations? If so, those charismatic megafauna come with a pretty hefty price tag—managing the world's tiger reserves costs more than $82 million annually (N. L. 2010). Then again, how can you place a price tag on the existence of a species, when once it is gone, it is gone for good? But if we do not take into consideration the annual cost of saving each individual animal of a given species—what some conservationists call ROI (return on investment)—what variables *should* we use?

FIGURE 13.2   Photograph from the mid-1870s of a pile of American buffalo skulls waiting to be ground for fertilizer.

Courtesy of the Burton Historical Collection, Detroit Public Library.

TABLE 13.1 Threats to Biodiversity

Residential & Commercial Development	Agriculture & Aquaculture
• Housing & Urban Areas • Commercial & Industrial Areas • Tourism & Recreation Areas	• Annual & Perennial Non-Timber Crops • Wood & Pulp Plantations • Livestock Farming & Ranching • Marine & Freshwater Aquaculture
Energy Production & Mining	**Transportation & Service Corridors**
• Oil & Gas Drilling • Mining & Quarrying • Renewable Energy	• Roads & Railroads • Utility & Service Lines • Shipping Lanes • Flight Paths • Air and Space Transport

Source: Adapted from Conservation Measures Partnership.

Biological Resource Use

- Hunting & Collecting Terrestrial Animals
- Gathering Terrestrial Plants
- Logging & Wood Harvesting
- Fishing & Harvesting Aquatic
- Resources

Human Intrusions & Disturbance

- Recreational Activities
- War, Civil Unrest & Military Exercises
- Work & Other Activities

Natural System Modifications

- Fire & Fire Suppression
- Dams & Water Management/Use
- Other Ecosystem Modifications

Invasive & Problematic Species & Genes

- Invasive Non-Native/Alien Species
- Problematic Native Species
- Introduced Genetic Material

Pollution

- Household Sewage & Urban Waste Water
- Industrial & Military Effluents
- Agricultural & Forestry Effluents
- Garbage & Solid Waste
- Airborne Pollutants
- Excess Heat, Sound, or Light That Disturbs Wildlife and/or Ecosystems

Geological Events

- Volcanoes
- Earthquakes/Tsunamis
- Avalanches/Landslides

Climate Change & Severe Weather

- Habitat Shifting & Alteration
- Droughts
- Temperature Extremes
- Storms & Flooding

-

Source: Adapted from Conservation Measures Partnership.

ECONNECTION 2: THE TRAGEDY OF THE COMMODITY

[I discussed] the theory of the tragedy of the commons—the belief that species extinction (and environmental ruin more generally) is exacerbated in those instances where natural capital has yet to be privatized. Rebecca Clausen and Stefano Longo (along with, more recently, Brett Clark) turn this thinking on its head, arguing for what they call the **tragedy of the commodity** thesis (e.g., Clausen and Longo 2012; Longo et al. 2015). Accordingly, rather than being our ecological savior, "commodification is a primary *contributor* to decline as well as an underlying *cause* for the failure of environmental policy prescriptions" to protect biodiversity (Clausen and Longo 2012, 231; emphasis in original). As the authors of this argument explain, "once the precedent has been set to view the value of a resource through the lens of a commodity, government regulations to help 'solve' the ecological problem will prioritize market-based solutions that accommodate capitalist needs for growth and accumulation" (232). As evidence of their thesis, they point to the AquAdvantage Salmon—selected by *Time* magazine as one of "The Best Inventions in 2010" (Clausen and Longo 2012). Here's a "solution" of salmon recovery and conservation that allows the status quo to continue, a technological fix that at least in the short term allows the treadmill of production to not miss a beat. In the long run, however, it is allowing biologically diverse natural salmon stocks to literally be gobbled up, along with their habitat.

Changing Definitions of Biodiversity

Early definitions of biodiversity tended to focus almost entirely on species diversity, in which case biodiversity was simply another way of saying "species richness" (see, for example, Lovejoy 1980). More recently, the definition of the term has expanded to include, along with species richness, genetic diversity (within and across species) and ecological diversity (which includes ecosystem services and habitat) (see, for example, Hunter and Gibbs 2007). Yet the problem doesn't lie just in deciding which criteria to include in our definition. It also stems from the inherent ambiguity of the criteria themselves. Take the concept—or, I should say, *concepts*—of species.

A review of the modern biological literature roughly two decades ago found at least twenty-four different species concepts (Mayden 1997), a figure that has no doubt increased in recent years, given the expanding literature on the subject. The **species problem**, as it has come to be known, refers to the inherent ambiguity surrounding the use and definition of the species concept. The three more widely utilized contemporary species concepts include the biological species concept (centering on the property of reproductive isolation), the ecological species concept (emphasizing speciation through ecological selection), and the phylogenetic species concept (focusing on the property of common descent). This all matters tremendously from a conservation standpoint, for ultimately which species concept we adopt affects the number of species we find.

It has been argued, for instance, that the biological species concept tends to overemphasize gene flow between populations and thus aggregates species together, while the phylogenetic species concept often splits such populations into distinct and thus potentially new species (Meijaard and Nijman 2003). This inflation and deflation of biodiversity levels based on which species concept is ultimately employed have been well documented. A team of researchers reanalyzed organisms utilizing a phylogenetic species concept that were earlier classified according to other species definitions (Agapow et al. 2004). The reanalysis yielded a species *increase* of 121 percent. Focusing on avian endemism in Mexico (birds that are found only in Mexico), another team applied two alternative species concepts: the phylogenetic species concept and the biological species concept (Peterson and Navarro-Siguenza 1999). Their findings indicate not only divergent levels of biodiversity based on which species concept was used but also divergent **biodiversity hotspots** (a biogeographic region with a significant reservoir of biodiversity that is under threat from humans), signifying where endemism is particularly concentrated. When the biological species concept was used, 101 bird species were found to be endemic to Mexico, with populations concentrated in the mountains of the western and southern portions of the country. Using the phylogenetic species concept, the endemic species total rose to 249, with population concentrations in the mountains and lowlands of western Mexico.

Equally problematic is the concept of "ecosystem"—a phenomenon, as mentioned previously, recently folded into biodiversity definitions. Maps of biologically diverse hotspots typically include tropical rain forests, for reasons related not only to species richness but also to the important ecosystem services, such as climate regulation and nutrient cycling, they provide. Wetlands and marshes, however, are typically ignored in these maps, even though they provide equally essential ecosystem services, such as nutrient cycling, erosion control, water purification, and storm protection. (See Ethical Question 2.)

And what about humans? Are we not a species who create and alter ecosystems? Shouldn't *we* factor into measures of biodiversity, other than being viewed as yet another thing that negatively affects it?

The Bombay Natural History Society noticed in the late 1970s that bird populations were on the decline in the Bharatpur Bird Sanctuary (what is today known as Keoladeo National Park) in Rajasthan, India. An accusatory finger was eventually pointed at cattle and buffalo, which were entering the preserve in sufficient quantities and disrupting what was believed to be an otherwise balanced ecosystem. In an attempt to correct the problem of decreasing bird populations, Bharatpur was declared a national park in 1981. This act was quickly followed by a ban on all grazing activities within the park. (Nine people were killed in the resulting riots that ensued as the park was cleared of its earlier human inhabitants.)

ETHICAL QUESTION 2: THE POWER OF CONSERVATION MAPS

A wealth of literature has emerged in the past thirty years examining the power embedded within maps (e.g., Edney 1997; Harley 1989; Wood 1993). For example, modern maps embody the commercial and political interests of Western European and North American nation-states. Most world maps place north at the top, have zero degrees longitude running through Greenwich, England, and are centered on either Western Europe, North America, or the North Atlantic. Maps can also reflect societal preferences for certain landscapes and ecosystems. For example, forests are far more frequently mapped than grasslands (Hazen and Anthamatten 2004). Yet even what's defined as *forest* is hotly contested. A mapped, legally defined *forest* may in fact not contain a single tree (Vandergeest 1996).

Similar to how world maps give readers the sense that political boundaries are natural and objectively given, conservation maps also tend to naturalize a static view of ecological and social systems. In other words, while the socioecological space being represented in conservation images is inherently fluid, once mapped these spaces take on a near timeless, permanent quality. Maps also tend to minimize differences across geophysical space. Harris and Hazen (2006), for instance, examined a widely distributed map created by the UN Environment Programme that visually depicts the spatial distribution of internationally recognized "protected" areas. Such global perspectives, however, risk endorsing the view that conservation spaces are comparable across what are in reality widely divergent areas. They point out how places of conservation in the United States and United Kingdom are often appreciably different. For example, as a result of divergent historical trajectories, national parks in the United States reflect the wilderness ideal (an image of nature devoid of human presence), while in the United Kingdom they are often populated agricultural landscapes. Although such spaces are radically different on the ground, these differences are washed away when viewed at the level of a global map. As argued in an article on the power of ecosystem service maps, "designing maps is thus a means of exercising power" (Hauck et al. 2013, 28). The authors go on to note that "the designer makes decisions on what to include and which scales are to be chosen" (28). One strategy then to avoid these pitfalls is to incorporate "a high degree of transparency with regard to the specific reasons for mapping" (28).

By the mid-1980s, something was amiss. Studies were beginning to indicate the seemingly impossible: bird diversity within the park had *declined further* since the ban on grazing (Vijayan 1987). By the early 1990s, it was irrefutable: biodiversity not only had declined since the grazing ban but was diving downward at an alarming rate. The absence of grazing animals, it turns out, had a disastrous effect on the ecology of the park. Weed species were taking over wetlands and choking canals, thereby reducing fish populations. As the open wetland habitat—a habitat that once attracted a tremendous mix of birds—was being overrun by a handful of fast-growing opportunistic plant species, avian species went elsewhere in search of more suitable places to nest. In 1991, in a stunning course reversal, the Bombay Natural History Society—originally the most vocal opponent on grazing in the park—concluded that, to avoid further weed takeover, grazing animals needed to be brought back. A report announcing this policy reversal admitted the shortsightedness of conservation policies that place humans apart from—rather than as a part of—biologically diverse ecosystems: "In the case of most wetlands in this country, [human] interaction with them has become almost inseparable and hence, [humans have] to actively manage them" (Vijayan 1991, 1).

ECONNECTION 3: THE IRREPLACEABLE BEE

Pollinators—honey and native bees in addition to certain birds, bats, and butterflies—not only provide a critical ecosystem service but are also an essential component to food security. Honey bees alone enable the production of at least ninety commercially grown crops in North America. Pollinators make possible the "growing" of 35 percent of the world's food and contribute more than $24 billion to the US economy (White House 2014). The number of managed bee colonies in the US has dropped over the past sixty years, from 6 million colonies in 1947 to just 2.5 million today. Crops like almonds are almost exclusively pollinated by honey bees. California's almond industry, which supplies 80 percent of the world's almonds, requires the pollination services of roughly 1.4 million beehives annually—that's 60 percent of all beehives in the United States (White House 2014). Unable to discern insect friend from insect foe, pesticides have had a major impact on all insect pollinators and are suspected of playing a significant role in what is known as colony collapse disorder (Chensheng, Warchol, and Callahan 2014; Doublet et al. 2015).

Biodiversity: The Fuel Driving Ecosystem Services

Biodiversity loss is our loss. Biodiversity may not make the world go around, but it certainly makes the planet inhabitable. Here I speak in a little more detail about some of the services provided by biodiversity.

Agriculture

No amount of technology and innovation could substitute for the ecosystem services provided by biodiversity in the production of food and fiber production (see ECOnnection 3). Biodiversity makes soil habitable for plant growth, as it is central to the breakdown and recycling of nutrients within this life-giving medium. Biodiversity also makes pollination possible and is essential for pest control, without which productivity losses would be even greater. Biodiversity may well also hold the key to future food security in light of climate change, as plant breeders will have to look increasingly into the gene pool to come up with varieties suitable to withstand and ideally thrive under a variety of agroecological conditions.

Forests

As with agriculture, commercial forestry depends on biodiversity for nutrient recycling and pest control. Some forests also generate revenue from hunting, the collection of wild food (e.g., berries and fungi), the collection of firewood, and bird watchers and nature photographers. Forests also offer spaces for recreation, itself a major revenue-generating activity. Last, there is an incalculable intrinsic value associated with these spaces, as they not only serve as sources of creativity and inspiration but also hold religious and cultural significance for populations around the world.

Fisheries

Waterways provide a provisioning ecosystem service in the form of fish catch. The fish catch, however, is heavily dependent on a functioning biologically diverse ecosystem that supplies nutrients, prey species, habitats, and a desirable water quality (Bullock 2008). There is also an intensely cultural component to fishing, as many societies have deep historical roots in this practice.

Water

Biodiversity performs an irreplaceable service in terms of both recycling nutrients and ensuring desirable water quality for agricultural use, fisheries, and human consumption. A significant amount of research has emerged in recent years documenting that species-rich aquatic ecosystems are more efficient at removing excess nutrients and even some pollutants from water than those with fewer species (Carnicer et al. 2015).

Atmospheric Regulation

Forests and other vegetation—and to a lesser extent all organisms—modify climate (though humans look to be the most influential organism). Plants and trees affect solar reflection, water-vapor release, wind patterns, and moisture loss. Forests help maintain a humid environment, as evidenced by the fact that half of all rainfall in the Amazon basin is produced locally by the forest-atmosphere cycle (Kozloff 2010).

Biocultural Diversity

As acknowledged by the United Nations Environment Programme, "biodiversity also incorporates human cultural diversity, which can be affected by the same drivers as biodiversity, and which has impacts on the diversity of genes, other species, and ecosystems" (UNEP 2007, 160). The term **biocultural diversity** speaks to an unmistakable and increasingly well-documented empirical fact: that cultural diversity does not merely parallel biological diversity but is profoundly interrelated with it (Maffi and Woodley 2010).

There is a subtle but noticeable disdain toward humans in many environmental texts in their noting only the ways in which humans threaten biodiversity. It is unquestionably true that we are the greatest threat to the earth's biodiversity. But this shouldn't lead to the conclusion that humans somehow represent an *inherent* risk to biological diversity. Granted, it's far easier to see the various ways in which we are mucking things up, as we read routinely about the latest species threatened or lost entirely at our own hands. Yet growing evidence points to how humans are also positively contributing to ecosystems and biodiversity levels.

There are two general approaches to biological conservation: **ex situ** and **in situ**. Ex situ conservation involves the sampling, transferring, and storage of a species in a place other than the original location in which it was found, like a zoo or seed bank. The other option is in situ conservation, which involves the management of a species at the location of discovery. The ex situ model is often what comes to mind (at least for most in the developed world) when people think of biodiversity conservation, which is understandable in light of the more than fourteen hundred seed and gene banks and more than one thousand zoos worldwide.

The popularity of the in situ model, however, has grown considerably among conservationists in recent decades. Proponents of the in situ approach argue that it provides a more complete form of conservation, in that it makes room for, unlike ex situ approaches, socioecological dynamics. It is no coincidence that most of the world's biologically diverse hotspots are also its **cultural hotspots**—biogeographic regions with a significant reservoir of cultural diversity that are under threat of extinction (Stepp et al. 2004). Research looking at indigenous populations in North America consistently notes a correlation between measures of biodiversity within a given region and its levels of cultural and linguistic diversity (Smith 2001; Stephenson et al. 2014).

Virginia Nazarea has extensively studied sweet potato farmers in the Philippines. At one site they were beginning the processes of commercializing production, while at another they remained firmly at the level of subsistence agriculture. She had hypothesized that commercialization causes a narrowing of genetic and cultural diversity among sweet potatoes raised. Her hypothesis was confirmed. Yet she also observed something unexpected. There was a large disparity between the two sites in terms of the number of varieties known or remembered, compared to the biodiversity that actually existed. At the commercial site, farmers had knowledge about a far lower percentage of sweet potato varieties than at the other site, having forgotten many that still existed and were being planted elsewhere in the country. This suggests a faster erosion of cultural knowledge than genetic diversity itself. Reflecting on this research, Nazarea writes how this finding signified that "in the context of agricultural development and market integration, knowledge may actually be the first to go" (2005, 62).

Sociologists MacKenzie and Spinardi (1995) argued a while back that nuclear weapons are becoming "uninvented" as a result of global nuclear disarmament trends and nuclear test–ban treaties. It is their contention that "if design ceases, and if there is no new generation of designers to whom that tacit knowledge can be passed, then in an important (though qualified) sense nuclear weapons will have been uninvented" (44). They are pointing, to put it simply, to the importance of putting knowledge to work. A lot of knowledge has to be acted out—literally *practiced*—for it to exist and be passed along to others. Try, for example, teaching someone to ride a bike with words alone—it just doesn't work. The same principle applies to our knowledge of biodiversity. This is why the term *biocultural diversity* is so apt, because the cultural knowledge tied to traditional crops is very much rooted in practice. Many traditional cultures are oral, meaning that much of this folk knowledge is not physically recorded (written down) anywhere. Once lost, there is a good chance this knowledge—and with it a piece of biocultural diversity—is gone forever.

Biopiracy

Although we often think about biological loss in the context of, say, extinction, this is not the only way it is experienced. In some cases, while the object of concern still exists (perhaps even thrives), the loss felt is the result of the misappropriation of biocultural knowledge. Enter **biopiracy**: essentially the loss of biocultural diversity through legal and sometimes illegal means.

It is estimated that developing nations would be owed $5 billion per year if they received royalties of 2 percent for their contributions to pharmaceutical research and another $302 million annually for royalties from agricultural products (see, e.g., Ramon 2011). Biopiracy—or what's called *bioprospecting* by those doing it—occurs when folk knowledge and biological artifacts are conjointly exploited for commercial gain without just compensation to those responsible for discovering or originating it. Although it's easy to chalk biopiracy up to the greedy actions of powerful multinational corporations seeking to exploit the knowledge and resources of indigenous populations, it is important to understand certain sociolegal realities that make such activities possible in the first place.

To begin with, patent law makes it exceedingly difficult for indigenous populations to call biocultural knowledge their own. According to patent law, no patent can be issued where prior art exists because of the statutory requirement that patents are to be granted only for new inventions on the basis of novelty and nonobviousness. An invention is generally not regarded as new if it was patented or described in a printed publication. **Indigenous knowledge**—or local knowledge, which is knowledge unique to a given community, culture, or society—however, has tended to be an oral and embodied effect, acquired through years of literally *doing* and applying that knowledge. As such, it is rarely ever written down. Its transmission occurs through storytelling, not book reading. The knowledge of these indigenous societies can thus often be freely plundered for private gain, as evidenced by corporations patenting and claiming as their own knowledge what had for centuries been part of the (indigenous) public domain.

One way indigenous groups are responding to this legal reality is by publishing their biocultural knowledge in large digital libraries, what are commonly known as Traditional Knowledge Data Libraries (TKDLs). Transforming this age-old embodied and oral knowledge into a written form turns it into something that patent law recognizes and that therefore constitutes prior art. Many countries—such as South Korea, Thailand, Mongolia, Cambodia, South Africa, Nigeria, Pakistan, Nepal, Sri Lanka, and Bangladesh—are following in the footsteps of India, which developed one of the first TKDLs in the late 1990s.

To what extent is biopiracy occurring? That's not easy to say, as a number of national laws, international agreements, and legally binding treaties make biopiracy illegal. So whatever is occurring is taking place under the radar. The most consequential legal structure to emerge to reduce biopiracy is the Convention of Biological Diversity (CBD), which was adopted at the Earth Summit of Rio de Janeiro in 1992. Its objectives are threefold: the conservation of biodiversity, the sustainable use of biodiversity, and the equitable sharing of benefits arising from the use of genetic resources.

Agreements reached through the CBD, however, do not apply to materials collected before 1992. Thus, any material in a gene or seed bank before 1992 can still be exploited for commercial ends without any money going back to the source country as compensation. Take the case involving a disease-resistant peanut from

Brazil. The peanut was first picked in 1952 by Alan Beetle. It was not until 1987, however, that Beetle's sample would be used for commercial ends. In 1987 the tomato spotted wilt virus (TSWV) was first detected in US peanuts. This virus severely injures or kills any peanut plant that it infects. It quickly spread throughout Georgia, Florida, Alabama, and South Carolina, seriously threatening the US peanut industry. Beetle's sample peanut was known to be resistant to TSWV and was quickly sought out for this trait by breeders. A number of peanut varieties have since been bred to be resistant to TSWV using this nut from Brazil. In fact, the germplasm from this nut was estimated roughly a decade ago to add at least $200 million annually to the US economy (Edmonds Institute 2006). Brazil, conversely, receives nothing. Nevertheless, as a recent report on the subject adds, "no laws were transgressed." Rather, this example speaks to a perfectly legal case of "pre-CBD biopiracy" (ibid., 3).

Even with CBD, however, biopiracy remains a problem. Let's look briefly at two recent well-publicized cases of biopiracy, involving Bt brinjal from India and herbal teas from South Africa.

Bt brinjal is a genetically modified strain of brinjal (eggplant) created by India's largest seed company, Mahyco, which also happens to be a subsidiary of the multinational company Monsanto. Bt brinjal has been engineered to be resistant to lepidopteran insects, particularly the brinjal fruit and shoot borer. According to the National Biodiversity Authority (NBA) of India, the development of Bt brinjal is a case of biopiracy, which means Monsanto and Mahyco could face criminal proceedings. The NBA charges these alleged biopirates with accessing nine Indian varieties of brinjal to develop their genetically modified eggplant without prior permission from the NBA or relevant national and local boards. This is a violation of the country's 2002 Biological Diversity Act, which provides for the conservation of biological diversity and calls for fair and equitable sharing of the benefits that arise out of the use of biocultural resources. (It is also illegal under the CBD.) By using the local brinjal varieties without permission, Monsanto and Mahyco weakened India's sovereign control over its resources while denying economic and social benefits to local communities under the benefit-sharing requirements of the Biological Diversity Act (Jebaraj 2011).

Example two: biopirated tea. Global food giant Nestlé is facing allegations of biopiracy after applying for patents based on two South African plants used in the making of herbal teas without first receiving permission from the South African government. This puts Nestlé in direct violation of South African law as well as the CBD. The controversy centers on two South African plants, rooibos and honeybush, commonly used to make herbal teas with well-known—and long-known—medicinal benefits. A Nestlé subsidiary has filed five international patent applications seeking to claim ownership over some of those medicinal benefits, such as using the plants to treat hair and skin conditions and for anti-inflammatory treatments. At issue is benefit sharing: namely, Nestlé believes it does not need to share any future profits that might be derived from these patents. Yet according to the 2004 South African Biodiversity Act, businesses must obtain a permit from the government if they intend to use the country's genetic resources for research or patenting. And these permits can be obtained *only* in exchange for a benefit-sharing agreement (ICTSD 2010).

Solutions

As biodiversity is threatened by multiple practices, pressures, and events, solutions directed at the problem of biodiversity loss must be equally multiple and diverse. I offer here two strategies that have had some success at enhancing biodiversity levels. In the space that remains, I discuss the practice of community conservation and agrobiodiversity conservation. These are not our only two solutions. Later chapters examine many of the other drivers of biodiversity loss and their potential solutions.

ETHICAL QUESTION 3: SUSTAINABILITY: FOR WHOM AND TOWARD WHAT END?

The term *sustainability* reminds me a lot of the term *nature*: we seem to talk endlessly about both but struggle when forced to offer a clear definition of either. *Social sustainability*, *environmental sustainability*, and *economic sustainability* are hotly contested terms. What they mean depends on whom you ask. For example, when we talk about social sustainability, do we mean improving social justice or reducing inequality or something else entirely? Or environmental sustainability: Do we mean zeroing out all ecological impact or just minimizing impact? If it is the latter, is everyone expected to reduce equally, or might those with the largest ecological footprints be asked to reduce more? Or economic sustainability: Does this mean simply that households and businesses need to be profitable, or does it also suggest a desire to reduce, for example, economic inequality?

What do you think about when you hear the term *sustainability*? If you're anything like my students, ecological sustainability likely comes to mind before social sustainability (and this is even among sociology students). Can you think of instances where an ecologically sustainable practice might not be socially sustainable?

Community Conservation

The modern conservation movement emerged in Europe in the nineteenth century. The wilderness model, around which so many of the world's national parks are built, came shortly thereafter out of the United States. Although these top-down—which is to say they are typically implemented and overseen by the state—conservation methods have had their successes, they are not without their problems.

For one thing, conservation has historically been viewed as separate from development. Indeed, in some camps they are antithetical to each other. The social costs of these conventional models of conservation have been great. Removing, sometimes forcibly, indigenous populations—like Native Americans in the United States and Parakuyo and Massai pastoralists in Tanzania—from lands they have lived on for centuries for purposes of "saving nature" is morally repugnant. But also, looking beyond the morality of these acts, the science refutes the ecological soundness of such policies. As the earlier case involving the Bharatpur Bird Sanctuary in India shows us, there may be better ways of conserving biodiversity than by removing people from the equation.

A paradigm shift of sorts is taking place in conservation and developmental circles. On the one hand, it is becoming clear that developmental policies that overlook conservation are unsustainable in the long run and ultimately offer no relief from threats to biodiversity. On the other hand, conservationists are beginning to understand that they can no longer afford to ignore the impoverishment they may be causing when they exclude human populations from habitats they are seeking to conserve. In fact, what we've learned is that those indigenous populations that conservationists have been so busy evicting over the past century may hold the key to truly sustainable development (see, e.g., Garcia, Rice, and Charles 2014; see also Ethical Question 3).

This is where community conservation comes into the picture (see ECOnnection 4). As generally practiced, community conservation is place-based and highly participatory. There are different "flavors" of community conservation, as there are many different ways to define community involvement when it comes to conservation. This variability is captured in Table 13.2. As illustrated in the table, levels of community involvement can run the spectrum: from low, where an agency is in charge, to high, where independent community-centered groups develop their own initiatives as a result of a crisis or problem.

TABLE 13. 2 Citizen Involvement in Conservation Decision Making

	Low (full control by agency in charge)		High (full control by stakeholders)	
Process	**Information Sharing:** Builds awareness by telling people what is planned	**Consultation:** Identifies problems, offers solutions, and obtains feedback to broaden knowledge base allowing for better top-down decisions	**Co-Directed:** Involves and actively engages stakeholders to contribute ideas and opinions when deciding best way to move forward	**Independent Community Initiatives:** Groups are enabled to act, in terms of process as well as outcome
Activity of Citizen Group	**Passive:** Receptors of information	**Marginally Engaged:** Predetermined phase is devoted to seeking public input	**Equal Players:** Involvement throughout entire processes	**Directing:** Groups set agenda and determine direction and outcome of project
Outcome	**Information Dissemination**	**Weak Participation**	**Strong Participation**	**Determination**

Citizen involvement can take many different forms. Some options offer little more than a façade of "involvement" (as illustrated by the "low" end toward the left of the table), while others (far right or "high" end of the table) put communities firmly in the driver's seat. Source: Forgie, Horsley, and Johnston (2001) and Trotman (2008).

Arguably the most publicized community conservation success story comes out of Tanzania. It involves two woodland reserves, both of which were being poorly conserved under previous management regimes. In 1994 and 1995, communities located near the edge of the forests secured the return of control over woodlands they had previously informally managed for generations.

As one of the few remaining tracts of the Miombo woodlands in the Babati District, the Duru-Haitemba woodlands were targeted to be turned into a forest reserve as early as 1985. (The Miombo woodlands stretch in a broad belt across south-central Africa, extending from Angola to Tanzania.) The intention was to protect the forest against further deforestation by deploying government forest guards to prevent expanding human settlements. By taking control, local governments were promised a steady source of revenue through the issuing of licenses for timber and pole-wood extraction, which would be granted to people living adjacent to the forest (Wily 1999).

The plan met significant opposition among local people whose livelihood was dependent on that tract of forest. There were also concerns about the plan's feasibility. As experience has shown, it is unrealistic to expect low-paid forest guards (many of whom are recruited from the same rural areas they are expected to police) to monitor the forest's border from villagers in need of forest products for basic subsistence. By the early 1990s, an agreement was reached to find a more acceptable management strategy. The solution ultimately involved allowing and assisting each of the eight villages that border the woodlands to take full rights and responsibility for its conservation.

ECONNECTION 4: SOCIOECOLOGICAL BENEFITS KNOWN TO ARISE FROM COMMUNITY CONSERVATION

First Benefit: Strengthens Communities

- builds local skills, interests, and capacities
- builds a sense of stewardship and community capacity for environmental problem solving that will remain with the community
- builds community cohesion
- increases the likelihood that the community will be able to solve future problems on their own

Second Benefit: Approaches Are Tailored to Local Needs

- As opposed to top-down approaches, which tend to serve nonlocal interests, community conservation can be highly responsive to unique community and environmental needs by incorporating local knowledge, and strategies and solutions will likely be well suited to local socioecological dynamics.

Third Benefit: Positive Outcomes for Individuals

- Knowledge of and relationship with surrounding ecosystems are enhanced.
- Working with others can have therapeutic benefits.
- Building social ties with others enhances individual well-being.

Fourth Benefit: Increased Likelihood of Local Acceptance and Sustainable Outcomes

- There is an increased likelihood of successful implementation when actions and decisions are viewed by those involved as responsible and appropriate.
- As local populations rely on having a healthy surrounding ecosystem, they have an incentive to be sure they get conservation strategies right.

Fifth Benefit: Efficient Use of Resources

- Enforcement and monitoring are often done cost-effectively, as informal social norms, trust, and a shared commitment to success are linked positively to compliance.

Adapted from Trotman (2008) and Wily (1999).

The results have been unmistakable. The forests show visible signs of gain, as most of the earlier unregulated in-forest settlement, charcoal burning, and illicit timber harvesting have ceased. The size of the woodland has actually increased. In the Duru-Haitemba Forest, which had previously suffered the most damage, the return of understory shrubbery, grasses, and bees points to improved forest health. In other parts of the forest, increases in wildlife biodiversity are being recorded. Hundreds of young village men have volunteered to patrol the protected areas, at zero cost to the government, out of a vested interest in the health of the forest (see, e.g., Lupala et al. 2015; see also Case Study 1).

Agrobiodiversity Conservation

Agrobiodiversity—all forms of life directly relevant to agriculture, including crops and livestock but also many other organisms, such as soil fauna, weeds, pests, and predators—is the result of natural and human selection processes, involving farmers, herders, and fishers over millennia. The future of food security, it is widely believed (Cairns 2015), hinges on agrobiodiversity. Agrobiodiversity gives us options when responding to whatever threats to food production we can expect to face in the future. Phenomena that can fall under the category of agrobiodiversity include harvested crop varieties, livestock breeds, fish species, and nondomesticated (wild) animals used for food; nonharvested species in production ecosystems that support food provision (like soil microbiota, pollinators, and other organisms such as earthworms); and nonharvested species in the wider environment that support food production ecosystems (such as species in a waterway that encourage the process of water purification).

CASE STUDY 1: PARTICIPATORY FOREST MANAGEMENT IN KENYA

Kenya has widely embraced participatory forest management, a variation of community conservation. Because of its track record, it is believed that this approach not only effectively achieves sustainable forest management goals but also simultaneously involves stakeholders whose livelihoods depend on the forest (Mbuvi et al. 2015). Participatory forest management is supported under the Forest Act of 2005. This act provides for the establishment, development, and sustainable management of forest resources for the socioeconomic development of the country. The avenues through which Kenyans in general, and Kenyan forest communities in particular, can directly or indirectly participate in the management and monitoring of their forests include the following: as members of community forest associations, as representatives appointed to the forest conservation committees, as representatives appointed to the Board of the Kenya Forest Service, and as individuals. The Forest Act of 2005 also allows forest communities to constitute up to 50 percent of the representation in the forest conservation committee that oversees the management of a recognized forest. The law further provides for community representation on the board of the Kenya Forest Service.

MOVEMENT MATTERS 1: OPEN SOURCE SEED

On April 17, 2014, on the campus of the University of Wisconsin, Madison, the Open Source Seed Initiative (OSSI) released twenty-nine seed varieties under an open source pledge printed on all OSSI-distributed seed packets. It reads as follows:

> This Open Source Seed Pledge is intended to ensure your freedom to use the seed contained herein in any way you choose, and to make sure those freedoms are enjoyed by all subsequent users. By opening this packet, you pledge that you will not restrict others' use of these seeds and their derivatives by patents, licenses, or

any other means. You pledge that if you transfer these seeds or their derivatives you will acknowledge the source of these seeds and accompany your transfer with this pledge. (quoted in Kloppenburg 2014)

In other words, any future plant that's derived from these **open source seeds** must be freely available. They cannot be patented, licensed, or commodified in any way, even in those instances where they have been bred or genetically modified into something new.

Irwin Goldman, professor of horticulture at the University of Wisconsin, Madison, was one of the organizers of the event. For him, OSSI is about restoring the practice of sharing that was once the rule among plant breeders around the world. In his own words, "If other breeders asked for our materials, we would send them a packet of seed, and they would do the same for us." Regrettably, he further notes that because of intellectual property rights "that way of working is no longer with us" (quoted in Charles 2014). For other members of the movement, the rationale of open source goes even deeper. For Jack Kloppenburg, professor of sociology at the University of Wisconsin, Madison, open source is a way to reshape our very food system: "The problem is concentration, and the narrow set of uses to which the technology and the breeding are being put" (quoted in Charles 2014). Within the first month after its launch, OSSI had received over two hundred orders from eight countries (Shemkus 2014). June 2015, after a three-day meeting near Hyderabad, India, saw the birth of Apna Beej (Hindi for "Our Seeds"): OSSI now has a sister organization, Open Source Seed System India (OSSSI). (See Figure 13.3.)

FIGURE 13.3   Pictured above is Indian attorney and prominent intellectual property rights activist Shahlini Butani. Six months prior to this picture being taken in June 2015, she was skeptical of open source seeds. She is now a vocal advocate, believing open source seeds encourage innovation and enhance biodiversity while respecting farmer livelihoods.

Jack Kloppenburg and Shahlini Butani.

CASE STUDY 2: THE SEED BANK THAT MAKES MEMORIES

The Seed Savers Exchange (SSE) is a US-based heritage seed bank in northeastern Iowa (see www.seedsavers.org). Founded in 1975, the SSE is a nonprofit organization that both saves and sells heirloom fruit, vegetable, and flower seeds. On this 890-acre farm, called the Heritage Farm, there are twenty-four thousand rare vegetable varieties, including about four thousand traditional varieties from eastern Europe and Russia; approximately seven hundred pre-1900 varieties of apples, which represent nearly every remaining pre-1900 variety left in existence out of the eight thousand that once existed; and a herd of the rare Ancient White Park cattle, which currently have an estimated global population below two thousand.

Although in part a gene and seed bank, the SSE is much more. Visitors can learn about the seeds being saved, including their history and how to cultivate the seeds and cook and prepare their harvest. If it's the right time of year, they can even experience how the fruits and vegetables taste. Indeed, calling SSE a memory bank doesn't go far enough, as many visitors find the organization also responsible for memory *making*. An example of this occurs at their heirloom tomato tasting workshop. During this event, participants get to not only taste more than forty different kinds of tomatoes but actively learn how to save the seeds of their favorite varieties for future planting (Carolan 2011a).

Agrobiodiversity is not only viewed as representing one of the keys to future food security but also widely seen as central to any sustainable model of food production. There is compelling evidence that, through the implementation of agroecology farming techniques, an approach relying heavily on ecological principles rather than commercial inputs [...], agrobiodiversity can help increase crop productivity—potentially even outproducing conventional agriculture. Agrobiodiversity is also a key ingredient to the effective control of disease and pest outbreaks without the use of harmful chemical inputs (Gliessman 2015).

The promotion of agrobiodiversity can take many forms. Simply allowing farmers to save seed from one year to be planted the next is a good place to start, particularly since patents and other controls like so-called **terminator technology** (genetically engineered seeds that produce sterile plants) are making this increasingly difficult (Carolan 2010a; see Movement Matters 1). **Memory banks**, spaces that preserve not only genetic material but the skills to grow and save seeds and prepare the fruits of those labors, also help promote agrobiodiversity by ensuring that future generations have a working knowledge of this species diversity (see Case Study 2).

Agrobiodiversity (or more specifically agrobiocultural diversity) can also be promoted and enhanced through activities related to urban agriculture, whether those gardens are located in, for example, Denver (Carolan and Hale 2016); Chicago (Taylor and Lovell 2015); Moshi, Tanzania (Schlesinger, Munishi, and Drescher 2015); or Rio Negro, Brazil (Emperaire and Eloy 2015). One study examining urban agriculture in migrant neighborhoods in Chicago found their gardens to be quite diverse, though the level of biodiversity varied by ethnicity group. African American gardens demonstrated the highest food plant richness (with an average of 16.3 food crops per garden), followed by Chinese-origin gardens (14) and Mexican-origin gardens (8.6) (Taylor and Lovell 2015). Cultural tastes and household-specific ethnic cuisine preferences also often compel urban gardeners to grow and thus preserve certain species not easily acquired at grocery stores and food markets (Carolan and Hale 2016). More than just a source of affordable food, these gardens also supply households with ingredients necessary for the making of certain cultural dishes, thus helping ensure both plant species and cultural survival.

Although humans pose the gravest threat to biodiversity, at the moment we are also its greatest potential ally. Once we accept our rightful identity as being part of nature, rather than seeing ourselves independent of it, new possibilities open up. These links are particularly conspicuous between agricultural systems and ecological ones, given the former's grounding (pun intended) in the latter. Agriculture, when done ecologically—*agroecology*—can go a long way toward preserving the ecological integrity of systems while helping to safeguard biological as well as cultural diversity and enhancing long-term food security.

Important Concepts

- agrobiodiversity
- biocultural diversity
- biopiracy
- community conservation
- ex situ and in situ conservation
- memory banking
- open source seeds
- participatory forest management
- tragedy of the commodity

Discussion Questions

1. What are the links between cultural and biological diversity?
2. Conventional agriculture has become a monoculture within a monoculture, where fields are populated by not just one crop but one variety of a single crop. What are some of the forces driving this specialization?
3. Can we rely entirely on zoos and gene banks when it comes to preserving our biological heritage?
4. Why isn't community conservation more popular in a country like the United States?

Suggested Additional Readings

Cocks, M., and F. Wiersum. 2014. "Reappraising the Concept of Biocultural Diversity: A Perspective from South Africa." *Human Ecology* 42(5): 727–737.

Dickman, A., P. Johnson, F. van Kesteren, and D. Macdonald. 2015. "The Moral Basis for Conservation: How Is It Affected by Culture?" *Frontiers in Ecology and the Environment* 13(6): 325–331.

Lynch, M., M. Long, and P. Stretesky. 2015. "Anthropogenic Development Drives Species to Be Endangered: Capitalism and the Decline of Species." In *Green Harms and Crimes: Critical Criminology in a Changing World*, edited by R. A. Sollund, 117–146. Critical Criminological Perspectives. Hampshire, UK: Palgrave Macmillan.

Relevant Internet Links

- www.biocultural.iied.org/about-biocultural-heritage. Resource seeking to promote "resilient farming systems and local economies" through a biocultural diversity lens.
- www.conservation.org/how/pages/hotspots.aspx. Excellent resource to learn more about biodiversity hotspots.
- www.gaiafoundation.org. The Gaia Foundation is committed to regenerating cultural and biocultural diversity and their website is rich in resources for those interested in the subject.
- www.ted.com/talks/lang/en/e_o_wilson_on_saving_life_on_earth.html. Video of well-known biologist E. O. Wilson talking about biodiversity and conservation.

Suggested Videos

- *Drop in the Ocean?* (2015). In less than fifty years, ocean life as we know it could be completely done for. This not only means dead oceans, but a dead ecosystem, and mass deaths of all who depend on it.
- *The End of the Line* (2010). Examines the subject of overfishing, suggesting the possibility of nearly fishless oceans by 2048 if sustainable fishing practices are not implemented soon.
- *The Fight for Amazonia* (2012). From the heart of the Amazon jungle comes a three-part series examining the strides being made to save the world's most endangered rain forest.
- *Queen of the Sun* (2010). A film on the honeybee crisis and colony collapse disorder.
- *Rachel Carson's "Silent Spring"* (1993). Though more than twenty years old, this production from the PBS series *The American Experience* offers an excellent historical lesson for anyone not familiar with this landmark book and its pioneering author.
- *Salmon Confidential* (2013). What's killing British Columbia's wild salmon? Watch this video and find out.

References

Agapow, P., O. Bininda-Emonds, K. Crandall, J. Gittleman, G. Mace, J. Marshall, and A. Purvis. 2004. "The Impact of Species Concept on Biodiversity Studies." *Quarterly Review of Biology* 79:161–179.

Booker, A., D. Johnston, and M. Heinrich. 2015. "Value Chains of Herbal Medicines—Ethnopharmacological and Analytical Challenges in a Globalizing World." In *Evidence-Based Validation of Herbal Medicine,* edited by P. Mukherjee, 29–44. Amsterdam: Elsevier.

Bullock, C. 2008. "The Economic and Social Aspects of Biodiversity." Government of Ireland.www.environ.ie/en/Heritage/PublicationsDocuments/FileDownLoad,17321,en.pdf.

Cairns, M., ed. 2015. *Shifting Cultivation and Environmental Change: Indigenous People, Agriculture and Forest Conservation.* New York: Routledge.

Carnicer, J., J. Sardans, C. Stefanescu, A. Ubach, M. Bartrons, D. Asensio, and J. Peñuelas. 2015. "Global biodiversity, stoichiometry and ecosystem function responses to human-induced C–N–P imbalances." *Journal of Plant Physiology* 172:82–91.

Carolan, M. 2010a. *Decentering Biotechnology: Assemblages Built and Assemblages Masked.* Burlington, VT: Ashgate.

– – –. 2011a. *Embodied Food Politics.* Burlington, VT: Ashgate.

Carolan, M., and J. Hale. 2016. "'Growing' Communities with Urban Agriculture: Generating Value Above and Below Ground." *Community Development.* DOI: 10.1080/15575330.2016.1158198.

Charles, D. 2014. "Plant Breeders Release First 'Open Source Seeds.'" NPR, Apr. 17. www.npr.org/sections/thesalt/2014/04/17/303772556/plant-breeders-release-first-open-source-seeds.

Chensheng, L., K. Warchol, and R. Callahan. 2014. "Sub-Lethal Exposure to Neonicotinoids Impaired Honey Bees Winterization Before Proceeding to Colony Collapse Disorder." *Bulletin of Insectology* 67(1): 125–130.

Clausen, R., and S. Longo. 2012. "The Tragedy of the Commodity and the Face of AquAdvantage Salmon." *Development and Change* 43(1): 229–251.

Conservation Measures Partnership. 2012. "Threats Taxonomy." Accessed May 17. www.conservationmeasures.org/initiatives/threats-actions-taxonomies/threats-taxonomy.

Costanza, R., R. d'Arge, R. de Groot, S. Farber, M. Grasso, B. Hannon, S. Naeem, K. Limburg, J. Paruelo, R. O'Neill, R. Raskin, P. Sutton, and M. van den Belt. 1997. "The Value of the World's Ecosystem Services and Natural Capital." *Nature* 387:253–260.

Costanza, R., R. de Groot, P. Sutton, S. van der Ploeg, S. Anderson, I. Kubiszewski, S. Farber, and R. Turner. 2014. "Changes in the Global Value of Ecosystem Services." *Global Environmental Change* 26:152–158.

Dell'Amore, C. 2013. "20,000 Species Are Near Extinction: Is It Time to Rethink How We Decide Which to Save?" *National Geographic*, Dec. 16.

Doublet, V., M. Labarussias, J. Miranda, R. Moritz, and R. Paxton. 2015. "Bees Under Stress: Sublethal Doses of a Neonicotinoid Pesticide and Pathogens Interact to Elevate Honey Bee Mortality Across the Life Cycle." *Environmental Microbiology* 17(4): 969–983.

Edmonds Institute. 2006. "Out of Brazil: A Peanut Worth Billions (to the US)." Edmonds, WA, March. www.edmonds-institute.org/outofbrazil.pdf.

Edney, M. 1997. *Mapping an Empire: The Geographical Construction of British India, 1765–1843.* Chicago: University of Chicago Press.

Emperaire, L., and L. Eloy. 2015. "Amerindian Agriculture in an Urbanising Amazonia (Rio Negro, Brazil)." *Bulletin of Latin American Research* 34(1): 70–84.

Forgie, V., P. Horsley, and J. Johnston. 2001. "Facilitating Community-Based Conservation Initiatives." Science for Conservation Report no. 169. Department of Conservation, Wellington, New Zealand. www.doc.govt.nz/upload/documents/science-and-technical/Sfc169.pdf.

Garcia, S., J. Rice, and A. Charles, eds. 2014. *Governance of Marine Fisheries and Biodiversity Conservation.* Hoboken, NJ: Wiley.

Gliessman, S. 2015. *Agroecology: The Ecology of Sustainable Food Systems.* 3rd ed. Boca Raton, FL: CRC.

Harley, B. 1989. "Deconstructing the Map." *Cartographica* 26:1–20.

Harris, L., and H. Hazen. 2006. "Power of Maps: (Counter) Mapping for Conservation." *ACME: An International E-Journal for Critical Geographies* 4:99–130.

Hauck, J., C. Görg, R. Varjopuro, O. Ratamäki, J. Maes, H. Wittmer, and K. Jax. 2013. "'Maps Have an Air of Authority': Potential Benefits and Challenges of Ecosystem Service Maps at Different Levels of Decision Making." *Ecosystem Services* 4:25–32.

Hazen, H., and P. Anthamatten. 2004. "Representation of Ecoregions by Protected Areas at the Global Scale." *Physical Geography* 25:499–512.

Hunter, M., and J. Gibbs. 2007. *Fundamentals of Conservation Biology.* 3rd ed. Malden, MA: Blackwell.

ICTSD (International Center for Trade and Sustainable Development). 2010. "Food Giant Nestlé Accused of Biopiracy." *Bridges Trade BioRes* 10(10): 3. ictsd.org/downloads/biores/biores10-10.pdf.

Jebaraj, P. 2011. "Development of Bt Brinjal: A Case of Bio-Piracy." *Hindu*, Aug. 10.

Kloppenburg, J. 2014. "The Unexpected Outcome of the Open Source Seed Initiative's Licensing Debate." Open-Source, June 3. opensource.com/law/14/5/legal-issues-open-source-seed-initiative.

Kozloff, N. 2010. *No Rain in the Amazon: How South America's Climate Change Affects the Entire Planet.* New York: Palgrave.

Longo, S., R. Clausen, and B. Clark. 2015. *The Tragedy of the Commodity: Oceans, Fisheries, and Aquaculture.* New Brunswick, NJ: Rutgers University Press.

Lovejoy, T. 1980. "A Projection of Species Extinctions." In *The Global 2000 Report to the President*, edited by G. Barney, 2:328–373. Washington, DC: US Government Printing Office.

Lupala, Z., L. Lusambo, Y. Ngaga, and A. Makatta. 2015. "The Land Use and Cover Change in Miombo Woodlands Under Community Based Forest Management and Its Implication to Climate Change Mitigation: A Case of Southern Highlands of Tanzania." *International Journal of Forestry Research* 459102. www.hindawi.com/journals/ijfr/2015/459102/abs.

MacKenzie, D., and G. Spinardi. 1995. "Tacit Knowledge, Weapons Design, and the Uninvention of Nuclear Weapons." *American Journal of Sociology* 101(1): 44–99.

Maffi, L., and E. Woodley. 2010. *Biocultural Diversity Conservation: A Global Sourcebook.* London: Earthscan.

Mayden, R. 1997. "A Hierarchy of Species Concepts: The Denouement in the Saga of the Species Problem." In *Species: The Units of Biodiversity*, edited by M. Claridge, H. Dawah, and M. Wilson, 381–424. New York: Chapman and Hall.

Mbuvi, M., J. Musyoki, W. Ayiemba, and J. Gichuki. 2015. "Determining the Potential for Introducing and Sustaining Participatory Forest Management: A Case Study of South Nandi Forest of Western Kenya." *International Journal of Biodiversity and Conservation* 7(3): 190–201.

Meijaard, E., and V. Nijman. 2003. "Primate Hotspots on Borneo: Predictive Value for General Biodiversity and the Effects of Taxonomy." *Conservation Biology* 17:725–732.

Mora, C., D. Tittensor, S. Adl, A. Simpson, and B. Worm. 2011. "How Many Species Are There on Earth and in the Ocean?" *PLOS ONE* 9(8): e1001127.

Nazarea, V. 2005. *Heirloom Seeds and Their Keepers: Marginality and Memory in the Conservation of Biological Diversity.* Tucson: University of Arizona Press.

N. L. 2010. "What's Up Pussycat? Saving the Tiger." Babbage (blog), *Economist*, Nov. 24. www.economist.com/blogs/babbage/2010/11/saving_tiger.

Peterson, A., and A. Navarro-Siguenza. 1999. "Alternative Species Concepts as Bases for Determining Priority Conservation Areas." *Conservation Biology* 13:427–431.

Pimm, S., C. Jenkins, R. Abell, T. Brooks, J. Gittleman, L. Joppa, P. Raven, C. Roberts, and J. Sexton. 2014. "The Biodiversity of Species and Their Rates of Extinction, Distribution, and Protection." *Science* 344(6187): 1246752.

Ramon, K. 2011. "Debates on Protecting Traditional Knowledge in an Age of Globalization." In *Interdisciplinary Perspectives in Political Theory*, edited by M. Kulkarni, 189–215. Thousand Oaks, CA: Sage.

Schlesinger, J., E. Munishi, and A. Drescher. 2015. "Ethnicity as a Determinant of Agriculture in an Urban Setting: Evidence from Tanzania." *Geoforum* 64:138–145.

Shemkus, S. 2014. "Fighting the Seed Monopoly." *Guardian* (London), May 2.

Smith, E. 2001. "On the Coevolution of Cultural, Linguistic, and Biological Diversity." In *Biocultural Diversity: Linking Language, Knowledge, and the Environment*, edited by L. Maffi, 95–117. Washington, DC: Smithsonian Institution Press.

Spilsbury, R. 2010. *Deforestation Crisis*. New York: Rosen.

Stephenson, J., F. Berkes, N. Turner, and J. Dick. 2014. "Biocultural Conservation of Marine Ecosystems: Examples from New Zealand and Canada." *Indian Journal of Traditional Knowledge* 13(2): 257–265.

Stepp J., S. Cervone, H. Castaneda, A. Lasseter, G. Stocks, and Y. Gichon. 2004. "Development of a GIS for Global Biocultural Diversity." *Policy Matters* 13:267–270.

Taylor, J., and S. Lovell. 2015. "Urban Home Gardens in the Global North: A Mixed Methods Study of Ethnic and Migrant Home Gardens in Chicago, IL." *Renewable Agriculture and Food Systems* 30(1): 22–32.

Trotman, R. 2008. *The Benefits of Community Conservation: A Literature Review*. Report prepared for the Auckland, New Zealand, Regional Council, Dec. www.arc.govt.nz/albany/fms/main/Documents/Auckland/Volunteers/Benefits%20of%20community%20conservation.pdf.

Tuck, S., C. Winqvist, F. Mota, J. Ahnström, L. Turnbull, and J. Bengtsson. 2014. "Land-Use Intensity and the Effects of Organic Farming on Biodiversity: A Hierarchical Meta-Analysis." *Journal of Applied Ecology* 51(3): 746–755.

UNEP (United Nations Environmental Programme). 2007. *Declaration of the Rights of Indigenous People*. Sixty-First Session, UN General Assembly, New York.

———. 2008. *State and Trends of the Environment, 1987–2007*. New York. www.unep.org/geo/geo4/report/02_Atmosphere.pdf.

Vandergeest, P. 1996. "Mapping Nature: Territorialization of Forest Rights in Thailand." *Society and Natural Resources* 9:159–175.

Vijayan, V. 1987. *Keoladeo National Park Ecology Study*. Bombay: Bombay Natural History Society.

———. 1991. *Keoladeo National Park Ecology Study, 1980–1990*. Bombay: Bombay Natural History Society.

White House. 2014. Fact Sheet: The Economic Challenge Posed by Declining Pollinator Populations. Office of the Press Secretary, Washington, DC, June 20. www.whitehouse.gov/the-press-office/2014/06/20/fact-sheet-economic-challenge-posed-declining-pollinator-populations.

WHO (World Health Organization). 2012c. "WHO Definition of Health." Geneva. Accessed May 19. www.who.int/about/definition/en/print.html.

Wilson, E. O. (1992) 1999. *The Diversity of Life*. New York: Norton.

Wily, L. 1999. "Moving Forward in African Community Forestry: Trading Power, Not Use Rights." *Society and Natural Resources* 12(1): 49–61.

Wood, D. 1993. "The Power of Maps." *Scientific American* (May): 88–94.

Discussion Topics

1. Why is biodiversity important?
2. What are the ramifications of declining biodiversity?
3. Identify four threats to biodiversity, and discuss potential approach to solutions.
4. Discuss the interaction between culture and biodiversity.
5. What are the two major solutions advanced by the author regarding the loss of biodiversity?

CONCLUSION

This article explains the important role that sociology plays in the investigation of social problems. The contribution of sociology to social problems is unique through its perspective, which is sociological imagination. Coined by C. Wright Mills, the concept of sociological imagination refers to the ability to establish a link between "biography" and "history." That is, sociological imagination enables us to understand that our personal troubles are connected to public issues. In a sense, this unique perspective of sociology allows uncovering or discovering the influential effects of social structure on social problems, which leads to theory formulation: theorizing. A social theory can be defined as a systematic, disciplined, and logical explanation of social phenomena, such as social problems. The process of theorizing occurs in three major steps: (1) Identify a problem ("the something ain't right"); (2) Describe the nature of the problem, its manifestation, and implications; and (3) Provide a description of how the problem can be solved and the impact of the solution on society.

UNIT 6

APPROACH OF SOLUTIONS TO SOCIAL PROBLEMS

Introduction

This unit focuses on the potential solutions to social problems. Social movements are identified as instruments used to bring about social changes necessary for structural problems we are facing in society. Defined as outside groups of institutionalized power that use conventional and unconventional methods to reach their goals by Almeida in his article, titled "*Social Movements: The Structure of Collective Action*," a social movement can be used as a catalyst to disrupt the status quo. In this article, Almeida describes types of social movements and their characteristics. He also discusses the process by which social movements come into existence and their structures.

In the second article of this unit, titled "*Conclusion: Mounting Crises and the Pathway Forward*," Almeida reiterates his thoughts about social movements as a pathway forward in our current world with its increasing problems linked to inequality. However, he implores, social movements face three major threats: economic inequality, increasing authoritarianism, and ecological crises.

Social Movements: The Structure of Collective Action

Paul Almeida

Paul Almeida, "Social Movements: The Structure of Collective Action," *Social Movements: The Structure of Collective Mobilization*, pp. 1-18, 181, 187-220. Copyright © 2019 by University of California Press. Reprinted with permission.

Editor's Introduction

This article titled "Social Movements: The Structure of Collective Action" by Paul Almeida focuses on social movements. This article was selected to be included in this text because social movements are important for bringing about social changes necessary for more equitable society, a sine qua non condition for the reduction of poverty, which is one of the major causes of social problems. After reading this article, you will gain a working definition of social movements and identify different social movements in the United States.

The Structure of Collective Action

The voluntary coming together of people in joint action has served as a major engine of social transformation throughout human history. From the spread of major world religions to community-led public health campaigns for reducing debilitating vector-borne diseases at the village level, collective mobilization may lead to profound changes in a wide variety of contexts and societies. At key historical moments, groups have unified in struggle in attempts to overthrow and dismantle systems of oppression and subordination, as observed in indigenous peoples' resistance to colonialism and in rebellions launched by enslaved populations. In the twenty-first century, collective action by ordinary citizens around the world could prove decisive in slowing down global warming and in supporting planetary survival. In short, the collective mobilization of people creates a powerful human resource that can be used for a range of purposes. In this [reading] we explore a particular type of collective action—social movements.

The study of social movements has increased markedly over the past two decades. This is largely the result of theoretical and empirical advances in sociology and related fields as well as an upsurge in collective action in the United States and around the world. The variety of mobilizations examined by students of social movements ranges from the anti-Trump resistance to antineoliberal and austerity protests in Asia, Africa, Europe, and Latin America. Already by 2011, global protests reached such a crescendo that *Time* magazine crowned the "Protester" as the "Person of the Year" (Andersen 2011). Then, in stunning fashion, citizens broke the record for the largest simultaneous demonstrations in the history of the United States, with the women's marches in 2017 and 2018. With so much social movement activity occurring in the twenty-first century, some experts predict we are moving into a "social movement society" (Meyer 2014) or a "social movement world" (Goldstone 2004).

On the basis of the best systematic evidence available from global surveys and "big data" collections of protest events over time (Ward 2016), social movement activity continues to be sustained around the world at heightened levels in the contemporary era (Dodson 2011; Karatasli, Kumral and Silver 2018). Indeed, over the past two decades groups engaging in social movement activities have not just proven to be impressive by their scale and intensity of mobilization, but have also transformed the social and political landscapes in the United States and across the globe. A brief sketch of some of the largest movements, including the anti-Trump resistance, immigrant rights, and movements for economic and climate justice, exemplifies these claims.

Women's March and Anti-Trump Resistance

The Women's March against the newly inaugurated Trump administration in early 2017 represented the largest simultaneous mass mobilization in US history, with the organizers, in the opening of their mission statement, explicitly stating a threat to the protection of rights, health, and safety as the primary motive for the unprecedented demonstrations.[1] Activists repeated the marches again in January 2018 with equally impressive levels of mobilization. The initiators of the mass actions strived for an intersectional strategy to unite women and others against structural exclusions along the lines of race, class, gender, and sexuality. The Women's Marches were held in hundreds of US cities and drew between four and five million participants (see figures 14.1 and 14.2), including people in dozens of countries outside the United States. The movement immediately evolved into the "Resistance" and has sustained mobilizations against subsequent exclusionary policies and public gestures by the Trump administration against immigrants, women, racial minorities, religious minorities, and LGBTQ communities (Meyer and Tarrow 2018).

1. www.womensmarch.com/mission/

FIGURE 14.1   Locations of Women's March, 2017.

Compiled by author from

FIGURE 14.2   Women's March, 2018.

Compiled by author from

Immigrant Rights

Between February and May 2006, the immigrant rights' movement burst on to the public scene in dramatic style with massive demonstrations and rallies in large and small cities in dozens of US states (Bloemraad, Voss, and Lee 2011; Zepeda-Millán 2017). The participants found motivation to take to the streets from new legislation (House Bill 4437) passed in the Republican-dominated U.S. House of Representatives that would make living in the United States without proper documentation a serious criminal offense for the undocumented, as well as for those aiding them. The impending negative consequences associated with this legislation mobilized communities throughout the national territory, with several cities breaking records for protest attendance. The resources used to mobilize the movement included organizations of churches, radio stations, public schools, and an emerging pan-Latino identity (Mora et al. 2018). With some of the demonstrations drawing up to a million participants, Congress backed down and shelved the legislation in a stalemate between the House and the Senate. The power of mass collective action had prevented the implementation of a punitive law that potentially would have led to widespread disruption of working-class immigrant communities in the United States. A similar campaign emerged in the summer of 2018 against the Trump administration's policy of family separation of immigrants seeking asylum at the US-Mexican border, with protest events reported in over seven hundred cities.

Movements Around the Globe for Economic Justice

Between 2000 and 2018, from the advanced capitalist nations of Europe and North America to large swathes of the developing world, citizens launched major campaigns against government economic cutbacks and privatization of social services and the state infrastructure—or what economists and sociologists call the economic policies of *neoliberalism*. Labor flexibility in France, austerity in Spain, Portugal, and Greece, and economic reforms in Argentina, Brazil, China, Costa Rica, and India all drew hundreds of thousands of people to public plazas and mass demonstrations demanding protection of their *social citizenship rights*—the basic right to a modicum of economic welfare provisioned by the state (Somers 2008).

The global movement for economic justice took off in the wealthy capitalist nations in the late 1990s and early 2000s with major protest events outside of elite financial summits in Seattle, Prague, Davos, Doha, Cancun, Quebec City, and Genoa. The mobilizations kept up steam by aligning with movements in the global South via the World Social Forum network. In July 2017 the global economic justice movement mobilized over one hundred thousand people to demonstrate against the G20 economic summit in Hamburg, Germany. Similar types of street demonstrations occurred in the United States over economic inequality between late 2011 and early 2012 with the occupation of public squares in the "Occupy Wall Street" movement. Privatizations of water administration, public health, telecommunications, and energy catalyzed some of the largest mobilizations in South America, Asia, and Africa over the past two decades. Taken together, there has been a recent upsurge of movements around the world struggling for more equitable forms of economic globalization (Almeida 2010a; Castells 2015; Almeida and Chase-Dunn 2018). On the dark side of politics, we also find that extremists and populist demagogues use the heightened inequities associated with economic globalization and free trade to mobilize right-wing and racist movements in the United States, South America, and Europe (Berezin 2009; Robinson 2014).[2]

2. Conservative movements in the USA would be another major collective mobilization over the past decade. The Tea Party movement emerged rapidly on the political scene in the first of months of 2009 immediately following the historical

Even though the base of the movement includes white working-class groups, it has large funders and does not represent the most excluded social groups in the United States.

Transnational Movement for Climate Justice

Since 2000 a worldwide movement has gained momentum in an attempt to slow down global warming. The "climate justice movement" seeks a global accord among the world's nations for an immediate and drastic reduction in carbon emissions. By 2006 the climate mobilizations had reached multiple countries on every continent. Climate justice activists use cyber networks and social media to coordinate with hundreds of nongovernmental organizations, concerned citizens, scientists, and environmental groups around the planet to hold public gatherings and demonstrations demanding governmental and industry action to reduce greenhouse gases. The global mobilizations usually take place in conjunction with annual United Nations-sponsored climate summits in order to place pressure on national leaders to act (including an enormous street march of four hundred thousand persons in New York City in 2014). Between 2014 and 2018 alone, the climate justice movement successfully mobilized thousands of protest events in 175 countries on multiple occasions—the most extensive transnational movement in history.

These four movements demonstrate the multiple facets of social movements discussed in the pages that follow. They all involve *sustained challenges seeking social change using resources to maintain mobilization*. All four movements first mobilized in reaction to real and perceived *threats to their interests*. Finally, and perhaps most germane here, the movements resulted in deep changes within the societies they operated in. The Women's Marches sent a powerful message that all attempts to deepen social exclusion by the newly elected Trump administration would be met with massive resistance. The immigrant rights movement forced anti-immigrant politicians to backpedal from their legislation as the mobilizations spilled over into a movement that fights for other immigrant rights issues, such as the right to education and employment for immigrant youth—the "DREAMers' Movement" (Nicholls 2014)—a comprehensive immigration reform act that provides a path to citizenship, and an end to the policy of family separation of asylum seekers. Economic austerity protests have swept several new left-wing political parties into executive power and parliaments in South America and southern Europe. The climate justice movement forced a long-awaited global treaty on carbon emissions at the end of the 2015 Paris Climate Summit.

Defining Social Movements

The four movements portrayed above clearly exhibit properties of social movement activity. Throughout this

inauguration of Barack Obama to the presidency. The first coordinated actions on a national scale occurred on April 15, 2009 (tax day), and were followed up by aggressive protests in the summer of 2009 during town hall discussions of Obama's new national health insurance program (Van Dyke and Meyer 2014). By late 2010 the Tea Party had shifted emphasis to electoral politics, winning major contests at the local and national levels. The trend would continue in national and local elections in 2012 and 2014, respectively (Vasi et al. 2014). By 2016 several Tea Party candidates competed in the Republican primary for president of the United States. As the Tea Party moved into electoral politics, it transformed the US two-party system by polarizing the Republican Party into an establishment branch and a libertarian branch Skocpol and Williamson 2012), prior to the rise of Trumpism.

text, we will work with the following definition: *A social movement is an excluded collectivity in sustained interaction with economic and political elites seeking social change* (Tarrow 2011). In such situations, ordinary people come together to pursue a common goal. Social movements are usually composed of groups outside of institutionalized power that use unconventional strategies (e.g., street marches, sit-ins, dramatic media events) along with more conventional ones (petitions, letter-writing campaigns) to achieve their aims (Snow and Soule 2009). The outsider status and unconventional tactics of social movements distinguish them from other political entities, such as lobbying associations, nonprofit organizations, and political parties (though these more formal organizations may originate from social movements). Most people participate in movements as volunteers and offer their time, skills, and other human resources to maintaining movement survival and accomplishing goals. Throughout this book, I will emphasize the *exclusion* of social groups from institutional, economic, and political power as a primary motive for engaging in social movement actions.

Social movements range from community-based environmental movements battling local pollution, to women's movements organized on a transnational scale attempting to place pressure on national governments and international institutions to protect and expand the rights of girls and women (Viterna and Fallon 2008). The modern social movement form arose with the spread of parliamentary political systems and nationally integrated capitalist economies in the nineteenth century (Tilly and Wood 2012). Before the nineteenth century, collective action was largely based on local grievances at the village level and mobilization was sustained for shorter periods of time (Tilly 1978). Nonetheless, we observe important forms of collective mobilization throughout human history (Chase-Dunn 2016). The core movement elements of *sustained collective challenges* by *excluded social groups* attempting to protect themselves from *social, political, economic, and environmental harms* form the basis of our definition of social movements and drive the largest campaigns of collective action in the twenty-first century.

The Core Movement Elements

Sustained Collective Mobilization

Social movements are collective and sustained over a period of time. How and why individuals come together to pursue common goals provides much of the content of this book. The larger the scale of collective action, the longer the mobilization should endure to be considered a "movement." Local neighborhood and community movements may last for only a few months or a year as they tend to have short-term and specific goals, such as preventing pollution from a nearby facility or demanding street lights for nighttime safety. Larger national-level mobilizations likely need to sustain themselves for at least a year to be considered a social movement. In contrast, a single demonstration or protest does not constitute a social movement. At the same time, collective actors must find ways to maintain momentum and unity. Preexisting organizations, social relationships of friends, neighbors, the workplace, schools, ethnic ties, collective identities, and a variety of resources assist in prolonging the mobilization process.

Excluded Social Groups

Social movements are largely constituted by groups with relatively less political and economic power. Their exclusionary status provides the rationale for taking the social movement form (Burawoy 2017; Mora et al.

2017). Non-excluded groups benefit from more routine access to government and economic elites in terms of having their voices heard, and are *relatively* more likely to receive favorable resolutions for their grievances via petitions, elections, lobbying, and meetings with officials. Excluded groups (along racial, economic, citizenship, and gender lines, among many others) lack this routine access and may at times resort to less conventional forms of seeking influence to gain the attention of authorities and power brokers.

Social, Economic, and Environmental Harms

A central motivation for social movement mobilization involves real and perceived harms. A critical mass of individuals must come under the threat of a particular harm, such as discrimination, job loss, or environmental health, that motivates them to unify and launch a social movement campaign, especially when institutional channels fail to resolve the issue at hand. Opportunities may also arrive to reduce long-standing harms, such as decades of discrimination or economic exploitation (Tarrow 2011). Social movement mobilization is much more likely to materialize when large numbers of people mutually sense they are experiencing or suffering from similar circumstances. This was precisely the case for the 2006 immigrants' rights protests discussed above. Millions of citizens and noncitizens came under a suddenly imposed threat of criminal prosecution for their undocumented status or for aiding nonlegalized immigrants. This led to mutual awareness among immigrant communities and to rapid mobilization (Zepeda-Millán 2017).

Throughout the text, I will emphasize these three core movement elements of (1) collective and sustained mobilization, (2) social exclusion, and (3) threats as key dimensions in characterizing social movement activity.

Basic Social Movement Concepts

As in most subfields of sociology and the social sciences there is a vernacular or jargon for discussing key social processes and terms. The field of social movements is no exception. As we progress deeper into the study of social movements in this book, new terms will be introduced and defined. To begin, some of the principal concepts used to discuss social movements are presented below.

Grievances and Threats

An initial condition for social mobilization centers on shared grievances. In other words, people collectively view some facet of social life as a problem and in need of alteration (Simmons 2014). A wide variety of grievances have ignited social movement campaigns, including police abuse, racial and gender discrimination, economic inequality, and pollution. At times, communities experience grievances as "suddenly imposed," stimulating mobilization in a relatively short time horizon (Walsh et al. 1997). Recurring instances of suddenly imposed and shocking grievances were behind the anti–police abuse demonstrations in the United States between 2014 and 2015 following jury acquittals or dramatic videos that went "viral" on social media and the internet. These incidents catalyzed the Black Lives Matter movement into a new round of the struggle for racial justice in the United States (Taylor 2016).

At my home institution, the University of California, Merced, many students experienced the surprising presidential election results of November 2016 as a suddenly imposed grievance. The university is composed of a large majority of students of color, many coming from immigrant families. The following e-mail I received from a student the day after the elections demonstrates how the unexpected election results immediately led to some of the largest protests in the history of the new campus:

> Good morning Professor Almeida,
>
> As professor of the social movements, protests, and collective action class, I thought I'd inform you of the protest that occurred on campus last night. At about 11:00 pm, students on UC Merced classifieds on Facebook, posted that they would organize to speak up against the results of the presidential election. Students started getting together in the main entrance of the university, they advanced through the summits and the sierra terraces encouraging students to come out of their rooms. The students continued walking through scholars lane and finally gathered around the New Beginnings statue. It was there that the organizers informed the students that there would be another protest today at 10:00 am in front of the library. Afterward, the students walked back downhill chanting…. Students were also seen holding signs with words in Spanish such as "la lucha sigue" and "marcha". The crowd of students gathered once again in the summits courtyard, where the organizers reannounced the protest that will take place today and where the students continued their chants. A few trump supporters were seen during the protest, but the organizers reminded the students that "this is a peaceful protest". The entire protest lasted about two hours.

We will later discuss how grievances move from the individual to the group level. But even in this short e-mail we can see elements of the structure of collective action discussed throughout this book, including the role of Facebook and social media, everyday organizations such as the dorms, and the appeals used to bring more people into demonstrations. Another important issue related to grievances […] is whether people are responding to an intensification of grievances (*threats*) or to new possibilities (*opportunities*) to reduce longstanding grievances.

Strategy

The actual planning of demands, goals, tactics, and targets as well as their timing is part of an overall social movement strategy (Maney et al. 2012; Meyer and Staggenborg 2012). Once the collective action process moves from grievance formation to actual mobilization, social movements will likely formulate a set of *demands*. Demands are communicated to power holders as a means to negotiate and attempt to address and reduce the original grievances. Scholars also use the term "claims" interchangeably with movement demands. Demands or claims are often written in formal letters during negotiations, as well as displayed on banners and chanted in unison during protest rallies, or publicly stated during press conferences held by social movement leaders. Social movements increasingly express demands and claims via various social media platforms (e.g., Facebook, WhatsApp, Twitter). Demands may be communicated in very specific terms, such as raising the salaries of fast-food workers to a fixed wage amount (e.g., $15 per hour), as observed in recent strike campaigns in the United States.

Goals are generally conceived as broader than a set of demands (though they often coincide); for example, the larger goal of a "living wage" and "economic justice" for fast-food industry workers. Goals and demands are also categorized from reform minded to radical—from changing part of a government policy to calling for the complete transformation of a society, the latter acting as a common aim defining revolutionary social movements. [... G]oals provide a way to measure movement success in achieving social change in terms of specified objectives.

Social movements also employ a variety of *tactics*—a repertoire of actions from teach-ins and educational workshops to media events (such as press conferences) and street demonstrations. Tactics range from the highly conventional, such as petitions and letter-writing campaigns, to the highly unconventional and disruptive, such as "die-ins," sit-ins, and traffic obstruction. At times, tactics may escalate to the level of violent acts, as in the case of riots, revolutions, and terrorism. Classifying tactics into conventional, disruptive, and violent is a useful categorization scheme. It leads to interesting questions about the conditions shaping the type of tactic and its effectiveness in mobilizing people, influencing public opinion, and achieving stated goals.

As another component of their overall strategy, social movements eventually *target* institutions to present their demands. The targets are often multiple and commonly involve some part of the government such as city councils, school boards, state agencies, the courts, and congressional and parliamentary bodies, which may be the final arbiters of the conflict. Depending on the nature of the movement, a variety of targets may be drawn into the campaign, including the mass media and other institutions (schools, hospitals, churches, private industry).

Coalitions

Collective actors often join with other groups to extend mobilization to other regions and sectors of society. When a collectivity aligns with at least one other group to engage in collective action, a *coalition* has formed. The formation of social movement coalitions raises intriguing research questions about their composition and consequences for mobilization (Van Dyke and McCammon 2010; Van Dyke and Amos 2017). At first glance, a coalition of multiple social groups (e.g., students, immigrant rights organizations, women's associations, environmentalists) appears to strengthen the level and size of mobilization by publicly exhibiting that several sectors of society are unified over a particular grievance or issue such as police abuse or a government's foreign policy in launching a military action. Large coalitions may be especially potent in struggles for democracy and human rights in authoritarian regimes by demonstrating that large segments of society oppose the prevailing lack of freedom and civil liberties (Schock 2005; Almeida 2005; 2008a). At other times, coalitions introduce new problems in sustaining collective action by trying to negotiate a consensus about strategy in terms of tactics, goals, and targets. This may lead to movement infighting and the rapid dissolution of mobilization.

Framing

The framing process incorporates many of the ideological and cognitive components of collective action (Snow et al. 2018). [... M]ovement leaders actively convey grievances to larger audiences in order to draw in more support for the movement and maintain commitments from movement participants. Movement ingenuity and creativity are put to the test in the way activists use existing cultural idioms and symbols to express social problems and motivate people into action.

The State

Throughout this work, I will use *the state* to refer to the government. The state may be local (e.g., city council), regional, or national. Social movements are deeply shaped by states, and at times movements have a profound impact in changing government policies and priorities. Different types of states often determine the possibilities for collective action and the forms they take. Repressive governments that do not allow citizens to form autonomous organizations or to assemble publicly place enormous obstacles for groups to initiate social movement campaigns. In some cases, governmental repression pushes groups into more radical demands and forms of mobilization. More-democratic states will likely tolerate social movement mobilizations and use softer forms of repression when trying to control or pacify mass dissent (e.g., manipulate the mass media, deny permits for demonstrations). Even at the local level in the United States there is wide variation among city governments and the amount of political space granted to excluded and marginalized populations.

Social Movement Organizations

Once social movements come into existence, they are likely to form organizations that support further mobilization (McAdam 1999 [1982]). We call these kinds of associations social movement organizations (SMOs) (McCarthy and Zald 1977; McAdam and Scott 2005; Minkoff and McCarthy 2005). The acronym SMOs has become so widespread in social movement studies that scholars often neglect to define the term. Examples of SMOs include the People for the Ethical Treatment of Animals (PETA), and the internationally active environmental organization Greenpeace. SMOs appear to be proliferating across national boundaries in the twenty-first century (Smith and Wiest 2012) [...].

These core social movement concepts are applied throughout this text. We can briefly start using these terms by returning to the Women's March and addressing the following questions: What were the grievances driving the largest mobilizations in US history? How would you describe the strategy of the organizers of the event? What were the central demands and goals of the marches? How would you classify the core tactic of the street march (conventional or disruptive)? What features did the organizers use in their framing strategies to bring millions out to protest? The maps in Figures 14.1 and 14.2 illustrate where the women's marches occurred in the 3,007 counties of the United States. Why did some counties have multiple women's marches while many more counties failed to produce even one event?

Major Themes in the Structure of Social Movements

[W]e explore [...] the multifaceted nature of social movements—the collective coming together of ordinary people to overcome exclusion and mount sustained campaigns for social change. We move from *methods* and *theoretical underpinnings* of social movements to the major subareas guiding the study of collective mobilization. These themes include *social movement emergence, collective action frames, individual recruitment and participation, the impacts of social movements,* and *the global spread of movement activities.*

Methods

While it might seem rather simple to identify a social movement on the basis of the concepts just outlined, systematically dissecting movement dynamics using social science methods is a challenging process. I [first] classify levels of social movement activity, from the microscale of everyday forms of resistance in small insular groups to the macroscale of mobilization spreading over entire societies and across countries. I next introduce the major techniques used in social movement research, including observation, interviews, newspapers, social media (Twitter, Facebook, WhatsApp, etc.), surveys, archives, and government statistics. Each method is directly linked to specific areas and dimensions of collective action, such as movement emergence and movement recruitment. Readers will be introduced to strategies on how to carry out collective action research, especially the appropriate techniques for collecting data for particular dimensions of social movement activity.

Theory

[This section] introduces the main theoretical explanations for social movement dynamics. Theories provide guides that reduce the social world to the most important features driving social movement mobilization. We review early models of social movements that failed to account for the unequal distribution of power and resources in modern societies. The universe of contemporary movement theories will be examined, including rational actor, new social movement, and political process frameworks. The now-dominant political process approach centers on the larger political environment and how differentially configured political contexts shape the likelihood of social movement emergence, forms of mobilization, and movement outcomes. Special attention is given to the negative conditions driving collective action within the political process tradition as movements in the twenty-first century increasingly respond to environmental, political, social, and economic threats. With social movement theories in hand, readers will have the tools to scrutinize elite and mass media accounts of real-time social movements in terms of their origins, motivations, and consequences for changing society.

Movement Emergence

[This section] examines how social movements are most likely to arise when a particular collectivity comes under threat or receives signals from the political environment that advantages may be forthcoming if groups decide to mobilize. In other words, either "bad news" or "good news" may motivate episodes of collective action (Meyer 2002). Under bad-news or threatening conditions, a community or population perceives that its situation will become worse if it fails to act and that it may lose collective goods (e.g., loss of land, rights, employment). In the good-news political environment, groups sense that they will acquire new collective goods if they act in concert (e.g., new rights, higher wages, greater environmental quality). Often, bad-news and good-news protest campaigns are triggered by government policies that signal to would-be challengers that the state is becoming less or more receptive to the issues most meaningful to the population in question.

Besides these motivations for movement emergence, some type of organizational base needs to be in existence to mobilize large numbers of people (McCarthy 1996; McAdam 1999 [1982]; Andrews 2004). These organizational assets may be traditional, such as solidarities based on village, religious, regional, or ethnic identities, or they may be associational, rooted in secondary groups such as labor unions, social clubs, agricultural cooperatives, educational institutions, and more formal social movement organizations (SMOs) (Oberschall 1973). Without preexisting solidarity ties and organizational links, either formal or informal, it is unlikely that threats or opportunities will convert into social movement campaigns. Hence, social movement scholars give special attention to variations in organizational resources across localities and over time in explaining social movement emergence (Edwards and McCarthy 2004; Edwards et al. 2018). More recent work in the resource mobilization subfield has expanded into sophisticated network analysis of the means by which a field of SMOs, potential participants, and sponsoring organizations are structurally connected to one another and how the variations in those structures affect social movement emergence (Diani and McAdam 2003; Diani 2015; Hadden 2015). The struggles of low-wage fast-food workers and the student movement against gun violence in the United States exemplify these dynamics.

Framing

[This section] features the framing perspective and how it derives from the interpretive tradition in sociology, with a special concern for the ability of activists to construct social grievances (Snow et al. 2014; Snow et al. 2018). It is now largely understood that injustice and organizational resources alone do not explain the timing and location of social movement mobilization. Movement leaders and activists must construct norm violations, grievances, and experiences of oppression and injustice in socially meaningful and convincing ways that will motivate the targeted populations to participate in collective action (Snow et al. 1986; Snow and Benford 1988). In other words, social and political activists must "frame" the social world in such a manner that it resonates with rank-and-file movement supporters as well as sympathizers and fence-sitters. We explore the creative ways that movements employ cultural artifacts, such as popular music, to reach their intended audiences of adherents and potential sympathizers. The framing perspective incorporates the human agency components of the collective action process.

Movement Participation

Social movement recruitment and individual-level participation draw on microlevel models of collective action. [This section] covers these individual-level dynamics in detail. Early explanations of social movement recruitment and participation emphasized the irrationality aspects of mass movements. Political movements of the unruly were viewed as fulfilling psychological deficits for movement participants—a kind of therapy to overcome sentiments of alienation and social strain inherent in fast-paced industrialized urban societies (McAdam 1999 [1982]). By the late 1970s and early 1980s, scholars began to look at more than just the beliefs and psychological profiles of movement participants. They also examined the microstructural context of mobilization, namely the social ties and networks of potential movement recruits (Snow et al. 1980; McAdam 1986). This newer empirical research found that movement participants were often highly socially integrated in their everyday lives and more likely to belong to civil society associations and clubs than those who did not participate in social movements. In addition, the connections individuals maintained with movement-sympathetic organizations and individuals made them much more likely to join a protest campaign, whereas those connected to organizations and individuals opposed to such activities were much more likely not to participate (McAdam 1986).

The most recent studies demonstrate how social networks interact with new political identities forged by political events (Viterna 2013). Further, movement mobilization occurs at a faster rate when entire groups and organizations are recruited en masse—a process termed "bloc recruitment"—as opposed to organizing single individuals one at a time (Oberschall 1973). Readers will develop a more pronounced understanding of the kinds of individual contexts, based on biography, ideology, networks, identities, and past collective action experience, that are more likely to condition one's choice to join social movement campaigns. Existing data sets on movement participation are also introduced, including state-of-the-art projects of collecting participant motivations in real-time protest demonstrations (Klandermans 2012).

Social Movement Outcomes

Perhaps the most important social movement arena involves movement impacts—the subject of [this section]. What kinds of changes in the political environment can be attributed to the existence and actions of a social movement? What aspects of social change can be explicitly associated with the activities of a movement? Students of social movements examine various dimensions of social movement outcomes. The enduring changes associated with movements include impacts on individual movement participants, changes in the political culture, influence on state policies, and "spillover" into other social movements (Meyer and Whittier 1994; Whittier 2004). In comparison to movement emergence, there is less scholarly consensus on social movement outcomes (Jenkins and Form 2005; Amenta et al. 2010). Often it is difficult to decipher the particular contribution of a social movement to a specific outcome while attempting to control for nonmovement influences. Despite these scientific shortcomings, major movements of excluded social groups in the United States and elsewhere have improved their circumstances. Constituents represented by such movements obtained major policy changes because large numbers of people engaged in social movement struggles, including the women's movement, the African American civil rights movement, the Mexican American labor and civil rights movement, and the LGBTQ civil rights movement, among many others.

Global South, Authoritarian Regimes, and Transnational Movements

[This section] focuses on movements in the global South and transnational movements (movements operating in more than one country). The majority of social movement studies concentrate on movements in industrialized democracies in the global North. However, a growing body of literature now exists on political contexts outside of the advanced capitalist states. The more stable forms of government in Western democracies allow for a greater upkeep of social movement organizations and more space to launch largely nonviolent campaigns. In nondemocratic and quasi-democratic nations (e.g., monarchies, dictatorships, military juntas, theocracies, authoritarian populism), where associational freedoms are proscribed and regular multiparty elections do not occur, scholars face challenges in explaining when social movements will arise and what forms they will take. One fruitful avenue investigates "cracks in the system," small political openings, or larger moves toward political liberalization in nondemocracies. These conditions often provide a conducive environment for a few activists in civil society to attempt to form civic associations and possibly even begin to seek small reforms. Other movements may be launched in institutions outside the purview of state control, such as religious institutions (mosques, religious schools, Catholic youth groups, etc.) or remote territories not completely controlled by the administrative state apparatus and army (Goodwin 2001). Foreign governments and movements may also support a fledgling movement in a nondemocratic context.

The expansion of transnational social movements that link members and organizations across more than one country is a major global trend over the past three decades (Smith and Wiest 2012). Two noteworthy transnational movements in the early twenty-first century are international Islamic solidarity and the global economic justice movement. Internationally connected Islamic movements benefit from the concept of *ummah*—the larger community of believers that links the Muslim world beyond national borders (Lubeck and

Reifer 2004; Roy 2006). With global migration flows and new communications technology, Islamic-based social movements easily mobilize internationally. Examples include transnationally organized insurgencies such as Al Qaeda or the Islamic State (ISIL). The *ummah* concept is also a powerful unifying force for nonviolent transnational antiwar and antidiscrimination movements in the Islamic world and diasporic communities, and it played a major role in the rapid diffusion of Arab Spring uprisings in 2011 against repressive governments.

The global economic justice movement (sometimes referred to by critics as the antiglobalization movement) is another major transnational movement that emerged in the late twentieth century. Supporters of this movement use global communications technologies to mobilize constituents. The global justice movement arose almost simultaneously with the expansion of the global internet infrastructure between the mid-1990s and the early 2000s. Several organizations in Europe and Canada, including the Council of Canadians, Jubilee 2000, People's Global Action, and ATTAC, began to work with nongovernmental organizations in the developing world to place pressure on newly emerging and older transnational governing bodies and economic institutions, such as the United Nations, the World Trade Organization (WTO), the International Monetary Fund, the World Bank, the Group of Eight (G8), and the European Union.

The demands of the global justice movement vary but tend to focus on economic justice, environmental protection, and the need for more transparency in decision-making among the elite transnational economic and political institutions mentioned above. Though the movement held several major protests in the late 1990s outside WTO and G8 meetings in Europe, a massive demonstration at the 1999 WTO meetings in Seattle, Washington, served as a breakthrough for the global justice movement. It was the largest sustained protest in an American city in several decades (Almeida and Lichbach 2003). Global justice activists coordinated the arrival of participants from around the country and the world via the internet and organized the protests in the streets of Seattle with cell phones. Dozens of countries across the globe also experienced protests in solidarity with the actions in Seattle. The success of the Seattle mobilizations provided a template for organizing dozens of similar global days of action in the twenty-first century during major international financial conferences, World Social Forums, free trade meetings, and climate change negotiations, including the 2017 G20 Summit in Hamburg, Germany, and the 2018 G20 Summit in Buenos Aires, Argentina.

The Conclusion ends our long journey through the field of collective mobilization dynamics by summarizing key features of social movements we have considered in previous chapters. The collective knowledge of methods, theory, emergence, framing, and movement outcomes accumulated from [this] is applied to particular case studies of movements emerging in the 2010s and likely in the 2020s. New frontiers of social movement research are also presented, including recent global patterns in the use of social media technology in recruitment practices, as well as transnational movements such as climate justice.

References

Almeida, Paul D. 2005. "Multi-sectoral Coalitions and Popular Movement Participation." *Research in Social Movements, Conflicts and Change* 26: 67–102.
———. 2008a. *Waves of Protest: Popular Struggle in El Salvador, 1925–2005*. Minneapolis: University of Minnesota Press.
———. 2010a. "Globalization and Collective Action." In *Handbook of Politics: State and Society in Global Perspective*, edited by Kevin Leicht and J. Craig Jenkins, 305–26. New York: Springer.
———, and Christopher Chase-Dunn. 2018. "Globalization and Social Movements." *Annual Review of Sociology* 44: 189–211.
———, and Mark I. Lichbach. 2003. "To the Internet, from the Internet: Comparative Media Coverage of Transnational Protest." *Mobilization* 8(3): 249–72.
Amenta, Edwin, Neal Caren, Elizabeth Chiarello, and Yang Su. 2010. "The Political Consequences of Social Movements." *Annual Review of Sociology* 36: 287–307.

Andersen, Kurt. 2011. "2011 Person of the Year: The Protester." *Time* 178(25): 52–89.

Andrews, Kenneth. 2004. *Freedom Is a Constant Struggle: The Mississippi Civil Rights Movement and Its Legacy.* Chicago: University of Chicago Press.

Berezin, Mabel. 2009. *Illiberal Politics in Neoliberal Times: Cultures, Security, and Populism in a New Europe.* Cambridge: Cambridge University Press.

Bloemraad, Irene, Kim Voss, and Taeku Lee. 2011. "The Protests of 2006: What Were They, How Do We Understand Them, Where Do We Go?" In *Rallying for Immigrant Rights: The Fight for Inclusion in 21st Century America.* Berkeley: University of California Press.

Burawoy, Michael. 2017. "Social Movements in the Neoliberal Age." In *Southern Resistance in Critical Perspective,* edited by M. Paret, C. Runciman, and L. Sinwell, 21–35. New York: Routledge.

Castells, Manuel. 2015. *Networks of Outrage and Hope: Social Movements in the Internet Age,* 2nd ed. Cambridge: Polity Press.

Chase-Dunn, Christopher. 2016. "Social Movements and Collective Behavior in Premodern Polities." Paper presented at the American Sociological Association Meetings, Seattle, August.

Diani, Mario. 2015. *The Cement of Civil Society: Studying Networks in Localities.* Cambridge: Cambridge University Press.

———, and Doug McAdam, eds. 2003. *Social Movements and Networks: Relational Approaches to Collective Action.* Oxford: Oxford University Press.

Dicken, Peter. 2011. *Global Shift: Mapping the Changing Contours of the World Economy.* New York: Guilford.

Dodson, Kyle. 2011. "The Movement Society in Comparative Perspective." *Mobilization* 16(4): 475–94.

Edwards, Bob, and John D. McCarthy. 2004. "Resources and Social Movement Mobilization." In *The Blackwell Companion to Social Movements,* edited by D. Snow, S. Soule, and H. Kriesi, 116–52. Oxford: Blackwell.

———, John D. McCarthy, and Dane Mataic. 2018. "The Resource Context of Social Movements." In *The Wiley-Blackwell Companion to Social Movements,* edited by D. Snow, S. Soule, H. Kriesi, and H. McCammon, 79–97. Oxford: Blackwell.

Goldstone, Jack. 2004. "More Social Movements or Fewer? Beyond Political Opportunity Structures to Relational Fields." *Theory and Society* 33: 333–65.

Goodwin, Jeff. 2001. *No Other Way Out: States and Revolutionary Movements, 1945–1991.* Cambridge: Cambridge University Press.

Hadden, Jennifer. 2015. *Networks in Contention: The Divisive Politics of Climate Change.* Cambridge: Cambridge University Press.

Jenkins, J. Craig, and William Form. 2005. "Social Movements and Social Change." In *The Handbook of Political Sociology: States, Civil Societies, and Globalization,* edited by T. Janoski, R. R. Alford, A. M. Hicks, and M. A. Schwartz, 331–49. Cambridge: Cambridge University Press.

Karataşli, Savaş, Kumral Şefika and Beverly Silver. 2018. "A New Global Tide of Rising Social Protest? The Early Twenty-first Century in World Historical Perspective." Presented at the Eastern Sociological Society Annual Meeting, Mini-conference on Globalization in Uncertain Times. Baltimore, MD, February 22–25.

Klandermans, Bert. 2012. "Between Rituals and Riots: The Dynamics of Street Demonstrations." *Mobilization* 17(3): 233–34.

Lubeck, Paul M., and Thomas Reifer. 2004. "The Politics of Global Islam: US Hegemony, Globalization and Islamist Social Movements." In *Globalization, Hegemony and Power: Antisystemic Movements and the Global System,* 162–80. Boulder, CO: Paradigm.

Maney, Gregory, Kenneth T. Andrews, Rachel V. Kutz-Flamenbaum, Deana A. Rohlinger, and Jeff Goodwin. 2012. "An Introduction to Strategies for Social Change." In *Strategies for Social Change,* edited by G. Maney, R. Kutz Flamenbaum, D. Rohlinger, and J. Goodwin, 11–38. Minneapolis: University of Minnesota Press.

McAdam, Doug. 1999 [1982]. *Political Process and the Development of Black Insurgency, 1930–1970.* Chicago: University of Chicago Press.

———. 1986. "Recruitment to High-Risk Activism: The Case of Freedom Summer." *American Journal of Sociology* 92(1): 64–90.

———, and W. Richard Scott. 2005. "Organizations and Movements." In *Social Movements and Organization Theory,* edited by G. Davis, D. McAdam, W. R. Scott, and M. Zald, 4–40. Cambridge: Cambridge University Press.

McCarthy, John D. 1996. "Constraints and Opportunities in Adopting, Adapting, and Inventing." In *Comparative Perspectives on Social Movements: Political Opportunities, Mobilizing Structures, and Cultural Framings,* edited by D. McAdam, J. D. McCarthy, and M. Zald, 141–51. Cambridge: Cambridge University Press.

———, and Mayer N. Zald. 1977. "Resource Mobilization and Social Movements: A Partial Theory." *American Journal of Sociology* 82(6): 1212–41.

Meyer, David S. 2002. "Opportunities and Identities: Bridge-Building in the Study of Social Movements." In *Social Movements: Identity, Culture, and the State,* edited by D. S. Meyer, Nancy Whittier, and Belinda Robnett, 3–21. New York: Oxford University Press.

———. 2014. *The Politics of Protest: Social Movements in America,* 2nd ed. Oxford: Oxford University Press.

———, and Suzanne Staggenborg. 2012. "Thinking about Strategy." In *Strategies for Social Change,* edited by G. Maney, R. Kutz Flamenbaum, D. Rohlinger, and J. Goodwin, 3–22. Minneapolis: University of Minnesota Press.

———, and Sidney Tarrow, eds. 2018. *The Resistance: The Dawn of the Anti-Trump Opposition Movement.* Oxford: Oxford University Press.

———, and Nancy Whittier. 1994. "Social Movement Spillover." *Social Problems* 41(2): 277–98.

Minkoff, Debra C., and John D. McCarthy. 2005. "Reinvigorating the Study of Organizational Processes in Social Movements." *Mobilization* 10(2): 289–308.

Mora, Maria de Jesus, Rodolfo Rodriguez, Alejandro Zermeño, and Paul Almeida. 2018. "Immigrant Rights and Social Movements." *Sociology Compass* 12: 1–20.

———, Alejandro Zermeño, Rodolfo Rodriguez, and Paul Almeida. 2017. "Exclusión y movimientos sociales en los Estados Unidos." In *Movimientos Sociales en América Latina: Perspectivas, Tendencias y Casos,* edited by P. Almeida and A. Cordero, 641–69. Buenos Aires: CLACSO.

Nicholls, Walter. 2014. *The DREAMers: How the Undocumented Youth Movement Transformed the Immigrant Rights Debate.* Stanford, CA: Stanford University Press.

Oberschall, A. 1973. *Social Conflict and Social Movements.* Englewood Cliffs, NJ: Prentice-Hall.

Robinson, William. 2014. *Capitalism and the Crisis of Humanity.* Cambridge: Cambridge University Press.

Roy, Olivier. 2006. *Globalized Islam: The Search for a New Ummah.* New York: Columbia University Press.

Schock, Kurt. 2005. *Unarmed Insurrections: People Power Movements in Nondemocracies.* Minneapolis: University of Minnesota Press.

Simmons, Erica. 2014. "Grievances Do Matter in Mobilization." *Theory and Society* 43: 513–46.

Skocpol, T., and Vanessa Williamson. 2012. *The Tea Party and the Remaking of Republican Conservatism.* Oxford: Oxford University Press.

Smith, Jackie, and Dawn Wiest. 2012. *Social Movements in the World-System: The Politics of Crisis and Transformation.* New York: Russell Sage Foundation.

Snow, David and Robert Benford. 1988. "Ideology, Frame Resonance, and Participant Mobilization." *International Social Movement Research* 1: 197–217.

———, Robert Benford, Holly J. McCammon, Lyndi Hewitt, and Scott T. Fitzgerald. 2014. "The Emergence and Development of the Framing Perspective or 25 Years since Publication of 'Frame Alignment': What Lies Ahead?" *Mobilization* 19(1): 23–46.

———, E. Burke Rochford, Steven Worden, and Robert Benford. 1986. "Frame Alignment Processes, Micromobilization, and Movement Participation." *American Sociological Review* 51: 464–81.

———, and Sarah Soule. 2009. *A Primer on Social Movements.* New York: Norton.

———, Rens Vliegenthart, and Pauline Ketelaars. 2018. "The Framing Perspective on Social Movements: Its Conceptual Roots and Architecture." In *The Wiley-Blackwell Companion to Social Movements,* edited by D. Snow, S. Soule, H. Kriesi, and H. McCammon, 392–410. Oxford: Blackwell.

———, Louis Zurcher, and Sheldon Ekland-Olson. 1980. "Social Networks and Social Movements: A Microstructural Approach to Differential Recruitment." *American Sociological Review* 45: 787–801.

Somers, Margaret. 2008. *Genealogies of Citizenship: Markets, Statelessness, and the Right to Have Rights.* Cambridge: Cambridge University Press.

Tarrow, Sidney. 2011. *Power in Movement: Social Movements and Contentious Politics,* 3rd ed. Cambridge: Cambridge University Press.

Taylor, Keeanga-Yamahtta. 2016. *From #BlackLivesMatter to Black Liberation.* Chicago: Haymarket Books.

Tilly, Charles. 1978. *From Mobilization to Revolution.* Reading, MA: Addison-Wesley.

———, and Lesley Wood. 2012. *Social Movements, 1768–2004.* Boulder, CO: Paradigm.

Van Dyke, Nella, and Bryan Amos. 2017. "Social Movement Coalitions: Formation, Longevity, and Success." *Sociology Compass* 11(7): 1–17.

———, and Holly McCammon. 2010. "Introduction: Social Movement Coalition Formation." In *Strategic Alliances: Coalition Building and Social Movements,* edited by N. Van Dyke and H. McCammon, xi–xxviii. Minneapolis: University of Minnesota Press.

———, and David S. Meyer. 2014. "Introduction." In *Understanding the Tea Party Movement,* edited by N. Van Dyke and D. S. Meyer, 1–14. Burlington, VT: Ashgate.

Vasi, Ion Bogdan, David Strang, and Arnout van de Rijt. 2014. "Tea and Sympathy: The Tea Party Movement and Republican Precommitment to Radical Conservatism in the 2011 Debt-Limit Crisis." *Mobilization* 19: 1–22.

Viterna, Jocelyn. 2013. *Women in War: The Micro-processes of Mobilization in El Salvador.* New York: Oxford University Press.

———, and Fallon Kathleen. 2008. "Democratization, Women's Movements, and Gender-Equitable States: A Framework for Comparison." *American Sociological Review* 73: 668–89.

Walsh, Edward, Rex Warland, and Douglas Clayton Smith. 1997. *Don't Burn It Here: Grassroots Challenges to Trash Incinerators.* University Park: Penn State University Press.

Ward, Michael. 2016. "Can We Predict Politics? Toward What End?" *Journal of Global Security Studies* 1(1): 80–91.

Whittier, Nancy. 2004. "The Consequences of Social Movements for Each Other." In *The Blackwell Companion to Social Movements,* edited by D. Snow, S. Soule, and H. Kriesi, 531–52. Oxford: Blackwell.

Zepeda-Millán, Chris. 2017. *Latino Mass Mobilization: Immigration, Racialization, and Activism.* Cambridge: Cambridge University Press.

Discussion Topics

1. Identify two social movements and discuss the primary factors that led to their emergence.
2. Identify two social movements discussed in the text and compare them.
3. What are the three core movement elements discussed in the text? Elaborate on them?
4. What is the main idea of this article?

Conclusion: Mounting Crises and the Pathway Forward

Paul Almeida

Paul Almeida, "Conclusion: Mounting Crises and the Pathway Forward," *Social Movements: The Structure of Collective Mobilization*, pp. 173-179, 185, 187-220. Copyright © 2019 by University of California Press. Reprinted with permission.

Editor's Introduction

This article titled "Conclusion: Mounting Crises and the Pathway Forward" explores the important role social movements play in social changes. This article was selected to be part of this text because it explains how social movements can contribute to the progression toward equity in the United states. After reading this article, you will be able to explain the methods and theories used to analyze the emergence and development of social movements and describe the challenges that these movements face.

Mounting Crises and the Pathway Forward

This book has introduced readers to the basic features of social movements and the specialized subfields within the discipline. The Conclusion offers suggestions on future directions of social movements and the mounting crises excluded groups face in the twenty-first century. While the new social media communication technologies continue to produce record-breaking national and transnational protests in the scale of mobilizations and provide evidence of the power in numbers, other challenges remain. The dark side of the new millennium includes rising inequality, a resurgence of authoritarian populism, and a deepening ecological crisis. Before turning briefly to these issues, we will look at promising new lines of inquiry in the major areas of movement research and the connections between these areas.

New Lines of Inquiry

Defining Social Movements

This text began by defining social movements as excluded social groups that mobilize using noninstitutional tactics to target political and economic elites. While this is a somewhat standard definition of social movements (Snow and Soule 2009; Tarrow 2011), much more work is required on the "exclusion" part of the classification (Burawoy 2017). Beyond economic, racial, and gender inequality and discrimination, social exclusion appears in a variety of forms (Mora et al. 2017). This includes exclusion based on religion, national origin, sexuality, citizenship status, disabilities, and many others. Activists and students alike need to better conceptualize the intersectionality of exclusions, as critical race scholars have carried out with race, gender, and class (Nakano Glenn 2004; Valdez 2011; Collins 2015; Terriquez et al. 2018). The focus may be to understand how to piece together movement coalitions across multiple forms of exclusion, and more important, how to sustain those coalitions.

Methods

In the arena of social movement methods, several advances are underway in analyzing collective action by excluded groups. One fascinating specialty continues to be in the field of social network analysis. The ties between individuals, organizations, and geographical regions offer several insights on where collective action likely emerges and then multiplies via diffusion mechanisms. The existence and strength of ties between individuals and organizations along with the network configuration of the entire social movement field allow students of movements to explore many scenarios and potential outcomes. New geographic information system software is just beginning to be utilized to demonstrate the significance of spatial ties in promoting popular mobilization. Another major opening for social movement methods resides in the vast amount of information (and its accessibility) available from information and communication technologies and social media. The possibilities of future contributions of internet and social media-based data in promoting and understanding movement emergence, protest event distribution, recruitment, framing, and coordinating transnational mobilization are truly astonishing.

Theory

Social movement theory continues in a vibrant state. The synergy of theoretical contributions over the past four decades is largely responsible for advances in explaining the timing and outcomes of social movements. More specifically, the conceptual contributions come from scholars in different specialty areas in the social sciences who have not permitted disciplinary boundaries to block theoretical collaboration in order to build better frameworks and models of collective action. These include social psychologists and scholars of religion; political scientists from the comparative politics tradition; historians of earlier rebellions; social anthropologists who highlight the role of culture in mobilization; and sociologists with advanced training in organizations, social network analysis, and comparative-historical methods. Indeed, the political process framework evolved by combining insights from resource mobilization approaches and the social psychological advances of framing theory. Continuing on this trajectory of combining complementary perspectives in theory building appears to be the best path forward.

The renewed emphases on collective identities and emotions provide additional perspectives for a multidimensional view of social movements to endure. Given the shrinkage of the state in the neoliberal period, scholars are also pushing theoretical frameworks to investigate movements targeting institutions beyond the political state, such as corporations, medical systems, and educational and religious bodies, showing the power of movements in multiple spheres of social life. Finally, this book has focused on many of the threats, or the "bad news," that communities confront; with so many of the major mass mobilizations of the past two decades driven by threats (e.g., war, climate change, economic austerity/inequality, and the erosion of immigrant and women's rights), we need to continue elaborating more precise understandings of how threats mobilize (such as magnitude, proximity, and scope of threat) and which conditions are associated with successfully preventing unwanted changes.

Emergence

Social movement emergence has been given more attention by analysts and activists than any other dimension of collective action. One fascinating area to explore with greater depth resides in the nonobvious institutions, organizations, communities, and networks that may contribute to the initial rise of a movement. We know that preexisting SMOs and labor unions often contribute to movement emergence. We know much less about why organizations, institutions, and networks not explicitly established for social movement mobilization, such as NGOs, neighborhood associations, public schools, or recreational clubs, become converted or annexed by activists to launch a protest campaign. Equally interesting, for both right-wing and left-wing movement emergence, is the role of elite groups in sponsoring mobilization, such as financial elites, political parties, bosses in patron-client relationships, and even criminal networks of narco-trafficking.

Framing

The framing perspective will largely advance through the accumulation of more empirical studies illustrating the social construction and interpretation of grievances in action. Framing work would benefit from exploring more real-world examples from the actual propaganda documents and cultural artifacts used by or left over from previous mobilizations. The tripartite task of diagnostic, prognostic, and motivational framing remains a useful categorical scheme to apply to the empirical evidence. Also, studying how various audiences absorb and react to framing strategies would provide greater comprehension of these processes and strike a better balance between the signalers (activists engaged in framing) and the receivers (targeted groups for mobilization) than currently exists.

Individual Participation

[T]he project Caught in the Act of Protest: Contextualizing Contestation (Klandermans 2012) [captures] individual participation in real-time demonstrations. Such designs provide high response validity because researchers implement the protocol while the participation is occurring. The standardization of the survey also allows for comparisons across types of demonstrations (e.g., climate change versus LGBTQ pride). The next phase for these kinds of designs centers on incorporating a comparison group of nonparticipants, those who came close to participating in the sympathy pool but failed in the end to attend a demonstration. In the twenty-first century, ordinary people are increasingly recruited online to participate in social movement activities. Knowing more about the mechanisms of receiving an invitation to participate via different social media platforms and about the origins of the invitation (from a friend or family member versus a stranger or SMO) will be a useful line of research for students and community organizations.

Outcomes

The study of social movement outcomes is essential for understanding how social change occurs. More work is needed on analyzing cultural outcomes and the outcomes of transnational movements in an increasingly globalizing world. Just as with the study of movement emergence, nonobvious aspects of movement outcomes also require further attention. In particular, movements that seem not to achieve their stated goals (or even appear to have failed) may have "hidden outcomes." Think about the 2017 and 2018 Women's Marches; they have not turned back many of the administration's policies, but they may influence future elections and the larger culture about sexual harassment and gender discrimination, and the increasing participation of women as electoral candidates. One of the world's largest mobilizations, the anti-war demonstrations in February 2003, did not stop the US invasion of Iraq, but the mass actions may have partially spilled over into the transnational climate justice movement and other campaigns coordinated on an international scale. Finally, more studies are required on the combination of conditions that result in favorable outcomes.

Global South

Social movements in the global South face so many obstacles. Finding the time and the resources to mobilize presents daunting challenges for ordinary people in poorer countries. One of the most pressing issues for movements in authoritarian states is to democratize the government. The heroic citizens in the Arab Spring mobilizations of 2011 largely focused on overthrowing nondemocratic regimes. Another major battle centers on the loss of social citizenship rights (access to social welfare, potable water, basic utilities, education, and healthcare). Even in the world's poorest countries, governments made efforts to expand the welfare state between the 1950s and 1980s. With the rise of the third-world debt crisis and the ideological dominance of economic liberalization, mobilizations are occurring across Africa, Asia, eastern and southern Europe, and Latin America to protect access to food and fuel subsidies, healthcare, education, and other benefits created in the period of state-led development. New transnational initiatives such as the World Social Forum and climate justice may be embryonic forms of generating more collective power and negotiating leverage for the global South.

Final Connections

All of the major themes and subareas of social movements considered above and throughout this text connect to one another. Defining movements, developing methods of inquiry, and constructing theoretical explanations begin the journey of understanding collective action. We use these fundamental tools to examine movement emergence, framing, individual participation, and outcomes. The framing perspective alone has stretched its analytical utility to applications ranging from movement emergence and recruitment to movement success. Students of collective action currently employ all of the social movement subareas to comprehend rebellions and collective resistance campaigns in the global South, including transnational movements. At the same time, struggles in the global South shape and inform current social movement frameworks by forcing scholars to account for the wide variety of political and economic contexts faced by protest campaigns in difficult circumstances.

Economic Inequality, Increasing Authoritarianism, and Ecological Crises

As the twenty-first century advances, excluded social groups face a number of major threats. Three substantial issues include the threats of economic inequality, increasing authoritarianism, and ecological crises. Social movement mobilization offers one pathway to attempt to slow these encroaching negative conditions. Globalization processes are creating new winners and losers in the world economy. In the global North, the globalized economy has launched new social movements against inequality and austerity, such as Occupy Wall Street in the United States and anti-austerity movements throughout Europe, as well as the ongoing global justice movement. Indeed, government-commissioned reports already predict that by 2030 the wealthiest 1 percent of individuals will own two-thirds of the world's wealth.[1] In the global South, free trade, privatization, austerity, land grabs, and labor flexibility have generated some of the largest demonstrations in the past three decades. Most of these struggles are carried out at the local and national levels. Stronger transnational ties are a minimum requisite to place pressure on international institutions and the most powerful nation-states to ensure a basic livelihood in a world with a growing population that must scrape out a precarious existence.

In the 2018 Rule of Law Index, 70 of the 113 countries sampled report an erosion in human rights, including the United States.[2] Scholars relate the findings to backlash mobilizations associated with economic globalization. Over the past two decades, right-wing political parties have used economic globalization, free trade, and international immigration in their framing appeals during election campaigns. Since the global recession of 2008–9, the appeals are gaining traction. Such framings have been associated with empowering right-wing movements and extremist extraparliamentary groups to become more assertive and public, resulting in upsurges in hate crimes and anti-immigrant violence. Much more research has been undertaken on progressive movements than on right-wing mobilizations. The reality of this academic imbalance has been manifested in scholars' inability to predict the resurgence of authoritarian populism in the new millennium. Equally important is for citizens to remain vigilant of eroding rights and prepared to defend constitutional protections and vulnerable groups via social movement mobilization.

Perhaps the biggest threat of all is ecological crisis, more specifically global warming and climate change. With the ten warmest years on record occurring since 1997 (with data going back to 1880), there is a scientific consensus that the planet is warming at an alarming rate. As the world already experiences monster storms and

---

1. See www.theguardian.com/business/2018/apr/07/global-inequalitytipping-point-2030.
2. See Will Bordell and Jon Robins. 2018. "'A Crisis for Human Rights': New Index Reveals Global Fall in Basic Justice." *Guardian* (US edition), January 31. www.theguardian.com/inequality/2018/jan/31/human-rights-new-rule-of-law-index-reveals-global-fall-basic-justice.

weather events, major droughts, massive wildfires and rising sea levels, the mounting ecological threats are pushing more collective action. Indeed, as of 2018 the transnational movement to turn back global warming (known as "climate justice") represents the largest social movement in human history. The movement is now coordinated in nearly every country on the planet and has successfully mobilized simultaneous actions across the globe since at least 2006. These transnational mobilizations occurred concurrently or just before major conferences and global summits on climate change, including the Paris Climate Agreement of 2015, which committed the nations of the world to reduce carbon emissions to the point of slowing global warming to less than two degrees Celsius in the present century. Even with the US withdrawal from the treaty, this incipient worldwide movement offers another glimpse of optimism for the future. If this emergent movement continues to grow, we can hope for many of the benefits provided by social movements, as discussed throughout these pages, on a global scale.

References

Burawoy, Michael. 2017. "Social Movements in the Neoliberal Age." In *Southern Resistance in Critical Perspective,* edited by M. Paret, C. Runciman, and L. Sinwell, 21–35. New York: Routledge.

Collins, Patricia Hill, 2015. "Intersectionality's Definitional Dilemmas." *Annual Review of Sociology* 41: 1–20.

Klandermans, Bert. 2012. "Between Rituals and Riots: The Dynamics of Street Demonstrations." *Mobilization* 17(3): 233–34.

Mora, Maria de Jesus, Alejandro Zermeño, Rodolfo Rodriguez, and Paul Almeida. 2017. "Exclusión y movimientos sociales en los Estados Unidos." In *Movimientos Sociales en América Latina: Perspectivas, Tendencias y Casos,* edited by P. Almeida and A. Cordero, 641–69. Buenos Aires: CLACSO.

Nakano Glenn, Evelyn. 2004. *Unequal Freedom: How Race and Gender Shaped American Citizenship and Labor.* Cambridge, MA: Harvard University Press.

Snow, David, and Sarah Soule. 2009. *A Primer on Social Movements.* New York: Norton.

Tarrow, Sidney. 2011. *Power in Movement: Social Movements and Contentious Politics,* 3rd ed. Cambridge: Cambridge University Press.

Terriquez, Veronica, Tizoc Brenes, and Abdiel Lopez. 2018. "Intersectionality as a Multipurpose Collective Action Frame: The Case of the Undocumented Youth Movement." *Ethnicities* 18(2): 260–76.

Valdez, Zulema. 2011. *The New Entrepreneurs: How Race, Class, and Gender Shape American Enterprise.* Palo Alto, CA: Stanford University Press.

Discussion Topics

1. What are some of the methods used when investigating social movements? Identify two, describe, and compare them.
2. Discuss the characteristics of social movement theory. What is the importance of theory in the study of social movements?
3. What are some obstacles faced by social movements in the global South?
4. Identify two current global social movements, describe their global challenges, and propose ways to bring about their expected outcomes.

CONCLUSION

This article explains the important role that sociology plays in the investigation of social problems. The contribution of sociology to social problems is unique through its perspective, which is sociological imagination. Coined by C. Wright Mills, the concept of sociological imagination refers to the ability to establish a link between "biography" and "history." That is, sociological imagination enables us to understand that our personal troubles are connected to public issues. In a sense, this unique perspective of sociology allows uncovering or discovering the influential effects of social structure on social problems, which leads to theory formulation: theorizing. A social theory can be defined as a systematic, disciplined, and logical explanation of social phenomena, such as social problems. The process of theorizing occurs in three major steps: (1) Identify a problem ("the something ain't right"); (2) Describe the nature of the problem, its manifestation, and implications; and (3) Provide a description of how the problem can be solved and the impact of the solution on society.

CPSIA information can be obtained
at www.ICGtesting.com
Printed in the USA
LVHW061534091222
734862LV00004B/29